1927

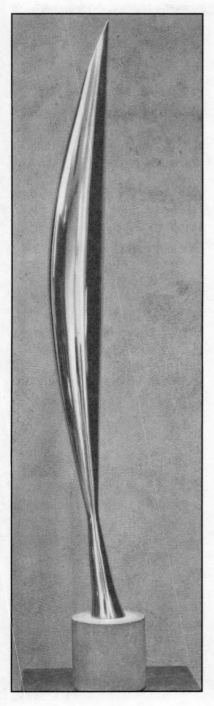

"If this is art, I'm a bricklayer," declared an art expert who recommended that Constantin Brancusi's "Bird in Flight" be considered merchandise, not art, by U.S. Customs and therefore subject to duty (*The* New York Times, *February 27, 1927). Photo courtesy the Museum of Modern Art, New York.*

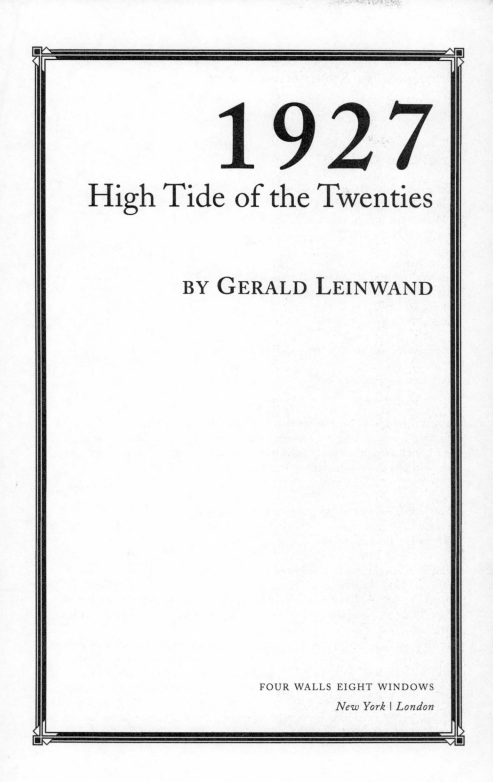

1927

High Tide of the Twenties

BY GERALD LEINWAND

FOUR WALLS EIGHT WINDOWS

New York | London

For my grandson, Spencer David Maslin

© 2001 Gerald Leinwand

Published in the United States by:
Four Walls Eight Windows
39 West 14th Street, room 503
New York, N.Y., 10011

U.K. offices:
Four Walls Eight Windows/Turnaround
Unit 3, Olympia Trading Estate
Coburg Road, Wood Green
London N22 6TZ, England

Visit our website at http://www.4w8w.com

First printing February 2001.

Library of Congress Cataloging-in-Publication Data:
Leinwand, Gerald.
1927/by Gerald Leinwand.
p. cm.
Includes bibliographical references and index.
ISBN: 1-56858-153-X
1. United States--History--1919-1933. 2. United States--Social conditions--1918-1932. 3. Nineteen twenty-seven, A.D. 4. Nineteen twenties. I. Title.
E791.L45 2000
973.91'5--dc21   00-034095

10 9 8 7 6 5 4 3 2 1

Printed in the United States
Typesetting by Precision Typographers

TABLE OF CONTENTS

Acknowledgements

I wish to acknowledge expert research assistance from Stephen Mihm, Mark Ladov, and Dan Prosterman, outstanding doctoral students in American History at New York University.

PROLOGUE

"Time," wrote the reclusive American philosopher Henry David Thoreau, "is but a stream I go fishing in." As a fisherman in time, I cast my fishing rod and fell hook, line, and sinker for 1927.

To readers who may be looking at 1927 through the lens of the millennium, what's in a date?

In 1927, Americans were confident that this was the year and America was the place where they would prosper. Americans in 1927 felt that the economic escalator was going up and that they need but hop aboard. America could do everything, its people could do anything, go anywhere, make a fortune, lose it and start all over again. In its New Year's Day editorial for 1927, even the staid *New York Times* seemed unrestrained: "The United States may be excused for thinking that it enters upon the New Year universally recognized as the most powerful nation on earth. Testimony on this point out of the mouths of others is overwhelming. Even those who dislike and envy us admit the facts."[1]

As one journalist of the day noted, "[T]he heavens have often conspired to make 27 a crucial number in the chronology of the western calendar."[2] He then went on to describe significant turning points in the history of civilization which took place in the year "27" during each century. While the writer may have taken journalistic license in interpreting the events of the past, the significance of his essay is that it reflects the sense of destiny and of chosenness with which Americans of 1927 thought of themselves.

Nineteen twenty-seven was, asserted historian Page Smith, "A remarkable year in which man-made events competed with natural disasters for public attention."[3] Like the spotlight that played on the crystal chandelier high over the heads of the marathon dancers covering them sometimes with bursts of color and at other times allowing them to glide into the shadows of the dance floor, so in 1927 Americans were bombarded with the staccato of rapidly developing events at home and abroad from the ever-bolder tabloids and from the newscasts of the still-infant radio.

With the sacrifices of the Great War over, Americans in 1927 were more intent than ever upon enjoying themselves. Optimistic Americans made generous use of the installment plan which deferred payments for the things they bought while offering instant gratification through their use. Looking at their world, historians Charles and Mary Beard saw an end to old puritanical values. "In the new order," they wrote, "prodigal members of the plutocracy set standards of reckless expenditure and high living which spread like a virus among all ranks of society, making the spending of money a national mania and casting the stigma of contempt on previous virtues of thrift, toil, and moderation."[4] While their President, Calvin Coolidge, told them that "the business of America is business," to Americans the business of America was to consume to their heart's content.

Like a great wine, 1927 was a vintage year. The issues of that year — evolved though they may be — seem for the most part to have stayed with us. The decade of the 1920s was one in which the pace of change accelerated as never before. Then, as today, scientific and technological marvels were such as to free Americans from their traditional moorings while utopian visions of a glorious future clashed with fear of an unknown and perhaps unknowable tomorrow.

Then, as today, Americans debated the role of immigrants, the liberation of women, opportunities for minorities. Tension between urban and rural America, between the virtuous country and the vulgar city, between evolution and creationism, and the role of religion in society and exactly how high the "wall of separation" between church and state in public affairs ought to be, were among the 1927 issues we revisit in our own time. While much has been made of American isolationism, in 1927 events abroad played importantly in the nation's press as Americans, then as today, debated what role the most powerful nation on earth should play in global events. The debates over foreign and domestic issues begun in those years were interrupted by the Great Depression, the Second World War and its aftermath. With the end of the Cold War, however, with a new sense of immediacy, we once again resume the debates begun in the 1920s.

If 1927 was the "high tide" of the twenties, then during that year could be found signs that the "good times" were nearing an end. But who would dare call attention to the chilling evidence if doing so might unleash a self-fulfilling prophecy and perhaps an economic collapse? Ostrich-like, Americans kept their eyes glued to the movies, their ears to the radio, their hands on the steering wheel, and their heads in the sand.

Gerald Leinwand
New York City

[1]The *New York Times,* January 1, 1927.

[2]Dunice Fuller Barnard, "Great Events Linked to Dates of '27," the *New York Times,* September 25, 1927.

[3]Page Smith, *A People's History of the New Deal: Redeeming the Time,* Vol. 8 (New York: McGraw-Hill Book Company, 1987), p. 164.

[4]Charles A. Beard and Mary R. Beard, *The Rise of American Civilization,* Vol. II, New Edition (New York: The Macmillan Company, 1927), p. 757.

THE YEAR IN REVIEW

January 1: Rain along the east coast of the United States did not dampen the spirits of the revelers who celebrated the arrival of 1927. Although a thousand extra police were on duty in New York City, traffic jams were the worst ever. Despite the Prohibition Amendment (XVIII) which forbade Americans from consuming, manufacturing, or importing hard liquor, beer, or wine, the celebrants had a good time as illicit "booze" was readily available. Eight revelers died of alcohol poisoning.

The celebrations were lavish, there was not a vacant hotel room in Manhattan, and tickets for the theaters of New York's Great White Way, as Broadway was then known, were difficult to come by. In 1927, two hundred seventy shows were to open, a record which still stands. Among them were "Countess Maritza," "Desert Song," "The Girl Friend," "Peggy Ann," "Connecticut Yankee," "Hit the Deck," "My Maryland," "Rio Rita," and "Show Boat." The New York Times *reported, "Prosperous with all confidence in the newcomer, New York gave a rousing welcome . . . to 1927 . . . ."*[1]

༺༻

Dubbing 1927 the "Year of the Big Shriek," popular writer Herbert Asbury concluded, "Not since the close of the World War has there been a year which produced such an amazing crop of big news as 1927 . . . ."[2] Of the reported events some showed America in all its glory, some showed America with all its warts.

Profile of a Year
• It was the year Charles A. Lindbergh, the Lone Eagle, captured the imagination of the nation and the world with his solo flight from New York to Paris. In the ticker tape parade held in Lindbergh's honor amid the skyscrapers of New York's financial district, more paper rained down on him, 1,750 tons, than on any other American so honored.

• The Italian immigrants Nicola Sacco and Bartolomeo Vanzetti, after numerous appeals and delays, were electrocuted in Charlestown, Massachusetts, for a crime in South Braintree, Massachusetts, that occurred seven years earlier.

• The nation's worst flood tore down the Mississippi River levees and flooded a land area about the size of Rhode Island with the loss of hundreds of lives and millions of dollars in property damage. Other natural disasters included the devastating floods in New England, and in St. Louis a blistering five-minute, 90-mile tornado killed 87, injured 1,500, and destroyed a thousand homes.

• In 1927 Ford produced the 15 millionth Model T. By year's end, in an attempt to recapture the automobile market in America which he was losing to General Motors among others, Ford introduced the Model A in a spectacular media blitz.

• If further evidence was needed that the age of the automobile had come to stay, the Holland Vehicular Tunnel under the Hudson River between New York and Jersey City, New Jersey, opened on November 12.

• Ruth Snyder and her lover Judd Gray, a corset salesman, were convicted for the murder of Albert Snyder, Ruth's husband. The trial made sensational headlines and titillated the reading public. A year later, the couple were electrocuted at Sing Sing Prison.

• The settlement of marital difficulties between "Peaches" and "Daddy" Browning fueled the passion of the times. These salacious stories were perfect grist for the new tabloid journalism. The *New York Daily Mirror* pandered to the public's taste for those who reveled in murder, mayhem, sex, and infidelity. The *Daily Mirror* devoted the entire front page to these stories, screaming in five-inch type: "Peaches' Shame!" and "Oh - Oh - Oh! Daddy Browning." Journalism such as this contributed to a huge increase in circulation during the year.

• The combined circulation of English language dailies in the United States rose to 38 million, about one copy for every two literate persons over ten years of age.[3]

• Actress Mae West, the sex symbol of her time, was fined $500 for her role in the play "Sex" and sentenced to ten days in jail.

• In South Dakota, Gutzon Borglum began working on Mount Rushmore to carve the heads of Presidents Washington, Jefferson, Lincoln, and Theodore Roosevelt.

• The American Telephone and Telegraph Company gave the first public demonstration of television in America. Herbert Hoover, Secretary of Commerce in the Coolidge administration, delivered a speech in Washington, D.C., that was seen and heard by a group of bankers in New York City.

• Duke Ellington's band opened at the Cotton Club in New York's Harlem. The show lasted for years.

` • Babe Ruth hit sixty home runs, a record that stood until 1961.

• Al Jolson, in *The Jazz Singer*, made the first "talkie." But the silent screen was not without excitement. In the still-silent *Flesh and the Devil*, starring John Gilbert and Greta Garbo, American viewers gasped at the sight of the first filmed soul kiss. That the more straight-laced objected made little difference. Americans wanted more of the same and got it.

• Robert Maynard Hutchins, at age 28, became the youngest Dean of Yale Law School and remained a formidable figure in American education.

• On May 16, 1927, the first Academy Awards awarded an "Oscar" to *Wings* for "Best Picture." Janet Gaynor, in *Seventh Heaven*, and Emil Jannings, in *The Way of All Flesh*, were chosen best actress and actor.

• Fans of boxing in 1927 paid two and a half million dollars to see Gene Tunney win a controversial decision over Jack Dempsey in the "greatest ring spectacle of all time."[4]

• Tennis was the most rapidly growing sport in America in 1927. The value of tennis goods produced by American manufacturers in 1927, the first year that tennis goods were listed separately in the census report, totalled $3,227,552.[5] Golf also grew spectacularly. Between 1927 and 1929, the manufacture of golf equipment gained 71.8 percent.

• In New York City, William S. Paley, a 28-year-old son of a Russian immigrant, took control of a money-losing radio network. He renamed it the Columbia Broadcasting System.

• An organization called the Motion Pictures Producers and Distributors of America, made up of Hollywood movie moguls, drew up a code of "good taste" in order to avoid government censorship of films. Under the direction of Will H. Hays, producers could not show the following on film: "any licentious or suggestive nudity," "miscegenation," "ridicule of clergy," "inference of sexual perversion," "indecent or undue exposure," and "excessive and lustful kissing." However, "actual hangings or electrocutions . . . brutality and possibly gruesomeness" may be shown "within careful limits of good taste." Movie makers innovatively skirted the guidelines.

• The Federal Radio Commission was created by Congress to oversee the newest form of domestic and international communication.

• "Scarface" Al Capone became the country's biggest bootlegger and controlled most its illicit liquor industry. He made $100 million in liquor, $30 million in the protection racket, $25 million in gambling, and $10 million in prostitution and other rackets. Most Americans did not seem to care.

• For those with a literary interest, 1927 was a bonanza year. P. G. Wodehouse wrote *Carry on Jeeves*, and William Faulkner wrote *Mosquitoes*. Ernest Hemingway wrote *Men Without Women*, a book of short stories, and Willa Cather, *Death Comes for the Archbishop*. Motivated by the extraordinary evangelism of Aimee Semple McPherson, Sinclair Lewis wrote *Elmer Gantry* to illustrate how high-pressure tactics of business had corrupted religion. Philo Vance became the "private eye" of the year and hero of Willard Wright's (S. S. Van Dine) *The Canary Murder Case*. In non-fiction, Will Durant's *The Story of Philosophy* surprisingly became a runaway best-seller. Thornton Wilder's *The Bridge of San Luis Rey* became the Christmas book gift of the year and won a Pulitzer Prize a year later. In 1927, Paul Green's play *In Abraham's Bosom*, a sympathetic treatment of the African American and the sharecropper, won the Pulitzer Prize for drama as did Louis Bromfield's *Early Autumn* for fiction. James Weldon Johnson wrote *God's Trombone: Seven Negro Sermons in Verse*, in which he described the spiritual world of Harlem.

• While there was a great deal of good literature, Americans preferred the lurid journals *True Story* and *Confessions*.

• At age 66, the notorious Lizzie Borden died of natural causes. Although she had been found not guilty of the murder of her father and stepmother in 1892, many of her neighbors continued to believe that she had gotten away with murder. The rhyme from which she could not escape was:

Lizzie Borden took an axe
And gave her mother forty whacks,
And when she saw what she had done
She gave her father forty-one.

• As an expression of newly won freedom, women bobbed their hair, wore skirts just above the knee, smoked cigarettes, and drank bootleg whiskey in public.

• Americans ate two million Eskimo Pies, and in March, this $25 million ice cream company went public.

• Despite the euphoria of the year, the suicide rate among American youth reached alarming proportions.

• Over a billion and a half dollars were spent on advertising, much of it designed to arouse feelings of guilt and anxiety over such matters of personal hygiene as body odor and bad breath.

• The beautician became a recognized professional, and in 1927, 18,000 income taxpayers listed themselves as beauticians.

• Reporting on the scene with biting criticism was H. L. Mencken, "the bad boy of Baltimore," whose *Mercury Magazine* achieved a circulation of 77,000. This made Mencken, according to Walter Lippmann, "the most powerful personal influence on this whole generation of educated people."[6]

• "Zyxt," a Kentish word which means "thou seest," became the final word in the final volume of the Oxford English Dictionary. To complete the project required seventy years, the talents of 130,000 people, and the expenditure of $250,000.

• The twenty-two newspapers of William Randolph Hearst, published in fifteen cities, reached 3,500,000 daily readers and 4,000,000 on Sunday.

• President Calvin Coolidge sent the Marines to Nicaragua and Dwight Morrow to Mexico to quell conflicts in Latin America.

• The optimism of the time was reflected in a worthy but unsuccessful attempt, in the Kellogg-Briand Peace Pact, to outlaw war.

• Americans could not keep themselves completely aloof from global affairs, as many would have preferred. Friends of the World Court prevailed and the United States Senate ratified adherence to the court by a vote of 76–17. President Coolidge soon approved the senate resolution.

• Population as a worthy field of study was recognized in 1927, when the first conference on world population convened in Geneva in August. During the conference, biologists and statisticians joined in developing a scientific base for the study of world population trends.

• While not yet sharply etched in the American mind, affairs in China began to reverberate in the United States and around the world. Chinese Communists attacked government fortresses and women and children needed to be evacuated from Hankow. Revolts broke out in Shanghai and Nanking, and American marines were sent to protect U.S. nationals and diplomats. Despite initial successes, the Communists under the leadership of Mao Zedong were defeated. Americans could not know that he would be the ultimate victor.

• Of the Italian dictator Benito Mussolini, Winston Churchill, then the British Chancellor of the Exchequer and later prime minister, remarked: "I could not help being charmed by his gentle simple bearing and his calm, detached poise . . . ."[7]

• In Germany, Houston Stewart Chamberlain was near death. His assertion of the superiority of the Anglo-Saxon race, along with his claim that the German race was being defiled by Jews, held great appeal for the Nazis. Hitler kissed the dying hand of the man upon whose theories his own were based.

• The German states of Bavaria and Saxony ended their ban on Hitler's public speaking. During the first ten months of the year, Hitler spoke publicly fifty-six times. Dr. Josef Goebbels, one of his most devoted followers, pledged that if the Nazi party could not win power legally, "Then we'll march against this government."

• The United States and Canada established diplomatic relations independent of Great Britain. The International Peace Bridge, which links the two countries at Buffalo, New York, opened with the Prince of Wales and Vice President Dawes presiding at the opening ceremonies. Today the two countries are squabbling about whether to build a new, state-of-the-art bridge, or renovate the old one.

• Meeting in Moscow, the 15th All-Union Congress of the Communist Party condemned all "deviation from the general party line as interpreted by Joseph Stalin," thus ceding to that despot effective control of the Union of Soviet Socialist Republics.

• Alexander Kerensky, head of the overthrown provisional government of Russia, came to New York City to live in exile.

• Mustapha Kemal Ataturk was elected president of Turkey and announced plans for the "westernization" of his country. Ataturk declared that Islam would no longer be the state religion, and men would abandon the fez and women the veil.

• Anthropologists found the origin of humankind in "Peking Man" and scientists and religionists continued to debate evolution and the theory of the universe's creation.

The distinguished journalist Elmer Davis described Americans of 1927 as the new "Chosen People."[8] But were they? Let us see.

Profile of a People

In 1927, some 118 million people lived in America. Substantially more than half (66 million) lived in urban areas, while about 52 million lived in rural areas. As in previous years, people continued to move from farms to cities and towns, but at a somewhat slower rate.[9] As of July 1, 1927, the farm population was about twenty-eight million or about three million less than what it had been in 1920. While the remaining farmers had no difficulty in providing enough food for a growing population, America was primarily an urban nation.[10]

Total immigration for 1927 was 323,885, while the number of those emigrating was 75,122. The effects of laws limiting immigration and favoring those from Northern and Western Europe, at the expense of those from Southern and Eastern Europe, began to impact the size and nature of the American population. Of the immigrants who entered the country in 1927, most were Mexican, German, Irish, English, Scotch, Scandinavian, and Hebrew. The majority of immigrants described themselves as unskilled laborers and tended to stay close to the places where they disembarked. The states receiving the most immigrants included New York, Texas, Michigan, California, Massachusetts, Illinois, New Jersey, Pennsylvania, Ohio, and Arizona.

America's population grew by only 1,545,000 from July 1925 to July 1928, compared with 1,800,000 between 1920 and 1925. Among the reasons America's population grew more slowly were the overall decline in immigration and the growing popularity of birth control. With an average of 2.41 children per family, America, by 1927, had entered into a period of much slower natural increase. "This is something new in our experience," wrote one demographer, "and will require many adjustments. . . . We are no longer as young as we once were."[11]

By 1927, life expectancy had risen to 59 years, a ten-year increase from 1900. However, suicide, especially among American youth, was a growing concern. In 1925, there were 12.1 suicides per 100,000 people in the United States; by 1932, that number had grown to 17.4. In New York City, the suicide rate during this period was somewhat higher: 14.4 per 100,000 in 1925, and 21.3 in 1932. In 1927, the suicide rate was 13.3 for the country as a whole and 15.7 for the City of New York.[12] Infant mortality was lower than in any previous year, with greater declines reported in rural areas as compared with urban areas. The decline in deaths from pneumonia, influenza, and tuberculosis, important killers in the earlier 1920s, helps explain the decline in the death rate for 1927. Death from cancer, however, showed a marked increase.

Between 1916 and 1926, marriages per 100,000 people declined from 93 in 1916 to 66 in 1926. Divorce, on the other hand, increased steadily from 113 per 100,000 in 1916 to 154 in 1926.[13] The term "companionate marriage" entered the vocabulary via former judge Ben Lindsey. This form of marriage allowed for divorce by mutual consent by a couple who postponed having children until they were sure they wished to stay married.

Havelock Ellis, the sex guru of the 1920s, applauded the greater economic independence of women and the greater freedom between the sexes before marriage. He concluded that "even if it has sometimes led to license, [sexual intimacy] is not only itself beneficial but the proper method of preparing for a more intimate permanent union." In his view, the greater facility of divorce encouraged more satisfactory marriages.[14] Ellis went on to express gratification over the growing use of contraception as a means of family planning and limiting excessive population growth. He declared, "To the United States ... belongs the honor of being first, among great nations, to assert, virtually, the international importance of birth control."[15]

Despite a failure rate of about 50 percent, the rubber condom grew in popularity and about two million were used daily.[16] According to research completed in 1927, the pessary used together with contraceptive jelly was more successful in preventing births.[17] Ellis deplored the continuing practice of preferring spinster teachers over married ones. "There cannot be the smallest doubt," he wrote, "that women who have had sex experience of their own and children of their own are incomparably better fitted to deal with the special difficulties of children than those who have not."[18] While Ellis was ahead of his time, his views gave encouragement to the growing independence of women, the use of family planning, and the abandonment of the prejudice against married women in teaching and in other professions.

As never before, the 118 million people who lived in America in 1927 were bombarded by the bewildering possibilities of the airplane, the motion picture, telephone, radio, and, above all, the automobile. On January 7, 1927, Walter S. Gifford, president of the American Telephone and Telegraph Company, and Sir Evelyn Mournay, Secretary of the British Post Office, spoke to each other by telephone thereby inaugurating the first commercial transatlantic telephone hookup. Thirty-one additional calls were made that day. These startling inventions fueled the economic boom of 1927. As reported in *Motor* magazine, there were 22,342,457 automobiles registered. In the United States there was one car to every five persons as compared with one car to 43 persons in Britain, one to 325 in Italy, and one to 7,000 in Russia. Paved highways were rapidly being built. Yet, by 1927, one could drive on paved highways only from New York to St. Mary's, Kansas. After that, dirt roads made soft by rain could be a problem as a car could easily get stuck in mud up to its hubcaps. Moreover, gasoline stations and rest stops were few and far between. The Federal Aid Road Act of 1916 offered money to states that would organize highway departments and match federal grants. In 1906 local governments were providing 96 percent of all highway funds; by 1927 they were providing only 53 percent while the states spent 37 percent, and the federal government 10 percent. Thus, automobiles were subsidized through federal monies to a far greater extent than were the railroads in the previous century.

In a national automobile show of that year one could find such models still being made today as the Buick, Cadillac, Chevrolet, Chrysler, Dodge, Lincoln, Oldsmobile, and Pontiac. Among those once-popular names no longer in pro-

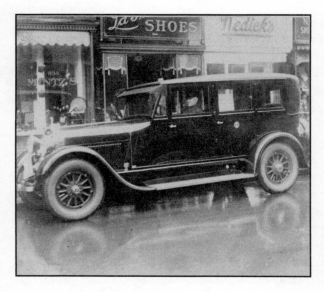

*President Coolidge's new
car—his first in twelve
years. From the collections
of the Library of
Congress.*

duction were the Auburn (production halted in 1936), Chandler (1928), Essex (1928), Hudson (1957), Hupmobile (1941), Packard (1958), Pierce-Arrow (1938), Rickenbacker (1927), Studebaker (1965), and Stutz (1934). The cars were cheap, even for the time. An ad featuring a Chrysler "50" in the *Saturday Evening Post* of May 7, 1927, asked, "Where can you find so much for $750?" Among the advertised features were a car that could do 50 miles an hour, reach 5 to 25 miles in eight seconds, and get 25 miles to the gallon. Some families who lacked indoor toilets and baths boasted an automobile. In New York, California, Ohio, Pennsylvania, Illinois, and Michigan, there were more than a million cars each.

But the hit of the year was the introduction toward the end of 1927 of Ford's Model "A." In 1927, half the cars on the road were Model "T" Fords, about ten million of them, some of which were brown but most black. When on December 2 Ford introduced the Model "A," a million people tried to see the new automotive phenomenon on the first day. Those who got close enough to see it found that the Model "A" had a self-starter. No need to wrench shoulder joints cranking up as one did with the Model "T." The gas tank was in front of the windshield, the dash had a speedometer, a gas gauge, and an ammeter. While the Model "A" was more powerful than the Model "T," what caught the fancy of the prosperous was that to meet the competition from General Motors and Chevrolet, the Model "A" was now available in different colors—red, green, yellow, and blue. Even the distinguished philosopher Reinhold Niebuhr was impressed, "Henry made a lady out of Lizzy,"[19] he said, that is, the "Tin Lizzy" as the Model "T" had affectionately been called.

In 1927, there were 21,716 automobile-related deaths. Mechanical failures, poor roads, and a paucity of road signs contributed to the high death rate. "In proportion to the number of vehicles today and the number of miles they were driven, the percentage is not as high today as it was then."[20]

Despite the growing use of the automobile, trolley mileage was still near its 1917 peak. There were plenty of financial backers for the electric railways who insisted that the modernized trolley provided more comfortable transportation than the automobile or the bus. But trolley usage had declined by four percent and many of the electric railway companies sought to keep themselves solvent by incorporating bus service into their transportation network. While the death of the trolley, as Mark Twain put it in another context, was greatly exaggerated, nevertheless, its future remained bleak.

The automobile was not alone in spearheading the Coolidge prosperity. Coolidge was the first president to speak to the nation by radio. From a standing start in 1920, when there was no radio broadcasting to the public, sales of radios grew in 1927 to $425.6 million so that by 1927, one-third of American households owned one.

Labor-saving household appliances proliferated, including the wall-mounted can opener, toasters, vacuum cleaners, heating pads, refrigerators, coffee percolators, waffle irons and washing machines. The American was indeed a "consumer in wonderland."[21]

Telling Americans about the wonders of the new labor-saving, fun-providing, status-creating products was the responsibility of a growing advertising business, which employed some 600,000 people. Industry spent well over a billion dollars advertising the fruits of the assembly line in newspapers and magazines, through direct mail solicitation, on radio, and in outdoor advertising on street cars and elsewhere. The *Saturday Evening Post* was the most prominent advertising medium of the times. The journal's average weekly circulation was two and a half million, which seemed to justify the $6,000 cost for a full-page advertisement in black-and-white. Of the more than 200 pages in each issue, three-fifths were taken up with advertising. The *Post* declined ads for liquor and cigarettes.

The "Average Man"

Since they spent such vast sums on advertising, American companies wanted to know more about the masses of people to whom they were trying to sell something. What did they want? How much would they pay? What did they need? How can they be motivated to spend their money? To provide some of the answers to these questions, Kenneth M. Goode (1880–1958), an advertising authority, and Harford Powel Jr. (1887–1956), a publicist, sought to provide the facts they thought advertisers needed to make their pitch to the American public. As one can see from the following, these advertising authorities had no illusions about the sophistication or intelligence of the masses of Americans.

"In the United States are about 118,000,000 people. Dropping the 5,500,000 who can't read or are in jails or hospitals, we have 112,500,000 left. Subtracting 23,000,000 million boys and girls under fourteen, we find, roundly, 90,000,000 still within range of ordinary advertising artillery. . . . This 90,000,000 contains, therefore, all the 'sales resistance'."[22]

Goode and Powel indicated that of every 100 American children, 36 were not attending school at all while 54 were in elementary school. There were seven out of every hundred attending public high school, three in public night and vocational schools, two entering college but only one remaining to graduate. "This means, first that only 64 per cent of the youth of America, coming customers, are at school at all. Even this 64 per cent does not receive a complete public-school education. Their schooling averages only seven and one-half years. College and university education reaches but two Americans in every hundred; and of those two, only one completely."[23] The authors concluded, "Although the various 'Alpha' intelligence tests rate the college freshman above the average man on the street, we don't find even the college graduate . . . any great highbrow."[24]

Among the examples of how little American consumers know, the Goode and Powel study found that fewer than 500 out of 1,047 students queried in Knoxville, Tennessee, knew where to locate the District of Columbia, while 95 percent did not know what the electoral college was. One student said, "It's a college where you take what you want." The authors feared that the growing popularity of film and radio threatened the reading of serious literature. "The mental standard for the moving-picture producer is the intelligence of the fourteen-year-old child."[25] "The average normal American," believed the advertisers, "celebrates his twenty-fifth birthday by shutting shop mentally and refusing to accept any new ideas." The result, they concluded, was that advertising copy aimed anywhere above the comprehension of an eighth-grade school child, about twelve to fourteen years of age, cut the readership in half.

Americans "go to the movies every other week; and about one in four listens to the radio perhaps an hour a day. They like dark blue as a color and lilac as a scent. Writing themselves, they use a vocabulary generally fewer than a thousand words although each can understand, in reading, maybe six times as many. In their aggregate action the element of intellect is practically negligible."[26]

As if to confirm this rather dim view, Harry L. Hollingworth, a Columbia University psychologist, concluded that the average American was "superstitious, ill-educated, conventional and mentally equal to a fourteen-year-old. . . ."[27] Conceding that the "average man" is an abstraction, nevertheless, tests administered by the Army to some four million soldiers and those given to employees in life insurance companies, police departments, colleges, and universities, indicated that:

• At the age of fifty-three or earlier the average man dies.

• The average man weighs 150 pounds and is 67 inches tall.

• In an age when brain weight is considered a measure of intelligence, the 1,300 gram weight of the average man, while weighing more than twice the weight of the great apes, is nothing to boast about.

• The average man's vocabulary includes about 7,500 words. If he has a whole minute for the problem, he will correctly answer when asked how many pencils can be bought for fifty cents if two pencils cost five cents.

• The average American leaves school at the eighth grade. He has a smattering of local geography and knows a little about history and a few elementary facts about physiology. He has no general knowledge of civics, science, politics, or literature.

• Following his father's example, the average man is a Methodist Democrat or a Baptist Republican. In industry he is likely to drift into the skilled trades but is not likely to have an occupation superior to that of his father.

• The average man does not take a great interest in religion, although he has concrete ideas about morality.

• Although the average man is often the victim of quacks, mediums, and salesmen who wish to sell him unsound investments, he "has great influence in determining what the next generation will be like."[28]

Advertisers noted that the average current annual income, divided evenly among men, women, and children, was $770. "No advertiser can go far wrong calculating his per-family average at $75 a week—with two people working to produce it."[29] Women and youth became primary consumers in society, with women responsible for four out of every five sales. "Whether married or getting pay for their work, women are the nation's purchasing agents."[30]

Rural America

"The American farmer," wrote William Allen White, "cut off his whiskers when he began cranking his car . . . He shaves as often as a lawyer . . . . When he goes to town in his Sunday suit, the American farmer looks no different from the merchant or the clerk, the doctor or the teacher."[31] The typical farmer had an education at about the sixth-grade level and had three or four children who attended school about seven months each year. While he owned a mortgaged farm, the farmer of 1927 was no peasant.

Rural America was becoming more prosperous and less remote. A survey of more than four hundred rural homes showed that one in four had been repainted within five years, and three in four had all the floors finished or covered with carpets or linoleum.[32] "The sagging window shutter, the peeling paint, the scuffed and splintered soft-wood floors of a previous generation, were almost as rare as the floorless log cabins of Lincoln's day."[33] Almost two farm houses in five had furnaces; one in ten running hot water; 15 percent modern bathrooms; three-fourths sinks with drains in the kitchen.[34]

In Edgar County, Illinois, a marketing survey described a prosperous type of farm community. Two-thirds of homes had phonographs and half had radios. "The aerial is already more familiar than the windmill."[35] There were nearly a million radio sets and ninety broadcasting stations, which relieved the isolation of farm work and offered weather data and better farming techniques.

Rural Free Delivery made it possible for the farm family to receive as much reading matter as the typical urban family. Ray F. Pollard, county farm bureau agent for Schoharie, New York, personally visited over one hundred farms in one hundred school districts to gain information on farmers' reading habits. He found they read 132 different newspapers and magazines. The average farmer in the area he canvassed received 9.82 "papers," 2.75 agricultural notices or leaflets, 1.87 weeklies, and 1.58 communications from farm organizations.[36] At the end of 1925, the rural circulation of the *New York Times* was estimated to be 75,205 daily.[37] Two-fifths of rural households had telephones to link them with the world. On December 31, 1926, the fiftieth anniversary of the telephone, there were an estimated 17.5 million telephones in the United States, serviced by 50 million miles of telephone wires and 300,000 employees. Approximately 20 billion telephone conversations were completed annually.[38]

However, the average rural household was still not as comfortable as its urban counterpart. The availability of electricity was limited, with the result that only about 9 percent used electric lighting, while 20 percent used gas, acetylene, or gasoline, and most of the rest still used the traditional kerosene lamp. Even in prosperous Edgar County, Illinois, only 15 percent had lighting superior to the kerosene lamp. The telephone was a party line, with the number of rings determining for whom calls were intended. Most farmers still depended upon the old wash tub—83 percent of farm households had no bathrooms and 85 percent had no sewage disposal whatsoever.[39] Kitchens generally had ice boxes, not electric refrigerators. Half of farmer households had no cupboards and dishes, as pots and pans lay on the kitchen table. The mail order catalogue was ubiquitous and goods were ordered from it on the installment plan.[40] Even though the farmer was not as well endowed with the labor-saving devices now readily available to his cousin in the city, "the automobile, the telephone, and the radio ended the traditional isolation, and the new machinery in both barn and kitchen reduced the burden of physical labor. Edwin Markham's 'Man with the Hoe' had become a small capitalist with a power plant."[41]

The farmer was rapidly becoming a business person. He was no longer merely a grower of wheat or a herder of cattle. He was in the wheat, cattle, or dairy industries and was concerned with "overhead, fixed charges, net income, quantity production, and turnover."[42] While work animals furnished more power than oil, steam, or electricity, reliance upon these animals was declining rapidly. As the horse population declined from 20 million in 1914 to 15 million in 1928, the number of tractors used on farms increased from 80,000 in 1918 to 853,000 ten years later.

Despite these gains, farmers grew uneasy. They knew they were not sharing in the general prosperity of 1927. Their urban relatives who had abandoned the farm to become doctors, lawyers, or merchants in the city appeared to be faring much better. Farmers knew their numbers were dwindling but were determined to hold on to political power by dominating the state and local government. But there was more on the mind of rural Americans than their economic well-being.

Among the reasons for concern was that the farm population was no longer quite so homogeneous as it once was. While in urban Illinois, for example, two out of three people were foreign born, in rural areas seven out of ten people were natives. They were white and Protestant and wanted to keep it that way. Although rural America's reservations about immigrant newcomers may have been no greater than those of city natives, white urban America prided itself on its ability to cope with diversity, the rest of the country still sought to hold that diversity at bay.

According to a report in the *New York Times* on February 13, 1927, there were 75,000 Jews on farms and many additional ones were seeking land. The Jewish Agricultural Society was frustrated in its attempt to satisfy the needs of all their co-religionists who sought to settle on the land and farm it. Of 885 applicants for farm land in 1927, only 80 bought property, as most could not afford to make the investment. The average cost per farm exclusive of livestock and equipment was $6,570, a sum Jewish immigrants could not raise.

Rural America was also uneasy about what appeared to be happening to their youth. Not only were many leaving the farm, but youthful behavior was becoming increasingly shameful. As one author wrote: "Recently I sat in a first-class hotel in a small city. Sitting across from me in the lobby was a girl in her teens. On each side of her sat a young man with an arm around her. She lolled back against the settee in a too-short skirt, her highly colored complexion was bought at a store and she was smoking a cigarette. Ten years ago the hotel manager would have unceremoniously driven the girl out of the hotel. Today the incident is so commonplace that no one paid any particular attention to it."[43]

But placing blame was not easy. Had the home become too lax? Were parents too permissive? Did the automobile provide too much opportunity for girls and boys to pet, or neck, or even "go all the way?" Did the automobile make society too mobile, thereby eroding the discipline associated with roots in one community? Why was religion no longer as powerful as it once appeared to be, and why did religious leaders appear to have less influence over youthful behavior than they once did?

While rural Americans could not provide the answers to these imponderables any more than could urban Americans, nevertheless they pushed two solutions. In the first instance, they proved influential in curbing immigration. In the second instance, rural Americans lobbied intensely for passage of Amendment XVIII to the Constitution in 1919, which prohibited the sale, use, and distribution of intoxicating beverages. There is little evidence, however, that these measures either raised the morality or improved the character of rural or urban Americans.

Urban America

Urban dwellers prided themselves on their relatively higher standard of living and tended to look down, often with derision, on the overall-clad "hayseed." As a result, there was considerable tension between city and country. H. L. Mencken, speaking for urbanites, crudely crystallized the tension when he wrote about the "humble husbandman" as a "tedious fraud and ignoramus, a cheap rogue and hypocrite . . . . a prehensile moron."

But a National Industrial Conference Board study showed that most city workers were just getting by, and many were not making it at all. The weekly expenditures of a typical office worker in Brooklyn—a costly town—showed that he paid "ten dollars to the landlord, fifteen to the grocer, butcher and milkman,

five to the clothing stores and nine to all his other creditors." His neighbor, working in a factory in Queens, would pay out somewhat less for essentially the same
standard of living.[44] The office or white-collar worker's weekly budget was about
$40 while the manual worker's was $36.

In response to the query, "What all is necessary to the trousseau of a bride
marrying a man of moderate means? He is a bricklayer and we expect to have a
five-room modern house." In her reply the journalist wrote that, among other
things, such a trousseau should include "six linen bed sheets and pillowcases,
summer and winter blankets, from six to twelve bath towels and as many smooth
towels, three or four ordinary table cloths and as many more 'for occasions,' eight
pairs of stockings (in three shades) and eight pairs of gloves to match, two hats,
four pairs of shoes, a raincoat and several dresses, one of them elaborate enough
to do for the evening."[45] While the rich were growing richer, the poor were also
growing richer. Can one really blame Calvin Coolidge, the president of the
United States, if he chose not to rock the ship of state?

Lucky Cal: Profile of a President

When Ronald Reagan became the fortieth president of the United States
(1981–1989) he hung a portrait of Calvin Coolidge, the thirtieth president
(1923–1929), over his chair in the cabinet room. It is not surprising that Ronald
Reagan found in Coolidge a kindred spirit. When Coolidge occupied the White
House, he seemed imperturbable. While Reagan declared, "It's morning in
America," Coolidge urged, "Don't sell America short."[46]

He was, moreover, the luckiest of men, "the darling of the gods," wrote
Mencken. He added, "No other American has been so fortunate or even half so
fortunate." On the day Coolidge was nominated for the vice presidency in 1920
as Harding's running mate, a Boston journalist told his colleagues that if Harding were elected he would be assassinated before he completed his first term.
When his colleagues reproached him for speaking so irreverently of the president
of the United States, the journalist replied, "I am simply telling you what I know.
I know Calvin Coolidge inside out. He is the luckiest, goddam, blank blank in
the whole world."[47] Others had a similar hunch, "Everything comes to Calvin
Coolidge in a most uncanny and mysterious manner."[48]

It was said that Coolidge could be silent in five languages. That when he
opened his mouth a moth flew out. Greeting him, said another, was like "shaking hands with a dead mackerel." Alice Roosevelt Longworth, daughter of
Theodore and for generations doyenne over the Washington, D.C., social scene,
declared that Coolidge must have been weaned on a pickle. William Allen White

thought he had been "weaned on a clothespin"[49] and seemed perpetually to be "looking down his nose to locate that smell which seemed forever to affront him."[50] His face was inscrutable and when he did smile, "the effect was like ice breaking in a New England River."[51] When the writer Dorothy Parker was told that Calvin Coolidge was dead, she asked, "How could they tell?"

In many ways, Coolidge was indeed the "odd fish" William Allen White called him. His frame was narrow and his height medium. His features were thin; his lips tightly pressed together as if he feared losing his teeth if he smiled. Reddish hair topped his broad forehead. He was an intensely private man who sought a public life; a farmer who preferred the company of those in business. He was rural born but spent most his life in cities of moderate size. He was a man of limited financial means but felt comfortable with the wealthy. Before being elected vice president he had never been to Washington, D.C. He was taciturn, withdrawn, undramatic, and undemonstrative. He lacked charisma, yet he was one of the most popular of presidents.

In 1927, Walter Lippmann, the distinguished journalist and essayist, portrayed Coolidge as the beneficiary of prosperous times. He wrote, "[The people] trust him utterly as they hear his voice on expensive radio sets; they praise him as they ride in expensive motor cars; they toast him at banquets where there is more food than can be eaten."[52] And even Mencken wrote in April 1933, after Coolidge's death, "He was revered simply because he was so plain just folks—because what little he said was precisely what was heard in every garage and barbershop."

Americans loved him because he was everything they were not. He was colorless, yet the times in which he was their president were among the most colorful in the nation's history. He was parsimonious. The people he served spent lavishly on automobiles, cosmetics, radios, and fashionable clothes. He lived prudently. He did not smoke. Prohibition kept liquor out of the White House when it did not keep liquor out of the mainstream of American life. In an age when sports were becoming an important national diversion, Coolidge played no games. He did not play golf or tennis, swim, bowl, or play billiards. He had no hobbies. As president, however, he did learn to fish for trout and exercised on a mechanical horse that he kept in the basement of the White House.

In an age of rampant political corruption, when prohibition was cheerfully ignored, Coolidge was incorruptible. He was dour and pessimistic; the people who elected him were lusty and optimistic. In an age of ballyhoo, he seemed the people's safe harbor. He was the "Puritan in Babylon," as William Allen White called him. In a raucous age, he was "Silent Cal."

He was the only president to have been born on the Fourth of July (1872). The date of his birth tends to fix him in time; his birthplace in the granite hills in remote Plymouth Notch, Vermont, tends to fix him in place. Today, the village is a Coolidge museum where one can still see the president's birthplace, the church his family attended, the small house in which Calvin was raised and which later became President Coolidge's summer White House. There's the Coolidge cheese factory and young Calvin's one-room school. Five generations of Coolidges are buried in the graveyard near Plymouth Notch.

On June 26, 1895, Amherst College in Northampton, Mass. awarded Calvin Coolidge his baccalaureate cum laude. There were seventy-six men in Coolidge's graduating class. It was Dwight W. Morrow, and not Calvin Coolidge, who was voted the one most likely to succeed. His roommate described him as "an ordinary American boy." Other classmates described him as "unostentatious in the extreme"; "not a fluent conversationalist, but rather a good listener"; "a man of character, both shrewd and straightforward"; "eminently methodical and got things done without the appearance of haste"; "constant in application, determined, simple, and independent." Lucius R. Eastman, a classmate, later said of him, "All of us came to like Coolidge as a comfortable table companion, but I do not think any of us rated him very high until the end of senior year. I think it would be stretching the facts a little to say that, other than having a high regard for him personally and recognizing his ability for quiet humor, we expected much from him, for we did not."[53] Yet, his Amherst experiences were central to his personality and he looked back fondly upon them. Coolidge, purportedly the most silent of presidents, could often be encouraged to talk warmly about his years at Amherst. He felt greatly honored when on May 28, 1921, he was elected a lifetime trustee of the college.

Although there is little in Coolidge's days at Amherst that would lead one to detect the batter out of which a president of the United States was made, by the time Coolidge became president upon the death of Warren G. Harding, he was one of the most experienced of American politicians. At a dinner when he was vice president, a distinguished woman inquired, "Mr. Coolidge, what is your hobby?" To which he replied, "Holding public office."[54] This was, indeed, the truth. He had held more elective offices than any other American president. He climbed the political ladder step by unostentatious step—city councilman, state assemblyman, mayor, state senator, lieutenant governor, governor, and vice president of the United States. Of the twenty elections in which he was a candidate he won nineteen. Despite the fact that he lacked the back-slapping gregariousness expected of a politician, he was one of the most effective vote-getters in

America's history. Rev. Jay T. Stocking, who knew him well at Amherst, wrote: "The last place in the world I should have expected him to succeed was politics."[55] But succeed he did.

Coolidge's success began with the decision he and his father arrived at jointly—that he should begin the study of law. However, studying law at a law school appeared prohibitively expensive. And so the decision was made that Calvin would prepare for the law in the old-fashioned way of apprenticing in the offices of a law firm. In 1895, Coolidge settled down to study law in the firm of Hammond and Field, Amherst alumni, in Northampton. By 1897, he appeared ready to practice in the Commonwealth of Massachusetts. He was twenty-five years old and a very eligible bachelor.

He was, however, in no hurry to get married. His career in law and politics came first. But during the winter of 1904–1905 he met another Vermonter, Grace Goodhue (1879–1957), a graduate of the University of Vermont, who had come to Northampton to teach at the Clark School for the Deaf. What followed was not exactly a whirlwind courtship. Nevertheless, it stimulated much gossip, since it seemed strange to that closely knit community to see this shy young man and the animated, attractive young woman apparently getting serious about each other. On October 4, 1905, a dreary rainy day, Calvin and Grace were married despite the objections of Grace's mother, who wanted her daughter to wait a year. But Calvin insisted that he had the resources to support a wife, and so the wedding went forward.

Grace's mother attributed Calvin's success to her daughter's qualities. Donald R. McCoy, a biographer of Coolidge, believes she may have been right. "She was a perfect helpmeet to a loving but often cranky husband. . . . Where he was dull, she shone. Where he was rude, she displayed strikingly good manners. Where he irritated people, she ingratiated herself with them. Where he turned men sour, she made them smile. Where he chilled women, she warmed them. In short, where he needed help she supplied it."[56] Although he was often an inconsiderate husband, Calvin was aware of his wife's contribution to his success. Writing in his *Autobiography* in 1929 he said, "She has borne with my infirmities and I have rejoiced in her graces."[57]

Even Vermont was sweltering in the heat on August 2, 1923, when Coolidge was on vacation at his father's house in Plymouth Notch. He had put in a hard day's work and the family went to bed at about nine o'clock. It was one way to beat the heat of that sultry summer night. The news services, which already knew of Harding's illness, were in Vermont "just in case" something happened to the president. Coolidge had never been particularly good copy and it was hot, dusty, and boring to watch the vice president pitch hay on his father's farm.

Since John Coolidge's home had no telephone, Plymouth Notch, Vermont, was almost the last community to get word of President Warren G. Harding's death. When Winfred A. Perkins, a telegrapher in a nearby post office, received word of President Harding's death, he called a Miss Cilley, a neighbor of the Coolidges. But she was fast asleep and did not respond to the ringing of the telephone. Perkins dressed, grabbed the telegram containing the news of Harding's death and sought out Coolidge's staff, which consisted of his secretary, Erwin C. Geisser, and his chauffeur, Joseph M. McInerney, plus William H. Crawford, a newspaperman, and together they raced over the darkened roads to deliver the message to the vice president.

They knocked on the front door of John Coolidge's house and awakened the seventy-eight-year-old man, who did not like being disturbed. When he heard what the message was all about he climbed upstairs and with a trembling voice called to his son. Coolidge awoke, read the telegram and heard himself called "Mr. President" by his father. Calvin and Grace Coolidge dressed and, perhaps as a shadow of self-doubt crossed his mind, he reassured himself, saying, "I believe I can swing it."[58] Before going downstairs the new president and his wife prayed.

By then, the village of Plymouth Notch was all lit up. Coolidge told the reporters that he had sent his condolences to Mrs. Harding and expressed his grief over the death of his "chief and friend." From the telephone in Miss Cilley's store, Coolidge called Secretary of State Charles Evans Hughes, who urged him to take the oath of office immediately. "It should be taken before a notary," said Secretary Hughes. Coolidge replied, "Father is a notary." "That's fine," Hughes concluded.[59]

In the modest sitting room of his home, Coolidge's father, dressed in his black Sunday clothes, administered the oath to his son. With his right hand raised and the other on a Bible that belonged to his mother, Calvin Coolidge repeated the oath: "I, Calvin Coolidge, do solemnly swear that I will faithfully execute the office of president of the United States and will, to the best of my ability, preserve, protect, and defend the Constitution of the United States. So help me God." And at 2:47 A.M. Coolidge signed the typewritten oath and his father affixed his notary seal. Mrs. Coolidge was tremendously moved, but the thirtieth president of the United States did not kiss his wife. He and Grace went back to sleep. While they slept, a telephone was put into John Coolidge's home.

As it turned out, when the Coolidges got to Washington, D.C., they discovered that John Coolidge was probably not eligible to administer the oath and so a new oath was quietly administered. But it was the oath administered by his father, taken in that simple home in rural Vermont, that contributed in important ways to the Coolidge legend.

Coolidge brought to the presidency a change of personality, not of policy. Where his predecessor had been gregarious, Coolidge was a loner. While Harding was warm and affable, Coolidge was cold and detached. The magnetic personality of Harding had been replaced by the sterile one of Coolidge. Coolidge was incorruptible while Harding, although personally honest, had been unable to see the corruption around him and tolerated a level of behavior among members of his administration that disgraced the nation. But Calvin Coolidge made no rash statement that he would clean out the Augean stables. As he did as mayor of Boston, or governor of Massachusetts, Coolidge tended not to take action until he was forced to do so. Coolidge determined, at the outset of his administration, to retain all of Harding's policies, but the change in tone and style in the White House seemed to the American public to be a change in substance as well. And, to a degree, it was.

Coolidge announced that he would continue the Harding policies of collecting all war debts of former enemies and allies ("They hired the money, didn't they," he said), restricting immigration, raising the protective tariff on behalf of American industry, urging additional credit legislation for the farmer, opposing bonuses to soldiers, and achieving further economy in government. He supported membership in the World Court but not in the League of Nations. Coolidge enjoyed no honeymoon period with the sixty-eighth Congress. Instead, he inherited and exacerbated relations with Congress as that body continued to hold the executive office in disdain. A maverick group of Republicans, together with Democrats, blocked Coolidge's proposals. During the first four months of the Coolidge administration, Congress did not adopt a single presidential initiative. When it passed the bonus bill for veterans, Coolidge promptly vetoed it and Congress, with equal gusto, overrode the veto. Congress was glad to adjourn in June and so its members were free to begin the presidential campaign of 1924.

Claude M. Fuess, who wrote a highly admiring biography of Coolidge, described the election of 1924 as "unimportant, uninteresting and unexciting." Why should it have been otherwise, inasmuch as the nation was enjoying genuine prosperity? For the 28.5 million American voters there was a choice of Calvin Coolidge (Republican), John W. Davis (Democrat), and Robert M. La Follette (Progressive), the populist senator from Wisconsin who had formed a third party.

The outcome was never in doubt. Coolidge remained way ahead in the polls and rode in on a tide of normalcy and prosperity. It was either "Keep Cool with Coolidge" or "Coolidge or Chaos." To the attacks of his opponents, Coolidge remained silent and smug, appearing too busy to campaign. Davis found himself in a futile fight with "Fighting Bob" La Follette and shadow boxing with Coolidge.

The victory was complete. In the Sixty-ninth Congress, Coolidge Republicans had a solid majority in both houses. The only shadow over the election of 1924 was that only 52 percent of qualified voters bothered to cast their ballots. Perhaps the price of prosperity was apathy. Nevertheless, as a result of the 1924 election, the accidental president became president in his own right.

On March 4, 1925, Calvin Coolidge took the oath of office. In the inaugural address that followed, the president sounded no clarion call to heroic action or to selfless sacrifice. He declared: "America seeks no earthly empire built on blood and force. No ambitions, no temptations lures her to the thought of foreign domination. The legions she sends forth are armed, not with the sword, but with the cross. The higher state to which she seeks the allegiance of all mankind is not of human but of divine origin. She cherishes no purpose save to merit the favor of Almighty God." While not inspired by these platitudes, the president's listeners were satisfied with what they heard because the president confirmed the rightness of their happy state. They had, the president said, achieved "a state of contentment seldom before seen." As a speech it is memorable only in that it was the first inaugural address ever to be broadcast to the nation over the radio. Gathering in clusters around their radios, more people heard their president address them than ever before.

If Coolidge had an underlying political philosophy, it was that "the chief business of the American people is business." Drawing on the dogmas of Professor Garman, his mentor at Amherst, Coolidge insisted that "the man who builds a factory builds a temple. . . . The man who works there worships there." On November 19, 1925, Coolidge spoke before the Chamber of Commerce of the State of New York. There he reiterated the awe in which he held business and thus came closest to defining his philosophy of the relations between government and business. "It is my belief," he said, "that the whole material development of our country has been enormously stimulated by reason of general insistence on the part of the public authorities that economic effort ought not to partake of privilege, and that business should be unhampered and free."[60]

As president, Coolidge was often described as "Silent Cal." Yet Coolidge made effective use of what we now call the modern media including radio, movie newsreels, public releases, as well as the press. His first State of the Union message to

President Coolidge greeting Boy Scouts at the White House. From the collections of the Library of Congress.

Congress, made in person in December 1923, was the first to be broadcast on radio. He held frequent press conferences, was patient with photographers, and was willing to pose for them in cowboy or Indian attire as the occasion required.

Writing for the *New Republic*, a reporter noted, "Mr. Coolidge, in his quiet way, pours into the microphone an average of 8,688 words a month, addresses by word of mouth or by special communication some seventy-five different kinds of public gatherings annually, unburdens himself each year of words enough in public addresses to fill two fair-sized novels, and preserves meantime a reputation as the silent man in the White House. . . . Mr. Coolidge is not a silent man, but a very noisy man. He is by no means economical with words. He squanders words. . . . His record for last year (1925) consisted of twenty-eight speeches as against Wilson's best with seventeen, but this was only the beginning."[61]

According to the *New York Times*, President Coolidge spoke to a radio audience equal in size to the entire population of the United States in 1865. His Washington's Birthday message was heard by more than 20 million people. On April 25, 1927, his address to the United Press Associations was heard by 10 million. When he decorated Colonel Charles Lindbergh with the Distinguished Flying Cross he spoke over a national hook-up of fifty stations to an audience estimated at 30 million.[62] By mastering the media, the president contributed to the Coolidge myths and legends and enhanced his growing popularity.

Thus, Coolidge caught the nation by surprise on August 2, 1927, while vacationing in Rapid City, South Dakota, when he announced that he would not run for reelection in 1928. He had been in office exactly four years. Even Grace Coolidge was surprised by the announcement. And once again, the man who even during his presidency seemed to avoid the spotlight found it shining on him as he willingly, even eagerly, prepared to abandon the highest office in the land. There were many, including his confidant Frank Stearns, who could not believe what they heard. There were some who thought it was a trick through which he might be more easily nominated or perhaps even drafted by his party. But Coolidge remained steadfast. Despite proddings of admirers, he declared to the Republican National Committee on December 6, 1927, "My decision (not to run) will be respected." And it was.

Had Coolidge chosen to run he surely would have been elected. Had he done so he, not Franklin D. Roosevelt, would have been the first to break with tradition and run for a third term. Breaking with traditions, however, was not the Coolidge way. But would it truly have been a third term? Apparently, Coolidge did not regard finishing Harding's presidential term as a "first term" in office. Yet the historian Mark Sullivan in an article in *World's Work* as early as 1925 urged "A Third Term for Coolidge." It was his view that the unwritten precedent of George Washington limiting a president to two terms no longer appeared appropriate to "modern America." At first Coolidge was grateful for the support he received and viewed a third term as a distinct possibility. But as his administration wore on, he appeared to grow tired of the presidency. For example, on New Year's Day, 1926, the president wrote his father: "I suppose I am the most powerful man in the world, but great power does not mean much except great limitations. I cannot have any freedom even to go and come. I am only in the clutch of forces greater than I am."[63]

The death of Calvin Jr. from blood poisoning on July 7, 1924, unnerved him. In his *Autobiography* he wrote, "When he went, the power and the glory of the Presidency went with him." The death of his father on March 18, 1926, left him insecure. While he did not openly express it, Coolidge probably loved his father more than any other person in his life. Colonel Edmund Starling, his chief Secret Service aide, interpreted a conversation he had with Coolidge in the spring of 1927: "The novelty of being president had worn off; the glory of it had gone with Calvin's death; there was no great national crisis which demanded a continuation of his leadership. From now on the office was more a burden than anything else. The steady grind of work was wearing him down, and the duties of the First Lady, plus Washington's weather, were weakening Mrs. Coolidge's health."[64]

Starling probably got it right when he noted the health considerations of the First Couple. The president, never really robust, was something of a hypochondriac. He had problems with his digestion and in May 1925, may have suffered a heart attack. Rudolph Max, a physician, reports that Coolidge had been warned by his doctors that because of his heart, he ought not subject himself to another four years as president.[65] The stifling summers in Washington, D.C., aggravated his bronchial asthma which contributed to a weakening of the heart.

Although Grace Coolidge had not been consulted, she too was ready to leave the White House and was subtly preparing the way for Calvin to do so. As early as March 1925, she began to crochet a bedspread eight squares long and six squares wide, one square for each of the forty-eight weary months she had to serve as the nation's First Lady.

In his *Masks in a Pageant*, William Allen White makes an ahistorical leap into Calvin Coolidge's mind when he writes that at the end of a hard day, as "the weariness of the flesh and the confusion of the spirit were riding him, he would come over to his wife, stand by her a second, looking down his nose drearily, then—one can almost see him opening his wide, handsome eyes to smile as he said: 'Let's go home, Grace.'" It is hard to believe Calvin was ever in such a reflective mood or that he shared his weariness with his wife. Moreover, few really thought the president handsome.

It has long been conjectured whether Coolidge anticipated the end of the bull market, the attendant stock market crash, and the era of the great depression. On one occasion, when visitors were urging him to reconsider, Grace interrupted, "Papa thinks there will be a depression." Coolidge was not well versed in matters of high finance and was content to let his Secretary of Treasury Andrew Mellon bolster confidence in American markets. But Coolidge understood, it seems, his essentially limited ability and his awareness that his route to the presidency had been in his ability to jump on the political escalator as it was going up. His intuition may have told him that Mellon could not be right all the time and that some difficult decisions would have to be made if desperate economic times were to come. He could sense that important issues were coming up before the nation and that during a "third" term, his powers to do anything about them would be more limited than ever.

In 1931, Coolidge wrote an article for the *Saturday Evening Post* in which he said, "When I announced my determination not to run for president in 1928, my decision had been made a long time. While I wanted the relief that would come to Mrs. Coolidge and me from public responsibilities we had for so many years, my action was also based on the belief that it was good for the country."[66]

But Coolidge did not find relief in retirement. As previously noted, he was not a man given to sports, hobbies, or recreation. He had been classically educated at Amherst and had, on his honeymoon, translated Dante's *Inferno*. However, he mostly confined his reading to newspapers; he did not enjoy concerts, ballet, or theater. Throughout his life, politics coursed in his veins, and when he gave it up he found little that gave him equal satisfaction.

Coolidge was jealous of Herbert Hoover and felt that the party ignored him in the convention at which the latter was nominated. Seven months after he left office the stock market crashed. The deepening depression for which he was being blamed irked and depressed him. He was urged time and again to speak on behalf of the party and its candidates, and he reluctantly did so on several occasion. In those public appearances, however, what his audience saw and heard was a man whose health was obviously declining. The election of Franklin D. Roosevelt and the philosophy of the New Deal deepened his depression and aggravated his medical condition.

Coolidge's health continued to deteriorate. His allergies weakened him and the afternoon naps for which he had become famous in the White House now included a second nap as well. His stomach continued to trouble him and he took an endless variety of medications both for his digestive system and for recurring headaches. Violent asthma attacks worsened his heart ailments.

A close friend described Coolidge's last day this way: "As they sat there talking he (Coolidge) said he was thirsty. The cook and maid were at hand as was Mr. Ross (his secretary), but he didn't like to be waited on—he went to the kitchen to get a glass of water himself. He heard the gardener in the cellar and he went down there to say something to him. The gardener was the last man he spoke to. . . . Leaving the gardener (he) went up to his bedroom. He took off his coat and waistcoat to shave, but sank to the floor. He was dead."[67] Grace found him when she returned from shopping about an hour and a half later. He died of coronary thrombosis on January 5, 1933.

Funeral services for Calvin Coolidge in Northampton were attended by President and Mrs. Herbert Hoover, Chief Justice Charles Evans Hughes, foreign diplomats, and members of the Cabinet and Congress. President Franklin Roosevelt was represented by his wife, Eleanor, and his son, James. A smaller party accompanied the body to Plymouth Notch, Vermont, where he was buried in the family plot.

His Place in History

History has not been kind to one of the most popular presidents. As the historian Peter Levin writes, "Coolidge, the success of his times, is a failure in history."[68] In a sense, Coolidge had the misfortune to be president at a time when to most Americans all seemed well at home and abroad. The nation was not looking for a bold leader and Coolidge complied with their wishes. In a letter to Frank Stearns he wrote, "When things are going along all right, it is a good plan to let them alone." By leaving things alone, Coolidge could not achieve greatness. Walter Lippmann, the most distinguished journalist of his day, noted Coolidge's "genius" for inactivity. "It is far from being an indolent inactivity," wrote Lippmann. "It is a grim, determined, alert inactivity which keeps Mr. Coolidge occupied constantly. Nobody has worked harder at inactivity, with such force of character, with such unremitting attention to detail, with such conscientious devotion to the task."[69] But, continued Lippmann, "this active inactivity suits the mood and certain of the needs of the country admirably."[70] While the American people were squandering their wealth on expensive cars and radios, often paying for them on the installment plan, Coolidge seemed to ease the nation's collective conscience, purge its guilt, and the people adored him in return.

Coolidge was not a constructive president, like Washington, Jackson, and Lincoln. But he does not belong with weaklings Pierce, Buchanan, Grant, and Harding. His place may be with John Quincy Adams and Rutherford B. Hayes or Grover Cleveland. How he might have fared in dealing with the stock market crash of 1929, and the prolonged depression which followed, makes for interesting conjecture.

A widely used college textbook of the 1930s had this to say about Calvin Coolidge. "So completely negative a man," wrote the historians Samuel Eliot Morison and Henry Steele Commager, "never before lived in the White House. . . . Yet this dour, abstemious, and unimaginative figure became one of the most popular of American presidents."[71]

In 1962, Professor Arthur Schlesinger Sr. published a poll in which seventy-five American historians ranked thirty-one of the presidents. Calvin Coolidge was ranked near the bottom as below average.[72] But the decade of the 1960s was one in which active government was considered a virtue. There was confidence that government action could ameliorate the lot of underprivileged Americans. Agitation that government ought to do something about civil rights led to passage of the Civil Rights Act of 1964, which banned discrimination in voting, jobs, and public accommodation. President Lyndon Johnson launched the "Great Society" programs and began his "war on poverty." In 1966, the government began Medicare, which paid part of the costs of medical care for those over sixty-five. Can one wonder that in such an environment, that historians found Coolidge an ineffective president?

However, when Ronald Reagan became president, revisionist historians began to take a closer look at the presidency of Calvin Coolidge. When President Reagan replaced a portrait of Harry Truman with that of Coolidge it was a symbolic advocacy of a less active role for government in American life. Like Coolidge, Reagan said he believed in strict economy in government and a more favorable climate for business activity.

Journalist/historian Paul Johnson continues the revisionist interpretation of the Coolidge presidency. "No president," he writes, "was better briefed on anything that mattered or less often caught unprepared by the doings of his team."[73] In Johnson's view, Coolidge was the most internally consistent and single minded of modern American presidents."[74] Johnson praises Coolidge's minimalism in government. Johnson approves of Coolidge's view that government activity not dictated by pressing necessity was likely to produce undesirable, or at least unforeseen, results.

Coolidge was an over-achiever. That is, little was expected of him by his father, his classmates, or his peers. He became president of the United States by accident but failed to use that bully pulpit effectively. The humorist Will Rogers insisted, "He didn't do anything, but that's what the people wanted done."[75] Writing a summary of Calvin Coolidge, his most balanced biographer wrote: "No nation has risen to heights of culture, spirituality, and material accomplishment based only on the virtues of soberness, thrift, industry, and honesty. This can also be said of individual men, and particularly of Calvin Coolidge."[76]

In 1927, H. L. Mencken wrote of Coolidge, "He will be ranked among the vacuums. It would be difficult to imagine a more obscure and unimportant man." Yet, when Coolidge died, Mencken appeared to have a change of heart. In writing the obituary for Calvin Coolidge, Mencken had this to say: "We suffer most when the White House bursts with ideas. With a World Saver [Wilson] preceding him (I count out Harding as a mere hallucination) and a Wonder Boy [Hoover] following him, he begins to seem, in retrospect, an extremely comfortable and even praiseworthy citizen. His failings are forgotten; the country remembers only the grateful fact that he let it alone . . . it may very well happen that Cal's bones now resting inconspicuously in the Vermont granite will come to be revered as those of a man who really did the nation some service."[77]

[1]*New York Times,* January 1, 1927.
[2]Herbert Asbury, "The Year of the Big Shriek," in *Mirrors of the Year 1927-1928* (New York: Frederick Stokes and Company, 1928), p. 191.
[3]Ibid., p. 196.
[4]Ibid., p. 198.

[5]Jesse Frederick Stekiner, *Americans at Play: Recent Trends in Recreation and Leisure Time Activities* (New York: McGraw-Hill Book Company, Inc., 1933), p. 67.

[6]Quoted in Frederick Lewis Allen, *Only Yesterday* (1931, reprinted New York: Harper & Row, 1959), p. 164.

[7]*New York Times*, January 21, 1927.

[8]Elmer Davis, "The State of the Nation," in *Mirrors of the Year 1927-1928*, p. 35.

[9]Ibid., p. 12.

[10]U. S. Department of Agriculture, *Yearbook of Agriculture: 1927* (Washington, D.C.: U.S. Government Printing Office, 1928), p. 28.

[11]Warren S. Thompson, "Population," in *Recent Social Changes in the United States Since the War Particularly in 1927*, ed. William F. Ogburn (Chicago: Chicago University Press, 1929), p. 9.

[12]John Kenneth Galbraith, *The Great Crash* (Boston: Houghton, Mifflin Company, 1961), p. 134. While there was a steady increase in the number of suicides, the author maintains that a spurt in suicides brought on by the Great Crash of 1929 is a myth.

[13]Ernest R. Groves, "The Family," in *Recent Social Changes in the United States Since the War Particularly in 1927*, ed. William F. Ogburn (Chicago: Chicago University Press, 1929), p. 162.

[14]Havelock Ellis, "The Family," *Whither Mankind: A Panorama of Modern Civilization*, ed. Charles A. Beard (New York: Longmans Green, 1927), p. 209.

[15]Ibid., p. 222.

[16]James F. Cooper, M.D., *Techniques of Contraception: The Principles and Practices of Anti-Conceptual Methods* (New York: Day Nichols, Inc., 1928), p. 52.

[17]Ibid., p. 187.

[18]Ellis, "The Family," p. 225.

[19]Reinhold Niebuhr, "Leaves from the Notebook of a Tamed Cynic," in *The Plastic Age (1913–1930)*, ed. Robert Sklar (New York: George Braziller, 1970), p. 327.

[20]Carl H. Giles, *1927: The Picture Story of a Wonderful Year* (New Rochelle, N.Y.: Arlington House, 1971), p. 230.

[21]Stuart Chase and F. J. Schlink, "Consumer in Wonderland," *New Republic* 49 (February 2, 1927): 293.

[22]Kenneth M. Goode and Harford Powel, Jr., *What About Advertising?* (New York: Harper and Brothers, 1927), pp. 102-118.

[23]Ibid., p. 88.

[24]Ibid.

[25]Ibid., p. 91.

[26]Ibid., p. 97

[27]"The Average Man," *Literary Digest* 93 (May 28, 1927): 21-22.

[28]Ibid.

[29]Goode and Powel, Jr., *What About Advertising*, p. 93.

[30]Ibid., p. 94.

[31]William Allen White, "Portrait of a Typical Farmer," *New York Times Magazine* (January 30, 1927).

[32]E. R. Eastman, *These Changing Times* (New York: The Macmillan Company, 1927), pp. 197-199.

[33]Ibid.
[34]Ibid.
[35]Ibid.
[36]Ibid., p. 24.
[37]Ibid., p. 22.
[38]Ibid., pp. 28-29.
[39]Ibid., p. 198.
[40]Preston William Slosson, "The Great Crusade and After: 1914-1928," *in A History of American Life,* ed. Dixon Ryan Fox and Arthur M. Schlesinger (New York: Macmillan, 1930), p. 217.
[41]Ibid., p. 191.
[42]Quoted in ibid., p. 192.
[43]Eastman, pp. 203–204.
[44]J. C. Lauae, "Cost of Living Shown for a New York Family," *New York Times,* February 13, 1927.
[45]*Washington Post,* July 26, 1928.
[46]Quoted in Jules Ables, *In the Time of Silent Cal* (New York: G.P. Putnam's Sons, 1969), p. 10.
[47]Ibid., p. 11.
[48]Ibid.
[49]William Allen White, *Calvin Coolidge: The Man Who Is President* (New York: The Macmillan Company, 1925), p. 11.
[50]Quoted in Allen, *Only Yesterday,* p. 150.
[51]Quoted in Edward Connery Lathem, *Meet Calvin Coolidge: The Man Behind the Myth* (Brattleboro, Vt.: The Stephen Greene Press, 1960), p. 7.
[52]Walter Lippmann, *Men of Destiny* (New York: The Macmillan Company, 1927), p. 16.
[53]Quoted in Claude M. Fuess, *Calvin Coolidge: The Man from Vermont* (Boston: Little, Brown and Company, 1940), p. 64.
[54]Quoted in Abels, *In the Time of Silent Cal,* p. 13.
[55]Quoted in Fuess, *Calvin Coolidge: The Man from Vermont,* p. 71.
[56]Donald R. McCoy, *Calvin Coolidge: The Quiet President* (New York: The Macmillan Company, 1967), p. 32.
[57]Calvin Coolidge, *Autobiography* (New York: Cosmopolitan Book Corporation, 1931), p. 13.
[58]Quoted in McCoy, *Calvin Coolidge: The Quiet President,* p. 148.
[59]Quoted in ibid., p. 149.
[60]Calvin Coolidge, "Government and Business," in *The Plastic Age: 1917–1930,* ed. Robert Sklar (New York: George Braziller, 1970), p. 275.
[61]Charles Merz, "The Silent Mr. Coolidge," *New Republic* 47 (June 2, 1926): 51.
[62]*New York Times,* September 4, 1927.
[63]Quoted in Fuess, *Calvin Coolidge: The Man from Vermont,* p. 373.
[64]Quoted in McCoy, *Calvin Coolidge: The Quiet President,* p. 383.
[65]Rudolph Max, M.D., *The Health of Presidents* (New York: G.P. Putnam's Sons, 1960), p. 349.

[66]Quoted in Fuess, *Calvin Coolidge: The Man from Vermont*, p. 392.

[67]Clarence Day, *In the Green Mountain Country* (New Haven: Yale University Press, 1934).

[68]Peter Levin, *Seven by Chance: The Accidental Presidents* (New York, 1948), p. 262.

[69]Lippmann, *Men of Destiny*, pp. 12-13.

[70]Ibid., p. 15.

[71]Samuel Eliot Morison and Henry Steele Commager, *The Growth of the American Republic, Vol II* (New York: Oxford University Press, 1937), p. 520.

[72]Arthur Schlesinger, "Our Presidents: A Rating By 75 Historians," *New York Times Magazine* (July 29, 1962): 12.

[73]Paul Johnson, *Modern Times: The World from the Twenties to the Eighties* (New York: Harper and Row, 1983), p. 219.

[74]Ibid.

[75]Quoted in ibid., p. 220.

[76]McCoy, *Calvin Coolidge: The Quiet President*, p. 3.

[77]Quoted in Robert Sobel, *Coolidge: An American Enigma* (Washington, D.C.: Regnery Publishing, Inc., 1998), pp. 416-417.

2
THE COOLIDGE PROSPERITY

February 11, 1927

"A Happy Birthday - Edison" were the words inscribed on employee lapel buttons during the exuberant festivities that marked the eightieth birthday of Thomas Alva Edison. Henry Ford, the 64-year-old billionaire automobile manufacturer and the birthday party's most distinguished guest, warmly embraced America's most renowned inventor.
President Calvin Coolidge sent the following letter to the octogenarian:

My Dear Mr. Edison:
I am very glad to have an opportunity to join with your friends throughout the world in extending hearty congratulations upon your eightieth birthday. To your energy, courage, industry and strong will the world owes a debt of gratitude which it is impossible to compute. Your inventions, placing the forces of nature at the service of humanity, have added to our comfort and happiness and are a benefaction to all mankind for generations to come. I trust that there are in store for you many more years of health and usefulness.

Very truly yours,
Calvin Coolidge[1]

Here are some of Edison's responses to selected questions from newspaper reporters:
"How does an idea for an invention occur to you?"
"A real new idea or a beautiful melody is pulled out of space, a fact which is inexplicable."
"Do you invent by intuition or by reason?"
"Stored-up experience is the principal thing, but the key to successful methods come unsolicited right out of the air."
"Is television possible?"
"Possible, but of very little general value. It's a stunt."'

Christmas 1927 was expected to wind up "in a veritable blaze of glory."[2] It did not disappoint. Buying for the month was estimated at about 10 percent higher than a year ago, making 1927 the third consecutive banner year for American business. Among the reasons for optimism was that Christmas bonuses to members of New York's financial community surpassed the $50 million figure of the previous year. Christmas Club accounts in the banks of New York City and vicinity had between $18 million and $60 million. Nationally, estimates for amounts in Christmas Club accounts varied from $250 million to $500 million.

Even farm communities, as judged by orders taken from mail-order catalogs and chain stores, reported good Christmas sales. Although there had been some concern about a recession in the farm belt, the buying power of farmers remained high because farmers were receiving about six percent more for their crops than in 1926.[3]

In 1927, Santa's sleigh was heavily laden with $200 million worth of toys. Of these, 90 percent were American made and were considered far superior to those imported from Germany and Japan. ". . . Children of ninety-three foreign countries will be made happy with American toys this Christmas."[4] Barring hip flasks and machine-guns, there were toys copied after nearly everything in the adult world, with special interest in wheeled toys such as automobiles, stimulated by Ford's introduction of the Model A, and airplanes, stimulated by Lindbergh's famous solo flight across the Atlantic the previous May.

Mark Sullivan, a distinguished journalist and chronicler of the early 1920s, observed that the dominant characteristic of the country at the end of 1927 was its "devotion to prosperity."[5] A huge electric sign at Columbus Circle in New York City admonished onlookers that: "You should have $10,000 at the age of 30; $25,000 at the age of 40; $50,000 at 50." "Let a Smile Be Your Umbrella" was a popular song of the year, and the economic indicators for 1927 demonstrated that most Americans had a great deal to smile about.

Living Standards

The Internal Revenue Service reported in 1927 that in the previous year Americans enjoyed the highest standard of living ever attained in the world. And Secretary of Commerce Herbert Hoover declared that the rate of real wages in the United States "remained higher than anywhere else in the world or than at any other time in world history."[6]

The Park Avenue Association noted with some pride that those living on New York's posh Park Avenue between Thirty-fourth Street and Ninety-sixth Street boasted an average income in 1927 of $75,000. The silk-stocking crowd, the report continued, annually spent $280 million on luxury items, including $20 million on jewelry and a like amount on luxurious foodstuffs. They spent $16 million on furs, $15 million on art and antiques, $10 million on automobiles, $15 million on travel, $18 million on dining out, and a whopping $54 million on shoes and women's wear.[7]

The automobile made Henry Ford the world's richest man, with holdings estimated at $1.2 billion.[8] John D. Rockefeller (oil) and Andrew W. Mellon (banking) were a distant second and third. In 1927, there were 15,000 millionaires in the United States, a growth from 4,500 in 1914 and 11,000 in 1924.[9] While the rich were growing richer, the average American was likewise growing richer. A $6,000 income per year put one in the upper five percent of the population and on this income a person could live very well.

In 1927, the per capita income was $2,010 for every gainfully employed person in the United States. The average per capita income of $770 was more than double that of 1914, when per capita income reached $320. According to the National Bureau of Economic Research, "The condition of the average person has been improving, from the economic standpoint, at a rate of seven percent a year during the past five years."[10] As a result, as 1927 drew to a close, a rather rosy economic scenario was predicted for America's immediate future.

In an article entitled "Feeling Prosperity's Pulse," the Literary Digest of November 12, 1927, summarized the positive feelings of many. Thus, bankers assembled at a convention in Houston, Texas, adopted a resolution that "there is nothing in recent developments to indicate that we are likely to have anything in the nature of a depression." The Alexander Hamilton Institute of New York anticipated "that industrial activity will strengthen during the next six months." The United States Department of Labor's official reports pointed to the fact that labor was generally well-employed throughout the country.

Secretary of the Treasury Andrew Mellon and Secretary of Commerce Hoover were particularly upbeat, although they tried to add a note of restraint. Mellon wrote, "While business is not as active as in most of 1926, it can hardly be said to be sub-normal, and the underlying fundamentals appear to be sound." He added, "the high prosperity of the year did not represent merely an upward swing in the business cycle, but was the result of general and permanent progress."[11] Hoover's views were read with extreme interest, since the commerce secretary had presidential ambitions.

In his presidential message to the first session of the Seventieth Congress,

Calvin Coolidge also weighed in on the side of optimism. "The country as a whole has had a prosperity never exceeded." He continued, "If the people maintain that confidence which they are entitled to have in themselves, in each other and in America, a comfortable prosperity will continue."[12]

At the thirty-ninth annual meeting of the prestigious American Economic Association in St. Louis on December 29, 1926, economist E. W. Kemmerer of Princeton University declared: "The facts remain that the United States has made great economic progress in recent years, and that at the present time the masses of our people probably enjoy greater prosperity and more comforts of life than do those of any other nation."[13]

In 1927, the wealth of America was as great as that of Britain, France, Germany, Italy, Russia, and all the rest of Europe combined. Never before had so many Americans had so much discretionary income. And they were enjoying their prosperity as rarely before. The radio brought news and music from afar, and the automobile ride into the country became commonplace. Nearly everyone in America's cities had electricity and could take advantage of electric refrigerators, vacuum cleaners, electric toasters, and clothes washers. Silk and rayon replaced cotton for women's lingerie and stockings. So widespread did the wearing of furs become that American women came to be known as "America's greatest fur-bearing animal."[15]

Americans went to the movies in droves. Spectator sports became a national religion. About half the population enjoyed the use of the motor car, compared with but a fraction in 1917. In 1927 there were 5.3 Americans per automobile compared with 196 Germans per automobile. There were 17.6 million telephones in use in the United States, as compared with but 5.9 million in use in 1910. With 6.5 million radios in use, compared with almost none in 1922, that was also rapidly becoming a common household appliance.[16]

Although Americans were living well in 1927, many thought they could live even better by making ever greater use of installment buying. One furniture store advertised: "You furnish the girl we'll furnish the home." Another announced, "Let us feather your nest with a little down." So much had the public become accustomed to installment buying that by 1927 about 15 percent of all goods were sold on credit, about six billion dollars' worth. At any given moment consumers were in debt for two or three billion. Over 85 percent of furniture, 80 percent of phonographs, 75 percent of washing machines, and most vacuum cleaners, pianos, sewing machines, radios, and electric refrigerators were bought by paying in installments.

Much debated was whether installment buying was good or bad for the economy of the nation. There were those who held that it stimulated prosperity and enabled ordinary men and women to enjoy comforts they could not otherwise afford. In a perverse sort of way, installment buying was viewed as a device that encouraged savings, in that consumers who had incurred a debt were motivated to save in order to repay it. And, for the most part, consumers of 1927 appeared to pay promptly what they owed. One large finance company reported that its losses were less than one-fifth of one percent on automobile sales.

Those who worried about widespread use of installment selling noted that the extension of credit came at a considerable cost to the consumer. Interest charged for installment purchases was far higher than one could get at a bank. However, getting bank credit was far more difficult for the consumer than getting credit from the local furniture and appliance store. There were some who feared that installment buying encouraged high-pressure selling, extravagance, and poor habits of consumption. The National Grocers Association complained that because of heavy payments due on large household items, the small grocer was often not being paid.

Likely as not, Christmas shopping for 1927 was done in chain stores. The ubiquitous five-and-ten-cent store dominated the retail market. What the chain store did was to bring to consumers in small towns the advantages of personal service at low prices made possible through mass purchasing.

By the end of 1927, the Great Atlantic and Pacific Tea Company had 17,500 groceries and did an annual business of $750 million. There was competition from chains such as Safeway and the Kroger Grocery and Baking Company. But the Piggly-Wiggly grocery chain pointed the direction of the modern supermarket. Here consumers could roam the aisles and make their selections at leisure without the interference of grocery clerks, and pay for what they had selected at a central checkout counter.

The F. W. Woolworth Company, with 1,600 branch stores that sold clothing products, was second only to the Great Atlantic and Pacific Tea Company. Woolworth's, as it was popularly known, sold $272 million worth of merchandise for nickels and dimes.[17]

Sources of Prosperity

European visitors found the high living standards of Americans a source of wonder. They appeared to recognize that for the mass of its people America had achieved a level of prosperity higher than anywhere else in the world. The

British journal *New Statesman* mused: "What, then, are the causes of America's abounding prosperity? America is by far the richest country in the world in developed and usable natural resources. . . . Then again, the United States is by far the largest Free Trade area in the whole world. For every product he can make, the American manufacturer has now a huge home market from which no tariff barriers can shut him out. . . . In the United States labor has always been scarce in relation to the demand for it. This has made it impossible . . . for the American capitalist to buy his labor cheap, in the sense of paying the laborer a low wage. . . ."

In 1927, the Director of the U.S. Geological Survey gloated: "Our country is blessed with an abundance of resources, soil, climate, water, mineral fuels, and ores of essential metals; and in natural wealth it is unrivaled with any other member of the family of nations. With hardly more than one-twentieth of the world's area and population, the United States has:

- More than one-eighth of the livestock of the world . . .
- Grows more than one-fourth of the world's supply of grain . . .
- Nearly two-thirds of its cotton, and one-tenth of its wool . . .

Our mines produce:

- one-half of the world's annual output of coal,
- one-half of the zinc,
- nearly one-half of the lead,
- more than one-half of the copper,
- more than two-thirds of the iron ore,
- almost three-fourths of the oil.

"Its energy resources are unequaled: already utilizing over one-third of the water power developed in the world and consuming more than one-half the annual supply of fuels, the United States is fortunate in the possession of un-mined reserves of coal and lignite nearly equal to those of all the rest of the world and also had more undeveloped water power than any other country except Siberia and the Congo region."[19]

In 1927, we boasted of the standard of living America's natural resources made possible. No sense of guilt, no concern that the resources might be used up and not be available for future generations. No concern that we were profligate in squandering the national treasure. In short, America considered itself blessed and Americans were encouraged to enjoy.

America's vast resources enabled automobile manufacturers to meet the burgeoning demand for the motor car. More than any other invention, the automobile not only contributed to American prosperity but altered lifestyles and value systems. Only the development of television and the computer can be compared with its impact on American life.

The automobile industry generated relatively high-paying jobs, triggered an interest in building roads rapidly, and developed a network of rail transportation so as to get the rubber, glass, and steel required by automobile manufacturers to the assembly plants. The automobile industry alone paid wages to about three and one-half million people, about six billion dollars a year. "Here, then, this single industry, non-existent a generation ago, which now provides nearly all the purchasing power of a body of consumers equal to the total adult population of Alabama, Arkansas, Colorado, and Connecticut...."[20] When in November 1927 the General Motors Company declared the largest single dividend in the history of the world, some $65 million, brokers and their clients cheered. Little wonder, then, that Main Street looked to Wall Street to augment its wealth.

Main Street Plays Wall Street

Secretary of Commerce Hoover warned investors to exercise care in their investments. But greed overcame caution as small investors were urged to "get aboard" as Arthur Brisbane, financial correspondent for the Hearst newspapers, implored in numerous editorials. If in 1925 speculating in land in Florida seemed to be the "smart" thing for ordinary investors to do, in 1927 it was the stock market. That by 1927 the Florida land-boom bubble had burst did not deter investors, who thought they were missing out on a good opportunity to make a financial killing by investing in stock and bonds. But as investors heard through rumor and hearsay that their neighbors were growing rich, it no longer seemed a game, much less gambling. The prudent thing to do was to use the few extra dollars to speculate in the financial markets. Tip sheets, purporting to give the innocent investors the "inside" information they would need to grow rich, often earned more than the investors they were urging to "play" the market. The *Saturday Evening Post* expressed the prevailing mood in the following lullaby:

O, hush thee, my babe, granny's bought some more shares,
Daddy's gone out to play with the bulls and the bears,
Mother's buying on tips, and she simply can't lose,
And baby shall have some expensive new shoes![21]

When the crash of 1929 finally came, so did the tune. A doggerel from *The Sucker's Mother Goose* went like this:

A flyer, a flicker,
A twelve o'clock ticker,
What wiped you out so soon?
I should have sold at ten o'clock
I stalled around till noon.[22]

Despite the risks of investing in the market, people began to put their money—even borrowing to do so—in stocks in ever greater numbers. One 1927 estimate held that 19 million Americans were shareholders. But in fact, the chief actuary of the U.S. Department of the Treasury estimated that only about three million Americans—less than 2.5 percent—owned securities in 1928.[23]

Two electric companies, in an effort to determine who their investors were in 1927, analyzed the sale of stock of some 13,856 purchasers. The nine largest groups of purchasers were the following:

Housewives	3,347
Miners	1,054
Clerks	949
Salesmen	401
School-teachers	336
Laborers	326
Stenographers	250
Farmers	237
Butchers	178[24]

The bull market was well underway in 1927. It was stimulated in important ways by the fact that investors could buy on margin. That is, they could borrow from their brokers to pay for stocks. In the 1920s, the Federal Reserve Board did not have the power as it now does to fix the margin requirements. Instead, individual brokerage firms did so. While some required prospective customers to pay at least half the price of the stock, others, greedy for profits and commissions, often sold large blocs of stock for a relatively small down payment. When these stocks declined in price, the investor lost all his or her investment unless he or she could provide additional funds.

Throughout 1927, speculation in the securities of giant public corporations grew rapidly. "Day after day month after month the price of stocks went up."[25] By the middle of the summer of 1927, the average of the leading industrials had reached 277 from 171 in January. During the week ending December 3, 1927, more stock changed hands than in any other previous week in the whole history of the New York Stock Exchange. By 1927, a real bull market was roaring ahead. Between December 1926 and December 1927, 577 million shares of stock were traded. Despite some "adjustments," prices of stocks rose by an average of 40 percent. But this represents an average only. Many stocks were winners and doubled or even tripled in price. Others, the dogs, dropped sharply and, by 1927, the high hopes of many investors were already dashed.

As the year progressed, the market needed assurances that all was well. Under Coolidge, the most frequent guests at the White House were the chief officers of America's great banks, utility companies, and those who controlled the natural resources of the nation including, coal, iron ore, copper, and timber. Likely as not, when these captains of industry emerged from their photo opportunity with the president, they issued optimistic statements about the soundness of the American economy and the reasonableness of stock prices.

Americans of those years were prone to listen to their "betters," such as Mellon, Rockefeller, and the president himself. Fueled by unrestrained optimism, the stock market continued to zoom, making paper profits for many. The Secretary of the Treasury, Andrew Mellon, a multi-millionaire who had made his money in finance, declared, "The stock market seems to be going along in an orderly fashion, and I see no evidence of over-speculation." When Calvin Coolidge, from his vacation retreat in the Black Hills of South Dakota, reassured the public on the stability of the market, the market jumped 26 points.

That the rich deserved their wealth and the poor their poverty was characteristic of the era. It was in this vein that Chief Justice William Howard Taft wrote to Associate Justice George Sutherland that the country was fortunate in having a president who was committed to allowing "the people to work out for themselves the prosperity they deserved." While a lower income tax made it possible for the wealthy to retain their earnings, the Coolidge administration boasted that because of lower income tax rates imposed in 1926, the burden of the income tax had been lifted from the lower and middle class. With an exemption of $3,500 for a married taxpayer, the number of Americans paying income taxes declined. By 1927, 98 percent paid no income tax. Although in 1927 closing quotations often competed for headlines with baseball scores, for the overwhelming majority of Americans playing the stock market was but a spectator sport. For most Americans, the real world lay on the assembly line, in the office, and on the farm.

Blue Collar

After an unusually cool and rainy August, the skies cleared for the Labor Day weekend of 1927 and millions of Americans left New York City by motor or rail and headed for the beaches or the countryside. Worries were readily put aside to enjoy the long weekend.

If the barons of American capitalism gloried that their time had come, American labor too was becoming more productive. The average industrial work week was declining from 47.4 hours in 1920 to little more than 44.2 hours in 1927. Real wages, that is wages after accounting for inflation, were likewise increasing. There was relative harmony between labor and capital as evidenced by the fact that strikes were few.

According to the Alexander Hamilton Institute's *Business Conditions Weekly,* the cost of living in 1927 was 64 percent higher than in 1914. But wages were 134 percent higher, so the average worker earned 2.34 times as large a weekly wage as before World War I. He was able, therefore, to buy 1.43 times as much with his wage as in 1914. This represented an increase in the standard of living of 43 percent. Greater productivity helped bring prices down, and a decline in working hours enabled workers to enjoy more of the goods and services they bought.[28]

In comparing the working classes of Europe and America, the writer H. G. Wells asserted: "In the United States the actual proletariat (defined as a degraded, propertyless class) must be a very small proportion of the population."[29] And James J. Davis, the Secretary of Labor, insisted, "The condition of labor was the best in the world as labor shared in the general high level of American prosperity."[30]

But the secretary was aware that American labor faced serious problems, the greatest of which was the threat of being thrown out of work because of the rapid introduction of mechanical inventions and improvements in machinery. "While we should continue to think about our wonderful machines," he declared in a Labor Day speech, "we must also think about our wonderful American workers. If we do not do this," he warned, "we may have discontent on our hands." He insisted that "with every labor-saving machine should come the invention of a way of utilizing the men displaced by the machine." Easier said than done, and Davis' prediction for the future of American labor was off the mark. "Today we are tossing aside skilled men at the age of 45 or 50 years because we think their skill is slipping. Tomorrow the machine will supply the skill and a man of 70 may operate it as well as a fellow of 25."[31]

In churches ministers spoke of the dignity of work as exemplified by Jesus' humble occupation as a carpenter. The Reverend L. H. Bell of the Methodist

Episcopal Church of New York asserted that the church had taken a courageous stand on the side of workers in the Passaic textile strike (see p. 53). Labor's success was due substantially to the efforts of Rabbi Wise, Norman Thomas, and others.[32]

William Green, president of the American Federation of Labor, sought to assure industrialists that his union was free from Communist influence. In a Labor Day tribute to Benjamin Franklin, he spoke of the patriotism of organized labor.[33] And in a radio address to the nation, Green sought to reassure the nation and American corporations that the purpose of the labor movement was not "the selfish use of massed wealth and power but the gradual advancement of the spiritual and intellectual growth of all the people." He went on to assert that labor would continue to fight for the end of unemployment, child labor, and industrial waste, and for collective bargaining, wage agreements, and compensation for workers hurt in industrial accidents.[34]

1927 was not good for militant labor. Instead, under the rubric of "welfare capitalism," big industry was urged to care for the health, safety, and security of its workers. In lieu of government-sponsored and tax-supported pension funds, some of the larger industries, especially railways, were privately financing pensions for their retired employees. These industry-sponsored pension plans, however, were fraught with more peril than promise. Because the financial burden was being voluntarily borne by industry, there was widespread concern that such pension funds would be the first to be withdrawn if the prevailing prosperity dissipated. Moreover, some were probably not actuarially sound, and for the masses working in small factories which could not afford a pension system, no security net whatsoever existed. Thus, while a valiant effort was made in some industries to provide insurance for workers, it was an initiative that could not diminish agitation for government-sponsored pensions. In less than ten years, the New Deal under President Franklin D. Roosevelt responded to the challenge.

In the euphoria of the 1920s there was some feeling that "big" labor and "big" capital need not be perpetual antagonists. If a mutuality of interests could be identified, why couldn't cooperation, rather than confrontation, prevail? John D. Rockefeller Jr. sought to demonstrate his enlightened views on the subject of labor—management cooperation. He offered an olive branch to labor: "If the labor movement, with its important contribution to collective bargaining . . . will do its share in outlawing industrial warfare, substituting partnership therefor; if those in its ranks who have long recognized the fallacy and harmfulness of the doctrine that the less work a man does in a day, the more days' work he will have, are all able to convince their associates that to secure the largest possible production is the best way to advance their own interests and maintain their self-respect; if more men of broad vision and high purpose respond to the opportunity for constructive leadership which labor unionism offers, it may be that the trade-union movement will enjoy the glory and honor of ushering in industrial peace."[35] If Rockefeller sought the cooperation of labor by identifying the attitude labor unions must take, labor's response quite naturally identified the changes in attitude to be made by industry.

The American Federation of Labor eagerly endorsed the principle of industrial cooperation: "Partnership, as Mr. Rockefeller very truly says, must be the basis of constructive relations between employers and employed." But, the A. F. of L. warned, "The essence of partnership is mutuality of confidence, responsibilities and duties. Either member of the partnership may be handicapped in what he may do by the shortcomings of the other. So the trade-union movement is prevented from rendering maximum service when employers do not enter into agreements with union representatives so that there may be clearly defined rights and conditions of employment which beget confidence, safeguarded by an agency controlled solely by the workers. Upon such a foundation may be developed the technique and agencies of cooperation. . . . Where employers are ready to make cooperation possible, trade-unionists are ready to do their part."[36]

Rockefeller's views were echoed by Owen D. Young, chairman of the General Electric Company. In a speech before the Harvard Business School he declared, "Here in America we have raised the standard of political equality. Shall we able to add to that full equality in economic opportunity? No man is wholly free until he is both politically and economically free. . . . I hope the day may come when these great business organizations will truly belong to the men who are giving their lives and their efforts in them, I care not in what capacity. Then they will use capital truly as a tool, and they will all be interested in working it to the highest economic advantage. Then men will be free in cooperative undertakings and subject only to the same limitations and chances as men in individual business. Then we shall have no hired men. That objective may be a long way off, but it is worthy to engage the research and efforts of the Harvard School of Business."[37]

Indeed, the objective of cooperation between labor and capital was a long way off. Neither "welfare capitalism" nor industrial cooperation between labor and capital were concepts whose time had come. Welfare capitalism could gain few converts among the overwhelming majority of industrialists. Instead, among most businessmen, there was widespread hostility to unions and active and often successful union-busting.

Industry was marching to the beat of the cash register and the assembly line. At best, organized labor was marching in place. Industrial prosperity, the rise in real wages of factory workers, unemployment brought about by technology, the falling demand for skilled workers, all contributed to the decline in labor union membership. It was not surprising, therefore, that there were growing indicators that all was not well in the ranks of labor. Economist R. C. Decter asserted that "at least ten percent of the population are usually subsisting on the barest margin of income over the minimum standard."[38] In 1927, the average hourly rate was $1.19 as compared with a $1.15 in 1926, or an average increase of four cents an hour.[39] For organized labor, 1927 was a year of stagnation and perhaps even of retreat. The ineffectiveness of labor unions especially in so-called "sick" industries may be seen in the sorry plight of the workers in Southern textile mills.

By 1927, the nation's cotton textile production was concentrated in the South, where 300,000 of some 1.1 million workers in all branches of the textile industry were concentrated. The most important segment of the business remained cotton, but rayon was growing in importance as mills responded to the fashion preferences of urban women. Women, wearing short skirts and fewer layers of underwear, contributed to the decline in the demand for cotton and rayon textiles. Desperate to hold on to their share of the market by remaining competitive with domestic and foreign competition, Southern mill owners were ruthless in the demands they made upon their workers. The power of the mill owners over labor was not unlike that formerly exerted by plantation owners over their slaves in the antebellum South. In Southern mill towns, the general prosperity of the nation could not be found.

The mill owners not only controlled what went on in their factory, they provided housing in which their workers lived, controlled the local government of the communities in which the houses were located, selected or owned the shops in which their workers could buy their daily necessities, and employed the clergy for the churches where their workers prayed, were baptized, and died. Workers in Southern textile mills were overwhelmingly white Anglo-Saxons, as racial segregation was the universal rule. Few whites, however poor, would agree to work in a plant in which African Americans were also employed.

Despite the harsh paternalism, the mill lured tenant farmers and migrants to the shop floors. Compared with earnings on southern farms, the mill was an attractive alternative. A 1926–1927 study of 500 families in Gaston County, North Carolina, showed that mill work, however ill-paid, still provided a better income than did work on the farm and had other attractions as well.

Mill workers could look forward to a more stimulating existence, contact with peers, better living conditions, and a sense of community. Moreover, mill owners often hired whole families rather than individuals, including women and children. The unit of employment was the family and, in the tight family structure of rural culture, this was not an unimportant attraction for those seeking to leave the farm. From the mill owners' point of view, the labor of children could be supervised by their parents who could also be responsible in case of accident or fatigue.

Company families lived in company houses which were located near the mill so that employees could hear the factory whistle at 5:00 A.M. Most of the houses had running water, inside toilets, and electricity, but virtually none had telephones. For this, the mill hand paid $4 per month, which was deducted from his pay. The rent was low, the coal cheap, medical service scant but also cheap, but wages were the lowest in manufacturing with the exception of tobacco. Hourly rates in mill towns averaged 29.1 cents while average weekly pay was $12.83. The census of 1927 showed that annual earnings in cotton textile industries in the South averaged $671, in contrast with $1,012 in the rest of the nation.

The ten- or eleven-hour day was typical and the twelve-hour shift not uncommon. In Gaston County, the typical work week was sixty-four hours. Night work was normal and included the work of women and children over fourteen. Periodically, to achieve maximum production and economies of scale, the "stretch out" system was imposed in which each mill hand was expected to tend an ever-larger number of work stations. In some of the worst mills, the floors were filthy, toilets revolting, and drinking water contaminated with the residue of tobacco spit. Chronic fatigue and the lack of safety devices on the textile machinery mill hands operated meant that the potential for accident, a torn finger, a broken ankle, or a lost toe, was ever-present. A popular ditty went:

I'm a-goin' to starve,
Everybody will,
'Cause you can't make a living
In a cotton mill.

Despite these conditions, organized labor had yet to make any headway. The mill owners were rabidly anti-union and because some unions were led by avowed Communists, the mill owners tended to equate any form of organized labor with Communism. Nor were the workers themselves any more likely to take to the idea of collective negotiation through labor unions. The isolation of rural Southern workers tended to confirm them in their individualism, to make them suspicious of organizers who came from the large cities of New York and Chicago, and to fly in the face of generations in which the individual and the nuclear family, not the group, was the center of all things good. The schools, churches, civil servants, and all with whom textile workers came into contact confirmed the negative attitudes toward labor unions.

"This country," a Southern mill hand declared in the mid-twenties, "is mighty quiet, but there is goin' to be a flutter before long."[40] One "flutter" came in 1927, when forty-one Southern churchmen drafted "An Appeal to Industrial Leaders of the South," in which they criticized the village system, long hours, low wages, night work for women and children, and the absence of collective bargaining. But the appeal met a wall of mill-owner silence.

On August 4, 1927, some 800 unorganized cotton-textile employees of Harriet Mill No. 1 in Henderson, North Carolina, struck to restore a wage cut imposed three years before. At the request of Bennett H. Perry, city attorney and lawyer for the mill, the lieutenant governor ordered two companies of the National Guard to the town on the 10th, one company commanded by a relative of the owners. Since there had been no provocation, the move was denounced in the press and the troops withdrew after two days. On the 13th, Alfred Hoffman arrived on the scene. He was in his early twenties, a heavy set, tough-minded but inexperienced organizer for the Hosiery Workers. Hoffman succeeded in signing up some five to six hundred workers of the United Textile Workers. On August 30, the mill evicted nine families of strikers from company houses and the strike collapsed.

In his book *The Lean Years*, from which these vignettes are drawn, Irving Bernstein notes that conditions in Southern textile mills in 1927 provided "a microcosm of all America in the somber decade to follow. . . . Here were problems of economic collapse—of poverty, of unemployment, of relief. Here too were questions of labor standards, of low wages, of long hours, of night work for women and children, of factory sanitation and company housing, of workmen's compensation. Here, as well, were the fundamental issues of collective bargaining. . . ."[41]

Between 1910 and 1929, in prosperity as well as depression, four million coal miners were out on strike at one time or another.

The agitation of strikers and the violent reaction of state police and company guards were symptoms not only of continuing labor turmoil in mines in Illinois, West Virginia, Pennsylvania, Colorado, and Ohio, but of the chronic and seemingly incurable sickness afflicting America's coal industry. On November 21, 1927, another feverish confrontation between coal miners and armed guards occurred when the Colorado State Police turned a machine gun on striking coal miners at the Columbine mine, thirty miles northwest of Denver. Three strikers were instantly killed; two died a short time later in a hospital. Twenty strikers, including two women, were seriously wounded. In New York, activists marched on the office of John D. Rockefeller Jr. in the mistaken belief that he was the owner of the struck mine and had ordered the response of the Colorado State Police.

The demonstrators could be forgiven if they believed the Rockefeller family was involved, inasmuch as in 1913 John D. Rockefeller Jr. had, indeed, taken an unyielding position against striking miners. What followed was what came to be called the Ludlow Massacre, when two dozen women and children who huddled for safety in tents as bullets were flying about them were burned to death by strike-breaking guards. In 1927, the memories of the Ludlow Massacre were still fresh, working and living conditions had not changed much, and another battle seemed to loom in the Colorado coalfields.

Living in company-owned houses, shopping in over-priced, company-owned stores, coal miners performed dangerous work in ill-regulated mines. By 1927, other sources of power such as oil and water, combined with more efficient furnaces, reduced the dependence of American industry on coal. The result was that wages remained depressed for miners and bankruptcy and foreclosure was an ever-present fear of owners. Operators lagged in investing in advanced industrial techniques and only reluctantly invested in reducing the risks of mining for their workers.

Under these conditions, American coal miners were ripe for unionization. Coal operators were stubborn in their refusal to negotiate. The American Federation of Labor, under the leadership of its president, William Green, called on President Coolidge to intervene in behalf of 150,000 striking miners and their 600,000 dependents. The federation protested the "intolerable and reprehensible" conditions found in the mines of Pennsylvania and elsewhere and the denial to "the workers' protection of life, liberty, and the pursuit of happiness" as they sought to ameliorate their circumstances. Union leaders pleaded for food, clothing, shoes, medicine, and shelter so that miners and their families could be at least partially protected during the coming winter.[42] Well before the Great Depression the depressed wages and working conditions and the violent, if unsuccessful, strikes were forerunners of what was to come.

From Flapper to Working Girl:
Women in the Workplace

By 1927, one in every five wage earners was a women, making a formidable army of more than 8.5 million working women. Working women could be found in 537 of the 572 occupational categories listed in the census of 1920. Included among such occupations were that of trapper, horse-trader, banker, technician, undertaker, lumberwoman, paperhanger, freight agent, street-car conductor, switchman and flagman, railroad laborer, longshoreman, stevedore, boatman, and deckhand. "Within the space of a single day, one can ride in a taxi driven by a woman, directed by traffic signals designed by a woman, to the office of a woman engineer, there to look out of the window and observe a woman steeplejack at her trade, or contemplate the task of the woman blacksmith whose forge was passed on the way. . . . Ten years ago a woman in Wall Street was an oddity; today women in Wall Street are almost as frequently met as on Fifth Avenue. . . ."[43] These examples of women at work demonstrate that some women, at least, were beginning to make inroads into a man's world. Yet, women faced a formidable array of problems in making their way in industrial America. In the competition of the market place, the business field was by no means a level one.

Professor Lillian H. Locke of Teachers College, Columbia University, complained that it was "practically impossible for a girl to meet her daily needs as to clothing and keep her health up to par on less than $2,000."[44] According to a study made in 1927, more than one-third of self-supporting "girls" lived in residence clubs and earned less than $1,000 a year. About one-fourth of the group studied spent $40 a year on beauty, cosmetics, hair bobs, and perfumes, and one in every five wore a fur coat. Mrs. Henry Moskowitz, vice president of the Association to Promote Proper Housing for Girls, sympathetically observed that "the working girl's . . . job and social life, perhaps her whole future, depend upon her ability to present an attractive appearance and she knows it."[45] But for whom were the working girls dressing? Were they dressing to snare a husband or land and keep a job?

The *Newark Evening News* commented, "Feminists may fulminate, but girls have not changed much in the last few centuries—the ultimate object is the trapping of the male." The *Brooklyn Eagle* was more evenhanded and observed that what women spent on clothing and beauty "belong among outlays for the business of getting a husband, perhaps, and in any case for the business of getting and keeping a position."[47] That women both out of necessity and desire were seeking to become self-supporting was slowly becoming evident and grudgingly acknowledged by the male-dominated world of business.

Women of 1927 were themselves divided on how best to pursue their goals and there was a great deal of ambivalence about what those goals should be. The veteran battler for woman suffrage Carrie Chapman Catt, in an article for *Current History* in October 1927, identified the goals of the women's movement as

follows: "What is the woman movement and what is its aim? It is a demand for
equality of opportunity between the sexes. It means that when and if a woman is
as well qualified as a man to fill a position, she shall have an equal and unpreju-
diced chance to secure it. . . . What will bring the revolt to a close? . . . [A]bsolute
equality of opportunity only will satisfy and therefore close the woman movement."[48] According to this view, the goals of the movement were to help women
escape from the male-imposed disabilities under which they continued to work.
While the expression "breaking through the glass ceiling" had yet to be coined,
clearly Catt was even then determined to break through it.

But in 1927 the hard-edged feminism of Carrie Chapman Catt was being
modified by a softer, if no less ambitious feminism of the "New Style Feminists"
who, wrote Dorothy Dunbar Bromley, were "young women in their twenties and
thirties . . . the truly modern ones, those who admit that a full life calls for marriage and children as well as career . . . convinced that they will be better wives
and mothers for the breadth they gain from functioning outside the home."[49]

The New Style Feminist wanted it all—home, husband, children, and family—but was less aggressive in the fight. According to Bromley, the admonitions
of the militant feminists to "Keep your maiden name," "Come out of the
kitchen," "Never darn a sock," were not worth arguing about. Nevertheless, concluded Bromley, the New Style Feminist "knows that it is her American, her
twentieth-century birthright to emerge from a creature of instinct into a full-
fledged individual who is capable of molding her own life. And in this respect she
holds that she is becoming man's equal."[50] But that equality was a long ways
off. If in 1927, slow progress was being made, the disabilities were likewise formidable.

During the 1920s the "emancipated" woman was more myth than reality. The
Nineteenth Amendment (1920) had given women the right to vote, but "the
Nineteenth Amendment had few immediate consequences for good or evil."[51]
Women continued to vote in smaller numbers than men and, when they voted at
all, they voted as their husbands did. While they did not vote as a bloc, they had
yet to learn the art and science of exercising political clout. But the success of the
feminist movement in gaining the franchise demonstrated that women would
begin to use their enfranchisement to secure both political power and economic
parity with men. While women were not yet fully engaged in the struggle for
equal pay for equal work, the flapper was on the way out and the working girl,
who became the career woman, was on the way in.

Because single women who worked outside the home were widely viewed as
working only on a temporary basis, that is, until a husband came along, wage dis-

crimination between men and women for identical jobs was the general rule. In testimony of the National Industrial Conference Board, the research organization of the large manufacturing interests, for December 1927, a representative month, the board quoted the following weekly wage figures:

Actual wages, all wage earners	$26.90
Actual wages, all males	29.35
Actual wages, male unskilled	24.12
Actual wages, male skilled	30.80
Actual wage, all women (skilled and unskilled not separated)	17.34[52]

For most women, working outside the home was a necessity rather than an opportunity. A 1927 study of "The Young Employed Girl" in Philadelphia reported on 3,867 working girls ages fourteen to sixteen, interviewed 500 of them, and visited the families of 263. All but ten turned over their entire pay checks to their families. Of the 263 families visited, 209 were in dire poverty because of the death or illness of parents, or because the fathers' income was inadequate to buy basic necessities. Often women in factories worked under harsh conditions for long hours with little protection for their health or safety. "The fact remains that the woman is nearly always the cheap or marginal worker, and that she is expected by the public and the employer to remain so."[54]

Because marriage for women was viewed as an alternative to a career, women who sought both a career and marriage were still widely viewed with suspicion. Strong prejudice continued against the career goals of married women. This was particularly true for college educated, professional women. The numbers of professional women, those who preferred to work outside the home, while caring for husband, home, and hearth were becoming increasingly important. The "supermom," a term not yet coined and a type not yet identified, began to make an impression, however slight.

In teaching, it was the general rule for a woman teacher to resign her position when she married. Moreover, among professional groups, women often occupied subordinate positions. Most elementary school teachers were women, most school administrators were men. In health care, men were doctors, women were nurses.

While the work of single women, including spinsters and widows, was taken for granted, there was considerable anguish about the potential for damage to the family when married women worked at a career outside the home. Alarmists were apprehensive that were married women to devote themselves to both career and family the latter would suffer at the expense of the former. Some even saw in the increasing interest of married women in a career a cause of the growing incidence of divorce (see p. 190). "The real clash of these opposing theories is in the gainful employment of women after they are married," and this, wrote Professor Emile J. Hutchinson, "is the heart of the economic problems of women today."[55]

"Generally speaking," wrote a male observer, "we have learned to expect that the children of gainfully employed mothers will be neglected, ill-disciplined, poorly nourished, and educationally irregular. Death-rates among the babies, truancy rates among the boys, and sexual immorality rates among the girls will be severely high."[56] Yet the author of the study was not altogether confident that the "out-working" of married women was really the cause of these domestic problems. He concluded: "We need much more light here before we can safely dogmatise as to the *causes* of the painful effects we see."[57]

One of the issues of the late twenties had to do with how much protection, if any, working women needed. By 1927, the federal government as well as state governments had passed laws attempting to ameliorate the conditions under which women worked. The alleged physical inferiority of women, or their potential for motherhood, led to laws which in some cases limited the number of hours they could work, the environment in which they could work, and the health and safety precautions which had to be taken. These laws were adopted to protect the "weaker" sex, but, of course, also hindered their employability.

The desirability of these laws was rarely questioned. Yet, as women ventured further into the workplace, concern grew among them that the laws designed to protect them also limited their opportunities. If men could work more hours than women, was it not more prudent to prefer to have men on the job? If fewer measures needed to be taken to protect the health and safety of working men, was it not wise to prefer to hire men? Women sought to have the protective legislation lifted while men sought to have the legislation applied to all workers, male and female, alike.

In a vast study published in 1928 by the Women's Bureau of the United States Department of Labor on "The Effects of Labor Legislation on the Employment of Women," the bureau concluded that while in some instances the protective legislation was helpful, in most cases "special laws . . . are not a panacea in increasing their (women's) welfare. . . ."[58] Women, the report held, were at a "crossroads." One road led to more protective legislation, the other led to none. But the bureau rejected both options and urged that the laws protecting women be extended to include men as well. "With forces united (with men) the progress of women, in the next twenty-five years, would hold promise greater than we dare now to prophesy."[59]

The trade union, however, was slow to accept the challenge of the working woman. In 1927, according to figures gathered by Dr. Leo Wolman of the National Bureau of Economic Research, of some 3 million women who were eligible for union membership, only 260,095, merely one in thirty-four American workers were organized into unions. The largest proportion of them were in the Amalgamated Clothing Workers Union, at that time not affiliated with the American Federation of Labor.[60]

Among trade union organizers "there was frequently a tacit understanding in the great brotherhood of man, that woman's place was in the home" and they were determined to keep her there.[61] Aggravating the problems of trade union activities for women was that the AFL considered itself a union for skilled workers, the working elite, while women, for the most part, represented both unskilled and temporary workers and were seen as not worth organizing.

But women too were partly responsible for being left out of unions. Women wage-earners had yet to perceive themselves as an important and permanent part of the labor force. In most of the industries in which women tended to find employment—domestics, stenographers, beauticians, hairdressers, clerks, and teachers—no unions existed. Moreover, even unions acknowledged and accepted the double standard in wage differentials between men and women working in the same job, for the same number of hours. Where trade union agreements with management were reached, wage discrimination became part of the contract.

But in 1927, this attitude was beginning to change. The Russian Revolution was but ten years old and conflict over the role of Communist ideology threw the American labor union movement into disarray and initially tended to discourage the recruitment of women as trade unionists. On the other hand, there were those who idealistically sought to organize women, African Americans, and other minorities of largely unskilled ranks into trade unions. Traditional unionists engaged in mortal combat with more radical wings, with many of the latter made up of militant women.

An example of the sacrifice may be seen in the historic strike of the textile industry in Passaic, New Jersey, in 1926–1927. The strike involved some 15,280 workers, of whom the majority were women. The issues in the strike included the low pay, the proposed additional salary reduction of 10 percent, bad housing, and excessive night work. The strike lasted more than a year, involved the raising and expenditure of several million dollars for relief funds, legal aid, and publicity. These efforts resulted in a union organization in a community where the idea of unionism had not existed before. At the beginning of the strike, thousands of women of different nationalities who could not understand one another and had nothing in common but their jobs in the same factory began to identify shared interests. After attending mass meetings, tramping on picket lines, working in food kitchens, attending classes in English, these women forged a union despite their differences in language, age, years of employment, family status, and ethnic origins.

The heroic efforts of women in Passaic, New Jersey set an example. In 1927, the textile workers of New Bedford, Massachusetts, likewise went on strike against a wage cut and for the privilege of forming a trade union. As in Passaic, the strike also involved several thousand women workers of multiple nationalities and lasted almost a year. In these efforts and in others that followed in 1928, working women demonstrated that the working woman was flapper no more.

Down on the Farm

During the Coolidge prosperity, "the farmer [was] not a gainer but a loser."[62] There was, during the 1920s, a general "thinning out" of the farm population as farmers moved to the city. Yet, according to the *Yearbook of Agriculture,* in 1927 "the exodus [from the farm] was losing momentum rapidly."[63] Farmers left agriculture for the city in the expectation of making a better living. But old age or physical inability to carry on the back-breaking labor farming required also contributed to the diminishing farm population. In some cases, whole families left the farm in the hope that their children would receive a better education.

While the wealth of the nation grew from $175 billion in 1910 to approximately $400 billion in 1927, the wealth of the average farmer was little greater than it was in 1910. Land values fell, machinery values fell, livestock values fell. While farm wealth gained less than 10 percent, the national wealth increased more than 50 percent.[64] In 1913, the amount of farm mortgages stood at $2.4 billion. By 1925 such indebtedness almost doubled. The ratio of indebtedness to the value of the farms was 27.3 percent in 1910 and 41.9 percent in 1925.

Farm labor, too, fared poorly. Between 1913 and 1925, farm wages increased 68 percent but costs of living during the same period increased 78 percent. While agricultural laborers lost ground during this period they came off better than farm owners. However, farmers suffered great and inequitable financial losses after 1920.[65]

Contributing to farmers' malaise was the paradox that while the farmer was in an economic bind, agriculture was becoming more efficient. Just before the outbreak of World War I, Henry Ford developed a compact tractor. By 1927, Ford was producing 650,000 small tractors, or about half those made in the United States to that time. The introduction of huge tractors and giant combines meant that fields put aside for animal feed could now be brought into production. A capital-intensive farm aggravated overproduction, contributed to a decline in land values, and made the farmer a capitalist—in some cases an absentee one. The family farm, while not yet a thing of the past, was waning.

In trying to improve the economic circumstances under which they lived, some farmers joined farm cooperatives and associations. Through these associations, they attempted to limit production in the hopes of raising prices for farm commodities. In some instances, they sought to utilize expensive farm machinery jointly. Mainly, however, in the 1920s farmers sought political clout through such organizations as the Farmer-Labor Party, to force the government to address their grievances.

But President Calvin Coolidge did not cooperate. Although he had been brought up on a farm, he showed slight sympathy for farm problems. More attuned to the community of big business, he generally supported protective tariffs which, in the eyes of the farmer, only increased the prices he paid for the commodities and machinery he needed while limiting his markets abroad.

In 1924, Oregon Senator Charles McNary and Iowa Representative Gilbert N. Haugen introduced the McNary-Haugen Farm Relief Bill. The measure proposed the formation of a Federal Farm Board to purchase the annual surplus of specified commodities (corn, wheat, rice, hogs, cattle, cotton, and tobacco) during the years of large output and either keep it off the market until prices rose, or sell it abroad at the prevailing world price. An equalization fee, the difference between the fixed domestic price and the free international price, was to be paid by producers of individual commodities in the event that the government suffered losses in selling at lower world prices. The bill suffered successive defeats in Congress but in 1927 was finally passed by both houses only to be vigorously vetoed by President Coolidge.

The president felt that the proposed measure would not help the farmer because, in his view, the promise of stable prices would increase production and decrease domestic consumption. He also felt bureaucratic difficulties would wreck the plan. Coolidge was concerned that setting a precedent for certain agricultural products would be adopted by other hard-pressed elements of the American economy including copper, lumber, coal, and textiles, all of which were hurting in 1927 despite the nation's general prosperity.

Moreover, his attorney general, John G. Sargent, held the bill was unconstitutional for a variety of reasons: (1) it required the president to select the Farm

Board from people recommended by representatives of the farmer; (2) its price-fixing provisions violated anti-trust legislation; and (3) the compulsory contribution of an equalization fee amounted to taking property without due process of law. In his veto message the president declared:

> The bill would impose the burden of its support to a large degree upon farmers who would not benefit from it. The products embraced in the plan are only about one-third of the total American farm production. The farmers who grow these commodities are themselves large consumers of them and every farmer consumes several of them. There are several million farmers who do not produce any of the designated products or very little of them, and they must pay the premiums upon the products designated in the bill.

The president ended his message by expressing concern about the unchecked delegation of powers to such a board.

The industrial and banking segments of the economy were more than satisfied with the Coolidge veto. The farmers were, of course, disappointed, and the issue of how best to help agricultural communities became an important one in the presidential campaign which was by then well underway. These were neither the best nor the worst of times for American farmers, yet the incongruities in American agriculture, the anxiety that all might not be well on the farm, set up some warning signals that perhaps despite the general euphoria all was not well with the American economy.

Warning Signs

The Wall Street crash and the subsequent Great Depression followed two years later, but those who cared to look could, in 1927, see warning signals of difficult times ahead. It's easy to say now that the sophisticated should have been sensitive to the fact that when assurances were needed to float the stock market upward, all was not quite so well. Although prosperity was widespread it was also uneven. Corporate profits rose faster than wages and unemployment was relatively high. According to a 1928 report of the Labor Bureau, Inc., a non-governmental organization which aimed "to serve the labor movement with facts for workers," unemployment rose to four million in 1927, up from one million just four years before. So severe was unemployment in 1927 that at the beginning of 1928, the director of the Charity Organization Society in New York reported that unemployment was more serious than at any time since immediately after the First World War.[66] To workers in industries such as coal, leather, and textiles, prosperity was a myth. In some factories, particularly in Southern textile mills, women and children as young as fourteen worked a seventy-hour week. It is estimated that about two million boys and girls under fifteen toiled in textile mills, cranberry bogs, and beet fields. Seventy-one percent of American families had incomes under $2,500.

Among those who sent up some warning signals was Yale economist Irving Fisher, who reported that in 1927 eight out of ten people earned little more than what they needed to live. He estimated that total income was $90 billion, and that 80 percent of the American population received a little more than half the income. The average income, he estimated, was about $2,550, but it took $2,432.39 for a family of five to live in the city. But since these figures were far better than what they had been in previous years, even Fisher reported that there was reason for "thanksgiving."

For a "fair" standard of living, the National Industrial Conference Board estimated that a worker's family of five required a minimum of $1,880 a year while an office worker's family of the same size required $2,119. The Labor Bureau of the United States Department of Labor set an annual total of $2,330.93 as a bottom level which a family cannot go below "without danger of physical and moral deterioration."[67] These figures demonstrate that despite the general prosperity of the nation, the overwhelming majority of Americans, both rural and urban, were barely getting by. Little wonder, then, that an editorial in the New Republic for January 19, 1927, warned of a "fading prosperity." "We see no way to stop the gradual slide downhill," continued the editorial, "except by a readjustment between retail prices on the one hand and farm and wage income on the other, such that the population may absorb the products which the steadily increasing capacity of industry is capable of turning out."[68]

The boom year of 1927 was, in fact, marred by a slight recession, as there was evidence that consumer spending was falling for the first time since 1921. Consumer incomes likewise failed to advance as sharply as in previous years. Although manufacturing output kept increasing, wages and salaries in manufacturing showed but small gains. Dividends and interest continued to increase as did the incomes of those working in the service occupations, finance, and government.[69]

The biggest decline in consumer spending came in durable goods, including electric refrigerators and other large household appliances. There was a sharp decline in the purchase of new automobiles. Residential construction, which had begun to decline in 1926, continued its decline through 1927. Spending by state and local governments likewise declined in 1927, and so the economy was deprived of the stimulus such outlays encouraged. For its part, the federal government used the surplus it generated to reduce the national debt and cut interest payments. "In view of these facts," George Soule asks, "anyone looking back over the figures is prompted to ask, not why the great depression began in 1929, but rather why it did not begin in 1927."[70]

One reason the depression was postponed was the relatively easy-money policy adopted by the Federal Reserve Board. In the spring of 1927, Montague Norman, the governor of the Bank of England, Jhalmar Schacht, governor of the Reichsbank and who would later serve in Hitler's government, and Charles Rist, the deputy governor of the Bank of France, came to the United States to urge the Federal Reserve Board to embark on a low interest policy to stem the flow of gold from Europe to America. In August 1927, the Federal Reserve Board obligingly lowered the discount rate from 4 percent to 3.5 percent, and purchased government securities in the open market, thus encouraging speculation and disguising the economic omens.

Adolph C. Miller was the only member of the Federal Reserve Board who disagreed with this policy. In later testimony before Congress he described the action of the Federal Reserve as "the most costly error committed by it or any other banking system in the last 75 years!" It is not altogether clear that Miller's harsh judgment on the action of the Fed is correct, or even that the Reserve Bank's action contributed in any important way to continued speculation in the stock market. What became clear, however, was that with easy money available, the stock market continued to soar, and some Americans got rich. "Everybody ought to be rich," John J. Raskob, the financier and later chairman of the Democratic National Committee which nominated Al Smith for president, later observed in a 1929 article in the *Ladies Home Journal,* just months before the crash.

Masking the strains in the economy of 1927 was the feeling that the nation had, at long last, mastered the technique of eliminating or at least leveling the business cycle. Profits generally continued to be satisfactory, wages were still good, the nation had been enjoying six years of prosperity, and there seemed to be no reason why prosperity should not continue. Free private enterprise, so it was thought, contained the inherent ability to correct itself as supply and demand made economic cycles less violent. President Coolidge and others in his administration, and many of the nation's leading economists, concurred with this rather sunny view.

꙰

[1]*New York Times,* February 2, 1927.
[2]Quoted in "A Record Breaking Christmas," *Literary Digest* 95 (December, 24, 1927): 44.

[3] Ibid.

[4] Ibid., p. 45.

[5] Quoted in Elmer Davis, "The State of the Nation," in *Mirrors of the Year: 1927-1928* (New York: Frederick A. Stokes, 1928), p. 47.

[6] *New York Times,* December 2, 1927.

[7] *New York Times,* January 28, 1927, p. 1.

[8] Ibid.

[9] Ibid.

[10] Quoted in "Our Incomes Doubled in 20 Years," *Literary Digest* 98 (March 5, 1927): 23.

[11] Quoted in "A Record Breaking Christmas," pp. 44-46.

[12] "Coolidge's Fighting Message for Prosperity," *Literary Digest* 95 (December 17, 1927): 5.

[13] E. W. Kemmerer, "Economic Advisory Worthwhile for Governments: Presidential Address delivered at the 39th annual meeting of the American Economic Association, December 29, 1926, St. Louis, Missouri," *American Economic Review* 17 (March 1927).

[14] William E. Leuchtenberg, *The Perils of Prosperity: 1914–1932,* 2nd ed. (Chicago: University of Chicago Press, 1993), p. 201.

[15] Ibid., p. 194.

[16] Preston William Slosson, *The Great Crusade and After: 1914–1928,* in *A History of American Life,* ed. Dixon Ryan Fox and Arthur M. Schlesinger (New York: The Macmillan Company, 1930), p. 181.

[17] Evans Clark, "Big Business Now Sweeps Retail Trade," *New York Times,* July 8, 1928.

[18] Quoted in "Reasons for America's Riches," *Literary Digest* 94 (August, 20, 1927): 16.

[19] George Otis Smith, "Natural Resources," in *Recent Social Changes in the United States Since the War Particularly in 1927,* ed. William F. Ogburn (Chicago: The University of Chicago Press, 1929), pp. 16-17.

[20] Quoted in "The Automobile—Key to our Prosperity," *Literary Digest* 98 (January 8, 1927): 56.

[21] Quoted in Havelock Ellis, "The Family," *Whither Mankind: A Panorama of Modern Civilization,* ed. Charles A. Beard (New York: Longmans Green, 1927), p. 32.

[22] Ibid., p. 34.

[23] "David M. Kennedy, *Freedom from Fear: The American People in Depression and War 1929–1945* (New York: The Oxford University Press, 1999), pp. 40–41.

[24] Ibid.

[25] John Kenneth Galbraith, *The Great Crash: 1929* (Boston: Houghton Mifflin Company, 1961), p. 13.

[26] Quoted in Page Smith, *A People's History of the 1920s and The New Deal: Redeeming the Time,* Volume 8 (New York: McGraw-Hill Book Company, 1987), p. 177.

[27] Robert H. Ferrel, *The Presidency of Calvin Coolidge* (Lawrence, Kansas: University Press of Kansas, 1998), p. 170.

[28] "Why We Are Living Better," *Literary Digest* 94 (July 23, 1927): 55-56.

[29] H. G. Wells, "The Way that Labor's Going," *New York Times Magazine* (September 4, 1927): 1.

[30] *New York Times,* September 5, 1927.

[31] Ibid.

[32] Ibid.

[33] Ibid.

[34] Ibid.

[35] H. B. Butler, "Industrial Relations in the United States," *Monthly Labor Review* 25 (September, 1927): 506.

[36] Ibid., pp. 506-507.

[37] Ibid.

[38] R. C. Decter, *Social Adjustment* (New York: Alfred A. Knopf, 1927), p. 20.

[39] U.S. Bureau of Labor Statistics, "Increase in Union Wage Rates in 1927," *Monthly Labor Review* 25 (November, 1927): 951.

[40] Quoted in Irving Bernstein, *The Lean Years: A History of the American Worker, 1920–1932* (Boston: Houghton Mifflin Company, 1960), p. 12.

[41] Ibid., p. 42.

[42] *New York Times*, November 16, 1927.

[43] Miriam Simons Leuck, "Women in Odd and Unusual Fields of Work," *Annals of the American Academy of Political and Social Science* 143 (May 1929): 166-167.

[44] "Clothes and the Working Girl," *Literary Digest* 93 (December 24, 1927): 24.

[45] Quoted in ibid.

[46] Ibid.

[47] Ibid.

[48] Quoted in Ethel Puffer Howes, "The Meaning of Progress in the Woman Movement," *Annals of the American Academy of Political and Social Science* 143 (May 1929): 15.

[49] Dorothy Dunbar Bromley, "Feminist New Style," *Mirrors of a Year*, ed. Grant Overton (New York: Frederick A. Stokes Company, 1927), p. 173.

[50] Ibid., p. 190.

[51] William E. Leuchtenberg, *The Perils of Prosperity*, p. 160.

[52] Quoted in Alice Rogers Hager, "Occupations and Earnings of Women in Industry," *Annals of the American Academy of Political and Social Science* 143 (May 1929): 70.

[53] Julie A. Mathaei, *An Economic History of Women in America: Women's Work, the Sexual Division of Labor and the Development of Capitalism* (New York: Schocken Books, The Harvester Press, 1982), p. 147.

[54] Hager, "Occupations and Earnings of Women in Industry," p. 73.

[55] Emilie J. Hutchinson, "The Economic Problems of Women," *Annals of the American Academy of Political and Social Science* 143 (May 1929): 132-136.

[56] David Snedden, "Some Probably Social Consequences of the Out-Working of Well-Endowed Married Women," *Annals of the American Academy of Political and Social Science* 143 (May 1929): 354.

[57] Ibid.

[58] Quoted in Elizabeth Faulkner Baker, "At the Crossroads in the Legal Protection of Women in Industry," *Annals of the American Academy of Political and Social Science* 143 (May 1929): 270.

[59] Ibid., p. 278.

[60] Theresa Wolfson, "Trade Union Activities of Women," *Annals of the American Academy of Political and Social Science* 143 (May 1929): 120.

[61]Ibid., p. 123.

[62]John M. Gillette, "Rural Life," in *Recent Social Changes in the United States Since the War Particularly in 1927,* ed. William F. Ogburn (Chicago: Chicago University Press, 1929), p. 154.

[63]U.S. Department of Agriculture, *Yearbook of Agriculture, 1928* (Washington, D.C.: U.S. Government Printing Office, 1928), p. 43.

[64]Gillette, "Rural Life," p. 152.

[65]Ibid., p. 156.

[66]Frederick Lewis Allen, *Only Yesterday: An Informal History of the 1920's* (1931, reprinted New York: Harper and Row, 1959), p. 242.

[67]*New York Times,* February 13, 1927.

[68]"Fading Prosperity," *New Republic* 49 (January 19, 1927): 237.

[69]George Soule, *Prosperity Decade: From War to Depression, 1917–1929* (New York: Harper and Row, 1968), p. 276.

[70]Ibid., p. 278.

[71]Quoted in Galbraith, *The Great Crash,* p. 15.

3
THE STATE OF THE UNION

March 4, 1927

"Don't ever tell us Friday is unlucky. Didn't Congress adjourn today? The Republicans died fighting to keep from being investigated. The voters would like to investigate both parties as to their sanity the last few weeks. And there would be no hung jury as to their decision.

March 6, 1927

"I notice all newspapers call it the adjournment of the Senate. It wasn't adjournment. They just give out. The big blow in Florida was a great local misfortune, but the big blow in the Senate was a national calamity. Even the Red Cross can't repair their damage. We got wind where we had paid to get wisdom. . .

March 7, 1927

"Well I just seem lost for comedy since Congress adjourned. I would keep them in session the year round for my business, but I have some consideration for people so I sacrifice my needs for the good of the country.

"I don't know where we will get our laughs from until next December, so if I am not funny it is because I have no example.

March 9, 1927

"Everybody out here (Beverly Hills, C.A.) is all excited about where Mr. Coolidge will spend his vacation.

"Put him on a farm with the understanding he has to make his own living off it, and I bet he will give the farmers relief next year. I offer mine for the experiment, and if he makes a go of it he is not a president, he is a magician."

Will Rogers[1]

❧

63

After Coolidge's startling announcement from South Dakota (p. 24), the dominant element in domestic politics in 1927 was the positioning of presidential contenders for the national elections the following year. Who, if not Coolidge, could best be counted on to hold the economic high ground which the nation then occupied? In jockeying for position for the presidential election of 1928, Alfred E. Smith, governor of New York, and Herbert Hoover, Coolidge's secretary of commerce, represented polarized visions of the future of America.

The Political Players: Alfred E. Smith (1873–1944)

He was born December 30, 1873, in a third-floor tenement above a German grocery at 174 South Street, in the shadow of the Brooklyn Bridge, then under construction. "The bridge and I grew up together," he later recalled. The Fourth Ward—New York's ethnically diverse but predominantly Irish community on the Lower East Side—formed his values and offered obstacles to overcome. Despite the run-down neighborhood in which he lived, filled as it was with cheap saloons, shabby dance halls, gambling rooms, brothels, and racketeering of many kinds, Al never became a rowdy. His Irish-American parents kept him clean, neat, and well-dressed. It was to become a life-long habit.

Before Alfred was ten, he became an altar boy and served regularly at the seven o'clock mass at his church. When he was eleven, he began selling newspapers to help support his family. At thirteen his father died and Alfred left school to take a variety of jobs to help keep the family together. He earned $3 a week as a helper to a truck driver, $8 a week as a worker in an oil factory, and finally $15 a week as a laborer in the Fulton Fish Market. This salary, considered substantial even for adult workers, made him something of a local celebrity. He always remembered his days in the fish market and in later speeches boasted that he had only one degree: the F.F.M. (Fulton Fish Market). By 1895, at the age of twenty-one, he was working in a pump works in Brooklyn.

At twenty-one, he still had no clear career goal in mind. The possibilities of a career in the theater fascinated him. But politics, not the theater, became the stage upon which he would play a starring role.

In the Irish Fourth Ward where Al Smith grew up, politics was a way of life and Tammany Hall was at its core. For many, politics was more a sport than an instrument of government. Political connections were a source of jobs. In an economic downturn, politics were a means by which the unemployed could tide themselves over: a basket of desperately needed coal to ward off winter cold, a bag of groceries to assuage the emptiness in hungry stomachs, or money for a respectable burial was often more than enough to tie the voters to the party. In this environment, political virtue was party loyalty and the coin of the realm was the political favor. In return, the party demanded that recipients of such largess remember the hand that fed them by showing up at the polling booth on election day and voting as the party leadership directed.

Al Smith found favor in the eyes of the political hierarchy of his community and in 1895 he was given a job as subpoena server in the Office of Commissioner of Jurors. In his new position, with an income of $1,000 a year, Al Smith was freed from the drudgery of ordinary labor and could concentrate on making a life and living in the politics of New York.

He could even contemplate marriage. For more than a year, he rode his bicycle from the Lower East Side to the Bronx to court the vivacious and attractive Katie Dunn. He overcame her family's objections (they didn't like the acting blood that still flowed in his veins), and the young couple were wed in 1900 and settled in Al's old neighborhood. By 1901 they were parents of two children.

By 1903, Al's service to the reform wing of Tammany Hall was recognized, and he was nominated and elected an assemblyman. In January 1904, on a dank and dismal evening, he arrived in Albany unprepared to live for an extended period of time away from home and family. He had even more to learn about the job of assemblyman and how it fit into the larger political scheme of things. Nevertheless, with the support of the Tammany political machine, he was reelected in 1904 and 1905. He was now a little more sophisticated, but not much, and still frustrated since he had made no speeches and the arcana of the bills and the procedures by which they would be voted upon eluded him.

But Al persevered. He was gradually recognized as a man who could be counted on. He developed a phenomenal memory, became an effective speaker and learned the essential art of accommodation and compromise. His range of acquaintances widened and he learned whom to see and what to do to get legislation important to him and to his constituents passed.

On Christmas Day 1910 "Sarsaparilla" Riley still stood at the head of the stairs of 207 Bowery greeting the seven thousand guests who turned up for a free holiday dinner. And, on his mother's birthday, "Big Tim" Sullivan still made his annual giveaway of two thousand pairs of shoes. But times were changing. In 1910, reformers in many parts of the nation were growing in public esteem and gaining public office. In New Jersey, Woodrow Wilson, president of Princeton University, became the Democratic governor of that state. Could New York be far behind? Could the Democrats gain control of the governor's mansion and both houses of the state legislature? If so, would it be business as usual for the leadership of Tammany Hall or would some accommodation have to be made to its reform wing? Much as the Tammany chieftains would have preferred to manipulate the voter in their well-honed ways, reform could not be resisted.

Smith became the pivot around which the reform wing of Tammany eventually turned.

A departure in Smith's career came with his appointment as vice chairman of the New York State Factory Investigating Commission which was looking into the causes of and the remedies for the fatal Triangle Shirtwaist Factory fire in New York City. The Triangle Shirtwaist Factory, which occupied the eighth, ninth, and tenth floors of the ten-story building on Washington Place near Greene Street, in Greenwich Village, employed 600 workers, most of whom were young girls earning an average weekly wage of $15.40. To prevent alleged pilferage, the young employees were literally locked in on the factory floor with all exits save one closed to them. When fire broke out late one Saturday afternoon on March 26, 1911, the employees could not get out of the building quickly and 146 died. Smith's involvement in investigating the causes of the fire and in establishing rules to improve factory safety encouraged his lifelong interest in the working conditions and general welfare of laboring men and women.

Thus, when the 1911 session of the New York State legislature opened, it was no surprise that the Democrats of New York turned to Al Smith to put a reform face on Tammany Hall. As leader of the Democratic majority he also commanded respect in the assembly. Smith's reputation was further enhanced by his role in the New York State Constitutional Convention of 1915. The convention was attended by some of the ablest men of both parties, but no one matched Al Smith's virtuosity in the minutia of governing New York State. Elihu Root, a leader of the Republican delegation to the convention, declared: "Of all the men in the convention, Mr. Smith is the best informed man on the business of the State of New York."[2]

As a reward for his faithful service, Tammany's leaders named Smith their candidate for sheriff of New York—and because of their grip on the electorate, a nomination by Tammany was almost as good as an appointment. At that time, the office of sheriff was on the fee system and was worth at least $50,000 a year to the incumbent. For the first time in his life, Smith would be in a position to save some money.

In 1917, Smith was elected president of the board of aldermen and in 1918, at the Democratic state convention in Saratoga Springs, Alfred E. Smith was chosen as the party's candidate for governor of New York.

Between 1918 and 1928, Smith ran for governor five times and was successful in four campaigns. On January 1, 1927, Alfred Emanuel Smith was inaugurated for his fourth term as governor of New York. For that occasion the chair upon which Governor George Clinton had sat was dusted off, polished up, and made available to Al Smith, the only other governor of New York State to be elected to a fourth term.

Smith's record as governor was formidable. He surrounded himself with men and women of unusual talent irrespective of race, sex, or religion. Among those who served him well were his administrative assistant, Belle Moskowitz, Justice Joseph M. Proskauer, Frances Perkins, and Franklin D. Roosevelt—who in 1932 became the Democratic candidate for president. Governor Smith opposed book censorship legislation despite its Catholic backing, and he also opposed a bill to establish a loyalty oath for teachers. He reorganized state government, established an executive budget, cut taxes, advanced social legislation, regulated utilities, authorized the Holland Tunnel between New York and New Jersey, and established the Port Authority between the two states.

Through these measures, he gained the national limelight and in 1920 and in 1924 was earnestly considered as a possible nominee of the Democratic Party for president of the United States. At the 1928 Democratic Convention, Al Smith was nominated by Franklin D. Roosevelt. Although he realized being a Catholic (see pp. 209–211) worked against him, his hopes for victory over Herbert Hoover were high. However, in the presidential election of that year, Smith lost decisively. The turnout of 1928 was high: two-thirds of eligible voters went to the polls. Hoover received over 21 million votes while Smith received 15 million. In the Electoral College Hoover carried all but eight states and won by an electoral vote of 444 to 87.

Smith was bitter in defeat. He could not understand why he had been spurned by the American voters. He could not bring himself to believe that he lost because he was a Catholic. Nor did he believe that his Irish ethnicity and urban lifestyle, and opposition to prohibition, made a difference. So what if he pronounced "radio" as "raddio" and "hospital" as "horspital?" No one could convince him that the campaign tune "The Sidewalks of New York" did not resonate among voters in the great heartland of America. Nor could he believe that his origins in the Lower East Side, in the cradle of New York City, "Sin City," as it was widely viewed by the rest of America, would be held against him. After all, his own life had been exemplary by any standard of family or traditional values. He did not recognize that his lack of education beyond the eighth grade was not helpful, and he could not fathom the power of the Ku Klux Klan to foment intolerance in the nation he loved. The *St. Paul Pioneer Press* gloated after Smith's defeat that America's destiny was still in the hands of small town Americans "with their traditional conservatism and solid virtues. . . . Main

Street is still the principal thoroughfare of the nation."[3] But this would not last long.

The Political Players: Herbert C. Hoover (1874–1964)

Herbert Hoover, then secretary of commerce, described the Mississippi River flood of 1927 (see pp. 159–165) as "the greatest peace-time calamity"[4] ever to strike the United States. The July issue of the journal *World's Work* described it as "Our Greatest Domestic Disaster Since the Civil War."[5] New England, especially Coolidge's home state of Vermont, was likewise hard hit by floods of historic proportions. Hoover's zeal in aiding flood victims made him one of the most popular figures in the United States and in no small way was his launching pad to the presidency. "The great Mississippi flood," one writer wrote, "ruined the South and elected Hoover."[6]

Herbert Clark Hoover was the first president to be born west of the Mississippi; the first president who was a Quaker, and, except for military officers, he was the first civilian president whose first electoral position was the presidency itself. No president in American history spent so much time abroad prior to assuming office. When Hoover returned to the United States in 1917, he was truly a stranger in his own country.

Whereas Al Smith was the first candidate for the American presidency to be born in the inner-city, Hoover was born in the village of West Branch, Iowa, the second of three children born into the Quaker family of Jesse Clark and Hulda Minthorn Hoover. His mother was a schoolteacher, his father a blacksmith and dealer in farm implements. While his parents' circumstances were modest, in 1951, when he was seventy-seven, Hoover recalled: "I prefer to think of Iowa as I saw it through the eyes of a ten-year-old boy. Those were eyes filled with the wonders of Iowa's streams and woods, of the mystery of growing crops. They saw days filled with adventure and great undertakings, with participation in good and comforting things. They saw days of stern but kindly discipline."[7]

But these happy days were not to endure. His father died of typhoid fever in 1880 and his mother of pneumonia three years later. The Hoover children had to be separated from one another and so, at the age of nine, Herbert went to live on a farm with his paternal uncle. After a year with his uncle, the ten year old was shunted off to Newberg, Oregon, where he lived with Dr. Henry J. Minthorn, his maternal uncle. When the Minthorns moved to Salem, Oregon, young Herbert went with them. After school he worked as an office boy in Minthorn's Oregon Land Company, a business devoted to selling land to Easterners who yearned for a rural or Western experience. As time went by, Hoover's energy, industry, and efficiency made him an increasingly important employee.

It was through mining engineers who from time to time came to do business with the Oregon Land Company that Hoover began to take an interest in mining and to think about mine engineering as a career. But Hoover's limited resources seemed also to limit his opportunities to pursue the demanding and extended education a mining engineer required. Fortunately, he applied for admission to the newly founded college Senator Leland Stanford of California had built as a memorial to his son. Because the new college sought to attract students by not charging tuition, Hoover began to think that perhaps this was his great opportunity. So it was. But his mostly Quaker schooling was not entirely adequate to the demands of Stanford, and, in particular, his written English and grammar were especially poor. When he sat for the entrance examinations he failed the tests. But Stanford University in its first year was anxious to build a student body and so Hoover was given a second chance in the fall. After a summer of special tutoring he was conditionally admitted to Stanford's pioneer class. What kind of freshman was the university getting?

Herbert Hoover's Quaker upbringing was probably the most significant aspect of his world outlook. He was not a strictly practicing Quaker in that he did not believe in pacifism and as a youth he did have access to secular books. However, the Quaker doctrines of hard work, self-reliance, thrift, temperance, frugality, and the abhorrence of wasted resources as well as of wasted time were strongly ingrained in his character. Perhaps even more importantly for the man who later became president was the sense of individual effort and initiative within the confines of and with the encouragement of a supportive community. In place of a formal creed, Quakers believe in an inner light that is more important than Scripture. This inner light a Quaker must follow though all others may disagree.

Hoover never strayed far from the concept that within a community which voluntarily comes to the aid of those who are needy, the latter can be helped to make the most of their skills, character, and ability—and thus helped to independence. In later years Hoover spoke of "rugged individualism," but it was not individualism based on the ruthless survival of the fittest, but rather on cooperative efforts to enable each person to achieve all he or she is able to become. These views were refined over the years, but they also made it incomprehensible to Hoover, when the Great Depression struck in 1929, that voluntary cooperation among workers and business people might not be enough to ameliorate the plight of those hardest hit. The "inner light," as Hoover saw it, made him resist taking initiatives that might have eased the pain of harsh economic times.

According to his Stanford classmate and later admiring biographer, Will Irwin, Hoover was just under six feet, walked with a slight stoop, carried his head slightly to one side, and wandered about the campus with his eyes fixed upon the ground. He was never popular among the other students. He rarely initiated conversation or laughed out loud. "The crowning of his personality was his shyness."[8] But Hoover's years at Stanford were neither unhappy nor unsuccessful. By the time he left Stanford he had impressed his professors in the geology and mining departments enough so they had made it possible for him to work two summers for the United States Geological Survey and so obtain some much needed income and work experience in his field.

But upon graduation in May 1895, jobs in mining were hard to come by. Hoover had $40 in his pocket and an A.B. in geology, but the country was in the grip of a depression. In 1896, he went to work as a common miner in for the Reward Mine in Nevada City for $2.00 to $2.50 a day for a ten-hour night shift and a seven-day week. Working far underground, he shoveled a wet mixture of dirt and rocks into a cart and pushed it to the surface. At first his fellow laborers mocked this college-educated young man, but before long Hoover won them over. But business continued to drop for the Reward Mine, and Hoover was sacked.

He found steady employment at the Mayflower Mine, near Grass Valley. The shift boss advised him, "So you want to learn mining. There's only one way, get in there and dig. It can't be learned by sticking your nose in a book. You need a nose for gold. You'll develop it by working where the gold is."[9] Hoover dug, developed a "nose" for gold and other minerals, and embarked on a highly successful business career.

Through Louis Janin, a prominent mining engineer to whom he had been casually introduced by his geology professors, Hoover finally got his chance to work on an important mining project. In 1897, Hoover, now but twenty-three years old, was recommended by Janin to the distinguished British mining firm of Bewick, Moreing and Company in order to develop gold mines in Australia, where a gold rush was on. Hoover accepted the assignment and left the United States. His mining career took him to far-flung corners of the world, including Canada, Mexico, Chile, Russia, Mongolia, Burma, New Zealand, and China. In 1899, en route from Australia to a new job in China with the same firm, he stopped off in the United States long enough to marry Lou Henry, a Stanford graduate. The only honeymoon was to be the long journey to China. While he was advising the bureaucrats of the Heavenly Throne, the Boxer Rebellion began, and Hoover, along with thousands of non-Chinese residents, was evacuated by

American troops. By 1914 he was but forty, worth more than $4 million, and living in Palo Alto.

When World War I broke out, Hoover was in London on business but immediately began helping Americans who were stranded in Europe. In October, Hoover was asked to take charge of Belgian relief assistance to feed the hungry and help the poor. He accepted, and in a few months became a widely respected world figure. In administering Belgian relief he established working relations with all the belligerents. As a citizen of the United States, the most important neutral nation, he was on good terms with both Germans and the French and traveled freely between Paris and Berlin. Although but an administrator of a large-scale relief project, Hoover was treated as a head of state. As the war progressed, Hoover's reputation rose and a great engineer became a great humanitarian.

When the United States entered the war in 1917, Hoover was called upon by President Woodrow Wilson to continue his humanitarian efforts as United States food administrator. His assignment was to coordinate the procurement, supply, and distribution of food for the European allies and for the United States as well. Hoover's efficiency became legendary. After the war, Hoover continued his efforts to use American food to feed European refugees and to help with rehabilitation efforts. Hoover sought to use the power of food to dissuade other countries from following the Russian experiment with Communism. He warned against a harsh peace with Germany, since a supportive Germany would be needed to stem the Communist tide. While his views did not prevail, his popularity continued to grow. The economist John Maynard Keynes wrote of Hoover, the man and his views:

> Mr. Hoover was the only man who emerged from the ordeal of Paris with an enhanced reputation. This complex personality . . . imported into the Councils of Paris . . . precisely that atmosphere of reality, knowledge, magnanimity and disinterestedness which, if they had been found in other quarters, also, would have given us the Good Peace.[10]

So great was the popularity of Herbert Hoover at the end of the First World War that he was considered a serious contender for the Republican presidential nomination. But Hoover had been away so long that the party leadership looked elsewhere for its candidate. Warren G. Harding defeated the Democrat James Cox and shortly thereafter Harding invited Hoover to serve as his secretary of commerce. Hoover used the post, which he occupied for eight years, to augment his reputation and hone his ideas. Whether or not he had already been bitten by the presidential bug is unclear.

In 1927, Hoover was "Secretary of Commerce and Assistant Secretary of Everything Else."[11] In the process of expanding the scope of the commerce department, he became a veritable busy-body, looking over the shoulders of nearly all the other cabinet secretaries. Sometimes his dabbling into the affairs of other departments was welcome, mostly it was not. President Calvin Coolidge described him derisively as "the wonder boy" and insisted that he offered more unsolicited advice than anyone else and that most of it was bad.

Hoover sought to racially integrate the commerce department. African Americans were taken out of the basement offices in which they worked and were assigned to the census bureau over the bitter criticisms of Southern members of Congress. It was not so much that Hoover was above the racist views of his day, but his sense of fairness often conflicted with the conventional wisdom of his time in these matters and he sought to reconcile them. However, where his humanitarian instincts collided with his presidential ambitions he readily compromised.

Hoover was mindful that excessive gyrations of business activity could cause undue hardship. He set up commissions to seek ways and means to reduce the boom and bust characteristics of the business cycle. He organized a Committee on Recent Economic Changes in 1927 in an attempt to gain a statistical grasp of the problem. Hoover worried about the rising boom which began to peak in 1927 and the growing speculation in securities, and he urged Coolidge to take some action against a precipitous fall in the national economy. But true to his own values, Coolidge could not be nudged into action.

In February 1927, Congress passed the radio legislation recommended by the commerce department, and President Coolidge asked Hoover to choose the members of the commission to regulate that new medium of communication. In the same year, Hoover, working through the state department, held an international radio conference. He presided over the meetings which were attended by delegates from seventy-six countries. The radio treaties signed at that time have lasted through the years except in Communist countries.

"Herbert Hoover can do things more intensely personal with a more helpless, hopeless impersonality than almost anybody else."[12] As if aware of this element of his personality, Hoover was among the first to make widespread use of public relations specialists to make sure that his activities were well recognized. He was well aware of the power of radio to disseminate propaganda and more than most statesmen of his era he was not above using all the media as a means of keeping his name before the public.

It was no mere accident that in 1927, the year before the national election, Hoover was the most heralded public official in the country. He felt that it was especially important for the commerce department to cultivate the media, since it was upon the media that business depended for statistical data and other business information collected by that department. Toward that end, Hoover surrounded himself with able people who often came from the field of journalism. One such was Christian A. Herter, who was editor of the *Independent* and *Sportsman's* magazines and who later became secretary of state under Eisenhower. Harold Phelps Stokes, a veteran reporter for the *New York Evening Post* and *Washington Evening Post*, was another.

George Akerson, a Washington correspondent for the *Minneapolis Tribune* and a friend of Hoover's since 1921, also joined the commerce department. He was more responsible than anyone else for promoting Hoover's candidacy for the presidency. Akerson remained with Hoover as press secretary into the third year of Hoover's administration. These "private assistants" were paid by Hoover personally and very likely were unique in the history of the commerce department before or since. In 1921, Frederick Feiker, a technical journalist for General Electric Company, became a full-time press aid to Hoover. After nine months with Hoover, in 1927 Feiker became managing director of Associated Business Papers, Inc., an organization made up of 124 business and technical publications which reached more than 1.1 million people in industry and trade. But now he was in an even better position to help Hoover with his public relations activities. And Hoover enjoyed friendships with such prominent journalists as William Allen White, Mark Sullivan, Ida Tarbell, and Walter Lippmann.

Because of his widespread contacts in the media, some have accused Hoover as being nothing more than a publicity hound and a self-promoter. But this is not altogether fair. As secretary of commerce, he viewed it as his responsibility not only to expand the work of the department and make it more influential, but also to share its studies with the general public. To the extent that in promoting his department he was promoting himself as well, then the critics may have some justification. But a fairer interpretation is that Hoover was aware of his own shortcomings and his limitations as a public figure. He was never really ambitious for the presidency. "The whole idea," he wrote, "fills me with complete revulsion." That is not to say that he did not want to be president, but that he did not lust after it, and that he preferred that others promote his candidacy. When Hoover did become president, his journalist friends were among the first to turn on him for his failure to make an adequate response to the Great Crash of 1929 and the ensuing depression.

By 1927, Hoover was well aware of strong grass roots support for his candidacy. His Stanford buddy Will Irwin, who was then helping with relief operations during the Mississippi flood, asked Hoover if he was a candidate for the nomination. Hoover responded, "I shall be the nominee, probably it is nearly inevitable." But when asked what he would do should Coolidge decide to run again, he replied, "I won't get in the way—naturally." In September 1927, a month after Coolidge announced that he would not seek another term, Hoover consulted Coolidge about his plans for the presidency. It was only after receiving further assurances that the president meant what he said that Hoover unleashed his public relations contacts to clinch his nomination.[13] (See Chapter 1)

The Political Climate of 1927

In June 1927 Nan Britton's salacious novel *The President's Daughter* was eagerly read by Americans. Written by Harding's purported mistress, the proceeds of the book were to go to a little blonde girl, Elizabeth Ann Guild, allegedly Britton's child by Harding. Britton could produce little evidence to support her claims. That she had made love to Harding in a closet off the Oval Office was probably false, but because the American people did not put it beyond Harding to engage in such conduct, this episode and other questionable escapades were by and large accepted. While reputable bookstores would not openly carry the book, shops took a clue from methods used in the sale of illegal whiskey, and close to 100,000 copies of the book were sold.[14] The volume further eroded Harding's reputation, and the relatively large sales may indicate that the shallowness of political interest among Americans in 1927 was no less extensive than today.

There were, to be sure, domestic and foreign issues with which to wrestle. If Coolidge "chose to run" would his reelection be a third term and would he therefore be breaking the two-term tradition for the presidency set by Washington? And, if he did, was this desirable or undesirable for a democratic America? With the probable nomination of Al Smith to be the Democrats' presidential candidate in 1928, Smith's Catholicism and urban origins triggered a knee-jerk hostility born in prejudice and fanned by swaggering, hooded members of the Ku Klux Klan. Americans did not appear ready to take on in serious debate the broader issues of separation of church and state. This debate was not resolved until John Fitzgerald Kennedy ran for the presidency in 1960.

Nor were they troubled by rampant corruption in national and local politics. In 1927, "Colonel" Charles R. Forbes, an army deserter who had been appointed by the not-too-inquisitive Warren G. Harding to head the Veterans' Bureau, left the federal penitentiary at Leavenworth after serving twenty-one months of a two-year sentence. Upon his appointment he, along with accomplices, promptly began defrauding the American people of about $250 million. He was indicted in 1924, charged with the corrupt sale of liquor, narcotics, and government property, mostly in connection with building new veterans' hospitals. A committee of the U.S. Senate had heard previous reports of unparalleled waste, recklessness, and misconduct in the Bureau of Veterans' Affairs. Forbes' two-year sentence did not seem to match the enormity of the crime, yet no one really seemed to be concerned.

Thomas W. Miller, Harding's Alien Property Custodian, sold invaluable German chemical patents for a song. In 1927, he was dismissed from office, fined, and sent off to prison for theft and corruption. In 1924 persistent reports surfaced about illegal activities of Attorney General Harry Daugherty, one of Harding's cronies, a group known as the Ohio Gang. As a result of a Senate investigation led by Burton K. Wheeler of Montana which confirmed illegal sale of pardons and liquor permits, Daugherty was forced to resign. In 1927, Daugherty was released after a jury failed to reach a verdict.

Corruption on an even larger scale was revealed before the Senate Public Lands Committee in 1922, which was authorized to investigate leases on oil lands set aside as a reserve for the navy. The senate committee, ably chaired by Senator Thomas J. Walsh of Montana, disclosed that E. L. Doheny, a major oil operator, had "loaned" Secretary of Interior Albert Fall $100,000 in cash and given him government bonds and a herd of cattle for his ranch. The total bribe amounted to an estimated $308,000. The secretary in return secretly arranged a lease for him of Naval Reserve No. 1 at Elk Hills, California, on which the businessmen would make a huge profit. It was also revealed that an equally prominent oil man, Harry F. Sinclair, likewise "loaned" Fall $25,000 and later employed him at a large salary when he left the cabinet in 1924. Sinclair, in return, had secured a lease for Doheny of Naval Reserve No. 3 at Teapot Dome, Wyoming. In anticipation of these leases, Secretary of the Navy Edwin Denby had transferred the reserves from the navy to the Interior Department with the approval of Harding and support from Attorney General Daugherty. In return, the government obtained some oil storage tanks in Pearl Harbor, Hawaii.

In trials that followed, Doheny and Sinclair were acquitted of criminal charges. Denby, who did nothing illegal but demonstrated poor judgment, was encouraged to resign to relieve the administration of criticism. Secretary Fall was prosecuted and convicted of taking a bribe. He was fined $100,000 and imprisoned for a year. Thus, the bribe givers were acquitted while the bribe taker was convicted. Sinclair served several months in jail for refusing to testify before a senate committee. The acquittal of Doheny and Sinclair eroded faith in the courts and cynically seemed to prove that in American justice money talks.

But in February 1927, the government won its civil suit against Doheny. The courts decided that the Elk Hills lease had been obtained by fraud and that the government, therefore, did not have to reimburse him for the $12 million naval oil depot he had built at Pearl Harbor.

American Politics: Mediocrity Triumphant

Just as the Coolidge administration remained untouched by the scandals, so too did the mass of Americans remain serene in the face of scandal on the part of their political leadership. Few voters at the time took politics seriously. According to the historian and journalist Mark Sullivan, the dominant characteristic of Americans in the year was their "devotion to prosperity." Why be bothered with such hard issues as tariff reform, immigration legislation, regulation of monopoly, farm relief, and political corruption. If some of the political and corporate leadership could be believed, even poverty was on the verge of banishment. When Americans were enjoying themselves, why deal with reality when fantasy was so much more fun? The automobile gave most a freedom they had not heretofore enjoyed. The city dweller could get out into the country and the isolated life of the farmer could be broken up with occasional automobile trips to the city or to the markets. Americans went to the movies at least once a week and there they could be seduced by sensuous women and men who lived a style of life which seemed at times to be not altogether out of reach of the movie-goer.

In foreign affairs important issues were emerging, but Americans looked inward and their complacency could not be shaken. They were disillusioned with the results of their participation in World War I and sought never again to be suckered into the machinations of foreign entanglements. Interest in foreign affairs was at its nadir. When the Democrats charged the Republicans with a lack of a foreign policy, the issue "attracted only casual attention."[15] (See Chapter 5)

If the machinations in foreign capitals seemed not to concern Americans, what went on in their own capital was likewise seemingly irrelevant. The distinguished journalist Walter Lippmann, in a 1927 essay for the *Atlantic Monthly* entitled "The Causes of Political Indifference Today," held that "nobody is very much interested in the nation."[16] The political parties, Lippmann wrote, were united only on the principle of electing one of their own to local, state, and national offices.

In 1927, Dr. Nicholas Murray Butler, president of Columbia University, held that "for the first time in 2000 years the world is without a single great man."[17] Those American editors who disagreed with him pointed to Benito Mussolini, the Fascist dictator of Italy, the inventors Edison and Marconi, the developer of the airplane Wilbur Wright, the automobile mogul Henry Ford, and the play-wright George Bernard Shaw. Except for Mussolini, most of the others mentioned by American editors were not political figures. In the United States, political figures likewise seemed to fade after the more spirited administrations of Theodore Roosevelt and Woodrow Wilson. Warren Harding never aspired to greatness and did not know how to use or to care about using the bully pulpit of the presidency. Calvin Coolidge, Lippmann commented, was "contented with little things; he is hardly suited to large thoughts and large deed. He has not attempted them."[18] Alfred E. Smith, the very able and distinguished governor of New York, while locally popular, failed to cut a national figure. Herbert Hoover, who was nationally recognized, had never been tested in a popular election. Thus there were no "great men," let alone great women, to capture the imagination of the American masses and inspire them to come to grips with emerging problems.

Because of the amazing prosperity Americans were experiencing, it seemed easier for most people to go out and make money than worry about trying to improve their lot through political action. And why pursue political action when the "new capitalism" seemed more enlightened toward labor unions and more concerned for the welfare of workers? Forward-looking industrialists sought voluntarily to ameliorate the grievances of their employees. The new capitalist, Lippmann held, was not perfect but he was "less autocratic. He does not arouse the old antagonism, the old bitter-end fury, the old feeling that he was to be clubbed into a sense of public responsibility. He will listen to an argument where formerly he was deaf to agitation."[19] "For the great majority of men," Lippmann declared, "political ideals are almost always inspired by some kind of economic necessity and ambition."[20] Capitalism as then practiced seemed to be making people comfortably well off; there was no pressing reason for a realignment of "haves" from "have nots," and economic discontent could not be counted on as a mainspring for political activity.

As a result, it was relatively easy for politicians to evade the real issues, and the average citizen of 1927 appeared content that they did so. Since 1927 was an "off year" politically (that is, the presidential campaign would not emerge in full steam until a year later), politics remained essentially in the background. But some issues could not be totally ignored. Among these were separation of church and state and the trial of Italian immigrants Nicola Sacco and Bartolomeo Vanzetti. Equally divisive in 1927 was the national schizophrenia brought about by prohibition.

Prohibition: The Fight Over Booze

"It is here at last—dry America's first birthday," the Anti-Saloon League gloated in a press release on January 15, 1920. "At one minute past twelve tomorrow morning a new nation will be born. . . ." The statement continued, "To-night John Barleycorn makes his last will and testament. Now for an era of clear thinking and clean living! The Anti-Saloon League wishes every man, woman and child a happy Dry Year."[21] But the euphoria of the Anti-Saloon League was short-lived. Problems of enforcement immediately surfaced, and in the absence of accurate data no real evidence exists to demonstrate that Americans drank less while the prohibition amendment was in effect. According to one historian, "Prohibition represented the single most striking act of hypocrisy of the decade. Americans never drank so much; yet there was not a single major national political figure of old ethnic stock to go on record as clearly opposing prohibition."[22]

While we may today look upon the Eighteenth Amendment as a quaint and misguided attempt to mold America's character by modifying the drinking habits of its people, excessive consumption of alcohol had been an American problem since colonial days. During the last half of the eighteenth century "demon rum" became an important medium of exchange in the slave trade between the American colonies, the west coast of Africa and the West Indies. Liquor, not bread, seemed to be the staff of life. In the absence of anything better in their arsenal against disease, physicians often prescribed liquor as a form of nourishment, a disease preventative, a cure for illness, an elixir of youth, a pacifier of infants, a stimulant for the feeble and a restorative for the depressed, and an aphrodisiac for those with flagging libido. A tumbler of whiskey, not orange juice, was commonly taken upon awakening and a copious draft of flavored rum most assuredly helped one sleep better at night. Hard liquor warmed against the cold of winter and was a cool refreshment against the heat of summer. Little wonder that our forebears referred to liquor as "the good creature of God."[23]

Between 1880 and 1917, the American saloon was at its worst, "the devils' headquarters on earth." "As an institution," historian Herbert Asbury comments, "the saloon was a blight and a public stench."

It was dingy and dirty, a place of battered furniture, offensive smells, fly-blown mirrors and glassware, appalling sanitary facilities. It encouraged drunkenness; few bartenders hesitated to serve children, idiots, and known drunkards. It ignored the law. It corrupted the police, the courts, and the politicians. It was a breeding place of crime and violence, and the hangout of criminals and degenerates of every type. It was the backbone of prostitution; in every red-light district in the country the fixer, the big boss, was a saloon keeper. Usually he also owned brothels, and his bartenders were pimps and panders.[24]

It was to fight these excesses that the Anti-Saloon League was born. It was founded in Oberlin, Ohio, in 1893 by representatives of temperance societies and evangelical Christians. Among its more colorful leaders was Carry Moore Nation (1846–1911) who believed she had a divine mission to destroy the saloon. She was six feet tall, weighed 175 pounds, and when she supplemented prayer with direct action her hatchet-wielding forcefulness destroyed saloons in Kansas and elsewhere. She was a formidable foe, widely respected and feared.

The Anti-Saloon League became a formidable political lobby. Its approach was to pressure both parties into bringing about national prohibition, but until that happened, its strategy was to dry up the nation bit by bit—town, village, city, county, and state. Its success was finally crowned with the adoption of the Eighteenth Amendment in 1919.

From time to time in America's history, important issues are debated in an environment which transcends the specific arguments, the pros and cons of the issue. This was true of slavery in the 1860s, when those who opposed the abolition of slavery looked to retain the status quo and their privileged position and could not or would not recognize that the institution to which they so devoutly held was doomed. Prohibition in the 1920s was another such issue in that it involved the question of how far the power of government should be invoked to mold American morals and values. In today's debate over abortion may be found parallel issues of the role of government, especially a democratic government, in forming American lifestyles.

By 1927, however, it was clear that prohibition was not working as the Anti-Saloon League had anticipated. Crime was up (Chapter 5) and was in many ways related to illicit traffic in whiskey. Corn farmers were hurting and the pinch was being felt as taxable proceeds from the sale of liquor were drying up. Congress repeatedly failed to allocate sufficient funds for the agencies of enforcement. As Alice Katharine Fallows, the daughter of a bishop who had been favorable to prohibition, put it, "Now in the year of 1927 the drink problem is the liveliest ghost that ever trod a national stage. Not since the first man sipped fermented grape-juice from a gourd has there been more discussion about it than in the United States to-day. This settled question has developed into the greatest national issue since slavery threatened to tear the Union asunder. It is as full of potential dynamite as the Civil War in 1860."[25]

The debate over the effectiveness of prohibition was more than a controversy over how best to enforce it, or how to modify it, or even to repeal it. As with the issue of slavery in the 1860s, or abortion today, prohibition symbolically showed deepening schisms in American society. There were "wets" who were for the repeal of Amendment XVIII among both Republicans and Democrats. There were "drys" in the Democratic camp just as there were among Republicans. Prohibition was the arena in which urban and rural preferences and national policies clashed, not merely over the drinking of hard liquor, but over which values ought to dominate America in the twentieth century. In general, those oriented toward urban living favored proposals to repeal prohibition; and those in rural settings zealously favored its retention. Religious fundamentalists supported prohibition; those whose views were inclined to be secular favored its repeal. Those who urged that men and women should have the right to choose whether or not to drink hard liquor and so should not have their freedom taken away by the heavy hand of government fought for repeal of the prohibition amendment. Those who looked to government to help prevent the lifeblood of the nation from being weakened with alcohol continued to support the Eighteenth Amendment's sanctions.

The debate over prohibition was between those who recognized that the social and cultural dominance of small towns and family farms was rapidly disappearing—to be replaced by turbulent urban life with its many racial, religious, ethnic, and immigrant strands—and those who sought to hold back the tide of inevitable change. It was a debate also between those who welcomed the industrialization of America and the social transformation the automobile, radio, and airplane were making or about to make, and those who feared or could not reconcile themselves to the new environment.

On April 8, 1927, in a debate sponsored by the Roosevelt Club of Boston, Dr. Nicholas Murray Butler, a Republican and president of Columbia University, spoke in the affirmative while Senator William E. Borah, Republican of Idaho, took the negative on the question, "Should the Republican national platform of 1928 advocate repeal of the Eighteenth Amendment?" According to the *Literary Digest* for April 23, 1927, the event reminded newspaper editors of the Lincoln-Douglas debates over slavery. According to Butler, "The Eighteenth Amendment represents the worst possible way of attempting to deal with the evils of the liquor traffic and the saloon. It is in the Constitution as a matter of law, and it must be obeyed while it is there. But it is not binding upon my intelligence or my conscience and I shall leave no stone unturned to get it out." Senator Borah declared, "I believe the Republican Party should declare for the Amendment and for its enforcement, and make the same sublime and daring fight against this evil that it made against the evil of slavery, two evils which the immortal Lincoln associated together as the greatest evils of the human race."[26] Borah went on to observe that the Eighteenth Amendment had never been adequately enforced. "There is, my friends, in this country," Borah continued, "a deliberate, organized attempt to nullify the Constitution of the United States. It is just as well organized and just as intelligently led as was the nullification doctrine of John C. Calhoun."[27] Six of nine judges chosen by the *Boston Herald* gave the verdict in the debate to Senator Borah. Yet, by 1927, there was a growing feeling that prohibition needed to be modified or perhaps repealed.

By the beginning of 1927, five states with a total of 20 million people—New York, Illinois, Wisconsin, Montana, and Nevada—held referendums urging some substantial changes in prohibition. What was revealed was a nation sharply divided. Some voters recommended more stringent enforcement, others sought modification, and some outright repeal. Even ministers, social workers, and police officials whose fields of work might be expected to prefer prohibition were divided on prohibition. Economics professor Irving Fisher held that prohibition at its worst was better than no prohibition at all and that only one sixth as much liquor was poured down American throats as before the Eighteenth Amendment went into effect. On the other hand, "from college president to bootblack comes the unofficial information that drinking is increasing . . . . Then along comes Raymond Pearl, as great a statistician as we have in the country, saying in effect that moderate drinkers outlive total abstainers."[28]

In 1927, "tired of taking a halfway position," the Women's Committee for Modification of the Volstead Act changed its name to the Women's Committee for Repeal of the Eighteenth Amendment and adopted as its slogan "the restoration of the Bill of Rights."[29] In the same year, a movement for repeal was initiated among the members of bar associations, led by the New York City Voluntary Committee of Lawyers. The lawyers based their opposition to national prohibition essentially on legal grounds: "The Eighteenth Amendment is inconsistent with the spirit and purpose of the Constitution of the United States and in derogation of the liberties of the citizens and the rights of the states as guaranteed by the first ten amendments thereto."[30] Within two years similar action was taken by the bar associations of many other states.

Congress was quick to urge stricter enforcement of the Volstead Act but dragged its feet in appropriating the money needed to enforce it. Presidents Harding and Coolidge urged voluntary compliance with the law, but since Harding flouted the law quite openly, even serving hard liquor at state events, the general public could not be expected to comply voluntarily. Early enforcement attempts were designed as flamboyant media spectacles during which enforcement officers were pictured destroying casks of beer or smashing bottles of liquor. By 1927, however, there was a growing awareness that these grand gestures were not having their desired effect. As a result, in December 1927, officials of the Treasury Department ordered the abandonment of dramatic raids and the subsequent sensational advertising. "Quiet, orderly enforcement of the law rather than sensational efforts is the new policy of the Prohibition Bureau."[31] In order to try to improve the efficiency of the Prohibition Bureau, on April 1, 1927, Congress placed all employees under civil-service regulations.

Repeated efforts to improve the quality and the efficiency of the Prohibition Bureau were of little avail. When Seymour W. Lowman became head of the Bureau in September 1927, he complained that "his arm grew tired signing orders dismissing inefficient staff members." Enforcement officers of the Prohibition Bureau were admonished in October 1927 to use weapons only in self-defense. But the order to this effect was no more effective in 1927 than it was in years before and after. Prohibition enforcers seemed to acquire a kind of flamboyant swagger—as if in bragging about the size of the "fish" that was caught the public might forget all of those that got away.

Although the federal government called upon the states for help, it failed to provide the resources with which even the administration of the best-intentioned state might do so. In his Message to Congress on December 6, 1927, as he had done so many times before, President Coolidge urged states to take greater initiatives in the enforcement of prohibition. "Vigilance on the part of local governments would render enforcement efforts much more successful,"[32] he declared. But the states were not paying close attention.

The net result of eight years of earnest appeals from Washington was an appropriation by the states of $698,855 for enforcement in 1927.[33] In the same year, Congress appropriated $12 million. What did the federal government get for its money? In 1927, 50,250 prosecutions began, the courts imposed an average fine of $157.90, sent violators to prison for an average of 136.4 days, achieved a conviction rate of 70.3 percent, and imposed fines and penalties of nearly $6 billion.[34]

While revelers were welcoming the new year of 1927, the Department of Health in New York City reported that in the previous year at least 750 people had died from poisoned liquor. The report further noted that deaths from poisoned liquor were rapidly increasing. All deaths from poisoned liquor was an unintended consequence of the enforcement of a law the Anti-Saloon League had insisted upon: the Tax Free Industrial and Denatured Alcohol Act of 1906. It was passed by Congress at the urging of the League and manufacturers, who asserted that alcohol used in manufacturing should not be taxed at the same rate as that used for consumption. The high tax on alcohol required in some manufactures inhibited the development of new products and raised their prices as well. Congress, therefore, removed all tax on industrial alcohol, and on alcohol used in heating, lighting, generating power, or for artistic purposes. But to make sure that none of the non-taxed alcohol found its way into the drinking glasses of the masses, the alcohol was "denatured," to make it unusable as a beverage. In most instances, the denaturant used was methanol, commonly called wood alcohol. The Treasury Department, at the insistence of the prohibitionists, required that most industrial alcohol contain about four percent wood alcohol. That was not only enough to make the taste unpleasant, but enough to kill a person even if consumed in moderate quantities. According to one physician, three drinks containing four percent wood alcohol would be enough to lead to blindness. Dr. Nicholas Murray Butler described the use of denatured alcohol as "legalized murder." The humorist Will Rogers, mayor of Beverly Hills, California, quipped, "Governments used to murder by the bullet only. Now it's by the quart."[35]

There were some prohibitionists who held that those blinded or killed because they could not resist the lure of alcohol, even denatured alcohol, deserved their punishment. Ardent prohibitionists like Wayne Wheeler, Anti-Saloon League president, were unsympathetic. "People who drink bootleg beverages after the government has warned them of the danger," he declared, "are in the same category as the man who goes into a drugstore, buys a bottle of carbolic acid with a label on it marked 'Poison,' and drinks the contents."[36] But was death an appropriate punishment for essentially a minor violation of the law?

In the early weeks of 1927, Wheeler tried to modify his stern remarks and demonstrate greater compassion for those who were driven to break the law. But he was unsuccessful. Among the majority of Americans who were prepared to live with prohibition provided that its enforcement was porous, the prohibitionist began to be viewed as an extremist who cared little for human failings.

By 1927, support for the Anti-Saloon League was noticeably eroding. Its position was worsened by the death on September 5, 1927, at the age of fifty-eight of Wayne Wheeler, its crafty and respected president. Friends and foes alike paid tribute to this able leader of the temperance cause. It was Wheeler who designed the master strategy of the Anti-Saloon League to make the campaign for prohibition a bipartisan effort. The *Mobile Register* declared, "Wheeler was one of the first to see that Prohibition could never be achieved through the success of the Prohibition party. . . . The champion of the drys worked subtly to cause its acceptance by both great parties, thus making assurance doubly sure."[37] In commenting on the death of Wheeler and the prospects for a successor, the *New York Times* noted that prohibition was on the verge of especially difficult times and that a new head of the Anti-Saloon League would have a very different climate in which to work. "Fed by war psychology," continued the *Times*, "mistaken patriotism, by inexhaustible propaganda, by Utopian hope and political cowardice, the torrent of Prohibition swept over the country. The waters have been receding. A reaction has been gathering strength. A large part of the population is sick of Prohibition that can't prohibit, a Prohibition law grounded on absurdity, of an old evil continued in new forms and creating grave social and moral deterioration. It is unlikely that the inheritors of Mr. Wheeler's shoes will find Congressmen so docile as they were when they lived in terror of the League."[38]

On the morning of December 12, 1927, eighteen prominent middle-aged men met at the house of ex-U.S. Senator James W. Wadsworth in northwest Washington, D.C., to discuss launching a campaign against prohibition. The group that gathered at 28 Woodland Drive included Pierre S. du Pont, retired chairman of the board of General Motors and E.I. du Pont de Nemours Company; Charles H. Sabin, president of Guarantee Trust Company of New York; Senators Walter E. Edge of New Jersey and William C. Bruce of Maryland; Edward S. Harkness, philanthropist and heir to one of the nation's largest fortunes; and World War I Assistant Secretary of War Benedict Crowell. They spent a day and a half discussing repeal of the Eighteenth Amendment of the United States Constitution.[39] Although they formed the Association Against the Prohibition Amendment, prospects for repeal in 1927 still seemed extremely remote.

Sacco and Vanzetti: The Case that Will Not Die

On August 4, 1927, newsboys hawking their papers awakened the good people of Boston with the cry "Sacco-Vanzetti must die." The news was that Governor Alvan T. Fuller had chosen neither to intervene in the case nor grant clemency to Nicola Sacco or Bartolomeo Vanzetti who, six years before, had been tried and found guilty of first degree murder.

Until the O. J. Simpson murder case of 1995, the Sacco-Vanzetti murder case of 1921 was, without doubt, the trial of the century. In the O. J. case the accused was found not guilty of the murder of his wife and her boyfriend despite substantial evidence of his guilt. In the Sacco-Vanzetti case, a jury found two Italian immigrants, Nicola Sacco and Bartolomeo Vanzetti, guilty of murder despite inconclusive evidence and lapses in due process to which the accused were entitled.

The O. J. Simpson murder case became a stand-off between whites and blacks. The latter for the most part preferred to see an accused murderer go free, as a way of "getting even" for the frequent miscarriages of justice in American courts when accused whites were casually let off by an all-white jury despite substantial evidence that an African American had been murdered, raped, beaten, or lynched.

The Sacco-Vanzetti case took place in a climate in which new laws legislating significant restrictions on immigration had been imposed and friction between alien-born and native-born was deep. The notorious raids of U.S. Attorney General Alexander Mitchell Palmer against alleged alien subversives (1919–1921) brought about a Red Scare and encouraged a mood of mass hysteria against all things foreign. Because Sacco and Vanzetti were immigrants, the world media wondered whether newcomers to "the land of the free" would really get a fair trial. Because the two were anarchists, intellectuals at home and abroad wondered whether American jurisprudence could focus objectively on the facts of the case. But just what were the facts in the case? It is a question more easily asked than answered.

About three o'clock in the afternoon of April 15, 1920, Frederick A. Parmenter, a paymaster, and Alessandro Berardelli, his guard, were carrying two boxes containing the $15,776.51 payroll of the Slater and Morrill shoe factory from the company's office building to the factory through the main street of South Braintree, Massachusetts. They were fired upon by two men armed with pistols. Berardelli was instantly killed, and Parmenter died a day later.

As it swept by them, the murderers tossed the money boxes into a green touring Buick and made a fast getaway. Twenty days after the robbery and murders, Sacco and Vanzetti were arrested. Both were carrying guns. Vanzetti had a loaded revolver and four shotgun shells, and Sacco had a pistol with twenty-three cartridges. On May 5, 1920, they were charged with murder. The twelve-man jury, allegedly made up of "representative citizens," "substantial," and "intelligent,"[40] included a former chief of police, two real estate dealers, two machinists, a grocer, a mason, a stockkeeper, a clothing salesman, a mill operative, a shoe worker, a photographer, and a farmer. But who were the two accused men? Were they murderers? Thieves? Members of organized crime?

In 1908, more than 130,000 Italian immigrants emigrated to the United States. Nicola Sacco and Bartolomeo Vanzetti were among them. Sacco was born in 1891 in southern Italy to a prosperous farm family. In the United States he became a highly skilled shoe craftsman, made a good salary of $80 a week, and was happily married. The couple had two children: a boy and a girl born after Sacco's imprisonment. They lived in a small house with a carefully tended garden. At the time of Sacco's arrest he had $1,500 in the bank. Vanzetti, three years older, was born in northern Italy where he had been apprentice to a pastry cook. He came to America after his mother died. Vanzetti had no family and worked at odd jobs. At the time of the crime Vanzetti was self-employed as a fish peddler.

Both men were ardent anarchists who believed in armed insurrection, violence, assassination, and the use of dynamite to bring about their vision of a stateless society. Vanzetti was especially well read in the works of such anarchist writers as Prince Piotr Kropotkin. He was also well versed in the works of Karl Marx, Giuseppe Mazzini, the theoretician of Italian unification, Charles Darwin, Herbert Spencer, Leo Tolstoy, and Emile Zola. Sacco had no criminal record, but Vanzetti had been found guilty on July 1, 1920, of the holdup on December 24, 1919, of the paymaster of the J. O. White Shoe Company in Bridgewater, Massachusetts. During World War I both men had fled America to evade the draft. During the trial the only point at issue was, or should have been, were Sacco and Vanzetti the two who killed Parmenter and Berardelli or were they not? Although it was not pertinent to the case, few jurors could see them as other than foreigners, anarchists, and draft dodgers.

Because neither man spoke English very fluently, an interpreter had to be hired for them so that they could follow the activities in the court. However, during the years in which Sacco and Vanzetti sat in jail, they both improved their English speaking and writing skills, and Vanzetti, especially, became eloquent in his own defense and as a spokesman for anarchism. At their trial, which lasted about seven weeks, the accused were represented by Fred H. Moore, a Westerner whose fee was paid for by radical supporters who organized themselves into a Sacco-Vanzetti Defense Committee. Moore was not a member of the Massachusetts bar, and was unfamiliar with the ways of New England jurisprudence. As an attorney, he was a disaster for the accused in that he appeared to irritate Judge Webster Thayer. The result was that the benefit of the doubt often went to the prosecution.

The prosecution was led by the very aggressive Massachusetts District Attorney Frederick G. Katzmann. As a skillful, ruthless, and perhaps not altogether ethical prosecutor, he played on the anti-alien emotions of the jury and aroused their hostility toward the accused immigrants. In his questioning technique he often intimidated the ninety-nine witnesses who appeared for the defense. Fifty-five witnesses appeared for the prosecution. The evidence against Sacco and Vanzetti was not identical. The prosecution sought to prove its theory that Sacco did the shooting while Vanzetti was one of four accomplices, two of whom were in the getaway car. But neither side submitted evidence that was altogether convincing. Sacco insisted that at the time of the murders he had taken a day off from work to go to Boston to get a passport so that he could visit his father in Italy. The truth of this statement was supported by an official of the Italian consulate. Vanzetti claimed that he was selling fish as he did everyday. A number of witnesses came forward to confirm that they had bought fish from him that day. Experts likewise clashed over bullets taken from the bodies of the victims, but whether the bullets were fired from Sacco's pistol was likewise inconclusive.

In sending the case to the jury, Judge Thayer explained the functions and duties of the jury. While he emphasized the rights of all parties and sustained the claims of radicals to equal justice and indicated that the Italians are entitled to the same consideration as though their ancestors had been aboard the Mayflower, according to future Supreme Court Chief Justice Felix Frankfurter, who took up the cause of Sacco and Vanzetti, Judge Thayer paid only "lip service to the ideals of justice."[41] On July 14, 1921, after five hours of deliberation, the jury returned with a verdict of guilty.

For the next six years the Sacco-Vanzetti case became a story of appeals and denials. In the nation and around the globe, opinion was crystallized between the friends of Sacco and Vanzetti who protested their innocence and foes who insisted that justice was not served. The money for which the paymaster was shot was never found. Among the many reasons for appeal were lack of objectivity by the judge and foreman of the jury. The judge was overheard in private referring to Sacco and Vanzetti as "sons of bitches" and "dagos." He had boasted to a friend, "Did you see what I did to those anarchist bastards?" According to a veteran reporter, Judge Thayer's "whole manner, his whole attitude seemed to be that the jurors were there to convict the men."[42] The foreman of the jury, in advance of the trial, was heard to say that "the two 'ginneys' ought to hang anyhow, guilty or not."[43]

While he was in jail, Sacco was visited frequently by his wife and children. A fellow prisoner, Celestino F. Madeiros, who witnessed these visits, was moved to smuggle a note to Sacco which read: "I hereby confess to being in the South Braintree shoe company crime and Sacco and Vanzetti were not in said crime." Madeiros testified under cross examination that he was associated with the Morelli gang of Providence, Rhode Island, and claiming that he, along with members of the gang, were at the scene of the crime. The defense submitted more than sixty affidavits in support of the theory that the murders had been the work of the Morellis. But all this new information failed to trigger the compassion of Judge Thayer, who continued to deny a new trial.

After futile appeals, on April 9, 1927, Sacco and Vanzetti in the Court House at Dedham were sentenced by Judge Thayer to be electrocuted in the Charlestown Prison during the week of July 10.

In open court Vanzetti protested his innocence. He charged the judge with prejudice and concluded: "This is what I say: I would not wish to a dog or to a snake, to the most low and unfortunate creature of the earth—I would not wish to any of them what I have had to suffer for things that I am not guilty of. But my conviction is that I have suffered for things I am guilty of. I am suffering because I am a radical and indeed I am a radical; I have suffered because I was an Italian and indeed I am an Italian; I have suffered more for my family and for my beloved than for myself; but I am so convinced to be right that if you could execute me two times, and if I could be reborn two times, I would live again and do what I have done already. I have finished. Thank you."[44] The Vanzetti speech was printed in full in newspapers throughout the world. Many readers concurred with Vanzetti's beliefs and held that Sacco and Vanzetti's appeals had fallen on deaf ears because they were anarchists and aliens. The only appeal now was to Governor Fuller. Would he grant clemency? Would he seek to obtain a new trial?

On June 1, 1927, Governor Fuller startled the country by announcing the appointment of a committee to review the case. Its three members included A. Lawrence Lowell, president of Harvard University; Samuel W. Stratton, president of the Massachusetts Institute of Technology; and Robert Grant, former justice of the Massachusetts Probate Court. The Lowell Committee found that although Judge Thayer was guilty of a "grave breach of official decorum" because of his prejudicial comments about the defendants, nevertheless Sacco and Vanzetti were fairly tried. Just before midnight on August 3, the governor reached his conclusion in a formal document. He found the jurors to be thoroughly honest; insisted that there was no reason to find the trial unfair; he gave no credence to the Madeiros confession. He found the six years of delay to be inexcusable. He praised his committee as one composed of men whose reputations for intelligence and open-mindedness were above reproach. But on August 10, 1927, forty minutes before the two men were to be electrocuted, a stay of execution was granted until August 22 to allow for additional legal moves by the defense.

Poets, writers, and intellectuals poured into Boston and took up a vigil in behalf of Sacco and Vanzetti. Although anarchists and communists are theoretically mortal enemies, inasmuch as Sacco and Vanzetti in reaching over the heads of judge and jury appealed to American and world opinion as members of an oppressed proletariat, communist organizations came to their support and joined the Boston vigil outside the walls of Charlestown prison. Enemies of Sacco and Vanzetti mounted counter-demonstrations and mocked the condemned immigrants.

Appeals by the defense to individual members of the Supreme Court of the United States, including Associate Justice Oliver Wendell Holmes, Associate Justice Louis Dembitz Brandeis, and Chief Justice William Howard Taft, failed on various grounds. President Calvin Coolidge, on vacation in South Dakota, remained silent. Madeiros, whose life had been spared pending a new trial for Sacco and Vanzetti, was executed at nine minutes after twelve. Nicola Sacco was brought into the death chamber where he cried "Long live anarchy," and was electrocuted ten minutes later. Bartolomeo Vanzetti appeared seven minutes later and shook hands with his guards. He said, "I wish to tell you that I am innocent and never committed any crime. I thank you for everything you have done for me; I am innocent of all crime, not only this one. I am an innocent man. . . . I wish to forgive some people for what they are now doing to me." Just after one o'clock on the morning of August 23, 1927, three ambulances, under heavy guard, passed out of the prison gates.

Despite a cold, wet, late August day, five days after the electrocution, the funeral procession for Sacco and Vanzetti covered eight miles. Open cars carrying brilliant floral tributes rode among the 50,000 marchers who wore red armbands. The police, in black raincoats, let the procession go by, but enraged that the anarchists should be accorded a funeral fit for a monarch, diverted traffic into the line of march, threw up road blocks, and charged into the cortège and scattered the marchers. Few marchers reached the cemetery gates and those who did were abruptly thrust aside.

From the Death House of Massachusetts State Prison, Bartolomeo Vanzetti wrote on the day of his death to H.W. L. Dana of the Harvard faculty: "What I wish more than all in this last hour of agony is that our case and our fate may be understood in their real being and serve as a tremendous lesson to the forces of freedom—so that our suffering and death will not have been in vain."[45]

The trial of Sacco and Vanzetti is one of those stories that does not end. Its echoes resonate with us today. Nearly all Americans participated vicariously in the trial. There were those who overlooked the anarchism of the accused and believed that since they sought the betterment of humankind they could not possibly be guilty of the crimes with which they were charged. There were others who felt that even if there was substantial evidence of the guilt of Sacco and Vanzetti, it was clear that the accused had not been accorded their rights under the American judicial system. They deplored the climate of hostility toward immigrants as well as anarchists and felt that in such circumstances the Italians had not been accorded a fair trial. In 1927, as today, some Americans were opposed, in principle, to capital punishment and cared less about the guilt or innocence of Sacco and Vanzetti but believed that the death penalty should never be imposed. Finally, Sacco and Vanzetti became symbols of the radical left. The communists exploited the case for their own purposes and the extreme right saw in the trial a way to "teach the wops" and other newcomers a lesson that they had better "behave" in America. In the middle were the intellectuals, mostly liberal but inclined to the left, who saw in the case an opportunity to crystallize class divisions in America.

Were Sacco and Vanzetti guilty of the murders of the Braintree paymasters? In 1962, Francis Russell, citing ballistic tests and other evidence, concluded that Vanzetti was probably innocent while Sacco may have been guilty.[46] In 1977, the distinguished novelist Katherine Anne Porter, who had demonstrated fiercely fifty years before in behalf of Sacco and Vanzetti, wrote that she still was not sure whether or not they were guilty but believed that Sacco possibly was. She continued to insist, "Yet no matter what, it was a terrible miscarriage of justice. . . ."[47] But was it?

Francis Russell quoted from a registered letter he received from Ideale Gambera who told him about her father who died in June 1982 at the age of ninety-three. She explained that she could not come forward before because her father had sworn her to secrecy, and she did not dare break her promise while he lived. But now she felt free to say that her father had followed the case from its beginning. "Everyone [in the Boston anarchist circle] knew that Sacco was guilty and that Vanzetti was innocent as far as the actual participation in the killing. But no one would ever break the code of silence even if it cost Vanzetti's life." She went on to say that her father was one of four to whom District Attorney Katzmann had proposed that in exchange for $35,000 in cash, he would guarantee deportation to Italy of the accused as undesirable aliens. While her father disagreed, the other three urged that the deal be rejected and that the trial go forward. "Their argument was that this [the trial] would bring great publicity for the anarchist movement and that there was every chance that the men would go free."[48] Yet, much as one would like to write "finis" and let Sacco and Vanzetti rest in historical limbo, one cannot be sure that the case is really closed.

On Thursday, September 16, 1920, at one minute after twelve, a bomb exploded on the corner of Broad and Wall, the symbolic center of capitalism. Thirty died, two hundred were injured. It was the worst explosion to date in American history. Property damage reached over two million dollars.

The perpetrator was Mario Buda, an Italian anarchist and likely accomplice in the Braintree murders, and close friend of Sacco and Vanzetti. Upon learning of the indictment of his friends, Buda had vowed to retaliate against the institutions that were harassing his friends. He left Boston and went to New York City, where he hired a horse and wagon in which he placed a large dynamite bomb filled with heavy cast-iron slugs. Buda parked his wagon at the curb in front of the United States Assay Office and directly across the street from the House of Morgan. He climbed down from the wagon and disappeared just before the bomb went off. U.S. Attorney General Palmer called the incident part of a "gigantic plot." It was not. The New York Chamber of Commerce called it an "act of war." It was not. Director Flynn of the Bureau of Investigation described the bombing for what it was, namely, revenge for the prosecution of Sacco and Vanzetti. Buda was never caught. After the bomb blast he secured a passport from the Italian vice-consul and a few weeks later sailed for Naples, Italy. He never returned to the United States. In 1927, however, Buda was arrested by the Fascist government as a "dangerous anarchist" and sentenced to five years of imprisonment. But in the United States the bombings did not end.

Instead, as it became increasingly evident that Sacco and Vanzetti would not be spared, anarchist publications urged further retaliation. They were spurred on in their efforts by Sacco and Vanzetti. The latter, for example, urged: "If we have to die for a crime of which we are innocent, we ask for revenge, revenge in our names and in the names of our living and dead. . . . I will make a list of honor of the perjurers who murdered us . . . I will try to see Thayer dead . . . I will put fire into the human breaths." In the summer of 1927, Sacco wrote after Governor Fuller refused clemency, "We are proud for death and fall as the anarchists can fall. It is up to you now, brothers and comrades!"[49]

On June 1, 1926, a bomb went off at the home of Samuel Johnson in West Bridgewater. The bomb was probably intended for Samuel's brother Simon who called the police which led to Sacco and Vanzetti's arrest. On May 27, 1927, a package bomb addressed to Governor Fuller was intercepted in the Boston post office, no one was hurt and no one arrested. On August 6, 1927, bombs exploded in the New York subway, in a Philadelphia church, at the home of the mayor of Baltimore. On August 15, 1927, an explosion destroyed the home of Lewis McHardy, a juror in the Dedham trial of Sacco and Vanzetti. McHardy's wife and three children were thrown from their beds but escaped serious injury.

The bombings continued after Sacco and Vanzetti were executed. On May 17, 1928, a bomb exploded at the home of their executioner. The home was badly damaged but no one hurt. By the end of the 1930s, the Italian anarchist movement was fading rapidly. Yet, on September 27, 1932, the home of Judge Thayer was destroyed, probably by anarchists.

"Public opinion, in 1927, was not as conscious of its own significance and power, as it has since become."[50] While it was not the object of any real scientific analysis, it is estimated that eighty percent of ordinary men and women in Massachusetts felt that justice had been done and that Sacco and Vanzetti deserved their fate. Were Sacco and Vanzetti to be tried today, today's legal safeguards are such that it is unlikely they would have been found guilty and much less likely that they would have been executed. In Massachusetts, capital punishment is, in any event, no longer carried out.

In 1947, twenty years after the executions, Eleanor Roosevelt, Albert Einstein, and Herbert Lehman offered the state of Massachusetts a bas-relief plaque of Sacco and Vanzetti, done by the sculptor of Mount Rushmore, Gutzon Borglum. Their proffered gift was rejected by the governor. In 1959, a resolution of the state legislature to exonerate the defendants, as had been done for the "victims of the witchcraft hysteria who were hanged in Salem," failed adoption.

In 1977, however, Governor Michael S. Dukakis marked the fiftieth anniversary of the executions by proclaiming August 23, 1977, "Nicola Sacco and Bartolomeo Vanzetti Day." The governor's proclamation read in part: "I do hereby . . . declare . . . further that any stigma and disgrace should forever be removed from the names of Nicola Sacco and Bartolomeo Vanzetti from the names of their families and descendants, and so from the name of the Commonwealth of Massachusetts; and I hereby call upon all people of Massachusetts to pause in their daily endeavors to reflect upon the tragic events, and draw from the historic lessons to prevent the forces of intolerance, fear, and hatred from ever again uniting to overcome the rationality, wisdom, and fairness to which our legal system aspires."[51]

[1]James M. Smallwood, ed., *Will Rogers Daily Telegrams: Vol. I, the Coolidge Years, 1926–1929* (Stillwater, Oklahoma: Oklahoma State University Press, 1978), p. 64.
[2]Quoted in *New York Times,* October 4, 1944.
[3]Quoted in Lawrence H. Fuchs, "Election of 1928," in Arthur M. Schlesinger Jr., ed., *History of American Presidential Elections: 1789–1968, Vol. 3* (New York: Chelsea House Publishers in Association with McGraw-Hill Book Company, 1974), p. 2608.

[4]Quoted in "First Effects of the Mississippi Flood," *Literary Digest* 93 (June 18, 1927): 8.

[5]Quoted in "How Hoover's Forces Fought the Flood," *Literary Digest* 94 (July 30, 1927): 39.

[6]Quoted in David Burner, *Herbert Hoover: A Public Life* (New York: Alfred A. Knopf, 1979), p. 193.

[7]Quoted in Robert Sobel, *Herbert Hoover and the Onset of the Great Depression, 1929-1930* (Philadelphia: J. B. Lippincott Company, 1975), p. 24.

[8]Joan Hoff Wilson, *Herbert Hoover: Forgotten Progressive* (Boston: Little, Brown and Company, 1975), p. 11.

[9]Quoted in Dorothy Horton McGee, *Herbert Hoover: Engineer, Humanitarian, Statesman* (New York: Dodd Mead and Company, 1959), p. 31.

[10]Quoted in Sobel, *Herbert Hoover and the Onset of the Great Depression*, p. 31.

[11]William Hard, *Who's Hoover?* (New York: Dodd, Mead and Company, 1928), p. 18.

[12]Ibid., p. 10.

[13]Craig Lloyd, *Aggressive Introvert: A Study of Herbert Hoover and Public Relations Management, 1912–1932* (Columbus: Ohio University Press, 1972), pp. 84–85.

[14]Geoffry Perrett, *America in the 20s: A History* (New York: Simon and Schuster, 1982), p. 284.

[15]Louis Seibold, "The Political Year," in *Mirrors of the Year: 1927–1928* (New York: Frederick Stokes and Company, 1928), p. 129.

[16]Walter Lippmann, "The Causes of Political Indifference Today," *Atlantic Monthly*, in *Politics of the Nineteen Twenties*, ed. John L. Shaver (Waltham, Massachusetts: Ginn-Blaisdell, 1970), p. 166.

[17]"Is there a Dearth of Great Men," *Literary Digest* 94 (August 6, 1927): 12.

[18]Lippmann, "The Causes of Political Indifference Today," p. 168.

[19]Ibid., p. 170.

[20]Ibid., p. 171.

[21]Quoted in Charles Merz, *The Dry Decade* (Garden City, New York: Doubleday, Doran and Company, Inc., 1931), p. 51.

[22]Fuchs, "Election of 1928," p. 2589.

[23]Herbert Asbury, *The Great Illusion: An Informal History of Prohibition* (Garden City, New York: Doubleday and Company, Inc., 1950), pp. 1 and ff.

[24]Ibid., p. 114.

[25]Alice Katherine Fallows, "Bishops Beer: A Temperance Experiment and Its Bearing on Prohibition," *Century Magazine* (February 1927): 474.

[26]"The Butler-Borah Debate on Prohibition," *Literary Digest* 93 (April 23, 1927): 10.

[27]Ibid.

[28]Fallows, "Bishops Beer," p. 475.

[29]Merz, "The Dry Decade," p. 213.

[30]Quoted in ibid.

[31]Ibid., p. 248.

[32]Ibid., p. 276.

[33]Ibid., p. 277.

[34]Ibid., p. 333.

[35]Thomas Coffey, *The Long Thirst: Prohibition in America 1920–1933* (New York: W. W. Norton and Company, 1975), p. 198.

[36]Ibid., p. 199.

[37]"Prohibition After Wheeler," *Literary Digest* 94 (September 17, 1927): 6.

[38]Quoted in ibid., p. 7.

[39]David. E. Kyvig, *Repealing National Prohibition* (Chicago: University of Chicago Press, 1979), p. 1

[40]Felix Frankfurter, *The Case of Sacco and Vanzetti: A Critical Analysis for Lawyers and Laymen* (New York: Grossett and Dunlap, 1962), p. 8.

[41]Ibid., p. 65.

[42]Quoted in Barrington Boardman, *Flappers, Bootleggers, Typhoid Mary and the Bomb: An Anecdotal History of the United States from 1923–1945* (New York: Harper and Row, 1989), p. 76.

[43]F. Lauriston Bullard, "Sacco-Vanzetti," in *Mirrors of the Year 1927–1928* (New York: Frederick A. Stokes, 1928), p. 81.

[44]Thomas A. Bailey, ed., *The American Spirit: U.S. History as Seen by Contemporaries*, 2nd Edition (Boston: D. C. Heath and Company, 1968), p. 756.

[45]Marion Frankfurter and Gardner Jackson, *Letters of Sacco and Vanzetti* (New York: Octagon Books, 1971 reprint), p. 325.

[46]Francis Russell, "Sacco Guilty Vanzetti Innocent?" *American Heritage* 13 (June 1962): 5–9, 107–111.

[47]Quoted in Page Smith, *A People's History of the 1920s and the New Deal: Redeeming the Time, Vol. 8* (New York: McGraw Hill Book Company, 1977), p. 135.

[48]Francis Russell, *Sacco and Vanzetti: The Case Resolved* (New York: Harper and Row, 1986), pp. 12-13.

[49]Quoted in Paul Avrich, *Sacco and Vanzetti: The Anarchist Background* (Princeton, New Jersey: Princeton University Press, 1991), p. 212.

[50]Louis Joughlin and Edmund Morgan, *The Legacy of Sacco and Vanzetti* (Chicago: Quadrangle Books, 1964), p. 293.

[51]Quoted in Brian Jackson, *The Black Flag: A Look at the Strange Case of Nicola Sacco and Bartolomeo Vanzetti* (Boston: Routledge and Kegan Paul, 1981), p. 90.

4

AMERICA AND THE WORLD

April 7, 1927

At 2:15 P.M., television was demonstrated in New York City. Walter S. Gifford, President of the American Telephone and Telegraph Company, sat at a telephone and not only talked to Herbert Hoover, secretary of commerce, in Washington, D.C., 200 miles away, but saw him on a rectangular television measuring no more than two by two-and-a-half inches. It was, reported the New York Times in its front-page article, "Like a Photo Come to Life." But, cautioned the newspaper, "Commercial Use in Doubt."[1]

Secretary Hoover's face was sharp and distinct on the small screen. He spoke glowingly of the new invention. "It is a matter of just pride to have a part in this historic occasion. We have long been familiar with the electrical transmission of sound. Today we have, in a sense, the transmission of sight, for the first time in the world's history. Human genius has now destroyed the impediment of distance in a new respect and in a manner hitherto unknown. . . . ."[2] The secretary's wife then took a seat and talked to Gifford. "What will you invent next?" she said. "I hope you won't invent anything that reads our thoughts." Mrs. Hoover next lightly confided in Mr. Gifford: "I don't know whether this is a good invention or not. There are times when I talk over the phone and wouldn't want anyone to see how I look."[3]

The New York Times reporter wrote: "The demonstration of combined telephone and television, in fact, is one that outruns the imagination of all the wizards of prophecy. It is one of the few things that Leonardo da Vinci, Roger Bacon, Jules Verne, and other masters of forecasting failed utterly to anticipate."[4]

The televised image was far less impressive than the motion picture film then available. Occasionally, Secretary Hoover's face could not be clearly distingushed. The secretary might be forgiven for not being a polished television performer: as he looked down to read his speech, he was not aware that the lower part of his face was often covered up. When he moved, however, his face became clearly distinguishable. Near the close of his talk he turned his head and his features in profile became clear and full of detail.

Although it was far from a finished product, the demonstration was stll impressive.
"The thing that chiefly staggers the mind, was that all that traveled over the wire from
Washington to New York was a series of electrical impluses."[5] The New York World
rhapsodized, "In time millions of people may watch and listen to a Presidential inau-
guration, a championship football game, or even the clash of armies on a battlefield."[6]
It would take, *however, nearly twenty years before the prescient comments of the* New
York World *would come true. A great depression and a second great war conspired to*
delay television's commercial introduction.

While 1927 was a year of substantial technical progress in the field of television,
most Americans and many in business could not imagine how it would affect their
lives. David Sarnoff, however, devoted himself to the cause. The "Father of American
Television," as he was annointed by the Television Broadcasters Association in 1944,
piqued the imagination of Americans by his insistence that the advent of television
was imminent and with it would come a new way of looking at America and the
world.

In the August 14, 1926, issue of the Saturday Evening Post, *Sarnoff envisioned the*
possibilities inherent in television. He is quoted as saying: "The greatest day of all will be
reached when not only the human voice but the image of the speaker will be flashed
through space in every direction. On that day the whole country will join in every
national procession. The backwoodsman will be able to follow the play of expression on the
face of every leading artist. Mothers will attend child welfare clinics in their homes. Work-
ers may go to night school in the same way. A scientist can demonstrate his latest discov-
eries to those of his profession even though they may be scattered all over the world."[7]

On January 31, 1927, Sarnoff, a lieutenant colonel in the United States Signal
Corps Reserve, made a speech to the Army War College in which he called attention to
the possibilities of using television in future wars. "It is conceivable," he declared, "that
a radio-television transmitter installed in an airplane might be useful in transmitting
a direct image of the enemy's terrain, thus enabling greater accuracy in gunfire."[8] *While*
his listeners were too disciplined to scoff, the military audience widely believed that
Sarnoff's remarks made for an imaginative talk and interesting dreams but were far
from practical application. Yet, it was but ten years later, as the possibility of war
loomed in Europe, that some of those who heard his remarks met with RCA engineers
to adjust television for airplanes and battleships.

Aware of the success of the April demonstration of television, on June 8, 1927, in an
address before the Chicago Association of Commerce, Sarnoff told his audience: "With
the inspiring demonstrations recently made of television, or the art of distant seeing, we
have passed the point of conjecture as to its scientific practicability. It is an accomplished
fact. . . . The possibilities of the new art are as boundless as the imagination. . . . It is

the glory of man that he has never quailed before the apparently insurmountable obstacles of space and time. . . . "[9]

In 1927, Isoraku Yamamoto, the Japanese Naval attaché in Washington, D.C., returned to his homeland to push the development of naval aviation in Japan. It was under his leadership that the versatile and formidable fighter plane, the Zero, was developed. In 1940, though he was personally opposed to the war with the United States, he conceived and successfully executed the surprise attack by sea and air at Pearl Harbor and thus catapulted America into World War II.

The Tanaka Memorial
On December 26, 1926, Hirohito became Emperor of Japan and in April 1927, Tanaka Glichi (1864–1929) became that country's prime minister. Between June 27 and July 7, 1927, Tanaka Glichi convened a conference of important Japanese civilian and military leaders to discuss problems relating to Japan's interests in the Far East. On July 25, 1927, a summary of the conference, known as the Tanaka Memorial, was allegedly drafted by the prime minister and shared with Emperor Hirohito and was presumably approved by him. However, the contents of the Tanaka Memorial were not released until 1929, when the Chinese made the document public. Because no original copy of the Memorial has thus far been found, because the source of the disclosure of the document's contents is suspect, the Tanaka Memorial is widely viewed as a clever attempt by the Chinese to arouse anti-Japanese feeling in the West. Despite the questionable character of the document, it is of interest because it sums up views that were probably widely held in Japan's ruling circles.

Since the European War (WWI), Japan's political as well as economic interests have been in an unsettled condition. This is due to the fact that we have failed to take advantage of our special privileges in Manchuria and Mongolia and fully to realize our acquired rights. But upon my appointment as premier, I was instructed to guide our interests in this region and watch for opportunities for further expansion. Such injunctions one cannot take lightly. Ever since I advocated a positive policy toward Manchuria and Mongolia as a common citizen, I have longed for its realization. So in order that we may lay plans for the colonization of the Far East and the development of our new continental empire, a special conference was held from June 27th to July 7th, lasting in all eleven days. It was attended by all the civil and military officers connected with Manchuria and Mongolia, whose discussions resulted in the following resolutions. These we respectfully submit to Your Majesty for consideration. . . .

After describing the significant resources in Manchuria and Mongolia and deploring the limitations on Japan's freedom of movement in that area as a result of signing the Nine-Power Treaty at the Washington Conference, the Memorial argued that, on the basis of "self-defense,"

Japan cannot remove the difficulties in Eastern Asia unless she adopts a policy of "Blood and Iron." But in carrying out this policy we have to face the United States which has been turned against us by China's policy of fighting poison with poison. In the future if we want to control China, we must first crush the United States just as in the past we had to fight in the Russo-Japanese War. But in order to conquer China we must first conquer Manchuria and Mongolia. In order to conquer the world, we must first conquer China. If we succeed in conquering China the rest of the Asiatic countries and the South Sea Countries will fear us and surrender to us. Then the world will realize that Eastern Asia is ours and will not dare to violate our rights. This is the plan left to us by Emperor Meiji, the success of which is essential to our national existence.[10]

When in 1899 the United States annexed the Philippines in the aftermath of the Spanish-American War, the "Open Door" policy was pursued with general consistency until the outbreak of World War II. That is, the United States sought to maintain the territorial integrity of China and prevent that huge country's further division into spheres of great power influence. The Washington Treaties of 1922 pledged the signatories, the United States, Great Britain, France, and Japan, against further imperialism in China to maintain China's political independence. But such policies were more easily stated than enforced. During 1927, events were to play out in China which would have an important impact on American foreign policy. Despite a preference for isolation, the United States became increasingly involved in the affairs of that region, most notably at first in China.

China: The Danger Spot of the World

Commenting on events in China in 1927, a lengthy editorial in the *New York Times* concluded: "China has, in truth, become one of the 'danger spots' of the world."[11] Danger spot or not, to most Americans China remained mostly an exotic oddity. Many of the homes of the affluent were decorated with "chinoiserie" of dubious origin, quality, or taste. Americans noted some of the "quaint" customs of the "inscrutable" Chinese who read from up to down not right to left, whose men wore skirts and women trousers, whose mourners wore white and brides red.

But Americans also had a more substantial interest in China. For one thing, there was an idealized version of the Chinese emperor as despotic but benign and as a guardian of China's ancient philosophers such as Mencius, Lao-tze, and Confucius. A respect for the wisdom of ancient China grew among the American intelligentsia, and when America developed its China trade using vast clipper ships to make the dangerous journey from Eastern ports around the Straits of Magellan to China, Christian missionaries, educators, and doctors were often aboard. In addition to missionary activities, China also became a focus of private philanthropy such as the massive aid given by the Rockefeller Foundation between 1915 and 1947 to the Peking Union Medical College.

In the first quarter of the twentieth century, many of the Chinese patriots who promoted the growth of Chinese nationalism and overthrew the monarchy had been educated at American colleges and universities. Sun Yat-sen, often described as the "George Washington of China," graduated from a medical school in Hong Kong and traveled and studied widely in the United States, often under the guidance of John Dewey, the philosopher and educator. His wife, Ching-ling Soong, sometimes known as "China's Joan of Arc," graduated from Wesleyan College in Macon, Georgia, as did her sister and Mei-ling Soong who became the wife of Chiang Kai-shek. (Their brother, Tzu-wen Soong, better known as T. V. Soong, graduated from Harvard. He became a leading member of the Guomindang and contributed mightily to China's economic development.)

But if private philanthropy appeared generous, realpolitik was the prevailing foreign policy of the United States in its relations with China. If other countries were eager to exploit China's wealth by setting up spheres of influence in violation of China's sovereignty, the United States was not long in following this example. The good will generated by private philanthropy was often eroded by treaties which treated the Chinese as an inferior people and insisted upon special rights for Americans living and doing business in China. In 1884, legislation was adopted cutting off Chinese immigration, and the people of China were offended. And, when Chinese nationalism asserted itself as it did in the case of the uprising of Boxers (1898–1900) against foreigners, the United States joined British, French, Russian, German, and Japanese troops in forcibly ending the rebellion.

In 1912, the Chinese monarchy ended, and with it came the beginning of a long crisis. The details are complex, but at issue was the question of what or who could possibly replace the rule of the Son of Heaven. Under Sun Yat-sen's (1866–1925) leadership, the "sleeping giant" awakened. The Guomindang (Nationalist Party) became the political instrument with which Sun would seek to achieve his goals for China namely nationalism (the end of foreign oppression), democracy (political equality), and people's livelihood (economic opportunity).

Stating goals proved easier than achieving them. Japanese invaders, Chinese warlords, and other competitors to Sun's leadership threatened his dreams as well as his life. As a result, he needed an army of six hundred bodyguards to protect him. When he and other military leaders moved about the country, "they did so in big American Packards, with gun-toting heavies mounted on the running board."[12] Sun realized that for China at that time these goals were longshots at best. As he told his head bodyguard, a Canadian Jew known as "Two-Gun Cohen," what he merely wanted was "a China where there is no need to shut one's outer gate at night."[13]

In 1923, when appeals to other sources appeared futile, Sun Yat-sen sought and received material assistance from the Russian Bolsheviks.

An alliance between a Communist China and the Union of Soviet Socialist Republics would make Communism a formidable force not only among developing countries but in any country where the workers could be aroused to take violent action against their tormentors in government and industry. Out of the turmoil Communism could emerge triumphant. If history could repeat itself, then the success of the Bolsheviki in Russia in 1917 could be achieved once again in China. If Communism could be expanded to China, the Bolshevik theory of world revolution would prove feasible. But in 1927, the Soviet Union, now under the fist of Joseph Stalin, postponed this ambitious revolutionary agenda.

In 1924, a diplomatic agreement was reached between Sun Yat-sen's China and the Soviet government according to which, while Communism would not be introduced into China, nevertheless that country would recognize the Soviet Union. For its part, the U.S.S.R. abandoned extraterritoriality and all special treaty rights and concessions obtained in China under the Czarist regimes.[14] The Chinese Eastern Railway, formerly a joint enterprise, was made into a private corporation capable of making its own commercial decisions. Armed Soviet guards of the railway would be removed. With the adoption of these agreements, Soviet funds, military supplies, and military advisors streamed into China to support the Guomindang's efforts at national unity. Thus, Soviet Communism and

Chinese nationalism sought to use one another. The former expected that because of their destitute lives the masses of Chinese laborers, farmers, and petite bourgeoisie would be ripe for a Bolshevik-style revolution. The Chinese nationalists expected that, armed with Soviet assistance, including military officers, however self-interested, China would at long last be unified.

In March 1925, a year after this agreement, Sun Yat-sen died in Peking of an advanced cancer. In his former capital at Nanjing, a spectacular funeral was held for this national hero. In keeping with common Chinese practice, his remains were placed in the Green Cloud Monastery, a Buddhist shrine in the Western Hills a few miles outside of Peking. In November 1925, a group of the Guomindang, in the presence of their dead leader's coffin, resolved to expel the Communists from the Nationalist Party. But it proved to be easier to pass a resolution than to achieve a successful outcome.

One can only speculate on how Sun Yat-sen, had he lived, might have interpreted and carried out his agreement with the Soviet Union. But his death left a void that was filled by rancor and fighting between the Communist and non-Communist wings of the Guomindang, the traditional warlords of China, and the Bolsheviks.

Chiang Kai-shek (1887–1975), Sun's military aide and commandant of China's newly created Whampoa Military Academy, at first continued to cooperate with the Bolsheviks. But in 1927, the leadership of the Guomindang suspected that the Soviets were plotting to take advantage of widespread discontent and establish a Communist government in China. The Nationalists, under the leadership of Chiang, decided to thwart Bolshevik intentions. Chiang proceeded to oust the Communists first from power in the Guomindang and then from China itself.

Purging the Communists was a formidable task. And, as the National Revolutionary Army of the Guomindang gained strength in various areas of China, anti-Bolshevik sentiment manifested itself as anti-foreign hostility as well. As social and labor unrest mounted all foreigners were blamed for China's time of troubles. Deep-seated hatred of foreigners from Europe, America, and Japan surfaced and violence against factories and banks owned by foreigners broke out first in one city and then in another.

On January 3, 1927, there was rioting in Hankow, a city which the Communists of the Guomindang, over Chiang's objections, sought to make the seat of government. It was crowded with business people, journalists, missionaries, and educators, many of whom expected to see the Chinese Revolution metamorphose into a Communist victory. A crowd of workers attacked the foreign police of the city and occupied the British concession. Great Britain, recognizing that it could not retain its privileges in a hostile city, agreed to relinquish its concession not only at Hankow but also at the other Yangtze port of Kiukiang. This was an important first step in ridding China of foreign interlopers.

In Nanjing on March 24, 1927, members of the Nationalist Revolutionary Army murdered one American and injured a second. Five additional foreigners were likewise killed and many more brutally treated. In retaliation, American and British naval vessels shelled the city. The incident at Nanjing was a relatively minor episode, but the American press built it up to make readers believe that there was a "reign of terror" against Americans in China. On April 11, 1927, Great Britain, France, Italy, Japan, and the United States demanded that the commander of the troops responsible for the riot be punished; an apology from the commander-in-chief of the Nationalist Army; a promise that there be no more violence against foreigners or their property; and complete reparation for damage done. When the Nationalists declined to comply with all of these demands, the British government, supported by business interests in China, urged joint intervention and the application of sanctions. The U.S. State Department, under Secretary Frank B. Kellogg, wisely rejected intervention. The British backed down as well.

The Chinese Communist Party was well entrenched in Shanghai. It controlled most of the labor unions and had enormous influence among university students.

Secretary of State Frank B. Kellogg. Reproduced from the collections of the Library of Congress.

It had a formidable military force known as the Workers' Inspection Corps. But in Shanghai, the non-Communist opposition was also strong, and the circumstances in 1927 were ripe for a showdown.

A great deal was at stake in Shanghai, the "Paris of the East," as it was a city that collected forty percent of China's import duties and where foreign property was worth billions of dollars. It had a self-governing foreign community of 40,000 people, including 4,000 Americans. Foreign and Chinese businessmen joined forces to oppose a Communist takeover. It was here where Chiang Kai-shek ruthlessly broke the back of the Chinese Communist Party and set back the timetable for a Communist takeover of China.

As unrest mounted in Shanghai, the foreign business quarter began to resemble an armed camp. A curfew was imposed; barbed wire impeded the free flow of people and traffic. As Chiang's armies contemplated entering Shanghai, the American Pacific fleet hastened from Manila to Shanghai. The British sent a number of warships and 20,000 fighting men. The front page of the *New York Times* advised its readers that American Marines marched through Shanghai in a show of strength. But in recognition that this event may not be of singular importance to the paper's readership, the headline was shared with the announcement that "[Babe] Ruth Gets $210,000 for Three Years as a Yank!"[15]

After escalating clashes with the Communists, on April 18, 1927, Chiang Kai-shek established a national government with its capital at Nanjing. Chiang enlisted the aid of Du Yuesheng (1888–1951), a powerful gangster who lived in the French Concession, to purge the Communist Party in Shanghai. Du hired hundreds of thugs who, disguised as workmen, infiltrated the Chinese sections of Shanghai before dawn on April 12, 1927. Hundreds of Communists were executed and hundreds more captured, including Zhou Enlai, who later escaped. The Chinese Communist Party was forced to move its headquarters to Hankow.

The Shanghai coup was part of a broader conflict in many cities of China during the spring of 1927 in which anyone who got in the way of Chiang's soldiers was treated mercilessly. Vincent Sheean, an important American journalist who despised Chiang, described the wholesale massacres that took place in the province of Hunan where an estimated four to five thousand workers and peasants were butchered at the hands of Chiang's armies in an over-zealous attempt to oust the Communists. "Many were disemboweled, scores were boiled in oil, hundreds were shot or decapitated; almost all were tortured before death and mutilated afterwards."[16]

On July 15, 1927, the Communists were expelled from the Guomindang and, a few days later, the total separation of the two parties was proclaimed. Mikhail

Borodin, the formidable Soviet adviser to the Guomindang, and Madam Sun Yat-sen were forced to flee to the Soviet Union. While the Soviet advisors were forced out, some in disguise, many Chinese Communists fought on and a long civil war ensued, a war that did not end until World War II was over. Borodin optimistically declared, "Do not suppose that the Chinese revolution is ending or that it has failed. . . . Sooner or later, a year, two years, five years from now, it will rise to surface again. It may be defeated a dozen times, but in the end it must conquer."[17] On August 1, Zhou Enlai led a Communist military uprising in Nanchang, Jiangxi province. Although Zhou's troops were forced to leave the city of Nanchang four days later, August 1, 1927, remains to this day the birthday of the Red Army.

Attempting to seize power by force, Communist cohorts stormed Canton, burned a tenth of the city, and massacred many, but to no avail. The Guomindang counter-attacked in force on December 14, 1927, and in street-by-street fighting defeated the Communists. Most of the workers in the Soviet consulate in Canton were murdered. In the aftermath, Stalin ordered that Borodin, now "safely" in the U.S.S.R, be put to death.

By the end of 1927 the future for Communism in China looked bleak. Stalin essentially had abandoned his efforts at world revolution and seemed determined to follow a policy of "socialism in one country," that is, the U.S.S.R. But seen through the eyes of Mao Zedong (1893–1976), there were new opportunities for Communism in China.

In 1927, Mao was thirty-four, tall, and powerfully built. He was the son of a self-made peasant who ruthlessly rose to affluence to become a prosperous farmer and grain merchant. Like Hitler, Mao was mainly a nationalist to whom the enemy was the foreigner. In 1924, Mao took a Chinese friend to see the infamous sign in the Shanghai park, "Chinese and Dogs Not Allowed." In his earthy manner he commented, "If one of our foreign masters farts, it's a lovely perfume! Do the Chinese people know only how to hate the Japanese, and don't they know how to hate England?"[18]

In February 1927, after an inspection trip through Hunan, Mao predicted: "In a very short time, in China's central, southern and northern provinces, several hundred million peasants will rise like a tornado or tempest. . . . They will break all trammels that now bind them and rush forward along the road to liberation."[19] But his observations were premature.

If the city workers were lost to Communism, at least temporarily, it was clear that for the immediate future the revolution could survive only among the peasantry of the villages. Mao understood the importance of establishing an organized military force and not relying on spontaneous uprisings of workers and peasants. He became a warlord with armies of his own. He also recognized that in a country as vast as China, revolution would not come all at once but would be won gradually, first in one part of China and then in another over a period of many years.

By 1927 it was clear that the "sleeping giant" had awakened. Yet few Americans fully appreciated the significance of the events that were taking place in China. One who did recognize their importance was the American philosopher John Dewey. After spending some time in China during the dramatic events that were unfolding in 1927, he wrote: "[S]een in historic perspective, it is certain that the re-constitution of the life of the oldest and most numerous people of Asia will stand revealed as at least as significant as the transition of Europe out of medievalism into a modernized culture. Such questions as the bearing of the changes upon the special privileges of a few thousand foreigners, the control of India by Great Britain, and other features which are now conspicuous will fall into place as paragraphs in a volume."[20] Dewey's views were not shared by the American State Department, which groped for an appropriate foreign policy.

On the subject of American foreign policy toward China as formulated by Secretary of State Kellogg, the journalist Elmer Davis had this to say: "Like the woman of Samaria, who had no husband but had five, he has no Chinese policy at the moment of writing, but has had all the Chinese policies there are, one after another for a few hours each, in the past fortnight."[21] But establishing a consistent policy for China was no easy matter. For one thing, with which China did one establish a foreign policy? At one time or another, both the Communists and the Nationalists appeared to have the power to speak for China and at other times neither did. At times the seat of government was Nanjing, Peking, Canton, or Hankow. It was difficult even to know to which of these authorities the American ambassadors should be accredited. Kellogg said of U.S. policy toward China, "I have never in my life faced a problem that required more caution and firmness than this."[22]

One corner of American foreign policy was to maintain the Open Door policy (see p. 98). On January 27, 1927, Secretary Kellogg said with regard to China, "The United States is . . . prepared to enter into negotiations with any government of China or delegations which can represent or speak for China. . . . The United States is prepared to negotiate release of extraterritorial rights as soon as China is prepared to provide protection by law and through her courts to American citizens, their rights and property. . . ."[23]

During 1927, a year of upheaval for China, the United States acted with forbearance and restraint despite critical pressures from European, Japanese, and

American business interests to act more aggressively. This policy of restraint was generally popular with the American people who retained a soft spot in their collective hearts for China. Secretary Kellogg consistently refused to be stampeded into joint action with other Western powers against China. He refused, for example, to apply sanctions after the Nanjing incident. The secretary likewise refused to get hysterical over the menace of the Soviet Union to China. He sought on the one hand to protect American lives, while on the other negotiating the elimination of extraterritorial rights and the granting to China of full autonomy over its tariffs. He steadfastly discouraged the division of China into two separate countries, which in 1927 was a distinct possibility.

President Calvin Coolidge generally held himself aloof from the unfolding events in China. He failed to grasp their significance and left most of the details to his secretary of state. In the case of America's relations with Latin America and the Caribbean, Coolidge was far more assertive.

Nicaragua: America's First Jungle War

In 1898, when the United States seized the Philippines, the last stronghold of the once-great Spanish empire, America became a world power and, as a *Washington Post* editorial of that year expressed it, "the taste of empire is in the mouth of the people, even as the taste of blood in the jungle."[24] Philander C. Knox, President William Howard Taft's secretary of state, summarized American foreign policy in Mexico, Central and South America as "dollar diplomacy" by which he meant that in unstable areas, the State Department would have among its high priorities the promotion of American business interests.

As the world's greatest industrial power, the United States had particular interest in Nicaragua as a possible site of an inter-oceanic canal. For Nicaragua, such a canal would have been an economic benefit of enormous proportions. However, when in 1904 construction began on a canal between the Atlantic and Pacific in Panama, disappointment in Nicaragua was deep and resentment over American tactics in choosing to build the canal elsewhere festered.

When the authoritarian Nicaraguan President José Santos Zelaya probed for such interest as there might be in Japan or Germany to build a competing canal, the U.S. State Department determined that Zelaya was "a blot on the history of Nicaragua" and no longer an acceptable Nicaraguan president. In 1909, with the help of U.S. Marines, Zelaya was overthrown and the United States threw its support to the conservative General Juan Estrada who became president in 1911. But stability eluded Nicaragua and a series of dictators ruled Nicaragua through the early 1920s.

During this time, intervention by marines in Nicaragua and other Central American countries became an American addiction from which the United States could not "dry out" until 1933. With marines wielding the "big stick," Nicaragua became a virtual protectorate of the United States. Not only were Nicaraguan finances subject to U.S. control, but in 1916, according to the terms of the Chamorro-Bryan Treaty, "The government of Nicaragua [granted] in perpetuity to the Government of the United States, forever free from all taxation or other public charge, the exclusive proprietary rights necessary and convenient for the construction, operation, and maintenance of an inter-oceanic canal." While the treaty effectively prevented a foreign country from building a competing canal, it encouraged, as if further encouragement were needed, America's meddling in this Central American republic. Although the marines were withdrawn in 1925, unrest, and fear that Communism would be imported from Mexico and infect Nicaragua's 600,000 people, influenced President Coolidge to send the soldiers back to this impoverished land.

In 1926, the U.S. State Department supported as president/dictator of Nicaragua Adolfo Díaz, a leader of the Conservative Party. Mexico supported the former vice president of Nicaragua, Juan Bautista Sacasa of the Liberal Party, and proceeded to provide arms and war materiel to the armies fighting in the cause of the Liberal Party. For his part, Díaz had the support of Nicaragua's American-established and trained National Guard. The United States insisted that Díaz was the duly elected president of Nicaragua inasmuch as he had been chosen by the Nicaraguan Congress. Sacasa insisted that as a former vice president who had been forced to leave the country during a period of turmoil, he had a prior claim. Sacasa established a rebel government in December 1926, and, in the civil war that escalated, Coolidge injected the might of American marines. But Coolidge was insufficiently aware how severely he would be criticized at home and abroad for his uncharacteristically bold adventure.

On January 10, 1927, President Coolidge delivered a special message to Congress in which he tried to persuade that body of the prudence of his decision. The marines had been ordered to return to Nicaragua, he said, to assure the stability of the conservative government. That stability was essential, Coolidge insisted, to resist the infiltration of the Bolsheviks from their alleged base in Mexico. On January 12, 1927, Secretary of State Kellogg, in a report to the Senate Foreign Relations Committee, echoed his president's concern. In a document entitled, "Bolshevik Aims and Policies in Mexico and Latin America," Kellogg insisted the threat of the Communists was real and imminent.

But neither Coolidge nor Kellogg were entirely persuasive. Senator George Norris challenged the view of the administration with this parody based on the James Whitcomb Riley poem, "The Goblins."

Onc't they was a Bolshevik, who wouldn't say his prayers,
So Kellogg sent him off to bed, away upstairs,
An' Kellogg heerd him hollr, an' Coolidge heerd him bawl,
But when they turn't the kivvers down, he wasn't there at all.
"They seeked him down in Mexico, they cussed him in the press;
They seeked him 'round the Capitol, an' ever'wheres, I guess,
But all they ever found of him was whiskers, hair and clout;
An' the Bolsheviks'll git you ef you don't watch out.[25]

The *New York World* pointed out that American intervention was "another source of irritation, not only between the United States and Nicaragua, but between this Government and all Latin America, which has no love for imperialistic gestures from Washington."[26] The *New York Times* was more supportive of the administration. "We cannot be rightly charged with imperialism, disguised or avowed, since we have continuously discarded the policy of maintaining a large army and navy. Admittedly, we seek to guard our own. Without false pretenses, our hope is to enlarge our commerce and our influence. But all that we do has at least the motive of aiding and protecting the weaker republics of this continent, rather than of overruling or despoiling them. If this be imperialism, make the most of it."[27]

European newspapers were likewise quick to condemn the United States actions in Nicaragua. With a striking disregard for English history, the *London Saturday Review* remarked: "If it were customary in dealing with international affairs to call a spade a spade, we should by now be talking of the country which Mr. Coolidge represents as 'The United States of North and Central America.'. . ."[28] And the German *Vorwärts* sarcastically commented: "This is the Government which on every occasion from a high pedestal gives peace sermons to Europe and upholds the American example as ideal."[29]

Senators George Norris, William Borah, and Burton Wheeler, and other progressive Republicans and Democrats roundly attacked the administration. They called for detailed information on why the marines should be sent to Nicaragua and sought to introduce legislation to prevent the president from sending armed forces abroad without congressional approval. Resistance from Congress, turmoil in Nicaragua which the marines were not quickly able to quiet, growing controversy with Mexico, and fear of additional military involvement in China, led

Coolidge and Kellogg to cast about for a way out of the Nicaraguan geographic and political jungle. The president sent for Henry L. Stimson and asked him to go to Nicaragua and "straighten the matter out."[30]

Stimson had been secretary of war under Taft and in World War I had been a colonel in the artillery. On April 9, Stimson, his wife, and secretary sailed from New York and upon their arrival on the west coast of Nicaragua proceeded at once to the capital, Managua. The armies of the Conservatives led by Díaz and the Liberals (now under the able leadership of General Moncada) were engaged in a bitter civil war. Since there was deadlock between the major warring factions, there was some receptivity to American intervention.

On May 4, Stimson met with General Moncada under a large blackthorn tree near a dry river bed at Tipitapa, between the lines of the opposing armies. Moncada and Díaz agreed to an immediate and complete disarmament which would permit farmers to plant their crops, to grant amnesty to all persons in rebellion or exile, to return confiscated property to their original owners, and to organize a Nicaraguan police force on a nonpartisan basis under the initial supervision and command of United States military officers. The parties also agreed to hold elections in 1928 under American supervision. Stimson left Nicaragua on May 16, certain that he had achieved a remarkable agreement in short order and that he had ended the vicious civil war. But little did he know that the continued hostility of thirty-four-year-old Augusto Cesar Sandino (1895–1934), a minor lieutenant in Moncada's army, would give no peace either to the Americans or the Nicaraguans.

Sandino was a mestizo born out of wedlock to the wealthy coffee plantation owner Don Gregorio Sandino and Margarita Calderon, a household servant, on May 18, 1895. As a youngster he took advantage of his father's considerable library to become knowledgeable about classic literature. But after high school he went to work for a number of companies including Standard Fruit in Honduras, Nicaragua, and Mexico. The nationalist pride that flooded Mexico (see below) infected him with a sense of obligation to instill similar national pride among Nicaraguans.

When the Tipitapa agreement was signed, Sandino began a guerrilla war which lasted six years and became a model for Fidel Castro and Che Guevara. "I decided to fight," he said, "understanding that I was the one called to protest the betrayal of the Fatherland."[31] He designed a battle flag of red and black emblazoned with a death's head. He showed his arrogance, humor, and self-confidence in the note he wrote whenever he stole supplies from plantation and mine owners: "The Honorable Calvin Coolidge, president of the United States of North America, will pay the bearer $———."[32]

Although his action was condemned by Moncado, Sandino and a small band of devoted, hard-core followers started northward to the heavily forested mountain provinces near the Honduran border to regroup, seek reinforcements and material support from Mexico, and to fight again. Eventually he established a mountain fortress at El Chipote. Kellogg called Sandino a common outlaw, and to some, but by no means all, Americans, he was. But to a growing number of Nicaraguans, Sandino was a patriot and hero who would fight for them against the American imperialists. Some scholars see him as the first of the modern guerrilla organizers of a "people's army."

On July 16, his first important skirmish was at Ocotal, where he fought the U.S. Marines, who were led by Captain H. D. Hatfield. The day before the attack, Hatfield sent Sandino an ultimatum demanding that he surrender. "I will not surrender," Sandino replied, "and will await you here. I want a free country or death."[33] But Sandino did not wait. His guerrilla army made a frontal attack on the National Guard but strafing from a couple of obsolete U.S. planes led to heavy casualties and Sandino was forced to retreat. Never again would he make such a mistake. He retreated to his fortress and there sharpened the skills of guerrilla warfare.

As a master propagandist, however, Sandino attracted enough attention and enough recruits to be a thorn in the side of American policy in Nicaragua. As 1927 drew to a close, the marines determined to remove Sandino and his force of about a thousand men from the stronghold at El Chipote. But Sandino had learned from his mistake at Ocotal and on December 21, 1927, he ambushed the American marines with devastating effect. Again, only air power from obsolete two-seater Corsairs and de Havillands prevented the battle from being a total disaster for the American forces. When news of heavy fighting at El Chipote was received at Washington, D.C., orders were given to send reinforcements. With additional reinforcements, the marines eventually dislodged Sandino and his followers, but the rebels continued to harass American marines and the Nicaraguan National Guard. Finally, on February 21, 1934, when Sandino was in Managua for a peace conference, he was seized and shot by members of the National Guard. However, his name lives in the Sandinista movements which are still active in Nicaragua.

The journalist Carleton Beals, who was the only American to interview Sandino in early 1928, had this to say about him in 1965:

Throughout the vast Latin-American world, this century's outstanding hero is Augusto C. Sandino who for six years (1927-1933) fought for the inde-

pendence of Nicaragua against foreign invasion by the most powerful military nation in history—the United States. His David-Goliath exploits are
the theme of songs and ballads. He is celebrated in articles, biographies and
novels. His ghost has haunted every Pan-American reunion and every
good-will emissary from Hoover to Nixon. His fame reaches far beyond
Latin America. . . .[34]

In 1967, America and allied forces were bogged down in the jungles of Vietnam, evidence that the military had learned little from their experience forty
years earlier, when the U.S. marines and their native collaborators were bogged
down in warfare in the jungles of Nicaragua. Marines that President Calvin
Coolidge sent to Nicaragua on January 1, 1927, did not leave that country until
1933, and then did so without having achieved a clear-cut victory.

Neill Macaulay, an officer in Fidel Castro's army until he defected when Castro became a Communist, asserts: "[I]t was in 1927 that the last of Abdel Krim's
Riffs surrendered to the French and Spanish armies in North Africa and that
Luis Carlos Prestes' revolutionary column gave up the struggle in Brazil. The celebrated guerrillas of the nineteenth and early twentieth centuries, the gauchos of
the South American pampas, the Llaneros of Venezuela, the vaqueros of Mexico,
the desert warriors of the Middle East - had their day by 1927. The new guerrilla . . . avoided mass formation in the open . . . but moved about in small groups
under the cover of dense foliage. . . . The guerrilla who emerged in 1927 traveled
light, lived off the land, massed his forces for the attack. But after the attack he
dispersed into small groups. . . . He struck, usually from ambush, only when the
odds were clearly in his favor; otherwise he avoided combat. These tactics were
employed by Sandino in Nicaragua beginning in 1927. They are essentially the
same as the tactics of the People's Liberation Army in China, the National Liberation Front in Algeria, the 26th of July Movement in Cuba, and the Vietminh
and Vietcong in Vietnam."[35]

Mexico and the United States

Henry L. Stimson thought he had brought peace to Nicaragua but felt that his
achievement had been eclipsed by the media attention given to Lindbergh's solo
flight across the Atlantic. In Mexico, Dwight L. Morrow, a classmate of Calvin
Coolidge, would be more fortunate. Successful in bringing peace between the
United States and Mexico, he received widespread credit for his efforts. Morrow's
success had been achieved in part by capitalizing upon Lindbergh's immense
popularity and the storybook marriage of his daughter to the "Lone Eagle."

In 1927, America and Mexico stood poised for confrontation in some ways reminiscent of the years before the outbreak of the Mexican War (1846–1848). In those years, President James K. Polk thought that war would be to the advantage of a growing America. President Calvin Coolidge, while much exercised by what he perceived to be a violation of the rights of American business interests in Mexico, finally shunned the example of his feisty predecessor, resisted the arguments of his advisers who sought confrontation, and sought conciliation and compromise instead.

The origins of America's difficulties with Mexico in the 1920s may be traced to the 1917 adoption by that country of a new constitution. The new Mexican constitution had been enacted by a constitutional convention to improve the lot of impoverished Mexicans, to restore land to Indian villages, and to make primary education compulsory and secular, that is, free of the educational monopoly of the Catholic church. Labor was given the right to organize and bargain collectively. An eight hour day, an end to child labor, equal pay for equal work, and employer responsibility in cases of occupational accident or disease were all promised. "The Mexican Constitution of 1917 in effect declared war on all the most powerful groups of the past; the clergy, the hacendados, and employers."[36]

The purpose of Article 27 of the new Mexican Constitution was to prevent the remaining land, oil, and mining resources of that country from falling into foreign hands. But for a few years immediately after the adoption of the constitution, this provision was in limbo as enabling legislation had yet to be adopted. In 1925, when the Mexican legislature did so, that provision pinched American business interests which ran to Uncle Sam for relief.

According to the new laws, the Mexican government required every foreign oil operator to give up title in favor of a government concession lasting for fifty years. Moreover, the foreign operator could be granted such a concession only if there was evidence that the concern had performed a "positive" act before 1917 indicating an intention to make use of the land, oil, or mining resource.

The United States objected to the substitution of a concession for a title on the ground that this impaired a vested interest and because American companies could not, under the Mexican constitution, hold such concessions unless they waived their right to the diplomatic protection of the United States. The United States also objected to the concept of "positive acts." These provisions set the stage for confrontation between powerful American business interests and Mexico.

The United States was ill-served by James Rockwell Sheffield, its ambassador to Mexico. He embodied the worst elements of the American corporate elite, condescending and racist. He boasted that he had no knowledge of Spanish and was convinced that Mexicans were mainly an inferior race of "Latin-Indians." In a letter to Nicholas Murray Butler, president of Columbia University in New York City, he described the Mexican cabinet: "There is very little white blood in the cabinet . . . Calles (President) is Armenian and Indian; Leon almost wholly Indian and an amateur bullfighter; Saenz the Foreign Minister is Jew and Indian; Morones more white blood but not the better for it; Amaro, Secretary of War, a pure blooded Indian and very cruel."[37]

The American ambassador was, moreover, convinced that Mexicans were not only barbarians, but perhaps worse, were Bolsheviks as well. Despite the fact that the Mexican Constitution of 1917 had been adopted on May 1 of that year while Lenin did not come to power in Russia until six months later, he was sure that the Mexican Revolution had been Communist-inspired. He was convinced that the revolutionary government of Mexico, at the behest of the new Union of Soviet Socialist Republics, was exporting Communist propaganda to Nicaragua and other countries of Central and South America and fomenting revolution in those countries. These views were echoed by Secretary of State Frank Kellogg. It was against this background that from mid-1925 to mid-1927 the United States and Mexico conducted angry diplomatic correspondence.

Interventionists, those who feared the Bolsheviks, or opposed the secularism of the schools, or sought to strengthen the stranglehold of foreign investors in Mexico, sought the ear of the American president to urge him to send the marines to Mexico. But the Coolidge administration was not at all happy over the prospects of war with Mexico. American marines were bogged down in Nicaragua and there were marines serving in China. Many, perhaps most, in Congress opposed a more aggressive response to Mexico. Senator Joseph Robinson of Arkansas introduced a resolution in January 1927 calling for the arbitration of all differences with Mexico. Despite attempts of oil interests to block the action, the Robinson resolution passed readily, to the dismay of the hardliners.

The news media were likewise opposed to military intervention. Walter Lippmann, the best-known journalist of his day, led the way in urging a more conciliatory approach to Mexico. He was convinced that American business interests had to retreat in the face of rising Mexican nationalism. "It is indisputable," he wrote, "that the Mexican revolution arose out of Mexican conditions in an effort to correct Mexican evils, and that it takes place historically with that series of nationalist uprisings from China to India, from Egypt to Morocco, offer so profound a challenge to the supremacy of the Western Empires, and so deep a riddle to their statesmanship. One persistent motive in these uprisings is the desire to assert the national independence and the dignity of an inferior race. . . . This nationalism inevitably comes into conflict with the vested rights of foreigners."[38] The *Commerce and Finance Journal* was convinced that Kellogg, the Secretary of State, was seeking "Bolshevist spooks." The *Commercial and Financial Chronicle* urged the administration to be "scrupulous" about maintaining a conciliatory attitude toward Mexico.

According to international law, in refusing to accept the Mexican interpretation of the extent of American oil rights it is doubtful that the United States stood upon solid legal ground. Whether or not Coolidge understood this to be the case is not clear, but what is clear is that the president would not engage in a swashbuckling attack on America's neighbor.

In May, when it became plain that Coolidge was not about to accept Sheffield's harsh policy toward Mexico, the ambassador resigned. Coolidge turned to Dwight Morrow, his classmate at Amherst. After an exploratory discussion with Morrow in Washington, Coolidge informally offered Morrow the job. On July 14, 1927, in a note written in longhand from Rapid City, South Dakota, Coolidge formally requested Morrow to serve. In his letter, Coolidge may have given perhaps the vaguest hint that he was about to announce that he would not be a candidate for a third term. Coolidge urged his friend to consider the offer carefully. "I do not wish you to think of me personally at all," the president wrote, "but only of yourself, and make your decision without reference to whether I run again or not."[39] Dwight Morrow accepted the position as U.S. ambassador to Mexico on July 20 and in mid-August made further plans for his assignment by visiting with Coolidge at the summer White House in the Black Hills of South Dakota. Reportedly, Coolidge's final instruction to Morrow was, "Keep us out of war with Mexico."[40]

A longtime Coolidge stalwart, Morrow was admirably suited to the delicate task Coolidge assigned. The new ambassador to Mexico had been the most promising member of Coolidge's college class at Amherst. In 1914, he became a partner in J. P. Morgan and Company. Despite his roots deep in the conservative milieu of Wall Street, Morrow's views were quite liberal. Morrow impressed those who worked with him with his intellectual power, determination, and resourcefulness. "Nervous, vibrant, and magnetic,"[41] Morrow defused the U.S.-Mexico confrontation with aplomb. He cut his thirteen-year association with the House of Morgan on September 30, 1927. In his private railroad car he traveled in style and arrived in Mexico City on October 23.

After the usual exchange of diplomatic formalities he began work on October 29. His private wealth made it possible for him to build a mansion at Cuernavaca and to furnish it with interesting art and artifacts from the Mexican markets. He used what Spanish he knew to establish contact with ordinary people and broke through the reserve of President Calles. Unlike his predecessor, he liked Mexico and Mexicans and his warm feelings for the people were genuinely reciprocated. He flattered the ego of ordinary Mexicans and strengthened the prestige of its government when he showed America's foremost celebrities such as Charles Lindbergh and the humorist Will Rogers around the country. Under Morrow's expert direction, Lindbergh, as "Ambassador of the Air," was warmly received. So overwhelmingly enthusiastic was the response of Mexicans to Lindbergh that the *Philadelphia Evening Ledger* urged that all foreign affairs be turned over to airmen. The *New York Sun* suggested a new version of the old floral slogan: "Say it with flyers."[42]

Morrow's talent for negotiation paid off in a temporary solution to the oil crisis which was the primary issue facing the nation. In 1927, the Mexican Supreme Court, with a provocative push from Calles, ruled that foreign companies which had begun to work their sub-soil properties before 1917 might retain ownership. The United States gave up its objections to establishing concessions to lands obtained after that date. Mexico was thus able to uphold the theory of the nation's ownership of the sub-soil. The solution was by no means a permanent one but was subject to continuing negotiation and refinement over the years.

But Morrow's sense of the dramatic was reinforced when in December Colonel Charles Lindbergh flew non-stop on a solo flight from Bolling Field to Mexico City. Thus the American hero of the air inaugurated non-stop flights between Washington, D.C., and Mexico City. And, to make matters more romantic, this shy hero ended up marrying Anne Morrow, one of the ambassador's talented daughters two years later.

The Mirage of Peace

America's Secretary of State Frank B. Kellogg was seventy years old and near the end of a long and successful career in public service. Short, white-haired, with gnarled and shaking hands, Kellogg was a textbook example of the rise from near poverty to extraordinary success. He is a testimony of what American democracy makes possible.

Frank Kellogg migrated with his parents from New York State to Minnesota just after the Civil War. He had little formal schooling but studied law in a law office in Rochester, Minnesota. As an attorney he rose to some prominence as a trust-buster under President Theodore Roosevelt. He prosecuted the Standard Oil Company successfully and when the private sector made one handsome offer after another, he switched sides and became a corporation lawyer himself. In 1917 he began to serve as a United States Senator but was defeated in his attempt to win a second term. After his defeat he became the United States Ambassador to the Court of St. James (Great Britain) and in 1925 became secretary of state.

As secretary of state he was known to have a fiery temper and salty speech. When in April of 1927, he was besieged with advice from various organized peace movements on how to react to a rather self-serving offer of a treaty by the French foreign minister, Aristide Briand, he undiplomatically referred to those who were pressuring him as "goddamned pacifists." Nevertheless, the highlight of his tenure as secretary of state was the Kellogg-Briand Peace Pact, otherwise known as the Pact of Paris. Signed on August 27, 1928, it was during the previous year that the groundwork was laid for its adoption. It was the culmination of competing American proposals for world peace.

During the 1920s, idealism mingled with frustration in America's search for a course of action in global affairs. The frustration grew out of the recognition that World War I had not made the world "safe for democracy," and with people losing their lives in Asia and Latin America it was equally clear that World War I had not been the "war to end all wars" as Wilson had promised. In Europe, foreign policy frustration was evident in America's refusal to join the League of Nations—but it needed to know what was taking place in that body. Further difficulties were evident in America's prolonged and futile courtship of the World Court. America's idealism in foreign affairs, however, manifested itself in the efforts of a host of lobbying groups which sought perpetual peace.

Perhaps because 1927 was the tenth anniversary of America's entry into World War I, idealistic peace proposals were very much in the air. Pressure was building for the United States to make up for its failure to join the League of Nations by providing alternatives.

The Idealists

Among many, the Carnegie Endowment for International Peace was the most prestigious organization in the United States working for peace. Funded with a gift of $10 million by steel tycoon Andrew Carnegie, it was easily the most financially secure peace organization. In the fiscal year ending June 30, 1927, it spent $613,881, a huge sum for those days. Its monthly bulletin, *International Conciliation* was highly regarded and widely distributed among influential groups. In

1927, the Carnegie Endowment was headed by Nicholas Murray Butler, president of Columbia University. He was not only an academic giant, but a prominent Republican, and a force in domestic and international politics as well. He was a formidable speaker and the forces for peace could not have had a more visible or more distinguished spokesman. President Butler was ably assisted by the historian and equally effective public speaker Professor James T. Shotwell. While both Butler and Shotwell favored American participation in the League of Nations, they sought alternatives to achieve world peace when they recognized that the mood of the nation precluded membership in that body.

During the 1920s, essay contests on the subject of peace were widespread and generous prizes were offered. Schools and colleges likewise participated by way of urging their students to think about world peace. In 1922, Edward Bok offered a prize of $100,000 to the author of a winning peace plan proposed in not more than 5,000 words. Half the money was to be paid immediately, the other half only if there seemed to be an adequate degree of popular interest. As illustrative of the widespread interest in America in alternative peace plans, over a quarter of a million Americans wrote asking for details of the contest. Among the 22,165 entries were plans from William Jennings Bryan, the former secretary of state, and from Franklin D. Roosevelt, the future president. One Charles H. Levermore, the secretary of the New York Peace Society, won $50,000 of the award but since the plan did not elicit much interest, he did not get the other $50,000.

Smaller and more radical in their approaches were a host of peace organizations that made up in zeal what they lacked in financial support. The most distinguished of the radical groups was the National Council for the Prevention of War, which took the role as coordinator of the many radical peace groups organized around the country.

Women's groups were especially active in the peace movements of the 1920s. As one woman put it, having been instrumental in ending slavery, achieving the vote for women, and imposing prohibition on the nation, women were ready to take on new crusades. What better crusade than world peace. If women could abolish slavery, could they not also abolish war? The formidable Jane Addams was the head of the Women's International League for Peace and Freedom while her good friend Emily Balch was president of the American branch. As a mainly pacifist group, it urged its membership to attach to their income tax forms the legend that "part of the tax which is levied for preparation for War is paid only under Protest and Duress." Nor was Carrie Chapman Catt to be without a cause. In a speech to the League of Women Voters in Cleveland, she announced a cam-

paign against war. "The women in this room can do this thing!" she told her listeners.[43]

In 1927 these competing groups were unable to coalesce. Disarmament, arbitration of international disagreements, and the "outlawry" of war were among the
major ideas for securing world peace.

It seemed to the foreign policy makers of Europe and America that if the
means of fighting wars could somehow be reduced or eliminated altogether, then
perhaps the motivation to engage in war would likewise be reduced or eliminated. In the Washington Conference on Arms Limitation (1921–1922), called
at the initiative of England and America, a naval treaty was adopted to reduce
the number of capital ships (battleships and aircraft carriers) to a ratio of five
(United States), five (Great Britain), three (Japan), and 1.7 (France and Italy).
The result of the treaty was to leave Japan the dominant naval and military power
in the Far East in return for a promise not to take undue advantage of China's
weakness. For the United States, the agreement implied that at long last, America would enjoy naval parity with the "Mistress of the Seas." In short, Britannica
and America would now both rule the waves. As it turned out, both proved to be
rather naive assumptions. Japan continued to take advantage of China's weakness
(see pp. 100–104) and Britain was not about to surrender its preeminence at sea.

The ink was hardly dry on the Washington Naval Arms Limitation Treaty
when Great Britain began to build fast cruisers, a type of vessel not covered by
the agreement, as well as submarines and destroyers. American naval parity
eroded rapidly. By 1927, it was evident that something had to be done but
Coolidge, not known for extravagance or confrontation, was reluctant to ask
Congress for the funds to construct the ships that America could legally build
under the terms of the Washington Treaty. Coolidge proposed on February 10
that Britain, France, Japan, and Italy join the United States in another disarmament conference. Since the Washington Naval Arms Limitation Conference
appeared to have been beneficial to the United States in stemming an arms race,
perhaps another conference would succeed as well.

Britain and Japan accepted the invitation, but France and Italy declined. The
conference opened in Geneva on June 20, 1927. Kellogg's biographer noted,
"Rarely had a conference, called with such sanguine hopes, foreshadowed its own
failure as speedily as did the Three-Power Naval Conference of 1927."[44] American diplomats sought to extend the parity achieved in capital ships to smaller vessels and to reduce the tonnage of cruisers. Britain insisted on building not less
than seventy cruisers and were unwilling to allow the United States to build the

same number. Since their naval bases were far apart, the United States favored 10,000-ton cruisers with 8-inch guns. Great Britain favored 7,500-ton cruisers with 6-inch guns, since their naval bases were close together. The Japanese half-heartedly sought to mediate. It was in their interest to keep American ships out of the Pacific and they were glad to see that Great Britain refused to agree to an increase in America's naval clout. After six weeks of futile negotiations, the Geneva Conference broke up. Why did the conference fail?

The Geneva Conference failed because President Coolidge convened the conference without adequate prior preparation. Moreover, top naval officers had rather more to say than they should have with the result that ego, professional jealousy, and one-upmanship, rather than diplomatic accommodation, prevailed. The American admirals, it has been said, tended to "view the world through a porthole." The same could probably be said of the naval brass of England and Japan as well. Moreover, inasmuch as it was not in the interests of the American shipbuilders to limit the building of ships, their paid lobbyist, W. B. Shearer, was so successful in sowing discord that his activities at Geneva led some reporters to describe him as "the man who wrecked the Geneva Conference."[45] While this was an overstatement, nevertheless, Shearer's lobbying activities led to a senatorial investigation in 1929. But within a year and a half, Congress authorized fifteen new 10,000-ton cruisers. The naval arms race was on.

Alanson B. Houghton, widely regarded as one of America's best ambassadors, became a strong supporter of the war referendum movement. He was a Harvard graduate, a European-trained businessman, and a former congressman from New York. He served under Presidents Harding and Coolidge first as ambassador to Germany and then to Great Britain. In his commencement address to the Harvard graduating class of June 1927, he urged international agreement to a war referendum plan. He challenged the world to an experiment in democratic control certain in his belief that a durable peace could not be based upon force."[46] With Great Britain and America taking the lead he suggested that treaties be negotiated through regular diplomatic channels and an international conference and then be ratified by a referendum in each country. Gradually, the plan won support from newspapers such as the *New York Times, Boston Herald, New York Telegram and World, Brooklyn Eagle,* and *Christian Science Monitor.* The war referendum idea was widely popular because of consistent disillusion with what America had achieved by entering World War I.

It was also popular because it would act as a check on those little groups of men, munitions manufacturers, diplomats, and business interests, who, as some believe, have the power to plunge a nation into international conflict. However, pacifists were opposed to the idea because the proposal did not outlaw war altogether. As a matter of fact, proponents of the war referendum idea urged that America retain a substantial military deterrent. Moreover, since the war referendum movement would be limited to America's wars of aggression, even if an amendment to this effect had been adopted, it could not have been applied when Japan attacked American military bases in Pearl Harbor in the Pacific.

Another example of American idealism may be seen in the goal to "outlaw" war altogether. Since armaments could not be outlawed, as the failure of the Geneva Disarmament Conference demonstrated, perhaps war could be outlawed. In his *Survey of International Affairs*, the British historian Arnold Toynbee noted: "The enterprise of 'outlawing war' captivated the American imagination during 1927 and 1928, and this was undoubtedly the most important event of those two years."[47]

The Chicago attorney Salmon O. Levinson was the leading lobbyist for the movement to "outlaw war." With the passion with which William Lloyd Garrison thundered against slavery, Salmon Oliver Levinson thundered against war. "When he fastened his dark eyes on you and his fist beat a staccato on the table and his voice, filled with intense sincerity, rose . . . you recognized a new Hebrew prophet castigating the race, like Moses of old, for bowing down to a strange god—the god of war. . . ."[48]

As Levinson saw it, war was an illegal activity and could be stopped, that is outlawed, much as a person who commits a crime can be arrested and punished. War as a means of settling international disputes would no longer have any legal standing. No country could enlarge its borders, conquer another nation, or claim legal title to any territory through the use of arms. Included in his concept of outlawing war was the codification of international law and making aggressive war punishable as a crime. In support of this central idea went the development of sophisticated arbitration procedures for resolving international conflicts and the establishment of an international tribunal to enforce arbitration decisions. He further urged disarmament as well as the abolition of secret treaties among nations. Levinson opposed American membership in the League of Nations since, in his view, membership was more likely to entangle America in foreign conflicts and thus violate his pacifist beliefs.

Charles Clayton Morrison, the editor of the *Christian Century*, was among the foremost advocates of the "outlawry of war." His book on the subject, published in 1927, became the classic statement. "[T]he term Outlaw War sits like a tongue of flame upon many diverse groups, whose understanding of its technical meaning may not be identical, but for whom the term expresses a higher hope and a more uncompromising purpose than any previous proposal."[49] Morrison felt that America had a special responsibility to take the lead in outlawing war precisely because the United States, by failing to join the League of Nations, had a responsibility to develop a uniquely American way of assuring world peace. "[F]rom the standpoint of effective peacemaking, I hold," he said, "that it was a great day's work when this country decided not to be drawn into the European system. But no morally sensitive people can find satisfaction in a negationist attitude."[50] The American philosopher John Dewey and the historian James T. Shotwell were among those to whom the concept of outlawing war resonated favorably. It was an idea whose time had come.

On April 6, Levinson and his family left Cincinnati by train for New York. There they were to board the *Leviathan* to sail for Europe. His purpose in making the journey was to try to develop some momentum for his ideas abroad. From Senator Borah, who likewise became convinced that the criminalization of war was a good idea and had introduced into the U.S. Senate a resolution to this effect, Levinson obtained letters of introduction to influential leaders. En route to New York, Levinson read in the evening newspapers that Aristide Briand, the French Foreign Minister, had used the occasion of the tenth anniversary of American entrance into World War I to propose that France and the United States sign a treaty to outlaw war with one another. That he had used Levinson's term "to outlaw war" in this informal feeler of American interests, must have brought joy to the heart of its originator. The Associated Press quoted from the letter to Secretary of State Kellogg:

If there were any need for those two great democracies to give high testimony to their desire for peace and to furnish other peoples an example more solemn still, France would be willing to subscribe publicly with the United States to any mutual engagement tending to 'outlaw war,' to use an American expression, between these two countries. The renunciation of war as an instrument of national policy is a conception already familiar to the signatories to the Covenant of the League of Nations and the treaties of Locarno.[51]

Initially, the Briand message was not front page news in America. The text appeared on page five of the *New York Times* and on page twelve of the *Herald-Tribune*. There was much more interest in the Butler-Borah debate on prohibition (see pp. 80–81). As Ferrell put it, "Borah wished to outlaw rum rather than war, but Butler maintained that it was too difficult."[52] Nevertheless, after a delayed reaction the *New York Times,* partly prodded by a letter from Nicholas Murray Butler, came out editorially in support of the Briand overture.

Coolidge and Kellogg were irritated that Briand had chosen to appeal directly to the American people. Moreover, there was some feeling that Shotwell and Butler, who prodded Briand to write the letter and even may have drafted it, may have violated the Logan Act. Passed in the late 19th century, the Logan Act forbade any American citizen from negotiating with or influencing a foreign power without permission or authority of the American government. Nevertheless, neither Coolidge nor Kellogg were quite ready to invoke the Logan Act against distinguished citizens who had widespread support among influential peace groups in America. On June 20, the day the Geneva Naval Disarmament Conference opened, Briand sent Kellogg a draft treaty between the two countries based on his informal letter to the American people.

Briand's draft declared in Article 1: "The high contracting powers solemnly declare in the name of the French people and the people of the United States of America that they condemn recourse to war and renounce it, respectively, as an instrument of their national policy toward each other." Article 2: "The settlement or the solution of all disputes or conflicts of whatever nature or of whatever origin they may be which may arise between France and the United States of America shall never be sought by either side except by pacific means."

As Kellogg saw it, the Briand draft was a negative treaty of alliance, in that it forced America to adopt a policy of neutrality in the event of a war between France and any other country. Under the very clever Briand proposal, France could be assured that under no circumstances, even if France grossly violated American neutrality as Great Britain had done during the early years of World War I, would the United States enter war against France. But the options for the Coolidge administration were limited. On the one hand, Coolidge and Kellogg were right in being suspicious of the motives of Briand. On the other hand, having rejected membership in the League of Nations, the Coolidge administration did not want to place America in a position as being any less interested in peace.

Under pressure from peace groups and with the continuing euphoria surrounding the Lindbergh flight, Coolidge and Kellogg, after a delay of many months, had no choice but to respond to the overture of the French foreign minister. On December 28, Kellogg decided he had to respond to the Briand proposal. Kellogg shrewdly proposed to Briand that the two countries sponsor a multilateral rather than a bilateral treaty renouncing and outlawing war. Briand was furious with the Kellogg proposal but, as the winner of the Nobel Peace Prize for the Locarno treaties, he too could not now show that he was less committed to world peace than his American counterpart. Briand tried every trick in his diplomatic bag to defeat the intent of the Kellogg proposal. To no avail. If the peace groups were elated with the original letter to the American people, they were ecstatic over Kellogg's proposal to enlarge the number of signatories to the treaty.

The Pact of Paris, as the Kellogg-Briand Treaty was called, was signed in an impressive ceremony at Paris on August 27. Secretary Kellogg made a special trip to Europe and with fourteen other countries signed the pact in the Clock Room of the Quai d'Orsay Palace. The Senate of the United States ratified the Pact of Paris on January 15, 1929. Sixty-four nations signed the pact in due course.

The provisions of the Pact of Paris were as follows:

Article I: The High Contracting Parties solemnly declare in the names of their respective peoples that they condemn recourse to war for the solution of international controversies, and renounce it as an instrument of national policy in their relations with one another.

Article II: The High Contracting Parties agree that the settlement or solution of all disputes or conflicts of whatever nature or of whatever origin they may be, which may arise among them, shall never be sought except by pacific means.

Former President Hoover with President Coolidge and Secretary of State Kellogg (right) announcing the Pact of Paris. Reproduced from the collections of the Library of Congress.

Kellogg, who at first blush was skeptical that such a treaty could accomplish anything, became a convert to it. For his efforts, the secretary of state was awarded the Nobel Peace Prize. Little wonder then that Kellogg's disappointment was deep when he recognized that most signatories signed tongue-in-cheek. Britain made major reservations as it reserved for itself the right to defend its empire. Wars of defense were not denounced and China and Japan were in an undeclared war in Manchuria. But most Americans were eager to believe that they had taken a major step in assuring peace by outlawing war. During the debate over ratification, Senator Carter Glass of Virginia declared that although he was voting for the pact, he was "not willing that anybody in Virginia shall think that [he was] simple enough to suppose that it is worth a postage stamp in the direction of accomplishing a permanent peace."[53]

The Pact of Paris confirmed the influence of the peace movement in the formation of America foreign policy. Supporters such as Butler and Shotwell, who were advocates of the League of Nations, hoped the Pact would eventually move America further in the direction of joining that international body. Since the Pact of Paris failed to set up the legal machinery by which international disputes could be settled, perhaps membership in the League would provide such a mechanism.

Few if any diplomats believed that the Pact of Paris would end war permanently. Yet, it was a good response to the clamor to do something—anything—for America to show its positive intentions in the world arena by urging the nations of the world to renounce war. Moreover, to some degree the sentiments expressed in the Kellogg-Briand Treaty resonate in more recent times.

For example, when after World War II German and Japanese war criminals were brought before the bar of international justice, the attorneys sought to justify their case, at least in part, by asserting that the defendants had violated the Kellogg-Briand Pact when they led their countries into aggressive war. In a memorandum written by Colonel William Chandler to Secretary of War Henry L. Stimson on the legal yardstick by which the war criminals of Nazi Germany would be tried, the colonel noted: "So far as Hitler's argument that war was necessary to correct the 'Crime of Versailles' and to gain the 'Lebensraum,' necessary to Germany's existence, the answer is that these are the very issues of 'National Policy' which under the Kellogg Pact must be settled by peaceful means. . . . Thus, we would have a judicial interpretation of the Kellogg Pact to the effect that any person or group of persons who engage in such a course of conduct as that followed by the Nazis in connection with the present war are violators of the Pact and as such are common criminals, not subject to the protection accorded to a lawful belligerent by international law."[54]

While the historian Robert H. Ferrell asserts that the arguments for conviction under the Kellogg Pact seem "far fetched" in an age in which nuclear war threatens, what other recourse is there except for nations to renounce war as a means of resolving disputes? "What had been the dream of old Frank B. Kellogg became the common sense of mankind. Did it not sound like the Kellogg-Briand Pact recidivus when in 1955 fifty-two Nobel science laureates, seeking to rouse their fellow men to the dangers of nuclear war, . . . signed on their part a solemn declaration that 'all nations must come to the decision to renounce force as a final resort of policy'?"[55]

On May 21, Charles Lindbergh received a tumultuous welcome from the French when he landed his Spirit of St. Louis at Le Bourget airport after his non-stop flight from New York. When it was evident that the French fell in love with the boyish American hero, relations between the two countries, which had been chilly, began to thaw. Thus it was that the Treaty of Paris was made possible by the warm after-glow of the Lindbergh flight. The media blitz that accompanied Lindbergh's non-stop crossing of the Atlantic in a frail craft portrayed the journey as nothing short of a modern miracle. It seemed to imply that in America in the 1920s everything was possible. If crossing the Atlantic by air was a modern miracle, then were not all things possible, even the "miracle" of outlawing war?

❊

[1]*New York Times,* April 8, 1927.
[2]Ibid.
[3]Ibid.
[4]Ibid.
[5]Quoted in "Television Makes its Bow," *Literary Digest* 93 (April 23, 1927): 7.
[6]Quoted in ibid.
[7]Quoted in Eugene Lyons, *David Sarnoff: A Biography* (New York: Harper and Row, 1966), p. 208.
[8]Quoted in Albert Abramson, *Zworykin, Pioneer of Television* (Urbana and Chicago: University of Illinois Press, 1995), p. 59.
[9]David Sarnoff, *The Papers of David Sarnoff* (New York: McGraw-Hill Book Company, 1968), p. 91.
[10]See Arthur Tiedemann, *Modern Japan: A Brief History* (Princeton, N.J.: D. Van Nostrand Company, Inc., 1955), pp. 127-133.
[11]"Why China is 'The Danger-Spot of the World,'" *Literary Digest* 92 (January, 15, 1927): 8.
[12]Paul Johnson, *Modern Times: The World from the Twenties to the Eighties* (New York: Harper and Row, 1983), p. 193.

[13]Ibid.

[14]Extraterritoriality is the doctrine that requires that foreigners may be tried in courts of their own countries rather than in those of the country in which they live and work.

[15]*New York Times,* March 3, 1927.

[16]Vincent Sheean, "Moscow and the Chinese Revolution," *Asia* (December 1927): 1005–1006.

[17]Quoted in Page Smith, *A People's History of the 1920s and the New Deal: Redeeming the Time,* Vol. 8 (New York: McGraw-Hill Book Company, 1987), p. 167.

[18]Quoted in Johnson, *Modern Times,* p. 197.

[19]Quoted in O. Edmund Clubb, *Twentieth Century China,* 3rd Edition (New York: Columbia University Press, 1978), p. 135.

[20]John Dewey, "The Real Chinese Crisis," *New Republic* 50 (April 27, 1927): 270.

[21]Elmer Davis, "An Inexpert Looks at Asia," *Asia* 27 (April 1927): 289.

[22]Quoted in L. Ethan Ellis, *Frank B. Kellogg and American Foreign Relations, 1925–1929* (New Brunswick, New Jersey: Rutgers University Press, 1961), p. 106.

[23]Quoted in Stanley K. Hornbeck, "Has the United States a Chinese Policy?" *Foreign Affairs* (July 1927): 624.

[24]Quoted in John A. Booth, *The End and the Beginning: The Nicaraguan Revolution* (Boulder, Colorado: Westview Press, 1985), p. 27.

[25]Quoted in Donald R. McCoy, *Calvin Coolidge: The Quiet President* (New York: The Macmillan Company, 1967), p. 353.

[26]Quoted in *Literary Digest* 92 (January 8, 1927): 6.

[27]Quoted in ibid., p. 7.

[28]Quoted in *Literary Digest* 92 (January 29, 1927): 5.

[29]Quoted in ibid.

[30]Quoted in McCoy, *Calvin Coolidge,* p. 354.

[31]Quoted in Neill Macaulay, *The Sandino Affair* (Durham, North Carolina: Duke University Press, 1985), p. 61.

[32]Quoted in Richard O'Connor, "Mr. Coolidge's Jungle War," *American Heritage* 19 (December 1967): 39.

[33]Ibid.

[34]Carleton Beals, "In Quest of Sandino, Imperialism Still Rides," *Nation* (September 20, 1965).

[35]McCauley, op cit. p. 62.

[36]Lewis Hanke, *Mexico and the Caribbean* (Princeton, N.J.: D. Van Nostrand Company, Inc., 1959), p. 72.

[37]Quoted in Robert Freeman Smith, *The United States and Revolutionary Nationalism in Mexico, 1916–1932* (Chicago: The University of Chicago Press, 1972), p. 232.

[38]Walter Lippmann, "Vested Rights and Nationalism in Latin America," *Foreign Affairs* 5 (April 1927): 357.

[39]Claude M. Fuess, *Calvin Coolidge: The Man from Vermont* (Boston: Little, Brown and Company, 1940), p. 412

[40]Quoted in L. Ethan Ellis, *Frank B. Kellogg and American Foreign Relations,* p. 48.

[41]Fuess, *Calvin Coolidge,* p. 408.

[42]Quoted in Thomas A. Bailey, *A Diplomatic History of the American People*, 8th ed. (New York: Appleton-Century-Crofts, 1969), p. 680.

[43]For more on the peace movements of the 1920s, see Robert H. Ferrell, *Peace in Their Time: The Origins of the Kellogg-Briand Pact* (New Haven: Yale University Press, 1952), pp. 12-30.

[44]Quoted in Robert H. Ferrell, "Frank B. Kellogg and Henry L. Stimson," in Robert H. Ferrell, ed., *The American Secretaries of State and their Diplomacy, Vol. 11* (New York: Cooper Square Publishers, Inc., 1963), p. 93.

[45]Quoted in Lawrence A. Moretz, "The Battleship and Mr. Shearer," *Naval History* 4 (Fall 1990), p. 29.

[46]Quoted in Ernest C. Bolt Jr., *Ballots before Bullets: The War Referendum Approach to Peace in America, 1914–1941* (Charlottesville, Virginia: University of Virginia Press, 1977), p. 140.

[47]Arnold Toynbee, *Summary of International Affairs, 1928* (London: Oxford University Press, 1929), p. 10.

[48]John S. Stoner, *S. O. Levinson and the Pact of Paris: A Study in the Techniques of Influence* (Chicago: University of Chicago Press, 1945), p. 187.

[49]Charles Clayton Morrison, *The Outlawry of War* (Chicago: Willett, Clark and Colby, 1927), p. 29.

[50]Morrison, *The Outlawry of War*, p. 47.

[51]Quoted in Ferrell, *Peace in Their Time*, p. 71.

[52]Ibid., p. 74.

[53]Quoted in Ferrell, *American Diplomacy: A History* (New York: W. W. Norton and Company, Inc., 1969), p. 567.

[54]Bradley F. Smith, *The American Road to Nuremberg: The Documentary Record 1944-1945* (Stanford, California: Hoover Institution Press, 1982), pp. 72-73.

[55]Ferrell, *American Secretaries of State*, pp. 126–127.

5
CRIME IN AMERICA

May 18, 1927

The town of Bath, Michigan, a community of 300 families just seven miles north of Lansing, the state's capital, was the scene of the most violent school bombing in America's history. Michigan State College graduate Andrew Kehoe, a farmer, who served also as the treasurer of the Bath Consolidated grade school, described in the press as "demented," set the dynamite and fired the fuses that destroyed the west wing of the elementary school. A moment or two before the blast Kehoe was seen to race from the school and enter his automobile parked at the curb. Witnesses said that Kehoe sat in his automobile in front of the school and gloated as he watched the bodies of the children hurled into the air by the explosions he set.

The timely discovery and removal of additional dynamite and lighted fuses in the east wing of the school prevented still further deaths among anguished parents and firefighters who were making valiant efforts to save the children they could and to remove the bodies of the children they could not save. Had all the dynamite exploded as Kehoe had planned, all 260 children and many teachers would have perished in the inferno. In the nation's most deadly school massacre nearly forty children were killed as were six adults.

Apparently what drove Kehoe insane was the mortgage foreclosure on his farm. He was heard to complain that high school taxes made it impossible for him to keep up his mortgage payments. Portions of the body of Mrs. Andrew Kehoe was found in an outbuilding of the couple's farm where Kehoe had placed dynamite in his house, barn, and wagonshed. These buildings were destroyed in a subsequent fire. Evidence on the site seemed to show that Kehoe had killed his wife by smashing her skull and then throwing her body into the outbuilding.

As Kehoe watched from the seat of the car the mayhem he had wrought, he suddenly took a rifle and fired it into the dynamite-packed automobile. Kehoe was killed, as

129

were the school principal, the village postmaster, and two other men who were stand-
ing nearby.

Down on his farm searchers found a note which read: "Criminals are made not
born."

※

Few could quarrel with Al Capone's self-serving observation: "I make my
money by supplying a public demand. If I break the law, my customers, who
number hundreds of the best people in Chicago, are as guilty as I am. The only
difference between us is that I sell and they buy. Everybody calls me a racketeer.
I call myself a businessman. When I sell liquor, it's bootlegging. When my
patrons serve it on a silver tray on Lake Shore Drive, it's hospitality."[1] Prohibition
drove the consumption of alcohol underground.

Buyers and sellers of illicit alcohol thus became partners in unlawful activity
and so contributed to a widespread tolerance for crime.

Partners in Crime

It was well known that President Warren G. Harding had his own bootlegger
and that the entire cabinet had easy access to illicit alcohol. Supreme Court Justice Louis D. Brandeis was surely on target when he wrote, "Our government is
the potent, the omnipresent teacher. For good or ill, it teaches the whole people
by its example. Crime is contagious. If government becomes the law-breaker, it
breeds contempt for laws; it invites every man to become a law unto himself. . . ."
Americans were surely learning the wrong lessons from their government.

In the clash of values between urban and rural, which sparked the Volstead Act
in the first place, "The old order of the country gave way to the new order of the
city. Rural morality was replaced by urban morality, rural voices by urban voices,
rural votes by urban votes."[2] The clash in values created a climate in which crime
and near-crime existed side-by-side. A kind of collective winking occurred at
those laws which seemed to pinch and shackle the pleasures and amenities of a
cultivated, self-disciplined, well-to-do urban people.

With the close of the Western frontier, the new frontier in America sometimes
seemed to lie in the underworld. The machismo of the cowboy in the eyes of
some found a soulmate in the bootlegger and his cohorts. In a discussion on control of weapons, for example, the *Chicago Tribune* expressed a view widely held in
the Western states that a revolver is "a domestic utensil, as normal as a frying-
pan, or a part of every gentleman's personal equipment, like a tooth-brush."[3]

It was surely consistent with the prevailing widespread tolerance for crime that in 1927 the state of Missouri sought funds for a monument over the grave of Jesse James (1847–1882), the colorful outlaw of the post-Civil War era. The melodramatic nature of his raids on banks and trains elicited widespread admiration which grew into myth and song. "The Ballad of Jesse James" extolled the alleged Robin Hood quality of his exploits, his chivalry toward Southern women and generosity to men who had served the Confederacy. In 1926, Robertus Love wrote a biography which exploded some of the most beloved myths about Jesse James but contributed to the outlaw's metamorphosis from criminal to icon and role model for red-blooded American boyhood.

What to do about crime and criminals sparked interminable debate but little action, in part because in the 1920s newspapers, egged on by the tabloids, made the most of crime to sell papers. If there was no glamorous crime about which to write they glamorized the crime they had—as they did in the Snyder/Gray murder case.

In May, Ruth Snyder and her lover Judd Gray were found guilty of first degree murder by a New York jury for the death of Snyder's husband.

On July 24, 1915, Ruth May Brown had married her boss Albert Snyder, the art editor of *Motor Boating* magazine and thirteen years her senior. A daughter was born to the couple in 1917 and the family moved into a good residential neighborhood in the borough of Queens in New York City. But the marriage was not a happy one. Ruth resented her husband's insistence on keeping a framed photograph of his dead former fiancée in their bedroom and Albert resented the extravagance of his wife.

While on a shopping spree in Manhattan, Ruth Snyder was introduced to thirty-two-year-old Judd Gray, a salesman for the Bien-Jolie Corset Company. Gray, father of one child, unhappily married, was smitten with the bleached blonde flapper. Their assignations at the Waldorf-Astoria Hotel in New York City lasted two years when Ruth Snyder began exerting pressure on Judd Gray to help her murder her husband. She had tried to kill him on at least three occasions the year before, in order to collect on his $100,000 life insurance policy.

Reluctantly, Judd Gray bought a vial of chloroform, lengths of picture wire, and a five-pound sash weight. After a first attempt during which he lost his nerve despite downing a quart of liquor, Judd tried again on March 19, 1927. Carrying a satchel containing the murder weapons, Gray let himself into the Snyders' empty house, hid in his lover's closet, drank heavily, and waited for the Snyders to return from a party at 2:00 A.M. An hour later, Judd Gray struck Albert Snyder with the sash weight and, as the victim struggled, Judd Gray strangled him with a necktie, while his lover continued to bludgeon her husband. The killers stuffed Albert Snyder's mouth and nostrils with a rag soaked in the chloroform and bound his hands and feet with neckties. To make sure he was really dead, Ruth Snyder strangled her husband with the picture wire. They fled the scene of the crime but not before they ransacked the room to make it appear a murder/robbery.

The two were easily apprehended as the police uncovered inconsistencies in the story Mrs. Snyder told. When Gray was arrested at his hotel in Syracuse, New York, he broke down readily enough. The murder weapons were found, and the sensational trial of the couple began in the Supreme Court of Long Island City. It even had its comic moments:

Question to Ruth Snyder: "In other words, you want the jury to believe that you were a perfect lady? . . . You did nothing to make your husband unhappy?"[4]

Ruth Snyder's reply: "Not that he knew about." Some entrepreneurs did a brisk business selling miniature sash weights as tie clips while others attempted to sell phony tickets to the trial for $50 each.

The couple was found guilty and sentenced to death in the electric chair. During the appeals process that followed, Ruth Snyder converted to Catholicism in hopes that Governor Al Smith would not allow a fellow Catholic to be executed. Ruth wrote *My Own True Story—So Help Me God!* Judd wrote *Doomed Ship*, an account of his fall into alcoholism and crime. Their appeals were, however, denied and both were executed on January 12, 1928 (see also p. 248).

The Snyder-Gray murder did not merit the media coverage it received, however lurid and brutal the nature of the crime. But in 1927, the media exploited the information they had. Crime and criminals held a fascination for much of America. Through the lens of the media, the gangster often became a celebrity.

If Charles Lindbergh was the nation's hero of 1927, then Al Capone was clearly its anti-hero. When Al Capone and his eighteen bodyguards went to the races or a football game many Americans went out of their way to shake his hand. Some even stood and cheered. "What were they cheering about?"[5]

Al Capone: Public Enemy Number One

Three Sicilians, guests of Al Capone, were dining in style at a $25,000 dinner he gave in their honor. Rich red wine washed down the exquisitely prepared meat, pasta, and antipasto. The setting was the Hawthorne Inn, a hotel Capone owned in Cicero, Illinois, a town he also owned. The guests were having a rousing good time when some time after midnight Capone rose from his chair, his humor and good nature gone. The raucous laughter and camaraderie of a few moments before faded, replaced by an eerie silence. Having checked their guns in the checkroom, the guests were unarmed. Capone's bodyguards grabbed the guests, lashed them with wire to their chairs, and gagged them. Al Capone reached around for his baseball bat, walked around the table and with both hands methodically brought the bat down upon his guests, one at a time, crushing heads, shoulders, chests and arms. A Capone bodyguard administered a merciful shot to the back of the head of each guest. Their offense: suspected disloyalty to the 1927 king of the underworld.

Al Capone grew up in Brooklyn in the shadow of the recently completed Williamsburg Bridge in 1899. It was not in those days a particularly tough neighborhood but Irish, Italian, and Jewish gangs defended their turf from the enemy. It was more or less a rite of passage, an expression of machismo, for urban urchins who had few other outlets for their energy and libido. The corner of Broadway and Flushing, the stamping ground of the Italian gang, was where Al Capone sought unsuccessfully to make his mark. The youthful Al was quiet and withdrawn, with little tendency toward brutality. He was widely viewed as a youth of unexceptional talent, a classy dresser and a splendid dancer. How then, did this fop become the notorious gangster of later years? According to his biographer Laurence Bergreen, it was syphilis that made Al Capone "larger than life."[6]

Before World War I, syphilis was rampant in America. What AIDS is today, syphilis was to the early 1900s. Approximately ten percent of the draftees for World War I were found with the disease. About twenty percent of those with syphilis think they have been cured only to find that their disease is but in a latent stage which could last twenty or more years. Al had no way of knowing that he was one of the unlucky twenty percent in which the disease entered its latent stage. It later seriously affected his personality. "The special swagger and the vehemence associated with Capone—the sudden outbursts of violence, as well as his reckless gambling—were the results of his incurable disease. The Capone we remember was the creation of the disease that had magnified his personality."[7]

Johnny Torrio introduced Al Capone to Frankie Yale, known as Brooklyn's "Prince of Darkness." Only six years older than Capone, he was already infamous and feared, having allegedly killed a dozen or more men. Among Frankie Yale's more notorious enterprises was the tawdry Harvard Inn in Brooklyn's seaside resort of Coney Island. Its most impressive feature was a twenty-foot bar which occupied nearly the entire length of one wall. One night, a year after working at the bar, Al could not take his eyes off a beautiful Italian girl. He leaned over and said in a loud voice, "Honey, you have a nice ass, and I mean that as a compliment." Her male companion, Frank Gallucio, turned out to be the beauty's brother. In the melee that ensued, Galluccio drew a four inch knife from his pocket and inflicted slash after slash on Al Capone's cheek and neck. He was left with three large scars which earned him the nickname "Scarface," one which he hated and which his associates could utter only at their peril.

On December 30, 1918, when their baby was already three and a half weeks old, Al Capone and Mae Coughlan were wed in the church St. Mary Star of the Sea near the Brooklyn waterfront. Despite his association with prostitutes and mistresses, despite the racketeering, bootlegging, and the accompanying gangland violence, Al always remained devoted to Mae and she to him.

Chicago's most notorious hood in 1919 was the brothel keeper "Diamond Jim" Colosimo. Because Chicago was well covered with his brothels, Colosimo sought help and invited Johnny Torrio, Capone's godfather, to come to Chicago to help out. It was Torrio who brought Capone to Chicago as well.

Capone arrived in Chicago in 1919, the same year that congress passed the very unpopular "noble experiment" prohibiting the consumption of alcohol. Chicago, the bawdy city of the "big shoulders" as Carl Sandburg called it, became symbolic of the gang violence which seemed to permeate the nation. Through the "Roaring Twenties" Chicago was the scene of nearly five hundred gang-related killings. Not one murderer was brought to trial.

Al Capone went to Chicago as a lowly procurer and manager for the Four Deuces Saloon and brothel at Number 2222 South Wabash Avenue. On winter nights he could be seen with his coat collar turned up, his hands deep in his pockets. He would fall into step with a pedestrian and mumble: "Say, pal, want to drink some good beer? Got some nice-looking girls inside here." But prohibition and Al Capone were made for each other, and he would leave his evil mark on that city and the nation.

When prohibition went into effect at midnight January 16, 1920, Colosimo recognized that illicit liquor, not prostitution, was likely to be the bigger source of revenue. With a well-honed organization already in place, Colosimo sought to become a major player in the business of furnishing Americans with beer and whiskey. But "Diamond Jim" would have been well-advised to stick to prostitution. On the morning of June 20, Colosimo was shot to death. Although speculation was rife that Colosimo was killed by men within his own organization, no one was ever prosecuted for the crime. "Diamond Jim" was buried with the ostentation to which he had grown accustomed in life. Among the hundreds of mourners at the $20,000 funeral were eight Chicago aldermen, three Cook County judges, and two United States congressmen.

Torrio took over the Colosimo brothel empire and, with Al Capone as his partner, successfully provided his customers with booze as well as girls. Al's brother Ralph (Bottles) Capone was likewise brought into top management. Torrio and the Capones pushed their enterprises into the Chicago suburbs and before long made the nearby suburb of Cicero their own. Here, without interference from the police or mayor, they manufactured real beer and opened gambling casinos. By 1923, Torrio and Capone were at the top of their form. In the spring of 1924, the man of their choice was elected mayor of Cicero and the chief of police was the one they preferred.

If "Scarface" Al Capone went to Chicago to make his mark in the world as hoodlum, racketeer, and bootlegger, Vincenzo Capone made his way to the village of Homer, Nebraska, there to take up his life as a government agent assigned the task of enforcing prohibition. Vincenzo was twenty-seven at the time, known as the "lost" Capone, having run away from the family at age sixteen to join the circus. He had served with distinction in World War I and had medals for sharpshooting to prove it. He remade himself as Richard Hart, after his screen idol of the day William S. Hart. While Al and his brothers adopted a life of crime, Richard Hart was determined to be as unlike his brothers as he possibly could. In 1919, Richard Hart married Kathleen Winch and the couple had four children. While his origins remained a closely guarded secret, even from his wife, the Hart family became a respected one in Homer. In 1920, Hart became a law enforcement officer for the state of Nebraska with a special responsibility to enforce the prohibition laws in that state. And he did so with a skill and flair that drew on his talents as an army sharpshooter and in due course earned him the flamboyant nickname "Two-gun Hart."

In 1923, Hart's rapid progress as an enforcement agent came to an abrupt end. In a shootout, he was charged with shooting a fellow prohibition officer. In the inquiry that followed the evidence was inconclusive but enough of a shadow fell over Hart's career that while he remained an officer of the law, he was no longer on the fast track as a prohibition fighter. Throughout the inquiry, Hart's origins as Vincenzo Capone, Al Capone's older brother, was never revealed. When Richard Hart read the Chicago newspapers about the murder of Frank Capone—"Gunman Kills Gunman" read the headline—he first became aware of the entirely different career the other members of his family had chosen. Nevertheless, after fifteen years, Richard Hart made a visit to his family in Chicago. During that visit newspapermen were astonished to learn that Richard Hart was not only Al Capone's brother but as "Two-gun Hart" was notorious as a law enforcement officer as Al Capone was a racketeer. When asked if he would arrest his brothers for bootlegging, he announced that he surely would if the Capone family ever set foot in Nebraska.

Fortunately, Richard Hart was never put to the test. The blood relationship to his family lured him back to Chicago year after year, but he was never lured into the criminal underworld. In the words of Laurence Bergreen, a Capone biographer, "Good and evil [were] inseparably linked by a fraternal tie."[8]

By the age of twenty-five, Al Capone was living in splendor. He traveled with his bodyguards in a steel armored, seven-ton, $20,000 chauffeur-driven limousine built especially for him by General Motors. The windows were of bulletproof glass, the fenders could not be dented. His Cadillac had special combination locks so that his enemies could not force the door open to plant a bomb inside the car. His car become a toy, an office, a status symbol. Nor did Capone travel alone. When he drove through the streets of Chicago his limo was preceded by a scout car, and by another carrying a car full of bodyguards. "There goes Al Capone," said one pedestrian to another in some awe as the magnificent vehicle drove by.

He bought custom-made suits of pea green, powder blue, and lemon yellow from Marshall Field for which he paid $135 each. Capone had the right-hand pockets of his suits reinforced to support the weight of a revolver. He preferred the gaudy colors as well for his made-to-order monogrammed shirts, royal blue silk pajamas and underwear from Sulka. The monogram A. C. could be found on his silk sheets, handkerchiefs, shirts, and underwear. He lavished diamond jewelry upon himself, including a diamond tie clasp and stick pin, watch and chain, and belt buckle. On his middle finger he wore a $50,000, blue-white, eleven carat diamond ring. He was rarely without his fedora and pearl-gray spats.

His foppish wardrobe could not hide his roly-poly stature reminiscent of an over-stuffed chicken. He was 5 feet 10 1/2 inches tall and weighed 255 pounds.

> Mountains of pasta and Niagaras of Chianti had deposited layers of fat, but the muscle beneath the fat was rock-hard, and in anger could inflict fearful punishment. . . . He moved with an assertive forward thrust of his upper body, the shoulders meaty and sloping like a bull's. His big round head sat on a neck so short and thick as to be almost undifferentiated from his trunk. His face looked congested, as if too much flesh had been crammed into the available frame. His hair was dark brown, the eyes light gray under thick, shaggy eyebrows, the nose flat, the mouth wide, fat-lipped and purplish. A scar ran along his left cheek from ear to jaw, another across the jaw, and a third below the left ear. . . .[9]

He was sensitive about his disfigurement and for photographers he would show his right and unscarred profile. One dared not call him "Scarface" in his presence. He much preferred his associates to call him "Snorkel," slang for elegant.

He threw fabulous parties for hundreds of guests at a time. The famous and the infamous, from the worlds of entertainment, business, and government accepted his invitations. Capone was something of an opera buff, but the music that moved him was jazz. It was through his efforts that by 1927 Chicago became the center of the world of jazz and every prominent jazz musician of the day was eager and proud to appear in his clubs.

The real center of Chicago's government was in the Capone suite at the Lexington Hotel. The lobby was constantly under the surveillance of his lieutenants. Other guards stood outside each elevator landing. Bodyguards toting .45 caliber revolvers under their jackets became more numerous as one sought entry into Suite 430, the nerve-center of the Capone underworld empire. From here, with the aid of his Russian-born accountant, Jake "Greasy Thumb" Guzik, Capone owned or managed an enterprise consisting of breweries, distilleries, speakeasies, warehouses, fleets of boats and trucks, nightclubs, gambling houses, horse and dog racetracks, brothels, labor unions, and business and industrial associations, together producing yearly revenue in the hundreds of millions of dollars. "Cash was stacked about Room 430 in padlocked canvas bags, awaiting its transfer to a bank under fictitious names."[10]

The year 1927 was a banner year for Scarface Al. "Capone was master of all he surveyed."[11] He had a near-monopoly of bootlegging and gambling in Chicago. He was one of the richest men of his time and the wickedest. When he said he owned the Chicago mayor and police, he was not lying. Mayor "Big Bill" Thompson was a pawn for Al Capone. "He has pioneered in the use of the truck and the telephone and the tommy-gun to unify American crime."[12] Capone showed versatility in all the rackets and gave meaning to the term "organized crime."

Yet Capone was a paradox. Some part of him yearned to be a Robin Hood in that he stole from the rich to give to the poor. During the depression he ran soup kitchens in Chicago supported out of his own resources. To seek some peace of mind and to escape from the tensions of Chicago, Capone often journeyed to Lansing, Michigan. He could have made another Cicero out of Lansing but he chose not to do so. Instead, the Capone the good people of Lansing came to know was "softspoken, impeccably groomed. . . . To them he was neither a pimp, gambler, murderer, nor racketeer. . . . He was a friend, a benefactor, and in some cases a savior."[13] Chicago's elderly and impoverished Italians often looked to Capone for help and many would have died had he not provided them with a place to live or food for their table. "Nobody ever gave him any special title, they never referred to him as 'Godfather,' they just called him Al."[14] In Chicago Heights he supported generously the church of Saint Rocco and from the windows of his bulletproof Cadillac he threw silver dollars. Little wonder that they cheered when Al and his bodyguards appeared in public. In 1930, in a student poll taken at the Medill School of Journalism in Evanston, Al Capone was listed among the ten most outstanding personages in the world. The others were Benito Mussolini, Charles Lindbergh, Admiral Richard Byrd, Bernard Shaw, Bobby Jones, Herbert Hoover, Mahatma Gandhi, Albert Einstein, and Henry Ford.

The U.S. attorney's office estimated that the Capone combine took in approximately $105 million a year. The amount broke down as follows:

Alcohol manufacture and sale	$60,000,000
Gambling	25,000,000
Vice and resorts	10,000,000
Other rackets	10,000,000[15]

But even this was not enough for Al Capone. In the early days of prohibition, Torrio, Capone, and O'Banion had been partners and shared the vast profits to be made in illicit booze. In an argument over sharing the loot, Capone and his allies struck first. On November 10, 1927, while Dion O'Banion was happily working in his flower shop, a front for his illegal activities, three Capone gunmen, passing themselves off as shoppers, shook hands with O'Banion and shot him to death. Al Capone and Johnny Torrio sent magnificent floral arrangements and attended the funeral. There were never any arrests and no one was ever apprehended or prosecuted for the crime. Instead, gunmen from competing gangs took the law into their own hands. In one ambuscade, John Torrio barely escaped death. Although severely wounded, he was frightened enough to flee to Italy. "If Capone had kept a diary, 1927 would be ringed in red as the banner year for plots against his life. . . ."[16] A dozen or more attempts were made to assassinate Capone but they all failed. The Chicago press reported that from 1923 to 1926 there were 135 gang killings. Although there were investigations, indictments, and trials, only one minor hoodlum was convicted.

In May 1927, in the case of United States v. Sullivan, the U.S. Supreme Court handed down a decision which would mark the beginning of the end of the Capone era. The decision essentially held that bootleggers would have to file income tax returns on their illegal income. The case reached the U.S. Supreme Court via Charleston, South Carolina, where lawyers for a bootlegger argued that a bootlegger did not need to file income tax returns because he was protected by the Fifth Amendment prohibiting self-incrimination. In writing for the majority Associate Justice Oliver Wendell Holmes declared: "We are of the opinion that the protection of the Fifth Amendment was stretched too far. . . . It would be an extreme if not extravagant application of the Fifth Amendment to say it authorized a man to refuse to state the amount of his income because it had been made in crime." With tongue-in-cheek Justice Holmes concluded, "It is urged that if a return were made the defendant would be entitled to deduct illegal expenses such as bribery. This by no means follows, but it will be time enough to consider the question when a taxpayer has the temerity to raise it."

Bootleggers and gamblers laughed at the idea of filing an income tax return. But the IRS would, in due course, have the last laugh. A Special Intelligence Unit under the direction of Elmer Frey now had augmented powers to pursue tax evaders among members of the underworld. Their first and most prominent target was Al Capone.

Eliot Ness was born in Chicago on April 19, 1903. He graduated from the University of Chicago where he had been a fine student, an outstanding tennis player, and something of an expert in jujitsu. In 1927, Ness entered the Chicago branch of the U.S. Treasury Department. A year later he was transferred to the Justice Department where he became one of three hundred agents assigned to the Prohibition Bureau. This division had the unenviable job of trying to rid the Windy City of illicit booze. Thus, Capone became the target of two federal investigations. The first was income tax evasion, which was the major concern of the Treasury Department. A task force led by Agent Frank J. Wilson set to work to find evidence that would hold up in a federal trial that Capone had, indeed, failed to file income tax returns. The Justice Department under U.S. District Attorney George Emerson Q. Johnson had the task of breaking up Capone's bootlegging activities. But the Prohibition Bureau, it was feared, was riddled with men who provided Capone with protection from law enforcement and information on when a crackdown was to take place. When Johnson cast about for an incorruptible law enforcement officer he chose twenty-six-year-old Eliot Ness. Ness was to select his own men, about a dozen of them, and dry-up the city of Chicago. Thus began the Chicago legend of the "Untouchables."

In a two-and-a-half year campaign against Capone, the Untouchables engaged in vigorous search-and-destroy operations against Capone's bootleg empire. Using a ten-ton flatbed truck equipped with scaling ladders and a giant steel ram with which to destroy breweries and distilleries, Ness jolted but did not destroy the Capone underworld organization. Because Ness made sure that the press was on hand to publicize the toppling of one Capone facility after another, he gained personal popularity and became a celebrity.

However, it was not the flamboyant techniques of Eliot Ness but the more pedestrian investigation into his failure to pay income tax that dropped the curtain on Al Capone. On October 6, 1931, Chicagoans flocked to the Federal Building to see "Public Enemy Number One" go on trial. On Saturday afternoon, October 17, 1931, the Capone case was given to the jury. Sixteen hours later, Capone was found guilty of willful attempt to evade payment of income taxes for the years 1925, 1926, and 1927. Capone's lawyers attempted to appeal the decision but without success. The court sentenced Capone to ten years in a federal penitentiary and an additional year in a county jail, and to pay $50,000 in fines and $30,000 in costs. "No other private individual in history was accused and probably guilty of so much and convicted of so little as was Al Capone."[17]

Capone was released from the penitentiary in eight years. He had been an exemplary prisoner mostly because he could be no other, in view of the syphilis which returned with a vengeance. Syphilis ate up his brain and he died a raving idiot at the age of forty-eight. Al Capone always feared dying in the street. He died in bed. In warm Miami Beach, a seven foot floral cross was placed beside a bronze casket. Capone's body was secretly brought back to Chicago where on a bitterly cold, wind-swept day, with the temperature below zero, he was buried in Plot 48 in Chicago's Mount Olivet Cemetery. The funeral was modest, the service lasted only five minutes as the church had forbidden a requiem mass or any elaborate ceremony. The simple tombstone read:

QUI RIPOSA
Alphonse Capone
Nato: Jan. 17, 1899
Morto: Jan. 25, 1947

A week before the death of Al Capone at the age of forty-eight, Andrew Volstead, the father of Prohibition, likewise died at the age of eighty-seven. To the end he believed that the prohibition of alcoholic beverages would improve the morals of Americans. But prohibition also made crime America's greatest problem.

Lawlessness: America's Greatest Problem

On a pleasant evening in 1927, Jacob Orgen, aka Little Augie, was standing on a corner in New York's Lower East Side, in conversation with Jack Diamond, his friend and new bodyguard, when an automobile raced down the street. The latter's warning shout was too late. Two pistols, thrust through the curtains of the automobile's windows, fired at close range and in a few minutes Little Augie lay dead upon the sidewalk. His friend, likewise hit, died in a hospital the next morning.[18] The police suspected that Little Augie was killed by the reorganized Kid Dropper mob whose leader, Nathan Kaplan, *aka* Kid Dropper, had been killed four years earlier. The rivalry between the Little Augie and Kid Dropper gangs had to do with criminal leadership in the Lower East Side of Manhattan.

Little Augie had been the last of the big-name mobsters in the Lower East Side. In 1923, when Kid Dropper had been released from police custody for lack of evidence, Louis Cohen, a bit player in Little Augie's gang who thought he could make a better place for himself in gangland's hierarchy of notables, boldly fired through the rear window of a taxicab and killed Kid Dropper as the latter relaxed in the back seat, relishing yet another escape from the criminal justice system. (Cohen went to Sing Sing for twenty years, and Little Augie assumed the dominant leadership of the gangs of the Lower East Side. But the price of such leadership was constant tension among rival gangs.) Fear among innocent residents of the Lower East Side that at any time they could be accidentally killed in a hail of bullets was understandable, in view of the thirteen gangland killings that took place between the death of Kid Dropper and Augie. Incidents such as these triggered growing interest in the extent and nature of crime in America.

The gang, an informal gathering of rival hoodlums, was often ethnically based and initially involved in petty crime. Gangs recruited members from school dropouts and the unemployed. Gang leaders often governed the members of their gangs like absolute monarchs. They ruthlessly punished those who violated the understood values of the gang and killed those who betrayed them. As the gang grew stronger, it cast about for politicians and lawyers who, for fat fees, would keep them out of the clutches of the law. Sophisticated gangs intimidated witnesses, bribed judges and juries, and sought to influence the outcome of elections by buying votes. In a 1927 study of Chicago gangs, Frederick Thrasher found no fewer than 1,313 active gangs comprising at least 25,000 members. Writing in *Harper's Monthly Magazine,* one authority on crime in America wrote: "Prosecuting criminals to-day is like trying to catch a 1927 automobile with an ox-team." Among the writer's concerns was that:

• Crime in America cost $13 billion . . . more than the total of the debts from the First World War.

• America maintained an army of half a million police, judicial and enforcement officials, to stand off an opposing army of two million criminals.

• In the "endless" war against crime, there were 12,500 fatalities a year.

• About 200,000 convicted criminals were in prison.

• In Chicago—that jungle of the underworld—six policemen were shot for every criminal who was hanged.

• In New York, the burglar had thirteen chances to one in his favor. In London, the odds were ten to one against him.

The author concluded, "We may have made the world safe for democracy but we certainly haven't made it safe for the law-abiding citizen."[19]

In the United States, there were 12,000 killings, or one violent death in every 10,000 in the 118 leading cities. Chicago had the most homicides at 510, followed by New York City with 340, even though it had about twice the population of Chicago. Writing in the *Spectator*, a New York City insurance publication, Dr. Frederick Hoffman declared, "Our murder record . . . is a most serious indictment of American civilization, and evidence of lawlessness which has no counterpart in any country in the world."[20]

The basis for its conclusion "Lawlessness Our Greatest Problem" and title of a major article in the *Literary Digest* for January 1, was a questionnaire sent by the National Economic League to members of its National Council, a group of men prominent in their communities. The members of the council were asked if they believed that an abnormal amount of disrespect for law existed in this country. Of those responding 1,480 answered in the affirmative and 105 in the negative. The question then asked was: "What in your opinion is most to blame; is it improper laws, lax enforcement, or the condition of public sentiment?" The responses were improper laws, 649; lax enforcement, 895; and condition of public sentiment, 1,065. In response to the query, "What specific laws . . . are most responsible?" prohibition was the overwhelming response given.[21] But by 1927, as if sensing that the Eighteenth Amendment might be repealed (see pp. 80–81), bootleggers began to seek other fields of illicit endeavor. As bootlegging waned, racketeering waxed. By 1927, the word "racketeer" was in widespread use.

At its simplest, racketeering may be defined as any scheme by which human parasites drain profit by intimidating legitimate business activity. It was but a short step from offering "protection" against violence or competition to demanding a portion of the profits. Thus, gangsters often muscled their way into legitimate business. In 1927, there were estimated to be ninety-one rackets in Chicago. Among the industries especially prone to the protection racket were: laundry, cleaning and dyeing, linen supply, carbonated beverages, barbers, bakers, coal, kosher meats, building material, paving, excavating, flour, tobacco, beauty culture, roofing material, municipal workers, garages, dairy products, demolition, perishable produce, long-distance hauling, distribution of ice cream, furniture storage, ash and garbage removal, machinery moving, railway express, lumber, florists, baggage delivery, janitors, commercial window washers, oil wagon drivers, electrotyping, and motion picture operators. The direct tribute paid to racketeers by every man, woman, and child of Chicago amounted to $45.[22] In 1927, there were 108 bombings and 379 murders, all of them likely by-products of racketeering.

There was a price list for inflicting a beating, a little more for eye-gouging or ear-slitting. To rub out an inconvenient but undistinguished competitor cost less than $100. For big jobs, killers were generally brought in from out of town. To kill a prominent person in business, the cost might be $5,000 and to kill a prominent city official, $10,000. To kill a president of a large corporation might require as much as $100,000.

Big business and big labor were likewise rife with racketeering. Harry Herbert Bennett's job at the Ford automotive plants was largely to keep Ford workers from organizing into labor unions. He did so by creating what the *New York Times* called the largest private quasi-military force in the world. It was made up of hoodlums and jailbirds recruited by former bootleggers. As early as 1927, Ford made an arrangement with the boss of Detroit's Sicilian bootleggers, Chester La Mare. What Capone was to Chicago, La Mare was to Detroit. He dominated a $215 million dollar bootlegging business, making it the state's second largest industry. La Mare was eventually convicted on a Prohibition violation in 1927, but Harry Bennett, intervening on his behalf, proposed that the judge allow Chet La Mare to be rehabilitated under the watchful eye of Henry Ford, "that great American folk hero and builder of moral virtue. . . ."[23]

Under the guise of attempting to "rehabilitate" former convicts, Bennett hired as Ford employees some eight thousand men with prison records. The main job of these men was not to build cars but to act as goons and strikebreakers. This task they enthusiastically performed through threats, beatings, and even killings of those who supported unions and especially of those labor union leaders who tried to organize the workers in the Ford factories.

If business resorted to thugs to protect them from labor unions, the latter were not long in responding in kind and recruiting thugs to protect them from the private armies of big business, to threaten workers who resisted calls to unionize, and to brutalize scabs.

On August 19, more than fifty non-union African American miners employed by the Pittsburgh Coal Company were hurled from their beds in the morning by an explosion which wrecked two buildings in West Elizabeth, Pennsylvania.

On July 8, two persons were rendered unconscious and four others had narrow escapes when a dynamite bomb exploded in front of the home of John McMahon, mine foreman of the Clinton Block Coal Company near Pittsburgh,

Pennsylvania. The dwelling was badly damaged by the blast and the entire neighborhood was rocked. Goons of the union were suspected as the act was a part of their campaign to force the company allow workers to organize.

During the silk mill employees' strike at Garfield, Passaic, and other towns in New Jersey in 1926 and 1927, numerous homes occupied by workers who refused to strike were dynamited and wrecked or damaged.

In the Twin Cities during the fall of 1927, the stagehands employed at the theaters went on strike in their attempt to win one day off in seven. The motion-picture operators were out in sympathy with them. On October 10, a bomb exploded in the Forest Theater, a movie house in the residential district of St. Paul, while the show was on. One woman was injured and over three hundred men, women, and children were thrown into a panic. On the same day the Logan theater in Minneapolis was bombed.

On August 19, during a labor-management conflict, a bomb went off at the Wright Theater at Guerdon, Arkansas, and caused $20,000 in damage. On November 8, the recently completed $1,700,000 State Theater of Hammond, Indiana, was completely destroyed by a dynamite explosion. A business agent of the Motion Picture Operators' Union was arrested and, according to the police, confessed to having had a hand in the plot. Others arrested and charged with having been connected with the bombing were the walking delegates of the Hod Carriers' Union and the Finishers' Union.[24]

The enemies of labor unions included not only owners of large and small businesses, but other unions and those workers who did not wish to unionize. Enemies of industry were mainly competitors and workers who sought to join labor unions and who were lured by labor union organizers to do so. Thugs, goons, and "gorillas" were paid to threaten and destroy the "enemy." In exchange, the industry or labor union paid the racketeer a monthly or annual fee for providing "permanent" protection. When unions or industry required no "protection" because all seemed to be well, the gangster hoodlums created problems by encouraging violence, arson, or bomb throwing. In these ways through an alliance with both business and labor and their political connections, gangsters found new opportunities in racketeering. Crime, its causes and cure, remained a lively topic during 1927 which saw a number of innovative efforts to deal constructively with the rehabilitation or punishment of criminals.

Crime and Punishment

There was little consensus about how best to reduce the level of crime. For one thing, there were some who did not agree that crime had at all increased.

The leading attorney of the day, Clarence Darrow, wrote that the extent of crime was very much overstated. The press overstated the extent of crime in order to sell newspapers. Advocates of law and order tended to overstate crime in an attempt to get the public stirred up enough so that their legislators would pass ever harsher methods of punishment. Darrow pointed out that "prisons are now filled with inmates who have only done something which a few years ago was perfectly legal." He had prohibition in mind. He pointed out further that the vast increase in the use of the automobile made criminals of those who violated motor laws in each of the states. As for the alleged increase in the incidence of rape, Darrow pointed out that the number of convictions for rape had increased because the age of consent had been raised from ten years of age to eighteen. Darrow concluded that what was luridly pictured as an army of criminals engaged in combat with organized society is in reality but an outgrowth of "poverty, hard luck, ignorance, maladjustment, and destiny."[25]

And Professor Joseph Mayer of Tufts College insisted that, comparatively speaking, there was no more crime in 1927 than there ever was, especially when one took into account the growing population and the vast increase in business activity. That there might be more crime in the United States than in comparable industrial nations he attributed to the fact that America remained a new and growing nation and that the frontier mentality continued to prevail. Moreover, he pointed out that America would not tolerate police espionage and the systematic registration of citizens as did some of the older nations "in which everybody is under surveillance from the time he was born to the hour of his death."[26]

On November 2 and 3, the National Conference on the Reduction of Crime was held in Washington, D.C., at the call of the National Crime Commission. In its two-day conference, those present considered four approaches for deterring crime. These were: (1) The effectiveness of police work in America, (2) American prisons and other punishments as a means of deterring crime, (3) Control of guns and other weapons, and (4) Crime viewed as a social disease. The latter was the perspective of the reform-minded participants in the National Conference. "The idea of looking at the criminal much as a doctor looks upon his patient is an essentially new idea in the handling of the crime problem."[27] But how to assess the mental responsibility of persons accused of crime?

Dr. L. Vernon Briggs of Massachusetts addressed the meeting, drawing on experiences in his home state, which had adopted the so-called "Briggs Law" some six years earlier. Massachusetts required that a board of psychiatrists examine any individual indicted for a capital offense or anyone indicted for a second time for a felony. Briggs believed that a board of psychiatrists, rather than a jury listening to the evidence of experts, was more competent to determine the mental fitness of the accused to stand trial and the fairness of the punishment imposed. Other states were urged to follow the example of Massachusetts.

Chief Justice William Howard Taft was, however, not especially supportive of this approach. It was his view that the victim of murder, theft, or violence was being forgotten. "We are all in favor, of course, of measures which will induce criminals to become law-abiding citizens, but we must never forget that the chief and first object of prosecution of crime is its deterrent effect upon future would-be-criminals in the protection of society." He continued, "We must not allow our interest in criminals to go to the point of making effective prosecution of crime and its punishment subordinate to schemes for reform of criminals, however admirable they may be."[28]

In 1927 the lack of reliable statistical data on crime and criminals stood in the way of making any intelligent judgment as to how best to proceed in fighting crime. In that year the Laura Spelman Rockefeller Memorial provided a grant to finance the creation of a workable system of uniform crime records. Many states likewise recognized the need for more detailed statistics on offenders, victims, and criminal justice procedures as well as a uniform method of reporting.

In a report on crime in New York City, the Crime Commission of New York State discovered that only 15 percent of all arrests on felony charges in 1925 led to punishment. And in all cases bound over to the grand jury in New York State, only 39 percent were finally punished. The state of Illinois followed the example of New York, as did the cities of Boston, Massachusetts, and Cincinnati, Ohio. The United States census bureau was engaged in 1927 in the first of a series of proposed annual censuses of those held in state and federal prisons and reformatories. Although Alabama, Florida, and Idaho failed to furnish reports and Delaware had no state prison nor reformatory, on January 1, 1927, there were 89,294 prisoners in state prisons and 6,803 in federal institutions. Between 1910 and 1927 there was a sharp rise in the number of prisoners. In 1910 there were 70.2 prisoners per 100,000 of population, in 1927 there were 79.2.

But what do these data represent? An increase in crime? Greater efficiency in the machinery of justice? Greater severity of sentencing? The year 1927 was a year of studying crime rather than one in which substantial advances were made in deterrence, reform of criminals, or the more equitable administration of justice. These studies do reflect, however, the enormous public interest in crime.[29] In the 1920s there was growing interest in applying the medical model to those convicted of a crime. Offenders were considered sick, mentally or emotionally, and prisons were to make a far better effort to reform the prisoner. Ideal prison programs were to compensate for childhood abuse, dysfunctional families, neglect, poverty, malnutrition, inadequate social or job-related skills. In short, ideal prisons were not to incarcerate inmates but cure them.

In 1867, Enoch Wines and Theodore Dwight concluded an extensive survey of American prisons. They reported that the whole prison system of the United States required "careful and judicious revision." They reported the regular reliance on corporal punishment, even torture for minor infractions. The report deplored the cramped quarters in which the prisoners were held and the overcrowding. In many prisons of the southern states, African Americans made up more than 75 percent of the inmates. They were generally assigned to harsh agricultural work in a prison system that was reminiscent of the worst elements of slavery on the plantation.

By the 1920s, however, little had been accomplished. Kate Richards O'Hare spent fourteen months at the Missouri penitentiary in Jefferson City in 1919 and 1920. In her 1923 book evaluating her experiences she described the cell areas as "very dirty and in most essentials, shabby and unsanitary." She wrote: "Every crack and crevice of the cellhouse was full of vermin of every known sort, which no amount of scrubbing on the part of the women could permanently dislodge." Rats "overran the place in swarms, scampered over the dining tables, nibbled [at the food], played in [the] dishes, crept into bed, chewed up shoes and carried off everything not nailed down or hung far above their reach." The dining room was equally filthy; the walls were "streaked with grime," and the ceiling was covered with fifteen years' accumulation of dead flies. The inmates were segregated and seated at long wooden tables infested with cockroaches. "The dishes were of rusty battered tinware, the knives and forks of cast iron, and the spoons were non-existent. If a woman wished to use a spoon she was compelled to buy it with her own money and carry it about. . . ." Health conditions were seriously neglected. No effort was made to separate inmates infected with contagious diseases, nor were disinfectants in use, with the consequences that all prisoners bathed in the same few tubs and frequently contracted highly contagious, even life-threatening diseases. O'Hare recounts an incident in she was ordered to bathe immediately after a woman infected with syphilis: "From her throat to her feet she was one mass of open sores . . . with clothes so stiff from dried pus that they rattled when she walked. A woman about whose neck live maggots had been working out of filthy bandages."[30]

In 1923, Joseph Fishman in *Crucibles of Crime* described widespread use of drugs among prison inmates and extensive drug addiction among men previously unaddicted before being sent to jail. Morphine, cocaine, heroin, and hashish were among the common drugs. These illegal substances were concealed in fruit, ice cream, under postage stamps, hems of handkerchiefs, or hidden in belts, in hollowed-out heels of shoes.[31]

In an attempt to deal more effectively with the causes of crime and the punishments for crime, state crime commissions were established and, in 1925, a National Crime Commission. These commissions were generally charged with the responsibility of gathering crime statistics and trying to make them comparable. They were to gather and disseminate data about homicides, arsons, thefts, and muggings. They were to keep records of the length of sentences and the length of time it took to get the accused a fair trial. The commissions sought to measure the rate of recidivism, that is, the rate at which a criminal once released commits another crime and is jailed once again. And they tried to establish a system of record keeping of those who had fallen through the cracks of the judicial system and measure the effectiveness of the juvenile courts.

During the 1920s, the belief was advanced that low intelligence was an important factor in the making of a criminal. During World War I, army recruits were required to take intelligence tests and the results were dismaying. Through a variety of similar tests, attempts were made to measure the intelligence of prisoners. But what to do when some of the tests revealed that the criminals were smarter than those who guarded them!

As the 1920s progressed, greater reliance was placed on psychiatrists and other behavioral scientists in a more systematic attempt at rehabilitation. By 1926, sixty-seven prisons employed psychiatrists and forty-five had psychologists. But these were so few in number in relation to the prison population that the programs were rendered ineffective. However, an outstanding example of the attempt at prison reform was made in 1927 at the Norfolk Prison Colony in Massachusetts. Building began in that year in an attempt to relieve the crowding at the old Charlestown prison. In a daring experiment some of the prisoners were put to work. The outside wall was built by prison inmates under the supervision of Howard Gill, an economist. Gill became so enthusiastic about what the prisoners had accomplished that he sought to apply the tools of psychology and sociology to reform the inmates and to build, insofar as possible, a normal community for them. New social, medical, psychological, and educational techniques were added to the traditional methods of industrial and religious instruction. Prisoners were classified and organized into groups of under fifty, each of which was housed and supervised by its own house officer. Every man had an individualized physical, mental, social, vocational, and avocational program.

Daily activities at Norfolk were recorded in a diary for the years 1927 to 1933. What they revealed was not encouraging. There was constant quarreling between those who were on the treatment and rehabilitation staff and those whose jobs were custodial in nature. Moreover, the social workers in those days lacked the knowledge and resources to bring about substantial rehabilitation. Nor could the prison deal with hardened offenders who initially were not supposed to be sent to Norfolk. In 1934, Gill was dismissed because of several escapes and the common criticism that Norfolk was too soft on criminals.[32]

In the high-flying economy of 1927, white-collar crime reached grave proportions. Tufts Professor Joseph Mayer noted widespread stock swindles, insurance scams, and frauds. Some took the form of land speculation, as in Florida; others involved wildcat mining without any remote chance of finding ore, or wildcat oil drilling with even less chance of finding oil, to say nothing of arson —which was both violent crime and, usually, insurance fraud. Every new invention, the radio, the automobile, and the airplane, attracted crooked professionals who sought to unload worthless stock in glamorous industries to an unwary public greedily eager to make a financial killing. Mayer estimated crimes of this nature cost the nation some $4 billion. Yet there was little outcry from the public. For one thing, small investors often did not know they had been "hoodwinked." They didn't really understand the market in which they were investing. Rules protecting the investor had vast loopholes and enforcement was uneven. Moreover, in the financial "gamble" might not the loser in one industry make up the loss by winning in another? And so the public was tolerant rather than indignant.

If the criminal was a victim of forces over which he or she had little control, was the convicted murderer likewise a victim? Should the convicted murderer be put to death? To what extent, if any, were there extenuating circumstances which would suggest compassion rather than capital punishment be in order? The latter became a topic of widespread public interest and debate.

On January 1, 1889, the legislature of New York State approved electrocution as the new means of carrying out capital punishment in a "quick and painless manner." On August 16, 1890, in New York State, William Kemmler became the first person to be executed by electrocution. The U.S. Supreme Court held that the electric chair did not violate the Eighth Amendment's prohibition against cruel and unusual punishments. By 1927, fourteen states had chosen to use the electric chair. In that year, moreover, Nicola Sacco and Bartolomeo Vanzetti were executed in the electric chair in Boston, Massachusetts (see pp. 84–92). Their electrocution let loose a re-energized debate over the merits of the death penalty as a deterrent against crime.

While a number of states had abolished the death penalty by 1927, the reform did not last, and hanging remained the most common form of capital punishment. In the words of an assistant district attorney who had initially favored the death penalty but in his later years opposed it, a "hang the dog" philosophy was the rule rather than the exception in the United States.[33]

In such a climate, hanging was also the preferred method of Ku Klux Klan members to intimidate African Americans. The worst of the crimes of the 1920s had to do with lynchings and burnings, fiery crosses and torching of homes of innocent people during a decade often described as the nadir of race relations in America.

꙰

[1]Quoted in Andrew Sinclair, *Prohibition: The Era of Excess* (Boston: Little Brown and Company, 1962), p. 220.
[2]Ibid., p. 5.
[3]"The Battle to Disarm the Gunman," *Literary Digest* 92 (February 19, 1927): 9.
[4]Quoted in Lois Gordon and Alan Gordon, *American Chronicle: Six Decades in American Life, 1920–1980* (New York: Atheneum Press, 1987), p. 70.
[5]"The Capone Era," *Life* 23 (February 10, 1947): 24.
[6]Laurence Bergreen, *Capone: The Man and the Era* (New York: Simon and Schuster, 1994), p. 46.
[7]Ibid., p. 45.
[8]Ibid., p. 125.
[9]John Kobler, *The Life and World of Al Capone* (New York: G. P. Putnam's Sons, 1971), p. 15.
[10]Ibid., p. 14.
[11]Fred D. Pasley, *Al Capone: The Biography of a Self-Made Man* (London: Faber and Faber Ltd., 1931), p. 158.
[12]Andrew Sinclair, "Introduction," in Pasley, *Al Capone*, p. 5.
[13]Bergreen, *Capone*, p. 177.
[14]Bergreen, *Capone*, p. 183.
[15]Bergreen, *Capone*, p. 236.
[16]Pasley, *Al Capone*, p. 153.
[17]"The Trial of Alphonse Capone for Income-Tax Evasion (1931)," in Francis X. Busch, *Enemies of the State* (Indianapolis: Bobbs-Merrill Company, Inc., 1954), pp. 175–176.
[18]Morris Markey, "Gangs," *Atlantic Monthly* 141 (March 1928): 296.
[19]Edward Hale Bierstadt, "Our Permanent Crime Wave," *Harper's Monthly* 156 (December 1927): 61.
[20]Quoted in "Our 12,000 Killings in 1926," *Literary Digest* 94 (July 2, 1927):12.
[21]"Lawlessness Our Greatest Problem," *Literary Digest* 92 (January 1, 1927): 24.

[22]John Gunther, "The High Cost of Hoodlums," *Harper's Monthly* 159 (October 1929): 539–540.

[23]Frank Browning and John Gerassi, *The American Way of Crime* (New York: G. P. Putnam's Sons, 1980), p. 395.

[24]Examples are from Louis Adamic, "Racketeers and Organized Labor," *Harper's Monthly* 161 (September 1930): 404–416.

[25]Clarence Darrow, "Crime and the Alarmists," in Grant Overton, ed., *Mirrors of the Year: A National Review of the Outstanding Figures, Trends and Events of 1926–1927*, p. 205.

[26]Joseph Mayer, "Crime in the Commercial Field," *Scientific Monthly* 24 (May 1927): 421.

[27]Watson Davis, "The Nation-Wide Campaign to Reduce Crime," *Current History* 27 (December 1927): 303.

[28]Ibid., p. 305.

[29]See C. E. Gehlke, "Crime," in William F. Ogburn, ed., *Recent Social Trends in the United States Since the War and Particularly in 1927* (Chicago: University of Chicago Press, 1929), pp. 169–184.

[30]Quoted in Morris Norval and David J. Rothman, *The Oxford History of the Prison* (New York: Oxford University Press, 1995), p. 177.

[31]Ibid.

[32]See ibid., pp. 181–182.

[33]Edwin Hedrick, "Hang the Dog," *Atlantic Monthly* 140 (September 1927): 338–348.

6

RACE IN AMERICA

June 27, 1927

About 3,000 African Americans and 1,000 whites from southeastern Arkansas gathered at Pine Bluff to thank Secretary of Commerce Herbert Hoover and others for effective relief work. When 200 women students sang "Swing Low, Sweet Chariot" tears filled Hoover's eyes.

Hoover had been aware that how effectively he handled the emergency of the great Mississippi Flood of that year would impact both his nomination and election. He was no racist, yet how Hoover responded to the racial issues growing out of the flood demonstrated that he shared the prevailing prejudices of his time and that his actions were motivated as much by his ambition to become the next president of the United States as from a desire to help the refugees.

For Hoover's presidential ambitions, the Mississippi Flood was a two-edged sword. On the one hand, it gave Hoover the publicity he needed to bring his name prominently before the public and the leadership of the Republican Party and to demonstrate that what he did by way of feeding hungry Belgians and others in Europe during the Great War could be repeated in his own country. On the other hand, the spotlight in which he worked would reveal his racial attitudes. Should blacks and progressives desert him because of alleged racial inequity, his candidacy could be doomed. Hoover would tread cautiously.

❧

To Americans of 1927, the year consisted not of fifty-two weeks, but, according to one enumeration, a hundred thirty-five weeks. Solid American citizens were expected to observe Better Speech Week, Courtesy Week, Fire Prevention Week, Honesty Week, Thrift Week, Walk-and-Be-Healthy Week, Apple Week,

Book Week, Canned Foods Week, Linoleum Week, Suspender Week, Reindeer Week, and Pharmacy Week. Badges, seals, stickers, and posters publicized the more influential "weeks."[1]

In 1926, Negro History Week was added to the list. By 1927, with the experience of two years behind it, the *Journal of Negro History* reported that the "second annual effort to invite attention to the achievements of the African American showed unusual progress toward the desired end of saving and popularizing the records of the race that it may not become a negligible factor in the thought of the world." Yet, the *Journal* article continued, "There should be no indulgence in undue eulogy of the Negro. The case of the Negro is well taken care of when it is shown how he has influenced the development of civilization."[2] After describing the activities in and out of school that were part of the observation of Negro History Week, the reporter noted the purchase of the A. A. Schomburg collection of four thousand books on African Americans made possible by a gift of the Carnegie Corporation. The books were placed in a special department of the 135th Street Branch of the New York Public Library to encourage research in African American life and history. After expressing thanks to leading daily newspapers which participated in the observance, the author concluded that Negro History Week "was one of the most significant movements ever started in the interest of the Negro race."[3]

A Day in the Life

Writing in the *Nation* of March 23, 1927, George S. Schuyler describes with tongue in cheek the daily humiliation of black Americans in that year. "I am black, unadulterated Negro. I do not regret it or go about with mournful countenance bewailing my lot. I do not clamor with the Garveyites for migration to Africa. On the contrary I enjoy life here in America. I glance at my white brother and sister with amusement tinged with pity.

> Entering a restaurant . . . the customers look up, shocked and annoyed. Eating stops. Breaths are caught. The silence is ominous. A worried waiter steps with an agitated inquiry. What do I want. (What would a person want in a restaurant?. . . .) I cannot help but enjoy all this. Over a hundred proud Nordics nonplussed by a lone Negro!
> Suppose I decide to go to a theater. If it be in the liberal North or East, I approach the ticket-window and ask for orchestra seats. . . . When seated I find that all the Negro audience is together. I indulge in a sardonic smile.
> Perhaps I am in the South. I wish to take a young woman to the theater.

She belongs to an old family. . . . She herself is a college graduate. Ordinarily I would be forced to buy orchestra seats with such a companion. . . . But Negroes can sit only in the gallery in this theater. Thus I am saved money, and what was designed as a humiliation is really a help. . . . I am not a snob. . . . All these things used to infuriate me. Now I have a sense of humor.

The street car affords similar amusement. There is an empty seat next to a rather dowdy female of the superior race. She is reading a tabloid. . . . I take the empty seat and open my *New York Times*. She glances disdainfully at me. . . and moves as far away as possible. That tickles me. I smile in my *Times*. She scowls in her tabloid.

Or, I'm in Memphis Tennessee. It is my first visit. I hail a [trolley] car. The sign says 'Front Entrance.' I start to climb aboard. Fresh from the North, I do not know that Negroes must enter from the rear as well as sit in the rear. The motorman . . . glances at me balefully. "Get in the rear door, boy!" he growls belligerently. . . . My heart leaps to my throat. Negroes have been beaten and jailed for no greater offense. . . .

There was the day in Paris, Texas. It was the policy of my paper to send my salary and expenses by telegraph at the end of the week. The clerk at the telegraph office has not sufficient funds to cash the order. . . . She endorses it and sends me across the street to the largest hotel to get it cashed. All the banks are closed. . . . I enter the hotel lobby and march toward the desk. I think only of getting my money and leaving town; Negroes have been burned at the stake here. "Take off your hat, boy!" The grating voice of the desk clerk sears me through. My heart leaps in my throat. I had entirely forgotten about the hat. Nearly everyone else has on a hat. I reach the desk. . . I politely tell the clerk my mission. He cashes the order. Handing me the bills he asks: "What are you—president of one of those nigger colleges?. . ." "No," I reply, "I am just a newspaperman. It's pretty hard for a boy to get a job as college president."

Once I was offered a good job in the New York office of a sugar company. The position was secured by a friend over the telephone. The only slip was that my friend neglected to mention that I was a Negro. When I walked into the palatial offices in the Battery Place Building, there was much conferring and studied courtesy. I enjoyed the whole thing hugely! Of course I didn't get the job.

Every night the Negro is in danger. I walk down a dark street or cut across the park. Suddenly, turning a corner, I come face to face with a white woman. Will she get frightened and scream? I never know. . . .

And so it goes—day in and day out, year in and year out, for a lifetime. Any Negro in America has similar experiences daily. Most Negroes, of course, are far too thin-skinned to delight in many of the situations within which they find themselves. . . . For my part, I would never be able to stand all this noise and smoke and stone and steel and machinery, if my blackness did not bring diversion and relief.[4]

Progress and Promise

Robert Russa Moton (1867–1940) was probably the most prominent African American of his day, having inherited the mantle of leadership from Booker T. Washington (1856–1915). Moton was a bear of a man who physically dominated any setting he was in. But he was a teddy bear, not a grizzly. Like Washington, his leadership style was one of waiting patiently for the whites to see the plight of blacks and do the right thing for them. When Washington died, Moton became principal of Tuskegee Institute in Alabama. As principal he continued developing Washington's preference for vocational rather than higher education. Moton also inherited what came to be called the "Tuskegee Machine," that is, he became the "political boss" through whom appointments of blacks at federal, state, and even local levels had to be cleared. He was conciliatory rather than confrontational, humble rather than proud; he was the "good Negro" with whom the whites could negotiate.

From Moton's perspective, conditions for the 10.5 million African Americans were by no means dire in 1927. In the *Annals of the American Academy of Political and Social Science,* he wrote, "At no time has the outlook for the Negro in America been as promising as it is today."[5] He described the network of agencies that had developed to improve the health and economic resources of African Americans. "Much of the restlessness and discontent within the race," he insisted, "is a consequence of [an] eager desire for improvement."[6] Moton boasted that holdings of black churches were not less than $200,000,000 while black churches spent $50,000,000 annually for religious activities as well as help to congregants. After paying tribute to his mentor, Booker T. Washington, Moton observed that black business enterprise grew from 20,000 in 1900 to 70,000 in 1927. "In every large city," he observed, "there is a Negro business section, containing usually a theater, a bank, an undertaking establishment, a printing shop, a haberdashery, a grocery, a drug store, a barber shop, office buildings and similar enterprises."[7] He pointed to black professional organizations in law, medicine, entertainment, journalism, and education. He paid tribute to the efforts of the National Association for the Advancement of Colored People to secure the defense of African Americans in civil and legal rights and of the National Urban League in securing improvement in employment, housing, and recreation. He noted the efforts of the Young Men's and Women's Christian Associations to help build facilities for colored people. That nearly all these efforts were segregated in nature did not appear to disturb him at all.

It is strange, however, that Moton spoke in generalities when he could have cited a number of improvements in African Americans' circumstances. He might have noted, for example, that on March 7, the U.S. Supreme Court in Nixon v. Herndon declared unconstitutional Texas legislation adopted in 1924 which specifically excluded blacks from Democratic primaries in that state. A majority of the court held that the Texas law was "a direct and obvious" infringement of Amendment Fourteen. "[I]t is too clear for extended argument," declared the Court, "that color cannot be made the basis of a statutory classification affecting the right set up in this case."

William Edward Burghardt Du Bois (1868–1963) was born in Great Barrington, Massachusetts. The few blacks who lived there were well integrated. The family lived in modest circumstances and young Will worked as a timekeeper in a local mill. When he graduated from Great Barrington High School in 1884 he was the only African American student in the class. Yet his obvious intellectual talents were such that he was encouraged by the school principal to enroll at Fisk University, in Nashville, Tennessee. It was in this all-black college that Du Bois first found himself in a community made up only of others of his race. He graduated with a B.A. degree, entered the junior class at Harvard, graduated with a B.A. cum laude in 1890, and received an M.A. degree in 1891. He spent two years at the University of Berlin in 1895 and received a Ph.D. from Harvard, the first African American to do so. He became one of the original founders of the National Association for the Advancement of Colored People. He remained a member of its board of directors, served as director of publicity and research, and editor of its journal, *Crisis* (1910–1934).

Du Bois recognized that the Washington/Moton style of black leadership was no longer adequate for the tasks ahead. He said: "[Booker T. Washington] stands as the one recognized spokesman of his ten million fellows, and one of the most notable figures in a nation of seventy millions." Yet, "Mr. Washington represents in Negro thought the old attitude of adjustment and submission. . . ." An attitude which has only achieved "(1) The disenfranchisement of the Negro; (2) The legal creation of a distinct status of civil inferiority for the Negro; (3) The steady withdrawal of aid from institutions for the higher training of the Negro." And, in words foreshadowing those of Martin Luther King Jr., Du Bois concluded his gentlemanly attack on Washington with these words: "[S]o far as Mr. Washington apol-

ogizes for injustice, North or South, does not rightly value the privilege or duty of
voting, belittles the emasculating effects of caste distinctions, and opposes the
higher training and ambition of our brighter minds,—so far as he, the South, or
the Nation, does this,—we must unceasingly and firmly oppose them. By every civ-
ilized and peaceful method we must strive for the rights which the world accords
to men, clinging unwaveringly to those great words which the sons of the Fathers
would fain forget: 'We hold these truths to be self-evident: That all men are created equal; that they are endowed by their Creator with certain unalienable rights;
that among these are life, liberty, and the pursuit of happiness."[8]

Writing in 1927, Du Bois agonized:

We have submitted in the United States to widespread customs, sometimes
written into law, and sometimes enforced by mob violence, which insult the
manhood and sense of decency of self-respecting human beings. In various
parts of the United States a traveler may be compelled to pay first-class for
third-class accommodations, may be publicly stigmatized and affronted
despite his dress, character and attainment, and simply because he has or is
suspected of having a Negro ancestor; families may be ousted from their
home and made to lose their property without due process of law; children
may be deprived of their proper education, youth kept from an opportunity
to work and age from the public enjoyment of wealth which it has helped
to create, not for any individual fault or failing, but because the majority of
the group, thus singled out for public insult, are descendants of slaves, and
therefore, as a class, less well-clothed, less well-educated, with smaller
incomes and more difficulties to encounter than other people.[9]

In recognizing how far the African American had yet to go to achieve reason-
able equality with other Americans, one writer noted, "The Negro began furthest
down and has had furthest to go in order to reach the common goal. The chat-
tel must become a person, the slave a freeman, the freeman a citizen, the citizen
an elector, while the elector must still fight his way to full fellowship. The halfway
stage has hardly yet been reached. . . . The government has recently spent forty
millions of dollars upon the enforcement of the Eighteenth Amendment with
dubious success. But it has not spent forty cents in forty years upon the enforcement of the Fourteenth Amendment, which is nullified with impunity. The Fif-
teenth Amendment is nullified by indirection and the Fourteenth by inaction on
the part of government. . . . The Negro attends separate schools and rides in separate cars in several states of the Union, but in few, if any instances, does he
receive equal accommodations and facilities. . . . ."[10]

The Mississippi River Flood:
A Case Study in Race Relations[11]

In April 1927, after many weeks of unusually heavy rainfall, the 1.24 million-square-mile Mississippi River basin flooded. Levees crumbled all the way from Southern Illinois to New Orleans, Louisiana. One and a half million people had to flee in search of higher ground. A billion dollars in property losses were sustained. The devastated area extended almost one thousand miles to the Gulf of Mexico and was from 50 to 150 miles wide. "Several hundred people died, and thousands of dead mules, horses, cows, and wildlife collected on log jams and raised the specter of epidemic. Earth tremors, electrical storms, and tornadoes added to the misery."[12]

President Coolidge recognized that his secretary of commerce was the logical choice to direct the massive recovery-and-rescue effort the situation required. On April 22, Coolidge appointed Herbert Hoover as chairman of the Special Mississippi Flood Committee. Hoover enlisted the assistance and the expertise of the American Red Cross, raised $32 million dollars from private sources and an additional $10 million from federal funds. He then set out by train to gain first-hand experience of the situation and to organize state and local relief committees. For three months, Hoover, America's "handy man,"[13] directed relief efforts using a Pullman car as his headquarters. One hundred fifty tent cities were created and at the height of the relief effort over 33,000 people worked under Hoover's direction.

High above the muddy river near the city of Vicksburg, Mississippi, were four camps for refugees from the Great Flood of 1927. These were Camp Hayes, Camp Juarez, Camp Louisiana, and Camp Fort Hill. At Camp Hayes, twelve hundred white refugees were sheltered in a neatly planned tent city with one family per tent. Each family member had a cot and each family had as many blankets as it needed. Most of the refugees were pitifully poor sharecroppers who were deeply in debt to a planter. Because they were white, however, they had privileges and amenities not available to black tenant farmers and sharecroppers who were in similarly dire straits. At Camp Hayes, the Church of Christ held religious services several times a day during the emergency, thus offering to the white refugees a sense of community, continuity, and hope. Said one white refugee, "I love this place, it is just like a camp meeting."

In Camp Louisiana, about two miles away, some 6,000 African Americans took refuge. Here, however, several families occupied a single tent. Cots were available only for the elderly and the infirm, but brown army blankets were plentiful and were available as needed. At Camp Fort Hill, another 6,000 black refugees were housed in a tent city very similar to that of Camp Louisiana. At Camp Juarez, some four hundred Mexicans were made safe in a rustic pavilion large enough to house the entire group. The most impressive thing about the black camps, declared an editorial in the *Crisis,* the journal of the NAACP, "was the incredible melancholy of the colored refugees. There was no laughter, no music, no Negro light-heartedness. They sat in silent apathy, or talked in low tones. They had come from scenes of horror, many of them greater than any white refugee knew, as the helplessness of the Negro exceeded anything known to whites."[14]

The American Red Cross proposed moving black labor to refugee camps. But this alarmed the white planters, for whom labor was the most important commodity. They insisted that the flood would not last very long and that they could take care of "their" black workers right on the plantation itself. So great was the fear that they would lose their laborers that the planters refused to cooperate with the Red Cross. In order to secure that cooperation, the American Red Cross agreed to return tenant farmers only to the plantation from which they had come. What this meant was that in effect African American refugee camps became virtual prisons, with the National Guard policing the movements of refugees, using guards and sentries around the clock for this purpose. The families required passes to leave the camps and were refused transportation except to the plantations on which they had worked. When a large plantation owner sought to retrieve "his Negroes" they were often forced to go at the point of a bayonet.

Nor was the system for distributing food, clothing and other necessities very efficient. The Red Cross furnished these necessities on a limited basis and distributed the supplies to needy black families through the plantation owner or through the storekeeper on the plantation. This was made to order for corrupt plantation owners to keep the Red Cross supplies for themselves or to sell to workers what had been freely allotted for them. Since the black workers had no cash of their own, they became further indebted to plantation owners, and so the dismal state of vassalage or peonage on the plantation was reinforced. Because blacks were often fed on food that had been spoiled, outbreaks of disease in the camps and on the plantation were common. Pellagra was especially widespread.

In a three part study of the circumstances in which black refugees found themselves, the National Association for the Advancement of Colored People described any number of instances of abuse. At the behest of the American Red Cross, National Guardsmen forced African American refugees to work without pay to clean up the camps. Failure to do so meant a beating. Such beatings were frequent despite repeated orders from National Guard officers that the guardsmen refrain

Refugees from the flooding of the Mississippi thronged the docks. Reproduced from the collections of the Library of Congress.

from doing so. Sometimes, the National Guardsmen lost control of the situation and shootings occurred as well.

From time to time, black refugees were forced to entertain the soldiers. As reported in the *Crisis*, a refugee from Greenville, Mississippi, reported, "on last Friday morning I was told to box another Negro boy by one of the soldiers on duty at Fort Hill. I replied that I did not want to box because my Mother told me not to. This soldier told me that he was going to make me box because I had stolen some oranges. I had two oranges in my pocket that I had gotten out of the basket where they had been thrown away. One of the soldiers then said, 'Go and get a case of oranges and make him eat them all, but Col. Tom Shaw pulled the gloves off of me and carried me down the hill, took my belt off and whipped me with it."[15]

On May 12, 1927, a refugee named Matilda Heslip was ordered to wash and iron clothes for a soldier who was about to leave camp on the noon train. Matilda Heslip insisted that it was impossible to wash, dry, and iron the clothing before the soldier left. She was ordered to do so nevertheless and to dry the clothes in front of the kitchen stoves. When she tried to do this a conflict arose with other refugees who were trying to prepare lunch in the same kitchen. A sergeant who tried to settle the matter ordered her out of the kitchen. She refused. The sergeant reached for a cot stick and struck the woman, whom he said had been insulting and impudent. Heslip was struck about the arm and the head and required three stitches. "Impudence is a sin," concluded the *Crisis*, "which cannot be forgiven in a Negro."[16]

Claude Barnett, who ran the Associated Negro Press which syndicated stories to 135 African-American newspapers, after spending some time in the flooded areas, reported to Hoover rumors of "injustice and scandal." From Jane Addams, the nationally prominent social reformer, and from other well-placed whites and blacks, charges of race discrimination mounted. They pointed to inequities in the distribution of food, blankets, cots, and tents. They complained that National Guardsmen were essentially keeping African Americans prisoner in the refugee camps. Hoover wired Henry Baker, head of the relief effort for the Red Cross working out of Memphis, Tennessee, to investigate the truth of these allegations. The reports Hoover received were uneven. That is, reports from some areas appeared to demonstrate that color lines had been at least temporarily obliterated. Others confirmed the worst examples of discrimination.

Enough examples of discrimination were uncovered so that the NAACP began demanding an explanation and began its own investigation. In an article written for the *Nation*, Walter White reported on his tour of the devastated area. He concluded that there was enough racial discrimination, forced labor, denial to blacks of the right of free movement, and the opportunity of selling their services to the highest bidder so "that, if persisted in, would recreate and crystallize a new slavery almost as miserable as the old."[17]

To respond to White's concerns, Hoover named a Colored Advisory Commission composed of sixteen prominent black men and two women. All names were proposed by Russa Moton and the commission was chaired by him. The appointment of Moton demonstrated that Hoover did not fully understand what was happening among African Americans. Moton, not quite the giant his predecessor Booker T. Washington had been, was, nevertheless, the most prominent African American of his day and very probably Hoover could not avoid working with him at some level. But Hoover did not realize that Moton's type of leadership involving carefully measured approaches to racial equality, and compromise with whites was waning. For example, on Moton's Commission there was not a single representative of the NAACP. The new African-American leadership under W. E. B. Du Bois and Walter White was rapidly becoming irritated with the leisurely pace in the improvement of black quality of life.

The rising black leadership was becoming more confrontational and less prone to compromise, more aggressive and less patient, more confident in the justice of the cause and less awed by white leadership, more skillful in using the media and less willing to "stand back." Thus, Hoover was caught in pressures from four sides: Moton representing the so-called "Tuskegee Machine"; Du Bois, representative of the NAACP; the white southern leadership, representing white supremacists; and progressive Republicans, who sought a greater measure of equity for blacks.

Surprisingly, despite the fact that the Moton Commission had been stacked with black conservatives, its report was more scathing in its criticism than had been expected. On June 13, Moton and his commission reported to Secretary of Commerce Hoover and to James L. Fieser, the director of Red Cross relief. The commission reported that many black refugees had been reluctant to talk to them for fear of beatings and other reprisals. Moton described the severity of the techniques of the mostly white National Guardsmen to keep the blacks in camp and to return them only to the plantations on which they had lived. The commission insisted that cots be provided for all refugees and that improvements be made in the way food, clothing, and other supplies are distributed. To ensure fair treatment of blacks, the commission urged that each camp form advisory committees and the appointment of at least two African Americans to the relief committee in each state. It is to Hoover's credit that he accepted the findings of the Moton Commission and sought earnestly to work with black leadership to ameliorate suffering.

Hoover developed a concept he thought would contribute to a solution to black vassalage. It became a model which he later drew upon to respond to the suffering growing out of the Great Depression of the 1930s. He was unsuccessful in both efforts.

Hoover envisioned the creation of a multi-million-dollar private land corporation to help blacks buy farms of their own. The corporation would be controlled and financed by Northern philanthropists and would begin its initial efforts with surplus Red Cross flood relief funds. It would buy land made idle by the flood and sell the land to sharecroppers of both races by making low-interest, long-term loans to them. Hoover imagined that before long tens of thousands of small, independent farms would be owned by landless whites and blacks. This was a breathtaking, indeed a revolutionary concept. Hoover estimated that an initial capital of $4.5 million would allow about 7,000 families to buy their own farms. As the independent farmers paid back their debts, the profits from interest could be used again and again to make new loans to other small would-be farm owners.

But Hoover shared his bold idea only with Russa Moton and a few others. Most of those who heard Hoover describe his plan were elated but were sworn not to release the details just yet. Moton, however, could scarcely contain himself, so great was his joy and so much confidence did he have in Hoover. In one or more speeches Moton began to hint at the resettlement plan. "I am not at liberty to give you details, but you will hear about it soon."[18] But Moton was wrong, blacks did not soon hear about the plan in any official sense and it died still-born.

Hoover had spoken prematurely. The Red Cross firmly informed the secretary that under no conditions would it release funds for the purpose of enabling blacks and other sharecroppers to buy farms of their own. The Red Cross viewed Hoover's visionary proposal as being outside the legitimate use of its funds. As the relief organization saw it, its task was solely to help those who were hurting and to do so within the existing equation between the races.

When Calvin Coolidge made his announcement that he did not choose to run for a third presidential term, Hoover became the front-runner for the nomination of the Republican Party. What opposition there was to his nomination from within the party dissipated because of Hoover's growing popularity ignited substantially by his perceived success in dealing with the great Mississippi flood relief. Hoover would do nothing to jeopardize his chances for the Republican nomination and his likely election as president of the United States. Under these circumstances he was not likely to take precipitous action that would erode his standing with conservative elements.

Conditions for flood refugees only seemed to worsen. A second report by the Moton Commission confirmed that discrimination in the distribution of Red Cross relief was unchanged. Hoover and the Red Cross, however, believed that for the 400,000 African Americans made homeless by the Great Flood, a great deal had been accomplished, even though Hoover's utopian vision of black families settled on farms of their own was never attempted. Moton and other black leaders did not disagree with this assessment, even though help for refugees was not all they thought it should have been. Moton did not voice his criticisms publicly and so helped ease Hoover's nomination and election.

In the 1920s, African Americans still had some clout in the Republican Party, or at least that segment of the party that traced its roots to Lincoln and Theodore Roosevelt. In some cities, blacks voted in a bloc strong enough to turn the tide in an election. Such was the case in Chicago, when in 1927 "Big Bill" Thompson won the election for mayor because of support from Al Capone and the city's growing African-American population. Although Hoover made no move to put his plan into action, lingering hopes that as president he might do so kept blacks voting

Republican. "The proposal that was to be the greatest boon for the Negro race since Emancipation lay waiting, and perhaps dying. Perhaps it was already dead."[19]

The Ku Klux Klan

In 1927, Clarence Darrow and Arthur Garfield Hays successfully defended Dr. Henry Sweet, a dentist, his brother, and eight other African Americans on the charge of murder. On September 8, 1924, Dr. Sweet and his wife and young baby moved into a home in Detroit. On September 9, a riotous mob stoned the house and a shot was fired and killed a white man in the street. All eleven blacks were arrested and charged with conspiracy to commit murder. A first trial of all the defendants together resulted in a hung jury. The defendants then chose to be tried separately and the State elected to try Henry Sweet first. Sweet was acquitted and in early 1928, the cases against the other defendants were dismissed. In his defense Darrow declared, "You know what this case is. You know why it is. You know that if white men had been fighting their way against colored men nobody would ever have dreamed of prosecution. And you know that from the beginning of this case to the end, up to the time you write your verdict, the prosecution is based on race prejudice and nothing else."[20]

In 1925, the Ku Klux Klan was at the height of its powers. With a membership of some 5,000,000, the Klan was able to muster 40,000 hooded Klansmen in a march on Washington, D.C. By 1927, however, the Klan had a membership of but 350,000. "Since 1927 . . . the Klan has appealed mostly to men on the bottom rung of the socioeconomic ladder, the kind least welcome in other fraternal orders. Men of any education and social respectability found Klan membership a handicap."[21]

From January 1, 1918, to January 1, 1927, American mobs lynched 454 persons. Thirty eight of these were white, 416 were African American, eleven were black women, three of whom were pregnant. Forty-two were burned alive, and the bodies of sixteen others were burned after death. Eight of the victims were beaten to death or cut to pieces.[22]

With the decline in Klan membership, lynchings also declined. By 1927, there were but eighteen lynchings in the United States, two of which were of whites and sixteen others of blacks. Even though one lynching is one too many, the NAACP, which had taken the lead in the campaign against lynching made note of the decline. But this is not to suggest that the year 1927 was free of racial conflict.

"Klansmen Riot in Queens," reported the *New York Times*. One thousand "knights" of the Klan and 400 of their women's auxiliary (Klavana) marched in white robes and hoods for four miles through the streets of Jamaica, Queens, to their reviewing stand. They were jeered and mocked by hostile crowds.

"Spectators from the 20,000 along the route of the Queens parade took sides. Women fought women and spectators fought the policemen and the Klansmen as their desire dictated. Combatants were knocked down, Klan banners were shredded, and at one point the Stars and Stripes, unwittingly, was trampled under foot."[23]

The Memorial Day parade in New York City was marked with tension as New York's finest sought to keep the Ku Klux Klan, African Americans, and Italian Fascists from confronting one another. Police clashes with the Klan continued sporadically throughout the day and the NYPD did manage to keep blacks in a tour bus bound for a picnic at Rockaway Beach safe from the Klansmen. The picnic-bound African Americans resented having their bus commandeered and they showed their displeasure. But no deaths took place that day in the police-Klan confrontation.

But violence that day did come from another source. Two Italians, endeavoring to catch up with their 400 black-shirted Fascist colleagues, were killed by an anti-Fascist group. Both men were war veterans. Joseph Carisi served with the American forces in France and Nicholas Amorosso with the Italian army. An Italian-American anti-fascist, Dr. Charles Fama, told the *New York Times* that the Black Shirts were taking orders from their leader in Rome, Benito Mussolini, and were opposed to "Americanism." He continued, "there is no reason why their propaganda should be spread in a Memorial Day parade."[24]

Despite dwindling national membership, Klan influences remained stronger in some states than in others. For example, the influence of the KKK remained strong in Alabama in 1927, making it, in the judgment of some, "the most completely Klan-controlled State in the Union. . . ."[25]

After the triumph of the Klan ticket in Alabama in 1927, its members felt free to indulge their eclectic hatred. Thus, a black woman was flogged and left to die; a white divorcee was punched into unconsciousness; a naturalized citizen was lashed for marrying a native-born woman, and a black man was beaten until he sold his land to a white man for less than it was worth.

One night in late June, Jeff Calloway, an illiterate orphan in his early twenties, was drunk in front of the Antioch Methodist Church, near Oneonta, some thirty miles from Birmingham, Alabama. A body of masked men emerged from the church, seized the young African American and whipped him mercilessly. He managed to find his way to a nearby house for the night and the next day his wounds were dressed by a doctor at Oneonta.[26] Under pressure from newspapers of Montgomery, Alabama, Governor Bibb Graves, an avowed Klansman, ordered his attorney general, also a Klansman, and law enforcement departments to find the culprits. At the trials of seven men charged with kidnapping and flogging Jeff Calloway, two defendants were found guilty and others entered pleas of guilty. Witnesses testified that the whipping of Calloway had been no casual or chance event but that the group was acting under official Klan orders. "In short, for perhaps the first time [the Klan] was caught red-handed."[27] The conviction of the first Klansman was considered so epochal an event in the life of Alabama that the newspaper, the *Age-Herald*, could compare it to the fall of the Bastille.[28]

In Aiken, South Carolina, three blacks, two men and one woman, the Lowmans, were accused of murder. They were hastily tried, convicted, and condemned. Their cases were taken up by a black lawyer from South Carolina, N. J. Frederick, who appealed to the Supreme Court of South Carolina which remanded the cases to the Circuit Court for trial. In the re-trial, upon a motion of Frederick, the judge directed a verdict of not guilty for one of the defendants. Probably the other two defendants would have likewise been found innocent. "But what happened? On that night a mob gathered and entered the jail through the connivance of the officers of the law and those two men and that woman were taken out and shot to death."[29] While the lives of the victims could not be saved, the NAACP took some solace from the fact that the *New York World* sent one of its outstanding correspondents to the scene of the crime so that the Aiken disgrace could be reported to the rest of the world.

In March 1927, when an African American was accused of attacking a white girl in Coffeeville, Kansas, whites told the black community that they intended to lynch the man and to march on the black section of town. Equipped with army rifles, tear-gas bombs, pistols, bayonets, and axes, the blacks left their section in company formation, dug small trenches at the entrance and stopped the white mob of 150 from seizing the suspect. Fighting broke out and continued for two days until three units of the National Guard arrived. Ten white men were killed and thirteen men and women were wounded.[30]

On June 13, two African American brothers, Jim and Mark Fox, accused of having slain their sawmill superintendent, were seized by a lynch mob, paraded through the streets of Louisville, Mississippi, and then doused with gasoline and burned to death at a telephone pole a short distance from town. A white would-be rescuer was seized and dragged away.

On November 30, Leonard Woods, a thirty-five-year-old black man, was lynched in Jenkins, Kentucky, by a Virginia mob of 400 men for allegedly murdering Hershel Deaton, a white foreman at a Kentucky mine. The mob broke into a rural Kentucky jail, placed a chain around Woods' neck and led him out into a courtyard, where a semi-circle of men shot him to death. The body was taken to the Virginia-Kentucky border where it was placed on a wooden platform, soaked in kerosene, and set on fire.

Also in May, a white mob in Little Rock, Arkansas, took John Carter, an eighteen-year-old black man convicted of slaying an eleven-year-old white girl, from the city jail, burned him, and dragged his body through the streets of the town. As a result of this violence thousands of blacks left town.[31]

On March 11, 1927, according to the *Chicago Defender*, Clarence Darrow was forced to flee Alabama after delivering speeches attacking lynching. At the Lyric Theater in a speech to the "best (white) people of the South," he declared that lynchings "are a disgrace to not only to the South but to the North and the entire United States." Suddenly there was a cry, "Lynch him!" When it became evident that the audience, now a mob, would not let him continue speaking, police with drawn weapons surrounded him and Mrs. Darrow and held the mob at bay.

In a speech at a school for an all-black audience, Darrow cautioned: "I can't help you. You will have to help yourselves. But I advise an attitude of defiance toward the white man who calls himself your 'friend.' How has he manifested his friendship? By hanging and burning you, by making you do his work and use his back door, refusing to let you enter the best hotels and use the best coach in the train, and making you sit in the rear of the street car. The only front place the white man has ever given you is in the battle line. There you can stop the bullets, but when you return home you can't use the sidewalks. . . ."[32]

In belated recognition of the evils of lynching, the Federal Council of Churches declared lynching an evil to be banished from America. February 12, Lincoln's Birthday, was dedicated as "Anti-Lynching Day." But it would take more than a prayer to curb the hate-filled hearts of the Ku Klux Klan. The KKK revival of the 1920s was a movement of hate—hate of blacks, Catholics, and Jews —but it was more. It was hate for modern America. The KKK outlook was one in opposition to both Darwin and Freud as these intellectuals were then understood or, more likely, misunderstood. Thus, the KKK disavowed such modern ideas as evolution, birth control, and education for women and minorities. They were threatened by industrial growth, alarmed at the perceived decline of the family farm, shocked by the permissive values of urban life, and resented the emerging role of women outside the home.

[1] *Boston Herald,* October 14, 1927. Quoted in Arthur M. Schlesinger, "Biography of a Nation of Joiners," *American Historical Review* 40 (October 1944): 20.

[2] Carter G. Woodson, "The Celebration of Negro History Week, 1927," *Journal of Negro History* 12 (April 1927): 103–105.

[3] Ibid., p. 109.

[4] George S. Schuyler, "Blessed Are the Sons of Ham," *Nation* 124 (March 23, 1927): 313.

[5] R. R. Moton, "Organized Negro Effort for Racial Progress," *Annals of the American Academy of Political and Social Science* 140 (November 1928): 263.

[6] Ibid.

[7] Ibid., p. 259.

[8] W. E. B. Du Bois, *The Souls of Black Folk* (New York: A. C. McClurg and Company, 1903), pp. 36–50.

[9] Du Bois, "Race Relations in the United States," *Annals of the American Academy of Political and Social Science* (November 1927): 7.

[10] Kelly Miller, "Government and the Negro," *Annals of the American Academy of Political and Social Science* (November 1927): 98-104.

[11] For more on the Mississippi Flood, see pp. 159–165.

[12] Donald J. Lisio, *Hoover, Blacks and Lily-Whites: A Study of Southern Strategies* (Chapel Hill: The University of North Carolina Press, 1985), p. 4.

[13] Ibid.

[14] "The Flood, the Red Cross and the National Guard: First Installment of an Investigation Made by the N.A.A.C.P. in May, 1927," *Crisis* (January 1928): 6-10.

[15] Ibid., p. 26.

[16] Ibid.

[17] Walter White, "The Negro and the Flood," *Nation* 124 (June 22, 1927): 689.

[18] Quoted in John M. Barry, *Rising Tide: The Great Mississippi Flood of 1927 and How It Changed America* (New York: Simon and Schuster, 1997), p. 385.

[19] Ibid., p. 393.

[20] Quoted in James Weldon Johnson, "Legal Aspects of the Negro Problem," *Annals of the American Academy of Political and Social Science* (November 1927): 94.

[21] William Peirce Randal, *The Ku Klux Klan: A Century of Infamy* (New York: Chilton Books, 1965), p. 224.

[22] Walter White, *Rope and Faggot* (New York: Alfred A. Knopf, 1929), pp. 34-35.

[23] *New York Times,* May 31, 1927.

[24] Ibid.

[25] Charles N. Feidelson, "Alabama's Super Government," *Nation* 125 (September 28, 1927): 311.

[26] Ibid., p. 312.

[27] Ibid.

[28] Ibid.

[29] Address of James Weldon Johnson before the Eighteenth Annual Conference of the National Association for the Advancement of Colored People. "Three Achievements and their Significance," *Crisis* 34 (September 1927): 222.

[30]Peter M. Bergman, *The Chronological History of the Negro in America* (New York: Harper and Row, 1969), p. 433.
[31]Ibid.
[32]Quoted in Ralph Ginzburg, *100 Years of Lynchings* (Baltimore: Black Classic Press, 1968), pp. 178-179.
[33]*New York Times,* October 29, 1927.

THE NEW WOMAN AND THE NEW MAN

7

July 4, 1927

In the summer White House in the Black Hills of South Dakota, President Calvin Coolidge, dressed in cowboy regalia, celebrated the Fourth of July and his own fifty-fifth birthday. A cowboy band played and a soloist serenaded: "We've come to say hello to you, our dear old friend Cal." Some two hundred journalists then enjoyed punch, ice cream, and a huge birthday cake.

In Paris, the transatlantic flight of Commander Richard E. Byrd and Clarence Chamberlin was celebrated at a dinner at the American Chamber of Commerce. In a radio address, Commander Byrd noted: "I want to say to America that if any American has doubt of France's high regard let him take a non-stop flight from America to France." Chamberlin modestly declared, "You may not believe it, but for me to give a short speech is harder than trying to fly the Atlantic." [1]

But as the Literary Digest *reported, in the United States the Fourth was "Not So 'Safe or Sane.'" The* Philadelphia Bulletin *wrote: "[I]t is too late to save the eyes of those who were blinded by fireworks, the skins of those who were burned, and the buildings that went up in smoke . . . the lesson of the wild and insane celebration just passed should not be forgotten another year."*

The New York Herald Tribune *reported that in New York City 300 people were injured from fireworks and there were 328 fire alarms, half of which were caused by fireworks. According to the National Museum of Safety, during the War for Independence, there were 4,044 American deaths. But in the years between 1895 and 1927, 4,500 Americans died in Independence Day Celebrations. "The god of patriotism does not demand human sacrifices on this day."* [2]

The historian Miriam Beard was encouraged that by 1927 women were springing "from allegory to life."[3] Tongue in cheek, she observed that heretofore the only women men admired were eight-feet tall, many tons overweight—the symbol for alma mater (while real women were kept off the campus)—or holding the scales of justice (while denying women the opportunity to serve on juries or become lawyers or according them equal protection of the law). "Man has protested," wrote Beard, "against the earning by modern woman of her own livelihood, yet for years he has placed her laurel-head on his dimes, quarters and fifty-cent pieces. He declared that her sphere was the home, but he put her out in the harbor, in public, as the Statue of Liberty."[4] But, Beard conceded, woman is moving from allegory to reality as she is doing the things which she once merely symbolized.

The Gibson Girl and the Flapper

In the 1890s the stereotypical young woman representing the ideal of femininity in the Gilded Age, was the large-breasted, well-rounded, somewhat plumpish

The New American Woman, from Ladies Home Journal, *November 1927.*

but tightly corseted Gibson girl as satirized for *Life*, a humorous weekly magazine, by Charles Dana Gibson. The Gibson Girl's hair was piled high on a patricianly small head; a slim neck and broad shoulders allowing vast expanses of décolletage, the carriage of a West Point cadet. She preferred an elaborate evening gown or the newly popular shirtwaist tucked into a straight skirt, the belted waistband of which showed her exquisitely small waist. The clothing of the Gibson Girl conveyed the message that her husband could support her well and so she did not have to work outside the home. The Gibson Girl's fashionable clothing testified to her husband's ability to support her. "For the Gibson Girl, grooming itself was her profession; to be her husband's prized possession was her career."[5]

The Gibson Girl took her cues in fashion and values from European royalty. She was the embodiment of women as bearers of children, makers of homes, devoted, affectionate, but obedient wives. She was taught to please men rather than herself. The ideals she embodied included innocence, dependence, helplessness, selflessness, goodness, and devotion to others. But these values encouraged ignorance of life's realities and downgraded the merits of education. Even in matters of childbearing and rearing, the Gibson Girl was aware of what was expected of her, but had little guidance in how to succeed at it. An anonymous feminist said that the average nineteenth century woman "contemplated sexual relations with the bitterest reluctance because she had to be sedulously guarded from knowledge of the fundamental reason of her being cast, suddenly and unprepared, into marriage." The Gibson Girl was solid, stable, a refuge in a storm; in short, the Gibson Girl was unflappable.

Unlike the Gibson Girl, the flapper was radiant, energetic, volatile, voluble, brazen. The Gibson Girl evoked the traditional moral code in America. That is, sex was in the background and women were subservient to the appetites of men and only reluctantly partook of sexual intercourse. The flapper flaunted her interest in sex and implied, at least, that she was available for sex for pleasure as well as for procreation.

What "modern" women sought to achieve was the abandonment of the double standard. If higher education was available to men, similar levels of education should be available to women. If men could choose careers in business and/or the professions, equal opportunities should be open to women. If men were free to stray sexually without criticism, women felt that such opportunity should be theirs as well.

The well-dressed flapper no longer took her cues from European royalty. Instead, she looked to Hollywood's movie stars. The flapper wore a tightly fitting felt cloche hat, two strings of beads, flesh colored hose rolled below the knees, bangles on her wrists, and unbuckled galoshes. She hid her breasts but wore kiss-proof lipstick as did Clara Bow in the 1927 movie "It."

Most symbolically, perhaps, was that the hemline of women's skirts rose from the ankle (1919) to above the knee (1927) "and was rightly taken as the index of the revolutionary change in morals and manners that accompanied and followed the war. . . ."[6] As the historian Will Durant noted, with a trace of sexism: "The short skirt is a boon to all the world except the tailors. What could be more delightful than the intriguing little movements with which the girl of 1927 pulls down her dress over her knees? Knees were once a luxury; now they are a necessity of the daily scene; no subway would be complete without them."[7]

Critics warned that when skirts rose above the knee and stockings were rolled below it, more naked flesh was immodestly revealed than at any time in history. The Young Women's Christian Association circulated a booklet called "Modesty Appeal" and urged women to dress more decorously. Fashion writers insisted that women had gone too far and should lower their skirts during the very next fashion season. Legislative bodies in Utah and Virginia sought to impose limits on hemlines and necklines but to no avail. Of these changes Carmel Snow, the fashion editor of *Vogue*, wrote: "Nobody ever again will think of clothes as designed for a creature who sits—she must walk about doing things. . . . [E]fficiency, simplicity, unity—these make for chic. And chic is the one thing sought by the modern woman when she thinks about clothes."[8]

As skirts were shortened, so too did women jettison encumbering petticoats and corsets. A survey in Milwaukee in 1927 of thirteen hundred working girls showed that fewer than seventy wore corsets. Silk or rayon stockings became almost universal and in hot and humid weather many women wore no stockings at all. Dress sleeves were shortened and in some cases vanished altogether.

Hair was worn short and long tresses were out. The "boyish bob" became the vogue and the barbershop, still a bastion for an all male environment, fell to women who found the barber more efficient than the hair stylist.

Seventy-three percent of women of the United States over eighteen years of age used perfume; 90 percent face powder; 73 percent toilet water; 50 percent rouge. In 1927, 7,000 kinds of cosmetics were on the market. The perfume and cosmetics industries, including lipsticks, talcum powder, hair tonics, and hair dyes, had grown six times what it was in 1917.[9] "Fortunes were made in mud baths . . . in patent hair removers, in magic lotions to make the eyelashes long and sweeping, in soaps that claimed to nourish the skin, in hair dyes that restored the natural color, in patent nostrums for 'reducing' and in all the other half-fraudulent traps of the advertisers for the beauty seeker."[10]

As eroticism shifted from the breasts (Gibson Girl) to the limbs (Flapper), the latter's costume also heralded a shift from women as wives and homemakers to competitors of men in business. Flappers' fashion made it possible for women to move around in the world of business, albeit at the lower rungs, as secretaries, stenographers, and telephone operators. The dress and grooming of the flapper not only enhanced sexuality but was efficient for work in an office and for businesslike activities with male and female peers. Black and beige were the preferred colors for the flapper as emerging businesswoman as well as coquette. The flapper, in short, wanted it all.

Some women began smoking in public. They "reach[ed] for a Lucky instead of a sweet!" and unhesitatingly entered speakeasies and consumed illicit alcohol. While data are hard to come by, researchers found that women born later than the turn of the century were twice as likely to have lost their virginity before they were married than women of the previous generation. College coeds generally made do with heavy breathing from necking and petting but a few went "all the way." Extra-marital sex also became more common. Possibly because of the relatively ready availability of sex from otherwise respectable women, a great many brothels lost their customers, as did street-walking prostitutes.

"I've kissed dozens of men," declared one of F. Scott Fitzgerald's heroines. "I suppose I'll kiss dozens more." Innocent, perhaps, by today's standards, the intent of the declaration was to shock the older generation—and shock it did. Petting in the back seats of enclosed automobiles, dating without a chaperone, dancing the latest craze, the Charleston, drinking illegal whiskey, defying adult authority and the traditions of the Judeo-Christian faiths, making heroes of hoodlums: the affluent youth of America, if not the immigrant poor, at least for a time succeeded in rewriting the rules of behavior and decorum. One writer, describing conditions in 1927, had this to say: "What a gulf separates even two generations! Mothers and daughters often understand each other's viewpoints so little that it seems as though they [aren't] speaking the same language." He goes on to note: "Changes are occurring throughout our whole social system. The education of youth in school and college changes from year to year. . . . Religion is no longer the unchanging rock of ages. . . . The family is becoming smaller. . . . Young people are marrying earlier and getting divorces more frequently. Restaurants and hotels are increasing rapidly in number, and apartments are becoming smaller. More and more women are working for pay outside the home. . . . And most perplexing seems to be our changing morality itself, for the detailed application of moral codes gives very uncertain advice on the new problems of conduct. . . ."[11]

From her abode in Paris, Gertrude Stein described the gifted young writers of her day as the "Lost Generation." Before long, her description was applied to the flapper era more generally. Perhaps Stein overstated the case, but the dominant mood in America appeared to be not so much that tomorrow would take care of itself but instead—who cares? The theme was best exemplified by Edna St. Vincent Millay:

My candle burns at both ends;
It will not last the night;
But, ah, my foes, and, oh, my friends —
It gives a lovely light.

Not only were women emancipated from the conventional morality, they were emancipated from the kitchen as well. A visit to an urban American home would have found a small, compact rather than roomy kitchen that was often so central to the rural home. An electric refrigerator took the place of the cool cellar. Nor was it necessary to store large amounts of food, since convenience stores were growing in number, in location, and in the variety of food in small quantities that could be bought.

In 1912, only 16 percent of Americans lived in dwellings provided with electric light. By 1927, 63 percent had electric lights. Household appliances were growing so numerous that 80 percent of the electrically wired homes had electric irons, 37 percent had vacuum cleaners, and more than 25 percent had clothes washers, fans, or toasters. Clean oil heating equipment began replacing the dirty coal furnace. In 1927, 100,000 American homes had oil furnaces and by 1928 the total of oil heaters in use in American homes was not less than 550,000 without counting those installed in stores, theaters, hotels, and public buildings. In view of the wide array of mechanical servants now available, the census would have done well to cease listing the American housewife as of "no occupation" and instead describe her as "household engineer."[12]

The era of the flapper, though not her influence, was short-lived. By 1927, the flapper as an American female type was on the way out.

The New Woman:
Flapper No More

The new woman of 1927 was neither feminist nor flapper but was indebted to both. The flapper opened wide the window of opportunity by attacking the double standard in American morality. She saw nothing wrong with smoking a cigarette, visiting a speakeasy for a drink of illegal spirits, or interpreting Freud as to allowing her to enjoy the pleasure of sex. For the most part the flapper was a product of the growing urban environment in which most Americans lived.

The new woman recognizes that the flapper is but a stereotype described by F. Scott Fitzgerald as "lovely and expensive and about nineteen," but is not entirely prepared to flaunt convention. The new woman admires the feminist for her courage but is uncomfortable with her zealotry. She honors the feminist for fighting her battle but believes the worst of the battle is over and that, therefore, it is not necessary to bear a grudge against men and that it is no longer necessary to throw hand grenades. The new woman concedes that a husband and children are necessary to the average woman's fullest development but believes with equal vigor that a career does not preclude motherhood. The new woman seeks happiness within marriage but without the stifling limitations customarily placed upon her. She expects marriage to be a monogamous partnership of equals in which both she and her husband shun promiscuity.

Advertisements in such magazines as the *Ladies Home Journal* for 1927 began to appeal to the new woman. "You think I'm a flapper but I can keep house," announced an ad for S.O.S., that "magic cleaner" of pots and pans. The advertisement continued, "If we get married, I'll keep house better than mother does hers. But I'm not going to turn into a slave. You men! You think drudgery is a sign of good housekeeping." The new woman never had to fear "dishpan hands" if she just used Lux soap. A "clean dazzling smile," Colgate noted, was women's "social weapon." Products for feminine hygiene, for undergarments, for hosiery, boldly appealed to the new woman.

Prominent women were called on to endorse products of various kinds. In the December 1927 issue of the *Ladies Home Journal*, Eleanor Roosevelt, whose husband, Franklin, was about to run for governor of New York State, endorsed the Simmons Beautyrest mattress. "The perfect gift," she called it. In another part of the advertisement she declared that it was "the most marvelous mattress in the world" and announced that she has one in her own bedroom "in our home in New York." Even automobile ads began appealing to the new woman. Thus Chrysler boasted that its automobiles anticipated "all that woman wants in a modern automobile."

By 1927 the new woman was still a work in progress. It was not what she had achieved, but she was able to dream of possibilities once believed altogether closed to her. While she had not arrived, she was free to experiment. She could experiment by trying to find the best means of squaring career with children, gaining an education while caring for husband and family, making a home for those she loved while not being enslaved to them either. Far from irresponsible, women approached their next steps with great seriousness of intent and purpose.

Although women had won the right to vote in 1920 when the Nineteenth Amendment was adopted, by the election of 1928 they did not vote with the discipline and in the numbers required to make them a formidable political factor. Yet political life was beginning to beckon. By 1928, seven women were in the Congress, 119 had been elected in 1928 as state representatives, and twelve were state senators.

Thus, at least one article conjectured, "Have We (Women) a Presidential Possibility?" After pointing out that in the 1870s the nominations of Belva Lockwood and Victoria Claffin Woodhull Martin had been viewed largely with amusement, the idea that the White House might one day have a woman in it was a thought no longer entirely derided. The author Ida Clyde Clarke admitted that while a woman president was no longer unthinkable, women of presidential character seemed relatively scarce. "Among the increasing number of women holding public office, none so far, had achieved such national popularity as would sweep her into the White House."[13]

Clarke went on to consider the feasibility of a number of prominent women who might aspire to the presidency. The first was the feminist leader Carrie Chapman Catt, the successor to the venerable Susan B. Anthony as president of the American Suffrage Association. But Clarke was doubtful that women fully appreciated her work, or that they would have united behind her candidacy. She saw three women as viable candidates: Anne Morgan, Alice Roosevelt Longworth, the "best informed American woman"; and Ruth Hanna McCormick—in the opinion of the author, the best presidential candidate.

McCormick, the daughter of Mark Hanna (once chairman of the Republican Party and the Svengali behind the election of William McKinley) and widow of Senator Medill McCormick of Chicago, had inherited political instincts. "I am a professional lobbyist, a ward-heeler, a favor-seeker, an office-seeker, and I hope something of a precinct boss."[14] She had already expressed an interest in the governorship of Illinois and a United States Senatorship. Her ambitions, she told Clarke, were not in appointive office but "to be elected in a fair fight on a clean-cut issue."[15]

While Ruth McCormick may be thought of as an example of the new political woman, the year 1927 was one in which new women emerged in a variety of fields.

• The aviator Blanche Hill, at the age of twenty-five, founded the Avion Corporation with John K. Northrup. It was this company that built the first all-metal aircraft.

• Twenty-one-year-old Louise Thaden won the first Woman's Air Derby. Within the decade her reputation as an aviator rivaled that of Amelia Earhart.

• Bryn Mawr professor Anna Wheeler was to be the first female mathematician honored by the American Mathematical Society.

• Marion Talbot, retired dean of the University of Chicago, served the first of two terms as acting president of Constantinople Woman's College.

• Lorena Hickok, a political reporter and editor of the *Minneapolis Tribune*, became a political reporter for the Associated Press. In this capacity, she developed a close relationship with Eleanor Roosevelt and later left the Associated Press for fear of being unable to report objectively on the administration of President Franklin Roosevelt.

• Journalist Dorothy Day, a pacifist in World War I, worked for such left-wing publications as the *Call* and the *Masses* but surprised her friends by becoming a Catholic. She agitated for peace and socialism through the Vietnam War. In 2000 Dorothy Day was proposed by the Vatican as a possible candidate for sainthood in the Roman Catholic Church.

• Elsie Eaves became the first woman associate member of the American Society of Civil Engineers.

• Phoebe F. Omlie was the first woman to receive a commercial pilot's license issued by the U.S. Department of Commerce.

• Ethel Waters became popular with all-white audiences as star of *Africana*, a Broadway show featuring jazz and blues music.

Despite these achievements, feminists, having won the franchise, now sought to have an equal rights amendment added to the constitution. Edna Kenton, after describing the pomp and dignity accorded to newly elected Governor Miriam A. Ferguson, the first woman governor of Texas, pointed out that a month before Ferguson had to petition the District Court of Bell County, Texas, to remove the disqualifications that might arise from her status as a married woman. According to Texas law, she first had to get her husband's permission to petition the court to have those disqualifications removed. Failure to proceed in this way might have invalidated such contracts that the governor might have signed in behalf of Texas, since a married woman in Texas was "but a living shadow, not of herself, but her husband—and, like a shadow, incapable of contracting or otherwise acting on her own responsibility."[16]

What was true in Texas was likewise true in other states of the nation. In Virginia and Rhode Island the father was the sole natural guardian of minor children with primary right to custody, control of their education, religion, and general welfare. In Alabama the father had preference as guardian of the child's property, and, in New York and Michigan, the father was entitled to the services and earnings of a minor child. The father's consent alone was sufficient to authorize the apprenticing of a child in Colorado, and the father alone was entitled to damages for the wrongful death of a minor child in the District of Columbia. In Massachusetts the father had first right to sue for damages for the seduction of a daughter, and the father had the right to will away the child from the mother in Georgia and Maryland. In the majority of the states the services of a wife in the home belonged to the husband. Thus, the right to vote did not also confer on married women equal rights with their husbands.

On December 2, 1923, the National Women's Party proposed to the judiciary committees of both houses of Congress a constitutional amendment which read, "Men and women shall have equal rights throughout the United States and every place subject to its jurisdiction." On July 13, 1927, a delegation from the National Woman's Party arrived at the summer White House in Rapid City, South Dakota, to enlist the support of President Calvin Coolidge for the Equal Rights Amendment.

But many "new women" were opposed to the Equal Rights Amendment. The League of Women's Voters felt that such a blanket amendment to the Constitution would be "self-defeating" and much of the protective legislation adopted in women's behalf would be withdrawn. What would happen to the minimum wage for women, to the statutory eight-hour day law for women, or to the guarantee of one day of rest? What would happen to protections afforded working, pregnant women, and what of penalties for rape? Some women feared the proposed Equal Rights Amendment would require a wife to support an incompetent husband. That kind of equality was not desired by all women.[17]

In February 1927, Margaret Culkin Banning lamented that women of thirty or forty "are younger than women of that age have ever been before, more confident of retaining their beauty, less burdened by housewifery, and better educated; and surely they are offered a more highly spiced and savory world than there has heretofore been spread before their sex, at least."[18] The author complained that these thirty-something women who could now vote had not fought for it. Not only did they take their vote for granted but they were using it ineffectually and sometimes not at all. Often they had to be shamed into casting their ballot. These women in their thirties share in common an "inertia" and demonstrated an "utter lack of response to the battle cries that used to get women into action."[19] The new woman, according to Banning, for all her accomplishments, was simply lazy.

For professional women, prejudice and opportunity existed side by side. In law, prejudice in employment persisted as most people preferred to seek legal advice

Margaret Bondfield (1873–1953), England's Minister of Labour and the first woman to be in the British cabinet, exemplified for many the New Woman of the day. Credit: Hulton Getty Picture Library/Archive Photos.

from men. In medicine, discrimination against women was flagrant. In higher education, of 4,700 full professorships, women held but four percent and served mainly in lower instructional ranks at lower salaries than men in the same rank. Yet the report from which these data were drawn concludes, "But a *coup d'oeil* over the path of sixty years of education development, should convince the most pessimistic that the progress made by women in the direction of equality of opportunity to learn and to achieve, is far greater and more significant than the inequities that still remain to be righted."[20]

If newspaper headlines are any yardstick, the emergence of the "new woman" continued to be viewed apprehensively by many Americans, women as well as men:

• "End of Monogamy Seen in Feminism." Professor William Montague of Barnard College predicted that feminism might eventually lead to the abolition of monogamy as we know it today.[21]

• "Finds College Girl as Good as Ever." Except that "golly," "darn," and "devil" punctuate her vocabulary, the Dean of Women at Cornell believed that the college girl of today is no worse than her predecessors.[22]

• "Women Inferior, Asserts Mussolini." They cannot create, they should never be taken seriously, but are a "Pleasant Parenthesis of Life."[23]

• "Modern Life Lessens Sex Fixity." According to Dr. Oscar Riddle of the Carnegie Institution of Washington, modern life may make women "grow less womanly and men less masculine."[24]

• "Governor [Alfred E.] Smith Yields to Feminism Trend," by making the same speech to girls graduating from high school as he did to boys graduating ten years ago.[25]

• "Would Have Girls Talk More Politics," declared Eleanor Roosevelt at a speech at the "good citizenship" session of directors and supervisors of vocational education in New York State.[26]

• "See Peril to Race in Birth Control." Eugenicists strove to show that birth control practiced by the more intelligent was dangerous, and that lack of birth control among the "inferior" groups of the population was also a danger to the race.[27]

• "Woman's Brain Not Inferior to Men's." Research scientists substantiated the life-long contention of Helen H. Gardener, a feminist who willed her brain to Cornell University, that women's brains are equal to men's.[28]

Margaret Sanger and the Birth Control Movement

Birth control, a term coined by Margaret Sanger, while widely practiced by affluent and educated Americans, was still neither generally known nor practiced by the impoverished. Catholic priests continued to thunder against birth control and the faithful were often torn between what they viewed as their obligation to their church and the physical demands of the body. It was Margaret Sanger's mission to extend knowledge of birth control to the many and by the time she died she had largely succeeded.

Margaret Sanger (1883–1966) was the sixth of eleven children born in Corning, New York, to Michael Hennesy Higgins, a rather rebellious, red-headed Irish sculptor. Margaret was seventeen when her mother, exhausted by poverty and excessive child-bearing, died. Despite the fact that the burden of caring for her siblings fell largely on her, with family encouragement she became a nurse. In the hospitals in which she served she learned that the greatest plague affecting women was giving birth to far too many children. She saw firsthand what repeated child-bearing did to the health of still comparatively young women, and the impact of having more children than they could possibly support on the quality of their family life. In her *Autobiography* she wrote, "In the hospital I found that seventy-five percent of the diseases of men and women are the result of ignorance of their sex functions. . . . So great was the ignorance of women and girls I met concerning their own bodies that I decided to specialize in women's diseases and took up gynecological and obstetrical nursing. . . . A few years of this work brought me to a shocking discovery—that knowledge of the ways of controlling birth was accessible to the women of wealth while the working women were deliberately kept in ignorance of this knowledge."

Margaret Higgins married William Sanger, an architect, and had three children. The family moved in a circle of radical intellectuals inclined toward socialism and anarchism. Among the inspirational leaders of this group were Eugene Debs, Ida Tarbell, Lincoln Steffens, and "Big Bill" Haywood of the International Workers of the World. It was Haywood who suggested that Margaret go to France where birth control was widely acknowledged and equally widely practiced. In France, Margaret Sanger studied methods of birth control while her husband studied painting. By 1914, she felt she had learned all that she needed to know in France and, leaving her husband behind, she returned with her children to the United States.

One of Sanger's biographers provides a striking description of her at about this period in her life. "Her green eyes were flecked with amber, her hair a shiny auburn hue, her smile always warm and charming, her hands perpetually in motion, beckoning even to strangers. . . . She had a quick Irish wit, high spirits, and radiant common sense. Men adored her."[29] And she was glad to leave William Sanger behind in Europe while she pursued her mission and men pur-

Margaret B. Sanger surrounded by supporters. Reproduced from the collections of the Library of Congress.

sued her. She divorced Sanger and married J. Noah H. Slee, a wealthy business-man.

She became editor of the *Woman Rebel*, a journal devoted to left-wing causes, but she also used the journal as a means of disseminating important information about birth control. It was at this juncture that she ran headlong into her neme-sis, Anthony Comstock (1844–1915), a crusader against vice, pornography, gam-bling, and obscene materials. He was instrumental in securing the passage of postal laws prohibiting obscene materials sent through the mails. Information about birth control was viewed as obscene and so could neither be sent through the mails nor otherwise distributed. As the secretary of the New York Society for the Suppression of Vice, Comstock's harassment of Margaret Sanger continued unabated until his death in 1915. Yet, his legacy of opposition to the dissemina-tion of birth control materials remained formidable throughout her pioneering years.

Sanger opened America's first birth control clinic at 46 Amboy Street, an immigrant neighborhood in Brooklyn, New York. In her *Autobiography* she wrote: "The morning of October 16, 1916—crisp but sunny and bright after days of rain—I opened the doors of the first birth control clinic in America."[30] But would the women come? It was not long before she found out. "Halfway to the corner they were standing in line, at least one hundred and fifty, some shawled, some hatless, their red hands clasping the cold, chapped, smaller ones of their children."[31]

Sanger's fight for reproductive rights for women had only just begun. The New York City police department's vice squad, a unit accustomed to raiding gambling dens and brothels, soon raided her clinic. Sanger was arrested for the first of nine times during the course of her crusade for birth control. But despite imprisonment, opposition from organized medicine, religion, and the press, and even ridicule from those she was trying to help, Sanger would not be deterred. In 1921, Margaret Sanger founded the American Birth Control League (ABCL). The ABCL became Margaret Sanger's platform for projecting her ideas.

In 1927, women members of ABCL were likely to be members of the American Association of University Women or the American Red Cross, while men were often members of such fraternal organizations as Kiwanis or Rotary. The 7,800 members of the organization were predominantly Protestant and middle to upper-middle class. Large numbers of them came from small towns. The group lasted until 1938, but by 1927 it had become truly national in scope and was at the zenith of its influence.[32]

By 1927, when birth control had developed enough momentum, Margaret Sanger organized the first World Population Conference in Geneva. The conference brought together for the first time doctors and social scientists who were concerned with worldwide overpopulation. In her preface to the *Proceedings of the World Population Conference*, Sanger wrote: "It has long been my desire to have the population question discussed from an international scientific standpoint, and it is with a feeling of some satisfaction that I am at last able to present to the public so complete and comprehensive a volume on this great question. . . ."[33]

Yet among the participants of the conference Margaret Sanger was a prophet without honor. The august scientists present did not relish having their names associated with a woman, much less a politically radical woman, and worse still, a woman whose scientific credentials could not match their own. (She was, after all, only a nurse!) Conference chairman Sir Bernard Mallet, under pressure from these scholars, agreed to remove the names of "all the workers" including that of Margaret Sanger, from the program. Uncharacteristically, so great was Margaret Sanger's wish to have the conference go forward that she humbly agreed to swallow her pride and acquiesce. In the *Proceedings of the Conference*, however,

Margaret Sanger was given credit for her initiative in launching the first serious study of population. An important by-product of the conference was the creation of the International Union for the Scientific Study of Population. Thus, between the growing vitality of the ABCL at home and the First Geneva Population Conference abroad, the year 1927 was an especially important one in the birth control movement.[34]

"Margaret Sanger," wrote her friend Mable Dodge Luhan, "was the first person I ever knew who was openly an ardent propagandist for the joys of the flesh." Mrs. Luhan wrote that to Margaret Sanger maturity meant "enjoying it (sex) with a conscious attainment of its possibilities."[35] By removing the fear of pregnancy, women could attain at least the same level of enjoyment through sexual intercourse as their male partners. In her book *Woman and the New Race*, Sanger wrote that women should break out of their repressive mentality and welcome sex as "the greatest possible expression and fulfillment of their desires. . . . This is one of the great functions of contraceptives."[36] Despite noteworthy advances in the birth control movement made in 1927, respectability, however, continued to elude Sanger as she could find little enduring support from the medical establishment, the eugenics movement or the feminist movement.

"Let Jake sleep on the roof," was the advice most doctors in 1927 were still giving women who sought to limit their pregnancies. As a nurse, Margaret Sanger understood well enough the need for physicians to become deeply involved in the birth control movement. But doctors were wary of her. Partly because she was a sexually liberated woman and a political radical who resorted to civil disobedience and willingly went to jail if need be, Sanger was not the kind of person with whom conventional and conservative doctors felt comfortable. Because she was not a physician, the membership of the American Medical Association kept their distance, some even going so far as to refer to birth control as medical quackery. As late as 1925 Dr. Morris Fishbein, editor of the *Journal of the American Medical Association*, asserted that there were no safe and effective birth control methods.[37] And Dr. Halliday Sutherland insisted, "The practice of contraception . . . is unnatural in terms of ethics and unphysiological in terms of biology. . . . It is in the same character as murder and sexual perversion. . . . Contraception," he continued, "is unphysiological because . . . it inhibits far-reaching physiological processes which result from normal intercourse, by reason of the absorption of certain vital substances which have a beneficial influence on the metabolism and health of the female."[38] Because there were no absolutely fool-proof methods of birth control, doctors felt free to attack the philosophy of contraception as well as its techniques, thus masking their sexism and intolerance of progressive political movements. Some physicians, on the other hand, deeply felt that not only were birth control techniques injurious to women's health, but with the removal of the ever-present possibility of pregnancy, birth control was injurious to the morals of women. Some physicians did take a middle road in that they willingly recommended contraceptive devices for women when, in their judgment, the health of their female patient was threatened. Yet, this was a strikingly hypocritical position for physicians to take. Affluent patients could be persuasive with compliant doctors who found some vague medical reason a convenient cover for providing contraceptives.

Margaret Sanger's wealthy second husband, Noah Slee, often supported his wife's efforts in dispensing birth control information and in making contraception an accepted aid in family planning and in women's health. Slee paid $10,000 annually to Dr. James F. Cooper to speak to groups of doctors on behalf of the ABCL. Because of Dr. Cooper's prestige as a physician he was often, but by no means always, attentively listened to by his medical audience.

Slee provided further help to the birth control movement. The Clinical Research Bureau, the research arm of the ABCL, discovered that the most effective means of contraception was a combination of a spermicidal jelly and a diaphragm. Sanger found the best spermicidal jelly in Germany and was soon able to have it duplicated in the United States. However, in the United States manufacturers were making a rather unsatisfactory cervical cap and the importation of the better diaphragm was illegal. Borrowing a page from the prevailing techniques of bootlegging whiskey, Noah Slee "bootlegged" better diaphragms from Germany to his Three-in-One Oil Plant in Montreal. From there, the illicit contraceptives crossed the Canadian border in oil drums. By 1925, an American firm agreed to manufacture the preferred diaphragm and the illegal traffic in contraceptives was suspended.[39]

That Margaret Sanger favored legislation to give licensed physicians exclusive authority to recommend birth control likewise whittled away at medical opposition. In 1925, endorsement of birth control by distinguished physicians at the International Birth Control Conference held in New York City shamed the president of the American Medical Association into doing likewise.[40]

Sanger's willingness to turn birth control over to the medical profession was more apparent than real. She was reluctant to give up control of a movement to which she had given her life and for which she had gone to jail. Moreover, she was certain that physicians would never use birth control as a means of liberating women as well as men from stifling sexual inhibitions. Sanger's reluctance forced her to look for other allies before capitulating altogether to the doctors.

For a time, she found such allies among doctors and other scientists who advocated eugenics as a means of improving the condition of the human race. Eugenics, a term coined by Sir Francis Galton in 1883, was a movement popular in the 1920s. Its advocates sought to encourage offspring among the physically and mentally alert segments of the population and to limit procreation among the genetically disabled or mentally retarded, the chronically ill, or the chronically criminal, mentally impaired, or impoverished. In America, during the 1920s the movement to control immigration as a threat to the "American race" was largely endorsed by eugenicists. Sanger, in her eagerness to get allies for the birth control movement, embraced the eugenics concept of selective breeding. More than once she spoke of how the improvement of the race could not be achieved without the widespread use of contraceptives to weed out those whose genetic dispositions doomed them and their progeny to crime, poverty, and squalor.

But Sanger and the eugenicists were uncomfortable bedfellows. Eugenicists tended to be politically conservative; Sanger was a political radical. While Sanger wanted birth control as a means of giving women control over their bodies, eugenicists viewed breeding as the primary, even the exclusive role of women. Most eugenicists felt that nothing short of sterilization would improve the "racial stock," and so they were opposed to birth control. Others looked upon contraception as compromise between sterilization on the one hand and unselective breeding on the other. During the decade of the 1920s, Sanger's views became more virulently racist in character. But the eugenics movement faded as it became tarnished with Nazism. Moreover, as birth control became more widespread, eugenics was replaced by family planning: wives and husbands would now agree on how many children to have, how many they could support, how to space them, and how to plan for safe delivery and the care of newborns.

While feminists of her day sought to encourage women to compete on equal terms in a man's world, Sanger held that women would exert more influence in their own sphere of home, hearth, and children. In propagating these views, she alienated feminists who, while accepting the need for contraception, refused to acknowledge that the best place for women was still in the home. She likewise alienated the moralists of her day who were convinced that sex was only for procreation.

In 1922, Katherine Benent Davis published the first statistical study of the use of contraceptives in the United States. She found that among the thousand married women interviewed, mostly college graduates or members of women's clubs, nearly 75 percent reported the use of contraceptives. And Robert and Helen Lynd, in their book *Middletown: A Study in American Culture*, found: "The behavior of the community in this matter of the voluntary limitation of parenthood presents the appearance of a pyramid. At the top, among most of the business group, the use of relatively efficacious contraceptive methods appears practically universal, while sloping down from this peak is a mixed array of knowledge and ignorance, until the base of ignorance is reached."[41]

Although birth control was widely practiced among the well-to-do and educated, it was not a subject many liked to talk about. Magazines often refused to take articles on the subject and radio was even more adamant in keeping public discussion of contraception off the air. Feminist groups likewise were reluctant to be associated with the birth control movement even as their members practiced it. Thus, the National Woman's Party in its 1927 platform refused to include a plank endorsing birth control for fear of splitting its membership and alienating supporters.

Ambivalence about what they were doing was widespread even among those who regularly resorted to contraceptives. On the one hand, they justified resorting to birth control as an important means of insuring the health of women and as a means of rearing fewer but better cared-for children. In the aftermath of World War I, it was taken as an axiom that if global population could be controlled, an important cause of war would be eliminated. But if married couples could engage in sexual intercourse without the responsibility of caring for children nine months later, what then would keep such marriages on a moral course? What would prevent the non-married from coupling promiscuously and what would that mean for the morality of Americans? What would happen to the American family? Charlotte Perkins Gilman, for example, in an essay written for the *North American Review*, worried that widespread use of contraceptives would lead to "a degree of sex indulgence without parallel in nature. . . ." Yet, she acknowledge that physicians were slowly accepting contraception as they see at first hand what the exhaustion of childbearing can do to the health of women. She acknowledged that economists liked birth control as a means of bringing population growth in line with available food supply. Eugenicists, she pointed out, likewise saw value in birth control as a means of bringing about a higher standard of offspring and a better quality of life for them. She concludes her essay, "Perhaps since birth is women's business it is right that she have some voice in discussing its control. . . . Mrs. Sanger's appeal for the overburdened mother is a just one; it is enough to warrant prompt action, to justify birth control; but there is more to be considered." What more is to be considered? How should a woman square her "duty to have children" with her right to decide "when, where and how many" to have? She conceded that the answer to this question "is not plain to most of us." She worried that "popular knowledge of preventive methods" would, in a "sex crazy" nation, lead to selfishness and indulgence, and that "rational continence" when necessary would become a value unknown.[42] In view of these doubts and contradictions, whither the American family in 1927?

Marriage and Divorce

In 1927, during the waning hours of its 1926 session, the Nevada state legislature hastily passed a law requiring but a three-month residency (instead of the six months previously required) to obtain a divorce. The more lenient requirement was quickly signed by the governor "before partaking of his grapefruit, toast and coffee thus assuring that his state would not lose the revenue from one of its chief industries." By reducing residence requirements for a divorce, Nevada was assuring that it would continue "catering to men and women who considered their better halves to be millstones about their necks." Nevada lawyers would have clients, cabarets would have patrons, shops would have customers, hotels would have guests.[43] By so doing Reno, Nevada, beat competition from Paris and Mexico to remain the divorce capital of the world.

But the hasty passage of legislation was criticized both within the state and throughout much of the nation, reflecting national concern about the stability of the family and the weakening of the marriage bond. In its January 8, 1927, issue the *Literary Digest* expressed concern about rising divorce rates. And in its December 3, 1927 issue it again expressed worry over the divorce rate. The *New York Times Magazine* for Sunday, December 18, 1927, ran a lead article by the distinguished sociologist W. F. Ogburn with the title, "Divorce: a Menace that Grows."

In 1926, Ogburn reported, 186,868 divorces were granted, ten divorces for every fifty-six marriages, a larger number than in any year in the previous half century. "More than one in six marriages of 1924-1926 will actually end in divorce in the next two generations. . . . If during the next half century the same rate of increase continues as in the last half century, then approximately one out of each thirty couples will be getting a divorce every year."[44]

There were more divorces, Ogburn noted, in urban areas than in rural ones, and more divorces granted in prosperous times than in depression, but causes for the growing rate of divorce, he conceded, were difficult to identify.

The ballot gave women the potential to wield political power. Growing use of contraceptives gave women the potential to control their own bodies. And divorce gave women the opportunity to get out of unsatisfactory marriages. While many feminists found sex degrading and destined to keep woman under male bondage, the sexual revolution of the 1920s contributed to making women equal partners within the home while fighting for equality outside it.

In 1927, Judge Ben Lindsey of the Denver family court noted that these tendencies led to the de facto existence of marriages that lasted merely for a term of years. Lindsey became convinced that conventional marriage no longer squared with the emerging realities between the sexes and the increasing necessity, if not always desire, for women to work outside the home. For him, companionate marriage was the route to take. Lindsey defined companionate marriage "as legal marriage with legalized birth control and the right to divorce with mutual consent for childless couples usually without payment of alimony."[45] The companionate marriage, the judge insisted was not "trial marriage." Since divorce would be by mutual consent, separation would not be easy. The government would augment the legal system with a House of Human Welfare, which the judge explained, would be staffed by specialists and would provide guidance in human behavior, sex and marital relationships. Nor, said Judge Lindsey, do "I propose two kinds of marriage. . . . [Rather] it would be the same marriage that at different stages may be 'Companionate.' At another time the same marriage may be 'Procreative. . . .'"[46]

Companionate marriage never caught on, but men and women continued to marry and continued, some of them, to get divorced. In an attempt to stem the tide of divorce, many states adopted waiting periods before matrimony. But such waiting periods were not especially successful. When in July 1927 a new California law was instituted requiring a wait of three days before marriage, ardent young couples swiftly took marital vows in Arizona or Nevada where the waiting period was not so severe.

For the nation as a whole, the most common age of marriage was twenty-five for a man and about twenty-two for a woman. Increased use of contraception helped keep illegitimate births relatively few in number and the relative ease of divorce tended to encourage marriage.

A sex manual in 1927, written to provide greater sexual satisfaction within marriage, gave specific instruction in sexual positions and in oral sex. As if in response to initiatives women were beginning to take in many fields of endeavor, the manual advised married women that in sexual matters "a certain feminine initiative and aggression brings a refreshing variety. Let her be the wooer sometimes, not always the wooed. She can be so while quite retaining her distinctive dignity and sweetness. This role of wooer can express her love in very desirable

ways and be intensely gratifying to the husband who feels that he not only feels
desire but inspires it."[47]

But what of the "new man?" Indeed, was there one? If his wife took the initiative in sexual matters was the husband now threatened? How did men react to
the socio-sexual revolution of their generation?

The New Man

"I've counted thirty-two fathers in three blocks, pushing perambulators!. . . .
Things certainly have changed since I was a girl. Why my father would no more
have pushed a pram on a public highway than he would have ridden in one himself." So observed a young grandmother on a sunny Sunday afternoon on New
York's Riverside Drive.[48]

In the emerging family of the 1920s, the father had to earn the respect of wife
and children by demonstrating an interest in family life. If he was to understand
the needs of his children and the new woman who was his wife, he had to make
himself knowledgeable about their problems. And, to the shock of some and to
the dismay of others, he did so. The new man, the modern father, began studying the rearing of children and the management of the home. He attended par-
ent-teacher conferences in his child's school and made up fifty percent of the
membership of the Parents Association of New York City, thus demonstrating
that the rearing of children and the management of the home was increasingly
becoming a fifty-fifty effort. Classes in parenting offered by colleges and universities and others offered by the Child Study Association of America and by the
American Association of University Women found that fathers were attending
these classes in ever increasing numbers. In an attempt to stem the rising tide of
divorce, the Young Men's Christian Association in Brooklyn, New York, began
offering courses in marriage and family relations to men who were about to be
married. So successful were these courses that twenty-five additional courses
were offered throughout the country.

As if to give further impetus to the institution of marriage the YMCA proposed in 1927 to evict bachelors who occupied cheap and comfortable rooms in
the Y's dorms for more than a year. The YMCA acknowledged that it hoped that
the new rule would increase the number of marriages. By being evicted, the single young man "can marry and . . . establish a home of his own. He can picture
for himself the comfort of such a home, the love of wife and children, good food,
the satisfaction of the homemaker."[49]

Many men of 1927, however, still had difficulty shedding the nineteenth-cen-
tury concept of masculinity. In sexual matters the new man, if there indeed was

one, was not clear as to what was expected of him. In the dating ritual men were still the ones who asked for a date and could do so again and again and with any number of women. But, with a liberated woman, how would a man act on a date? In a closed car, far from home, what was permissible? How far did liberated girls go and how far should male machismo aggressively pursue the advantage?

In earlier years, men and women rarely, if ever, spoke of sex. In the 1920s, especially among youth, sex was often just about the only thing they discussed. And, while in our own time we are accustomed to the use of four letter words by women as well as men, in the 1920s a new vocabulary developed so that "skirt," "sweet," "chick," "potato," and "gold digger" were among the more acceptable metaphors for young women. The distinguished journalist Heywood Broun hailed the liberation of women as an opportunity to tell ribald stories in their presence. "The woman who smokes and says, 'Have you heard this one?' is bringing about a better and cleaner America."[50]

In earlier days, men sought and married "virtuous" women. But, if women were sexually liberated and sought satisfaction in sex as in careers, how could a man distinguish between the virtuous and unvirtuous woman? Was a woman who had some pre-marital sexual encounters still virtuous? Did one propose marriage to such a woman? And, if a husband's wife were liberated, should a married woman tolerate an occasional marital infidelity on the part of her husband? And was she free to have an occasional dalliance of her own? "There was no model for appropriate behavior for a New Man to accompany a New Woman."[51]

Some women, as well as some men, did not view equality in the home as desirable. Others believed that America was becoming feminized and weakened. Perhaps in reaction, the Boy Scouts experienced a period of vitality and growth.

As the Boy Scouts of America prepared to celebrate their seventeenth anniversary on February 6 to 12, 1927, the organization could point to an enrollment of more than one million scouts and officials. One quarter of all twelve-year-old boys became Boy Scouts. "Over the sixteen years in which scouting was organized in America about three million boys and a half million men identified with this movement."[52] It was the largest male youth organization in America.

The Boy Scouts advertised themselves as the modern alternative to the passing of the frontier, the decline of the family farm, and the growing industrialization that threatened the small but independent person of business. Declared Daniel Carter Beard in *The Boy Scouts of America*: "The Wilderness is gone, the Buckskin man is gone . . . the hardships and privations of the frontier life which did so much to develop sterling manhood are now but legend and history, and we must look to the Boy Scout movement to produce the men of the future."[53]

The emergence of the "new woman" imposed changes even at West Point, that most conservative and distinguished training ground for American officers. If the brave deserved the fair, and if the latter smoked, could the former be denied? When in 1927 Superintendent Brigadier General March R. Stewart informed a Congressional committee that the ban against smoking had been officially lifted at West Point, the puffs of smoke demonstrated that even the military academy could not be untouched by the currents that created the "new woman" and the "new man."

Based on experiences in World War I, the West Point cadet could not be trained solely to deal with other professional soldiers. Instead, he had to be prepared to deal with reservists and conscripts, with men for whom the military was not a total commitment. The fledgling commissioned officer had to recognize that at times the tongue could be mightier than the sword in dealing with the public, the parents of the conscripts, and the legislators upon whom he relied for financial and moral support. While the military academy's cadets had to observe and enforce strict military rules—yet reject rigidity as a military virtue—"The new West Point graduate . . . will be more of a diplomat and less of a drill-master. . . ."[54]

One man who wrote anonymously to the *Nation* complained that women, in their zeal to find release from household drudgery by having careers, a satisfying love life, and adventure, shared a distorted view of how men lived. "My work, congenial as work goes," he wrote, "has involved a large element of drudgery." He continued, "I find my enthusiasms dimming, my objectives disappearing, my interests dying. . . . I long to sow a (carefully selected) crop of wild oats. I should like to have one (or more) passionate love affairs. . . . I should like to embark on an adventure to the South Seas. Instead I commute daily to the city. . . . I am not arguing that life is harder on men than on women, I merely assert that life from a masculine standpoint is not necessarily an unending round of Sunday dinners without dishwashing, that ever verdant series of love affairs without responsibility, that continuous vaudeville adventure and daring which literary ladies sometimes imply it to be. . . . There is no salvation to being born a male."[55]

❧

[1]*New York Times,* July 5, 1927.
[2]"The Fourth Not So Safe and Sane," *Literary Digest* 94, July 23, 1927, p. 12.
[3]Miriam Beard, "Woman Springs from Allegory to Life," *New York Times Magazine* (March 20, 1927): p. 12.

[4]Ibid.

[5]Kenneth A. Yellis, "The Flapper," in William L. O'Neill, ed., *The American Sexual Dilemma* (New York: Holt, Rinehart and Winston, Inc., 1972), p. 40.

[6]Gilman M. Ostrander, "The Revolution in Morals," in Joan Toff Wilson, ed., *The Twenties: The Critical Issues* (Boston: Little, Brown and Company, 1972).

[7]Will Durant, "The Modern Woman," *Century Magazine* (February 1927): 426.

[8]Carmel Snow, "Today and To-Morrow in Clothes," in Grant Overton, ed., *Mirrors of the Year 1927-1928* (New York: Frederick A. Stokes, 1928): 313.

[9]"How the World is Perfumed," *Literary Digest* 93 (April 9, 1927): 24.

[10]Preston William Slosson, *The Great Crusade and After: 1914–1918*, in Dixon Ryan Fox and Arthur M. Schlesinger, ed., *A History of American Life* (New York: The Macmillan Company, 1930), p. 155.

[11]William Ogburn, *Recent Social Changes in the United States Since the War and Particularly in 1927* (Chicago: University of Chicago Press, 1929), p. xii.

[12]Slosson, *The Great Crusade and After*, p. 137.

[13]Ida Clyde Clark, "A Woman in the White House," *Century Magazine* 113 (March 1927): 591.

[14]Ibid., p. 595.

[15]Quoted in ibid.

[16]Edna Kenton, "The Ladies Next Step: The Case for the Equal Rights Amendment," *Harper's Magazine* 152 (February 1926): 566.

[17]Charlotte Perkins Gilman, "Women's Achievements Since the Franchise," *Current History* (October 1927), p. 9.

[18]Margaret Culkin Banning, "The Lazy Thirties," *Harper's Magazine* 154 (February 1927): 357.

[19]Ibid., p. 358.

[20]Willystine Goodsell, "The Educational Opportunities of American Women-Theoretical and Actual," *The Annals of the American Academy of Political and Social Science: Women in the Modern World* (May 1929), Vol. CXLIII, #232, p. 13.

[21]*New York Times*, February 7, 1927.

[22]*New York Times*, February 13, 1927.

[23]*New York Times*, March 6, 1927.

[24]*New York Times*, May 6, 1927.

[25]*New York Times*, May 18, 1927.

[26]*New York Times*, May 26, 1927.

[27]*New York Times*, September 29, 1927.

[28]Ibid.

[29]Ellen Chesler, *Woman of Valor: Margaret Sanger and the Birth Control Movement in America* (New York: Simon and Schuster, 1992), p. 16.

[30]Margaret Sanger, *Margaret Sanger: An Autobiography* (Elmsford, N.Y.: Norton and Company, 1938), p. 216

[31]Ibid.

[32]See Linda Gordon, *Woman's Body, Woman's Right: A Social History of Birth Control in America* (New York: Penguin Books, 1977), pp. 295-298.

[33]Margaret Sanger, ed., *Proceedings of the World Population Conference* (London: Edward Arnold and Co., 1927).

[34]Max Hodann, *History of Modern Morals* (London: William Heineman Medical Books Ltd., 1937), p. 195.

[35]Mable Dodge Luhan, *Intimate Memories, Movers and Shakers,* Vol. 3 (New York: Harcourt, Brace, 1936), pp. 69-71.

[36]Margaret Sanger, *Woman and the New Race* (New York: Brentano's, 1920), p. 111.

[37]Gordon, *Woman's Body, Woman's Right*, p. 260

[38]Halliday Sutherland, "The Fallacies of Birth Control," *Forum* 77 (May 1927): 841.

[39]See David M. Kennedy, *Birth Control in America: The Career of Margaret Sanger* (New Haven: Yale University Press, 1970), p. 183.

[40]Gordon, p. 264.

[41]Robert and Helen Lynd, *Middletown: A Study in American Culture* (New York: Harcourt, Brace and World, 1956), p. 125.

[42]"Progress Through Birth Control," *North American Review* 224 (December 1927): 622-629.

[43]"Reno Divorces 1927 Model," *Literary Digest* (April 9, 1927): 13-14.

[44]*New York Times Magazine* (December 18, 1927): 1.

[45]Judge Ben Lindsey and Wainright Evans, *The Companionate Marriage* (Garden City, New York: Garden City Publishing Co. Inc., 1927), p. xiii.

[46]Ibid., p. xvi.

[47]Theodore H. Van De Velde, M.D., *Ideal Marriage: Its Physiology and Technique* (New York: Random House, 1926), p. 156.

[48]Grace Nies Fletcher, "Bringing Up Fathers," *Ladies Home Journal* (September 1927), p. 199.

[49]*New York Times,* January 30, 1927.

[50]Heywood Broun, "It seems to Heywood Broun," *Nation* 124 (November 2, 1927): 470.

[51]Kevin White, *The First Sexual Revolution: The Emergence of Male Heterosexuality in Modern America* (New York: New York University, 1993), p. 125.

[52]John W. Withers, "Scouting as a Vocation," *Journal of the National Education Association* (May 1927): 143.

[53]Quoted in Jeffrey P. Hantover, "The Boy Scouts and the Validation of Masculinity," in Michael S. Kimmel and Michael A. Messner, ed., *Men's Lives* (New York: Macmillan Publishing Company, 1989), p. 161.

[54]H. I. Brock, "Arms and the New Man at West Point," *New York Times Magazine* (February 27, 1927).

[55]"These Modern Husbands," *Nation* 124 (January 12, 1927): 89.

8

RELIGION OLD AND NEW

August 7, 1927

The International Peace Bridge connecting Buffalo, New York, with Fort Brie, Canada, was dedicated by United States Vice President Dawes and England's Prince of Wales, Prince George. The New York Times *reported that the ceremonies dedicating the bridge were elaborate and carried out with inspiring solemnity despite the fact that Dawes chose to use the occasion to chastise the failure of the Geneva Naval Conference to reach an agreement. Although some thought the vice president's remarks undiplomatic for a ceremonial occasion, nevertheless, the approximately 100,000 onlookers were enthusiastic. A vast radio audience listened in.*

"The ceremonies took place in Buffalo, but men, women and children, seated comfortably in parlors, on verandas, perhaps in ranch kitchens or on tenement roofs, were enabled by the marvel of twentieth century science to hear as distinctly, as if they had been standing on the bridge itself, the expressions of international friendship, the solemn repetition of the Lord's Prayer, the martial music that proclaimed the arrival of the heads of nations. The emotional spirit of the moment was carried to them on invisible waves traveling with the speed of light." Secretary of State Kellogg, New York's Governor Al Smith, and other dignitaries were present. Prolonged applause greeted the remarks of the Prince of Wales, who declared: "To seek peace and pursue it is the first and highest duty of this generation. . . ."[1]

August 10, 1927

At Mount Rushmore, South Dakota, President Calvin Coolidge dedicated the proposed memorial to Presidents Washington, Jefferson, Lincoln, and Theodore Roosevelt. The president, dressed in cowboy attire, ascended the mountain on horseback. He wore buckskin gloves, high cowboy hat, and Mexican spurs. The spurs he removed, but in his cowboy outfit made inspirational remarks. "We have come here," he said, "to dedicate a cornerstone that was laid by the hand of the Almighty. On this towering wall of Rushmore in the heart of the Black Hills, is to be inscribed a memorial which will represent some of the outstanding events of American history. . . ."[2] The sculptor, Gutzon Borglum, carved the first lines of the portrait of George Washington.

♨

"They can't make a monkey out of me," thundered William Jennings Bryan, the former Secretary of State and presidential candidate, to enthusiastic rural audiences who came to hear him inveigh against modernism, urbanism, immorality, and evolution. And President Calvin Coolidge ruefully observed on April 3, 1927, that at times it appeared "as though a popular familiarity with the Scriptures is not as great at the present time as it has been in American life." He was not far off the mark.

Competing with the Bible for the mind of America were scientists and historians who, through books, magazines and newspapers, encouraged disturbing ideas that did not square with biblical authority. No intellectual concept had greater impact on what Americans thought and what they believed than the controversy over evolution.

The theory of evolution seemed to place humankind on a small and inconsequential planet while its inhabitants had, like other animals, evolved from lower forms of life. Evolutionists held that humankind was merely an infinitesimal part of a grand scheme governed by natural law. Such a view seemed to dethrone men and women from the exalted position which they felt reserved for them by God. Evolution seemed to strike at the very roots of religious values to which most Americans continued to cling.

The Baptist Bible Union insisted "that the Bible was written by men supernaturally inspired, that it has truth without the admixture of error for its matter; and that as originally written it is both scientifically and historically true and correct, and therefore is and shall remain to the end of the ages the only and complete and final revelation of the will of God to man. . . ."[3] Most Americans would not go this far. Yet they accepted in the very marrow of their beings the idea that the universe was created by God in six days and that God had peopled it with men and women who were created in His image and for whom He had a special place. The theory of evolution seemed to represent a fall from grace.

Did this fall from God's grace tempt Americans to drink hard liquor excessively and be sexually promiscuous? Did evolution explain the growing preference of many women for the workplace, the allegedly growing disobedience of many children, the growing rates of divorce, and the growing preference for the sinful city to the virtues of rural life? Why was there a preference for Sunday baseball, rides into the country or to the seashore, rather than to church to sing traditional hymns or listen to God's word as their ministers interpreted it?

Many Americans, men and women who were not devout or regular churchgoers, felt adrift among forces they did not fully understand but with which they nevertheless disagreed. In looking for something familiar to cling to they thought they found it in traditional religion—especially in its more extreme fundamentalist forms. Writing in the *American Mercury* in 1925, H. L. Mencken wrote: "Heave an egg out of a Pullman window, and you will hit a Fundamentalist almost anywhere in the United States today."[4]

In 1927, Sinclair Lewis published *Elmer Gantry*, a scathing novel about a "bellowing bull who cavorts as an apostle of righteousness through 432 pages closely packed with seductions, irreverences . . . pot-shots at the preachers and dissections of the denominations."[5] This floridly handsome man of God has the gift of rhetoric, the charisma of a Saturday afternoon football hero, the charm of a Rudolf Valentino. He preaches morality and fornicates on the pulpit, from whence he preaches virtue as the route to salvation. "He lays siege to virtue instead of conquering vice."[6] So fierce was the storm created by this satire of fundamentalist preachers, that the public library in Kansas City banned the book, as did other public libraries as well. There was, of course, no Elmer Gantry. He was a character made up of the worst qualities Sinclair Lewis attributed to the preachers of his time. One such preacher, who might have been the female model for Elmer Gantry, was Aimee Semple McPherson.

Aimee Semple McPherson:
Prima Donna of Fundamentalism

On the afternoon of Tuesday, May 18, 1926, Aimee Semple McPherson, generally called Sister Aimee, the most prominent evangelist of her time, waved to her secretary and in her flowery green bathing suit dashed off to take a swim in the ocean off Ocean Park, California. By 6:00 P.M. newsboys were shouting a headline sure to help them sell huge quantities of papers. "Evangelist McPherson Believed Drowned!" they hawked. Despite desperate searches, no body could be found. About five weeks later, however, Sister Aimee reappeared in a small community on the Arizona-Mexico border alleging that she had been kidnapped and held for ransom. On her return, she was a celebrity, "the most famous woman in America."[7] How did she capture the imagination of Americans?

Aimee Semple McPherson. Courtesy *The New York Times.*

Aimee was born on October 9, 1890, in a farmhouse in Ontario, Canada. Her father, James Morgan Kennedy, came from a line of Methodist ministers. Her mother, Minnie Peau Kennedy, was the child of a Salvation Army missionary and his wife. Aimee's religious training began when she was three weeks old, as the rites, beliefs, and traditions of the Salvation Army were thrust upon her. As a teenager, however, she began to question the literal interpretation of the Bible. But on July 18, 1906, when Aimee was fifteen, she wrote a letter to the editor of the *Family Herald and Weekly Star of Montreal* in which she demonstrated that she had been saved "just in the nick of time." She wrote:

> I have for some time been an ardent student of the High School Physical Geography. All my life I have been trained in unwavering confidence in the teachings of the Holy Scriptures and God as creator of all things, and that God created man in His own image, a living soul. The teachings of the High School Geography tend to undermine and destroy this faith in God as a

Supreme being and Creator. Its doctrine is at direct variance with that taught in our Holy Bible. It leads us to believe that neither earth nor man were created by God, but by a process of evolution, man being a product of the animal kingdom. . . . [L]et me appeal to every student, to rally and stand by the sacred old truths which right away through the ages have withstood every storm, and risen triumphant above every blast in spite of the cold blooded reasoning of scientists. 'For what shall it profit a man if he gain the whole world and lose his own soul.'[8]

Twenty years later we find her still preaching these few simple principles.

At sixteen she attended a revival meeting led by the Pentecostal evangelist Reverend Robert Semple. She had come to scoff, but she stayed to be mesmerized by the handsome, spellbinding preacher. After a brief courtship, the two were married and the pair went off to carry the word of Christianity to the Far East. But the mission to Asia was unsuccessful. Aimee became pregnant with their first child and both she and her husband succumbed to malaria. Just three months after their arrival, Robert Semple died of the disease. A month later Roberta Star Semple was born. When her daughter was six weeks old, mother and daughter boarded the Empress of China and returned to the United States.

Aimee found solace in church missionary work and as Sister Aimee found her niche among the evangelists of her day. In 1912, she married Harold Stewart McPherson, a grocery salesman, and had a son, Rolf Kennedy McPherson, later to become his mother's successor. In 1921, she and her husband divorced, and Aimee resumed her missionary work with even greater zeal.

In 1923, in Los Angeles, she opened her Angelus Temple, capable of seating 5,000 people. Sister Aimee viewed her church as a center for evangelism as well as a house of worship. In her church, Sister Aimee emphasized sanctification, the gift of tongues, faith healing, and the imminent return of Christ. Branches of her church were built in various parts of the country, and in 1927 these branches and the mother church were incorporated as the International Church of the Four Square Gospel.

Sister Aimee was not bashful in publicizing her sermons. She guaranteed newcomers a preferred seat and urged regular members to stay away from her Sunday evening service so that there would be more seats available for new visitors and greater opportunity to convert them. Among her publicity techniques was to throw thousands of printed invitations from an airplane or to invite the public to watch her practice faith healing on a lion in the zoo. She stood on the back of a donkey and posed for photographers. The Angelus Temple entered floats in the Tournament of Roses parade in Pasadena, California.

These techniques brought criticism from other evangelists and from the public as well. Aimee was not deterred. In her view it was better to be ridiculed rather
than not to be noted at all. Nor was she deterred when male evangelists suggested
that God had not intended women to become preachers. She met this challenge
boldly by declaring, "Woman brought sin into the world, didn't she? Then surely
she should have the right to undo the work and lead the world to the Eden
above."[9] In 1924, she mastered the use of radio and became the first woman
preacher to use the radio to bring God's word to those who did not get to her
Angelus Temple. According to one observer, "Her radio spectaculars were mirac-
ulous. Hundreds of thousands of people were electrified with the certainty that
the broadcasts represented God's invasion into their personal lives. Thousands
believed they were miraculously healed when, at Aimee's urging, they placed
their hands on the radio receiver."[10]

By 1926, Sister Aimee was growing in fame but she was not yet a household
name. Her sudden disappearance and her abrupt reappearance made some question her integrity. Her claim that she had been kidnapped and held for ransom
did not ring true but could not be proven to be false. Where had she been? With
whom?

A grand jury investigation was launched in Los Angeles which turned out to
be a media riot.[11] For eighty-eight consecutive days, the hearings went on, and
for each of those days Sister Aimee's name appeared prominently in the press.
She reveled in her trial for perjury as each day's developments only made her
name better known in California and indeed, across the nation. Even the intellectual journals such as the *Nation* and the *American Mercury* began to carry serious stories about her work and her personality. But the publicity generated by
public debate in the press over precisely what had happened was made to order
for her temperament and she sought to capitalize on her notoriety to bring ever
more converts to God. The grand jury could not agree, the charges were dismissed, and her popularity spread—as she knew it would. When in November a
gubernatorial election was held in California, Sister Aimee received many write-
in votes.

Throughout the hearings and the attendant hoopla, Sister Aimee appeared
serene. She prepared her sermons with her customary care and preached in the
temple to overflowing audiences. But there was no doubt that she was gratified
to hear through the open window of her office the newsboys shouting, "Read All
About It: Aimee Wins." But Aimee Semple McPherson wanted more: she
wanted vindication among members of her immediate congregation and of those
who yet needed to be "saved."

On New Year's Day 1927, she proclaimed from her pulpit that she would begin a "vindication tour" to enhance her reputation. With help from Ralph Jordan, a newspaperman formerly with Hearst's *Los Angeles Examiner*, she embarked on a three-month lecture the theme of which was, "The Story of My Life," including her account of her disappearance. She preached in Colorado, Nebraska, Kansas, Missouri, Illinois, and Ohio. She prayed for deliverance of the modern world from enemies of the "old time religion," namely, the kidnappers whom she claimed had abducted her, district attorneys who were threatening to put her behind bars, and the proponents of Darwin and evolution. In 1927, she published *In the Service of the King*, a popular autobiography based on her sermons.

On February 18, 1927, she got off the train in New York, wearing "a full-length fur coat and a broad-brimmed slouch hat, a beaded bag on her arm." In the lobby of New York's McAlpin Hotel "she revealed a yellow suit with buttons and a collar of fine white fur, so exquisitely tailored, it got its own note on the society pages."[12]

In New York she preached in speakeasies and at the Three Hundred Club of Texas Guinan, the "queen of the nightclubs." There, mobsters, politicians, prominent businessmen, and famous athletes rubbed elbows. The speakeasy shook with vibrations from jazz music and the gyrations of dancers on the crowded floor. Sister Aimee was given a good table, served a glass of water and when she was invited to speak she said:

> Behind all these beautiful clothes, behind these good times, in the midst of your lovely buildings and shops and pleasures there is another life. There is something on the other side. 'What shall it profit a man if he gain the whole world, and lose his own soul?' With all your getting and playing and good times, do not forget you have a Lord. Take Him into your hearts.[13]

Her audience was moved. Not a glass clinked. Suddenly there was applause which lasted longer than her remarks. Sister Aimee had done what she always did best. That is, talk to sinners without judging them, because she was one of them. Nor was the impact of the publicity of her words and deeds lost upon her. She was the Evangelist in the Speakeasy and she invited all New Yorkers to come and hear her at the Glad Tidings Tabernacle at 325 West 33rd Street.

The *New York Times* was enthusiastic at her performance: "Her voice is a full-throated contralto.... She has an expressive mouth, even teeth and brown eyes that flash or are luminous with tears at will...."[14] Sister Aimee prayed that "this throbbing metropolis, home of the nation's greatest men, center of its greatest buildings and stores, known for its great culture, will some day be blessed as the home of the greatest revival churches."[15] Reporters followed her everywhere and peppered her with questions. These she answered with grace, candor, wit, and charm.

But she did not charm Paxton Hibben, a reporter for the sophisticated *New Yorker* magazine. He saw Aimee in quite a different light. "Aimee's mouth is very large indeed, her nose long and lumpy, her eyes small and ever-shifting. She is generous-breasted and broad-hipped, though the middle-aged spread is hidden by the cape she wears. Her legs belong to the school known as piano."[16] Hibben preferred the honesty of Texas Guinan to the duplicity he felt surrounded Aimee McPherson. In his essay he accused her of pandering to the press, of exploiting her listeners, of shaming them into making contributions most of them could not afford to make.

But Sister Aimee's charm and mystery came exactly because the public saw in her what they wanted to see. For example, a journalist for *Harper's*, an equally sophisticated magazine, describes her pulpit technique admiringly:

This was my first sight of Aimee Semple McPherson. From it I received the impression that in this unique house of worship called Angelus Temple in the city of Los Angeles the Almighty occupies a secondary position. He plays an important part in the drama to be sure; but the center stage is taken and held by Mrs. McPherson . . . this ample lady of early middle years, her soft curves concealing muscles like steel; a lady of flashing eye and quick movements and conspicuous reddish hair and ever-busy smile; a lady who gazing forth with satisfaction on an assemblage come to do her homage has the right to honest pride. . . . Semple McPherson is staging month after month, and even year after year, the most perennially successful show in the United States.

There's a blare of trumpets, and the murmur of more than five thousand people hushes sharply. A baton flickers. "The Stars and Stripes" flings itself in long red and white streamers of sound. Glances swing abruptly toward a staircase which comes down to the flower-decked platform. A figure descends—plump, tripping, balancing an armload of roses.

"There she is! That's her!"

The plump one trips forward to center stage, lifts the bouquet, her face wreathed in a garland of interwoven roses and smiles. Upon it plays the calcium-violet light, pink light, blue light, golden light. And now the vast gathering rises to its feet, breaks into clapping. The plump one bows to this side, to that, a focused center of roses, smiles, light, delight, applause, while the band fairly bursts its brass to hail her.

No, it's not a famous prima donna's opening night. It is not the entrance of a world-renowned tragedienne, or of a queen of the flying trapeze or the tightrope. It is she who outstrips all of these. It is "Sister."[17]

As with other fundamentalist preachers, Sister Aimee's theology was one of extremes. She took no prisoners. There could be no neutral ground. Her followers had to choose between purgatory or heaven, there was no in-between. Men and women are either saints or sinners. Among the latter were murderers, idolaters, sorcerers, liars, and evolutionists. She was a theologian, a preacher, an actress, an evangelist who urges a return to a simpler way of life. Yet by using publicity effectively, honing her radio skills, and brazenly asking for money and spending it essentially as she saw fit, she became the most influential evangelist of her time. "I fail to see why one cannot serve the Lord as well in pink silk as red flannel," declared one of her followers. [18]

Her audience consisted of the Middle West farmer or the small-townsman and his family. On every side there were old men and women with weathered faces. The men wore their Sunday best, the women were "often gaudy in the short, tight, adolescent garb that some salesperson has foisted upon them. . . . The couples drag tired old bones to the Temple and listen as if at the gates of Heaven itself."[19] There were some intelligent and educated persons who devoutly believed in Sister Aimee and worshipped at her feet.[20] But mainly her audience comprised men and women of limited education. Many were illiterate. To many in the audience, education was a catalyst of change and therefore suspect.

Aimee's funeral on Friday, October 6, 1944, at her beloved Angelus Temple still attracted throngs of people. They blocked traffic and cluttered the sidewalks. Many stood stoically outside on a warm fall day waiting to pass her coffin. Forty-five thousand did so. Lavish floral displays were everywhere and the newspapers noted the passing of one of the most influential women in American history. Her detractors, including at least one widely respected minister, believed "Christianity, as a whole, has suffered from the wound this misguided woman has inflicted in its very heart, to say nothing of the corruption that her power has worked in public office."[21] Aimee Semple McPherson remains a controversial figure. But as saint or sinner, she could not single-handedly push back the forces of modernism.

Fundamentalism in Retreat

In 1923, some states whose lawmakers were largely rural in background and inclined toward traditional interpretations of the Bible passed laws prohibiting public schools from teaching evolution. Of these, Tennessee passed the most

*The Scopes Trial as portrayed in
the* Literary Digest.

stringent law, banning the teaching of Darwinism in any public school in the
state. John Scopes, a young teacher of biology, deliberately violated the law in
order to test its constitutionality.

In the "Monkey Trial," held in Dayton, Tennessee, in 1925 a line was drawn
between fundamentalists and modernists. The American Civil Liberties Union
paid for Scopes' defense and recruited the eminent Clarence Darrow to lead his
legal team. William Jennings Bryan volunteered to lead the prosecution. Because
both Darrow and Bryan loved to wallow in the public spotlight, because they
were egged on by an army of journalists which included H. L. Mencken, the editor of *Mercury Magazine*, probably the most influential journal of the day, the
trial soon took on a carnival-like atmosphere.

In the trial, Clarence Darrow confronted William Jennings Bryan and "with little difficulty, made an unwitting fool of the former presidential candidate."[22] Bryan
did not know how Eve could have been created from Adam's rib, where Cain got
his wife, or where the great fish came from that swallowed Jonah. He said he had
never contemplated what would happen if the earth stopped its rotation. Under
relentless questioning by Darrow, Bryan revealed his lack of knowledge about theology generally and how superficial his knowledge was of other religious beliefs and

even of the origins of the Bible itself. Despite Darrow's wicked cross examination, Scopes was found guilty of teaching evolution and fined one hundred dollars. In 1927, however, the verdict was later reversed on a technicality.

Although the verdict reversal was little noted, the year 1927 may be said to mark at least a temporary retreat for religious fundamentalism in America. That year, the *Methodist Christian Advocate* reported that the waning of anti-evolution agitation was "a happy event for the Christian Church."[23] In July 1927, the president of the World's Christian Fundamentals Association, William Bell Riley, noted with regret that the activities of the World's Christian Fundamentals Association no longer made the headlines. [24]

In 1927, Harry Emerson Fosdick, the distinguished Protestant clergyman and nemesis of the fundamentalists, had, if not the last word, then certainly brought some closure to the fundamentalist-modernist-evolutionist controversy of the 1920s. Fosdick scoffed at the notion that religion was in decline. Despite fundamentalist fears that science, especially evolution, was eroding religious faith, Fosdick held that perhaps because of the wisdom of science imparted religion could return to spirituality. "To serve these values is to live a religious life, and to believe that these values reveal the creative reality, God, behind and in the universe is religion's central faith. Sciences may come and go, but religion so rooted will persist as long as the race does."[25]

Fundamentalists could not have it both ways. That is, they could not use the advances science and technology made possible while denouncing them at the same time. The radio made it possible for people to hear the word of God in churches from afar without leaving home. A study of 225 rural families in McHenry County, Illinois, showed that half had radio connection with some church on Sunday morning. Thus they could hear the sermons of some of the most dynamic clergymen, listen to the voices of the great choirs, hear distinguished soloists and organists. And, should they prefer to do so, the family could get into the automobile and drive some distance to a house or worship anywhere they wished and sample from among the wide variety of worship opportunities.

Because fundamentalism was largely, but not entirely, a revolt of rural America against urban America, the migration from farm to city eroded support for the fundamentalist position. A study of the National Bureau of Economic Research estimated than in six years ending January 1, 1927, farm population had been depleted by farm-town migration by almost 3.75 million people.[26] Thus, the population base for much fundamentalist sentiment was eroding as rural men and women came into the more pluralistic environment of the city.

Following the Scopes trial, religion and science made a modest attempt at rec-
onciliation. In 1927, the scientist Robert Andrews Milikan delivered a series of
lectures entitled "Evolution in Science and Religion," in which he declared that
modern science is learning "to walk humbly with its God." That is, he explained,
every scientific discovery revealed how much more there was to know so that "our
ignorance was increasing faster than our knowledge" leaving plenty of room for
religion and science to explain matters on their own terms. "It is as difficult," he
said, "to find a satisfactory definition of matter as of spirit." No matter how much
science contributed to pushing back the frontiers of knowledge, there was so
much that remained unknown and perhaps was even unknowable that there was
plenty of room for faith. Milikan believed that atheism was the greater enemy of
science, not the belief in God. "The field of science," he said, "is the field of fact
and the field of religion is the field of mystery." He concluded his argument by
saying, "There is no incompatibility between science and faith if you only have a
mind large enough to hold them both, but it requires some mind."[27]

The effort to keep both science and faith in mind was attempted by the blos-
soming movement of humanism. John Dewey, together with Harry Elmer
Barnes and thirty other prominent scholars, published a *Humanist Manifesto* in
1933 that was based on debates that took place in the 1920s. Humanists
believed that God was immanent, and that religion was merely an aspect of the
human experience. They were skeptical of the supernatural element in religion.
A humanist wrote in 1927, "Fundamentalism is skeptical of science, modernism
merely flirts with science; but humanism says that while science may give us
inadequate knowledge, it gives us all we have and we must make the most of
it."[28]

In October 1927, Dr. John H. Dietrich delivered a sermon to his Unitarian
congregation in which he developed the basic principles of what he called Unitarian Humanism. Humanism believes in the supreme worth of human life and
makes the effort to understand human experience. The primary concern of
Humanism is human development and accepts the responsibility for the conditions of human life. The Humanist makes no attempt to shove the responsibility
for the present miserable conditions of human life onto some God or some cos-
mic order. Dietrich concluded: "In some of its aspects humanism may not be so
comforting as the older forms of religion have been; but it will develop men, not
molly coddles. . . . So let us stand upon our feet like men and look fair and square
at life; and see the world as it really is, its beauties, and its ugliness, and be not
afraid of it. . . . [We] must heed that fundamental command of Humanism,
'Thou must do the good that thou cravest.'"[29]

Humanism failed to capture the soul of a still-religious nation. Its appeal was too cold, too intellectual, and left out so much of the natural world that science could not explain. Fundamentalism, for its part, fared somewhat better and it emerged after World War II as a powerful social force in America. However, the immediate future for American Protestantism was found in what may be called a moderate modernism, where what science could reveal was gladly accepted.

In 1927, an international conference was held by the major Protestant religious groups in the West at Lausanne, Switzerland. Known as the World Conference on Faith and Order, it sought to encourage pluralism in religion and to compromise on diverse theological viewpoints and practices. Preparations were also made for a National Conference on Comity participated in by most of the American Protestant denominations. The Conference was held the following year at Cleveland, Ohio. The aim of these conferences was to substitute the doctrine of mutual understanding for the doctrine of proselytizing. "However this new attitude is described, it doubtless represents an epoch in the history of religious development in the West. Either religion is becoming more tolerant or it is considered that from the functional standpoint all religions serve a common purpose and matters of detail difference are of little importance."[30]

These ecumenical efforts seeking religious toleration and pluralism were essentially limited to Protestant denominations. During the 1920s, Catholics and Jews remained largely out of the mainstream of the fundamentalist controversy. For these religions, the conservatism of fundamentalism sharpened religious bigotry and, in different ways and in varying degrees, these were not good times for Catholics and Jews.

Al Smith:
Can a Catholic Be President?

In April 1927, Charles C. Marshall, an attorney and a prominent New York Episcopalian, gave voice to a previously unspoken question: "Could a Catholic be president of the United States?" In the *Atlantic Monthly* of April 1, in "An Open Letter to The Honourable Alfred E. Smith," Marshall asked the New York governor and possible presidential nominee of the Democratic Party whether or not obedience to Catholic dogma could be squared with the principles of the Constitution of the United States. The letter was released by the *Atlantic Monthly* to the press and on the morning of March 25, 1927, all of the New York papers and many journals carried Charles C. Marshall's queries about reconciling the canons of the church with the laws of the nation.

Marshall recognized Governor Smith's distinguished career and his sense of fair play. Nevertheless, Mr. Marshall said, "through all this tribute there is a note of doubt, ... as to certain conceptions which your fellow citizens attribute to you as a loyal and conscientious Roman Catholic." These conceptions, Marshall continued, "are irreconcilable with that Constitution which as President you must support or defend, and with the principles of civil and religious liberty on which American institutions are based. . . . Citizens who waver in your support would ask whether, as a Roman Catholic, you accept as authoritative the teaching of the Roman Catholic Church that in case of contradiction, making it impossible for the jurisdiction of that Church and the jurisdiction of the State to agree, the jurisdiction of the Church shall prevail, whether, as statesman, you accept the teachings of the Supreme Court of the United States that, in matters of religious practices which in the opinion of the State are inconsistent with its peace and safety, the jurisdiction of the State shall prevail; and, if you accept both teachings, how will you reconcile them?" The Episcopal lawyer concluded that "to avoid the subject is to neglect the profoundest interests in our national welfare."

What was Smith to do? How should he respond? Should he respond at all? Smith's instincts and upbringing told him to make no response. Brought up in a city that was home to Jews as well as Catholics, blacks as well as whites, Asians as well as Eastern Europeans, the very air he breathed and the accents he heard from his earliest days had taught him to value the diversity of urban life. Because he would not question the religious or ethnic roots of others, he was taken by surprise that his Irish background and Catholic faith would become obstacles to his ambition to seek the Presidency of the United States.

Much as Smith would have preferred not to answer, Marshall's letter could not be ignored. Franklin D. Roosevelt thought that as a Protestant perhaps he was in the best position to draft a response. But the governor felt that he needed to frame the reply. With the aid of Father Francis J. Duffy, celebrated chaplain of the Sixty-ninth Regiment of World War I fame and a former professor of theology, Judge Joseph Proskauer, his aide Belle Moskowitz, and New York Secretary of State Robert Moses, he did so.

The caption placed over Smith's response was "Catholic and Patriot, Governor Smith Replies." "I am grateful to you," Governor Smith wrote, "for defining this issue in the open and for your courteous expression of the satisfaction it will bring to my fellow citizens for me to give 'a disclaimer of the convictions' thus imputed. Without mental reservation I can and do make that disclaimer. . . . I recognize no power in the institutions of my Church to interfere with the operations of the Constitution of the United States or the enforcement of the law of the land."

Smith continued, "You have no more right to ask me to defend as part of my faith every statement coming from a prelate than I should have to ask you to accept as an article of your religious faith every statement of an Episcopal Bishop, or of your political faith every statement made by a President of the United States. . . .

"I stand squarely in support of the provisions of the Constitution which guarantee religious freedom and equality. . . . I have exemplified that complete separation of Church and State which is the faith of American Catholics to-day." Smith concluded, "I believe in the worship of God according to the faith and practice of the Roman Catholic Church. I recognize no power in the institutions of my church to interfere with the operations of the Constitution of the United States or the enforcement of the law of the land. I believe in absolute freedom of conscience for all men and in equality of all churches, all sects and all beliefs, before the law as a matter of right and not as a matter of favor. I believe in the absolute separation of Church and State and in the strict enforcement of the provisions of the Constitution that Congress shall make no law respecting an establishment of religion or prohibiting the free exercise thereof. . . . In this spirit I join with fellow Americans of all creeds in a fervent prayer that never again in this land will any public servant be challenged because of the faith in which he has tried to walk humbly with his God."

In an editorial in the *Atlantic Monthly*, the Marshall-Smith exchange was praised as a useful public service because the candidate has answered "not deviously and with indirection, but straightforwardly, bravely and with the clear ring of candor. . . ." But Marshall's serious inquiry and Smith's equally candid response could not prevail in a nation in which the Ku Klux Klan encouraged religious bigotry and blinded the American people with religious prejudice and unjustified fears. The issue of whether a Catholic could be a serious presidential candidate would not be resolved until John Fitzgerald Kennedy ran for president in 1960.

Henry Ford and Anti-Semitism

In March 1927, a jury of six men and six women—four Catholics, two Presbyterians, a German Lutheran, a Baptist, a Congregationalist, a Universalist, a Christian Scientist, and one whose religion was not known—was impaneled in the U.S. Court at Detroit, Michigan, to try the $1,000,000 suit for defamation of character brought against Henry Ford by Aaron Sapiro, a Chicago lawyer and Jewish cooperative marketing head. Members of the Ku Klux Klan were excluded from the jury.

Henry Ford's anti-Semitism first became public when on May 22, 1920, his weekly newspaper, the *Dearborn Independent*, began a scathing series of articles attacking "international Jews." For ninety-one issues, the *Dearborn Independent* returned to this theme without let-up. Writers for Ford's newspaper wrote about the alleged corrupting influence of Jews on American morals, government, and economy. "The articles were a sustained outpouring of prejudice the like of which had never been seen in America, before or since."[31]

By requiring dealers in Ford automobiles to purchase the *Dearborn Independent*, circulation in 1923 stood at 700,000, or 50,000 greater than the circulation of the *New York Daily News*, the largest daily newspaper in the United States. But Ford dealers were not happy about being forced to buy the newspaper, and there is little doubt that the anti-Jewish articles injured the sale of Ford cars. While the extent of that injury cannot be ascertained, in 1922, perhaps because of pressure from President Warren Harding, or the benign influence of Ford's son, Edsel, the anti-Semitic articles abruptly stopped, only to be resumed in 1924.

This time the anti-Semitic articles dealt largely with the activities of Aaron Sapiro, a distinguished and rather volatile Jewish attorney from Chicago, who was helping farmers get better prices for their crops by forming farm cooperatives, something Ford opposed. Sapiro enlisted in his cause wealthy Jews including Bernard Baruch, Julius Rosenwald, David Levy, Otto H. Kahn, Mortimer Fleischhacker, and Eugene Mayer. From these names, some of whom were only marginally associated with Sapiro, writers in the *Dearborn Independent* concluded that there was a Jewish conspiracy to gain control of American farmers, particularly those engaged in growing wheat. "A band of Jews," declared the first sentence in the first article, "bankers, lawyers, moneylenders, advertising agencies, fruit-packers, produce buyers, professional office managers and bookkeeping experts, is on the back of the American farmer."[32] Although many non-Jews came to the defense of Sapiro and his associates, Ford's newspaper persisted in describing the group as "Jewish Combinations," or as "Jewish International Bankers."

The anti-Semitic prejudice expressed in these articles was quickly absorbed by much of rural America, eager to find a scapegoat for their financial distress. Among letters to the *Dearborn Independent* may be found views such as these: "The dirty devils of Jews should be run out of the country. . . . That skunk of a Jew (Sapiro) being allowed to do such things to this country. . . ."[33]

Articles containing pernicious attacks on Jews appeared in *The International Jew*, a compilation of anti-Semitic diatribes that had formerly appeared in the *Dearborn Independent*. These articles were widely translated and circulated and were welcomed by Jew-haters in France, the Soviet Union, and especially in Germany. Henry Ford's standing as an industrial humanitarian and an authentic hero from the heartland of America gave his anti-Semitism the ring of authority. Little wonder then that when Hitler came to power in 1933, he relied heavily on the anti-Semitic attacks written for Ford's *Dearborn Independent*. Henry Ford is the only American to be favorably mentioned in Adolph Hitler's screed, *Mein Kampf.*

The trial generated widespread interest as legal heavyweights and a mass of private detectives sought evidence against Sapiro. Ford hired six of the best trial lawyers in the country, led by U.S. Senator James A. Reed. Sapiro's legal team was led by William Henry Gallagher, an Irish Catholic lawyer prominent in Detroit. That Sapiro did not hire a "Jew lawyer" was a surprise to the Ford legal group. Sapiro financed his own legal activities and neither asked for nor received money from Jewish organizations, most of whom were reluctant to see the trial go forward for fear of further anti-Semitic backlash. The attempt of Ford's lawyers to separate Ford from the editorial policies of the *Dearborn Independent* failed, and Sapiro appeared on the verge of winning his case against Ford.

Henry Ford had no desire to take the witness stand. He was essentially a poor speaker and a shy man in public. It was to improve his public image that he launched the *Dearborn Independent* in the first instance. Ford dodged subpoena servers time and again, but finally one was successful when the server dumped a subpoena in his lap while he was at the Ford Airport for a celebration. Ford was to appear in court on April Fool's Day, but on Sunday evening, the night before he was to appear, he was injured in an automobile accident.

He had left his mansion and was driving alone in a Model T coupe when he was sideswiped by two men in a Studebaker. Ford lost control of his car as it veered off the road, jolted over a stone curb, plunged down a fifteen-foot embankment, and into a tree. But Ford was lucky. He was badly shaken up, but his injuries were not life-threatening. An attempt to keep the accident secret was unsuccessful. When Ford was admitted to a hospital for his injuries, the flamboyant newspapers of the day ran headlines of assassination plots or that Ford was near death. The accident, however, gave Ford's lawyers an excuse to say that Ford was in no physical condition to testify even though the doctors had released him to recuperate at home.

While the lawyers sparred with one another over Ford's ability to testify, some employees from the Ford Motor Company submitted affidavits to the effect that Sapiro had attempted to bribe the jurors and that one juror had accepted a package from Sapiro's lawyers. Actually, this accusation was the exact opposite of the truth in that it was Ford's private army of detectives that harassed the jury illegally. When one juror injudiciously remarked to a reporter that the Ford side seemed to be anxious to stop the case by getting to the jury, a declaration of mis-trial was inevitable. The judge adjourned the case for six months.

Now Ford had a chance to settle the case out of court. The financial settlement with Sapiro, which was modest enough, came to about $140,000, although nei-ther side disclosed the exact amount. Far more importantly, on July 7, 1927, on his sixty-fourth birthday, Ford published a personal apology to Sapiro and retracted all of his past attacks on the Jewish people. "To my great regret," he apologized, "I have learned that Jews generally and particularly those of this country, not only resent these publications as promoting anti-Semitism, but regard me as their enemy. Trustworthy friends with whom I have conferred recently have assured me in all sincerity that in their opinion the character of the charges and insinuations against the Jews, both individually and collectively, con-tained in many articles which have been circulated periodically in the *Dearborn Independent* and have been reprinted in the pamphlets mentioned, justifies the righteous indignation entertained by Jews everywhere toward me."

But in his six-hundred-word retraction, Ford went on to defend himself. He was not at all honest when he wrote that he really wasn't entirely aware of "the exact nature" of these articles and that it was only after a "survey" that he began to appreciate their falsehoods. "Had I appreciated even the general nature, to say nothing of the details of these utterances, I would have forbidden their circula-tion, without a moment's hesitation."[34] The historian Allen Nevins observes, "The idea that he did not know the content of the anti-Semitic articles is absurd."[35] Ford promised that he would publish no more of the offensive articles. He withdrew *The International Jew* from publication, although he could do noth-ing about the circulation of old copies. At the end of 1927, he stopped publica-tion of the *Dearborn Independent*.

Ford's retraction, despite the self-serving qualifiers, was well received both in and outside the Jewish community. He was praised as a "true repentant" and the composer Billy Rose went on to compose a song in honor of Ford's retraction of his anti-Semitism. The melody was entitled "Since Henry Ford Apologized to Me."

> I was sad and I was blue,
> But now I'm just as good as you,
> Since Henry Ford a-pol-o-gized to me.
> I've thrown a-way my lit-tle Chevrolet
> And bought my-self a Ford Coupe.
> I told the Sup-'rin-ten-dent that

The Dearborn In-de-pen-dent
Does-n't have to hang up where it used to be.
I'm glad he changed his point of view,
And I even like Edsel too,
Since Hen-ry Ford a-pol-o-gized to me.
My mother says she'll feed him if he calls
'Ge-fil-te-fish' and mat-zo balls.
And if he runs for President,
I would-n't charge a sin-gle cent.
I'll cast my bal-lot ab-sol-utely free
Since Hen-ry Ford a-pol-o-gized to me.[36]

To strengthen its founder's image as a former anti-Semite who had seen the light, the Ford Motor Company spent $150,000 worth of advertising in Jewish journals and newspapers. This was the first time Ford had advertised in publications sponsored by religious or ethnic groups. Ford also became a frequent guest at dinners honoring distinguished Jews and attended testimonials for Jewish dignitaries. But the depth of Ford's anti-Semitism became clear in the years after 1927 when he continued to support anti-Semitic publications and the organizations that published them. William Cameron, Ford's editor of the *Dearborn Independent*, became editor of *Destiny*, the magazine of the anti-Semitic Anglo-Saxon Federation of America. The new journal gained influence among fascists and Nazis and, like the *Dearborn Independent* before it, gave those organizations undeserved credibility. The new journal helped make the decade of the 1920's the zenith of anti-Semitism in America. In 1938, when Ford marked his seventy-fifth birthday, Adolph Hitler sent his personal greetings and awarded the automobile magnate the Grand Cross of the German Eagle, the highest honor the German government could bestow upon a foreigner.

The American Jewish Yearbook for 1928 was overoptimistic in its assessment that "the past year witnessed the practical cessation of all organized [anti-]Jewish propaganda."[37] Quite the contrary, anti-Semitism, often violent, persisted through the 1920s. In 1916, a Jewish medical intern at King's County Hospital in Brooklyn, New York, was bound and gagged by Christian interns, put on a train at Grand Central Station and was warned that if he ever returned he would be thrown into the East River. He did not return. No Jewish interns served at Kings County Hospital until 1925, when three were appointed. The interns were warned by their Christian colleagues that "This is a Christian institution and we will tolerate no Jews here." The three continued to serve but could not eat at the same table with Christians nor use the hospital tennis courts. Sometimes nurses refused to carry out their orders. On June 29, 1927, the Jewish interns were dragged out of their beds in the middle of the night, bound, gagged, and ducked in a bathtub of ice cold water by some twenty other young physicians at the hospital. In an investigation that followed the protests of the three Jewish interns, six of the perpetrators were expelled.[38]

In the decade of the 1920s the children of Jewish immigrants were prepared more than the children of other ethnic groups who had come to America to join the mainstream of American Protestant life. But becoming mainstream was no easy task. For one thing, the Bolshevik revolution was blamed on Jews because some of the leadership of that revolution were, indeed, Jewish. Americans also feared that excessive immigration was making the nation "less American," and so the flow of immigrants from lands whose people seemed difficult to integrate was severely curtailed. Pseudo-scientific theories of racial superiority, of the superiority of Nordic as opposed to Semitic types, contributed to a climate that made progress for bright young Jewish women and men very difficult and very slow.

It was in college admissions that anti-Semitism was most visible, as the Ivy League schools found that they too had "a Jewish problem" because too many young Jews were found eligible for admission. By admitting all Jews who qualified, they feared, it would be ever more difficult for them to turn out proper Protestant gentlemen. While Harvard President A. Lawrence Lowell openly acknowledged that Harvard would admit only a limited number of Jews, other institutions found rather creative ways of identifying Jews and establishing equally unique methods of denying them admission. At Colgate, the dean of admission felt that by having six Jews the college could not be called discriminatory and the mission of retaining a white, Anglo-Saxon environment would not be compromised. At Syracuse University between 1927 and 1931, Jews were placed in segregated dormitories. Applications asked for religious affiliation, or "Does your family observe strict Sunday observance?" Some asked for pictures in the belief that by determining the size of the nose one could identify Jewish applicants.

If prejudice against Jewish students was rife in the 1920s, such prejudice was even greater among faculty, especially at distinguished institutions. In 1927, the faculties of Yale, Princeton, Johns Hopkins, and the universities of Chicago, Georgia, and Texas each had one Jew. There were two each at Columbia and Berkeley, three at Harvard, and four at City College. "Fewer than 100 Jews were on the liberal arts and sciences faculties of American Universities in the mid-1920s and not many more a decade later."[39]

"No Jews need apply," was a common refrain in discriminatory advertising in the 1920s. Banks, insurance companies, publishing houses, architectural firms, oil firms, and drug companies all refused to hire Jews or severely limited their employability. Discrimination against Jews was the general rule among private clubs anywhere in the United States. Many hotels boasted that they accepted neither Jews nor tuberculars in the belief that by showing this level of discrimination they were also enhancing the prestige of their establishment.

America's Religious Beliefs

While views were changing, Americans remained a religious people. Bryan's concerns that modernism and evolution would erode America's faith were unwarranted. Led by the Federal Council of Churches of Christ, a liberal Christianity was growing in which denominational differences were less important than attacking social problems. The council fought both anti-Semitism as well as Jim Crowism. It called for social security and the right of workers to organize into labor unions.

Among students of liberal theological seminaries, polls showed that four-fifths denied that heathens and infidels would be damned. Only eleven percent believed in an actual hell, and still fewer, about eight percent, thought that the Bible was divinely inspired; four percent believed that the Bible was wholly free from legend. Only 25 percent believed in the Virgin Birth.[40]

In 1927 while fundamentalism was already waning, the results of a poll conducted by 200 newspapers of some 125,000 people on religious belief demonstrated that Americans were still a religious people. Ninety-one percent expressed a belief in God, although only 77 percent said they were active church members. On the other hand, 85 percent believed that the Bible is "inspired as no other book is inspired."

The questionnaire was prepared by a committee of one hundred clergy for the Church Advertising Department of the International Advertising Association to find out what Americans believed about basic religious questions. Dr. Charles Stelzley, director of the religious census, reported that since records were kept, Protestant church membership had steadily risen: in 1800, it was seven percent of the population; in 1850, 15 percent; in 1880, 20 percent; in 1900, 24 percent; in 1925, 26 percent. Data on Catholics and Jews were not published, but by 1927, total church attendance in the United States was estimated to include 43 percent of the entire population:[41]

"The Scopes trial shook American popular culture the way a hail storm shakes a tin-roofed Tennessee mountain shack."[42] But who won? And who lost? The trial appeared to demonstrate that while Scopes had been found guilty, science would triumph over religion, urban America would triumph over rural America, intellectualism over yokelism, knowledge over ignorance, modernism over fundamentalism, and the twentieth century over the nineteenth. But if modernism, urbanism, and evolutionism, seemed to win overwhelmingly in the trial of public opinion, the fact remained that the Tennessee Supreme Court had upheld an anti-evolution statute. This encouraged other states to try the same strategy. In an important sense it was just the beginning of muscle-flexing of the anti-evolutionists.

After 1925, pressure on state legislatures to pass anti-evolution statutes mounted rapidly, with the peak year coming in 1927. "In 1926, three states debated anti-evolution bills. In 1927, eighteen anti-evolution bills appeared in fourteen widely scattered states, an all-time high. . . ."[43] Most of these bills died in committee without ever being debated by the legislatures of the respective states.

The fundamentalist-modernist-evolutionist controversy of the 1920s faded but did not disappear. Under the cover of the Great Depression and as the clouds of World War II gathered, conservative churches became less militant. A less "in-your-face" strategy enabled fundamentalist churches to tend to their roots, hone their dogmas, build their infra-structure, and strengthen their financial base out of the public limelight. Despite scientific disclosures reinforcing now this and then another aspect of evolution, the issue of whether or not evolution should be taught in school remains perennial in American schools and politics.

As late as 1999, the Kansas Board of Education voted to discourage the teaching of evolution by informing educators of that state that no questions on evolution would appear on examinations administered to evaluate student achievement. For good measure, the board also eliminated from the curriculum the "Big Bang" theory of the creation of the universe which the French priest Georges Lemaître (1894–1966), first proposed in 1927.

The Lemaître concept that the universe might have erupted into being from a "primeval atom" and may still be expanding was at least partially confirmed in 1929 at the Mount Wilson Observatory in California, when the astronomer Edwin Powell Hubble observed astronomical data through his powerful telescope. The Big Bang has been elaborated upon, refined, and modified by other scientists. But because no one was present at the creation and we may never find out exactly what happened, fundamentalists assert that the Big Bang deserves no place in the school curriculum.

[1]*New York Times,* August 8, 1927.

[2]*New York Times,* August 11, 1927.

[3]Quoted in Charles and Mary Beard, *The Rise of American Civilization* (New York: The Macmillan Company, 1927), p. 782.

[4]Quoted in Norman F. Furniss, *The Fundamentalist Controversy, 1918-1931* (New Haven: Yale University Press, 1954), p. 40.

[5]"The Storm Over Elmer Gantry," *Literary Digest* 93 (April 16, 1927): 28.

[6]Ibid.

[7]Daniel Mark Epstein, *Sister Aimee: The Life of Aimee Semple McPherson* (New York: Harcourt Brace Jovanovich, 1993), p. 315.

[8]Quoted in Robert Bahr, *The Least of All Saints: The Story of Aimee Semple McPherson* (Englewood Cliffs, New Jersey: Prentice-Hall Inc., 1979), pp. 285-286.

[9]Quoted in ibid., p. 292.

[10]Quoted in ibid.

[11]Gordon Langley Hall, *The Sawdust Trail: The Story of American Evangelism* (Philadelphia: Macrae Smith Company, 1964), p. 192.

[12]Epstein, *Sister Aimee,* p. 318.

[13]Quoted in ibid., p. 319.

[14]Quoted in ibid., p. 320.

[15]*New York Times,* February 19, 1927.

[16]Paxton Hibben, "Sister Aimee," *New Yorker* III (March 5, 1927): 65.

[17]Sarah Comstock, "Aimee Semple McPherson," *Harpers* 156 (December 1927): 11-12.

[18]Ibid., p. 16.

[19]Ibid., p. 15.

[20]Ibid.

[21]Quoted in Bahr, *The Least of All Saints,* p. 3.

[22]George M. Marsden, *Fundamentalism and American Culture: The Shaping of Twentieth-Century Evangelicalism: 1870-1925* (New York: Oxford University Press, 1980), p. 186.

[23]Quoted in William B. Gatewood, Jr., *Controversy in the Twenties: Fundamentalism, Modernism, and Evolution* (Nashville: Vanderbilt University Press, 1969), p. 39.

[24]Ibid.

[25]Harry Emerson Fosdick, "Recent Gains in Religion," *World Tomorrow* X (October 1927): 391.

[26]Arthur E. Holt, "Religion," in William F. Ogburn, ed., *Recent Social Changes in the United States Since the War and Particularly in 1927* (Chicago: University of Chicago Press, 1929), pp. 186-187.

[27]Quoted in Dr. James J. Walsh, "Dr. Milikan and the Failure of Science," *Catholic World* 35 (September 1927): 721-729.

[28]See Curtis W. Reese, "The Faith of Humanism," *Open Court* 41 (May 1927): 270-277.

[29]Quoted in Harry Elmer Barnes, *The Twilight of Christianity* (New York: The Vanguard Press, 1928), pp. 456-459.

[30]Holt, "Religion," p. 185.

[31]Robert Lacy, *Ford: The Men and the Machine* (Boston: Little, Brown and Company, 1986), p. 205.

[32]Ibid., p. 214.

[33]Quoted in Reynold M. Wik, *Henry Ford and Grass-roots America* (Ann Arbor: The University of Michigan Press, 1972), p. 138.

[34]Quoted in Allan Nevins and Frank Ernest Hall, *Ford: Expansion and Challenge, 1915 - 1933* (New York: Charles Scribners' Sons, 1957), p. 321.

[35]Ibid.

[36]Quoted in Albert Lee, *Henry Ford and the Jews* (New York: Stein and Day, 1980), p. 83.

[37]Quoted in Leonard Dinnerstein, *Antisemitism in America* (New York: Oxford University Press, 1994), p. 100.

[38]Ibid., pp. 100-101.

[39]Ibid., pp. 87-88.

[40]Harvey Wish, *Society and Thought in Modern American Life* (New York: Longmans, Green, 1952), p. 449.

[41]"The Old Faith Still Strong in America," *Literary Digest* 92 (January 15, 1927): 31; "Just as Religious as We Used to Be," *American Review of Reviews* 75 (February 1927): 202.

[42]Edward J. Larson, *Trial and Error: The American Controversy Over Creation and Evolution* (New York: Oxford University Press, 1985), p. 72.

[43]Ibid., p. 75.

9

HEALTH AND EDUCATION

September 24, 1927

"Doctor Says Cigarette Smoking by Mothers Kills 60 Per Cent of Their Babies in Infancy." The newspaper's editors, perhaps making an intuitive leap in judgment that Dr. Chauncy L. Barber of Lansing, Michigan, might have been on to something, placed the accompanying article on the first page of the New York Times, *but below the fold.*

At the annual convention of the American Association for Medico-Physical Research held in Chicago in 1927, Dr. Barber asserted that the nervous system was easily poisoned by nicotine, and that it was possible for a person to get drunk on tobacco as well as on alcohol or opium. He attributed the increase of crime "to the use of narcotics in young people." As for infants, "A baby born of a cigarette-smoking mother is sick. It is poisoned and it may die within two weeks of birth. The post-mortem shows degeneration of the liver, heart and other organs. Sixty per cent of all babies born to cigarette-smoking mothers," he continued, "die before they are two years old."[1]

Dr. Barber's comments, however, did not go unchallenged by the medical profession. In a riposte, New York Health Commissioner Louis I. Harris declared, "I am sure that no scientific proof or justification has yet been brought forward to substantiate the alarming statements attributed to Dr. Barber. . . . I have never heard of any babies who died because their mothers smoked tobacco." Dr. Charles Hendee Smith likewise distanced himself from Dr. Barber's "alarmist" views. "A statement that attributes 60 per cent of the infant mortality to mothers who smoke is very far from the truth," he said.

And so, the Phillip Morris Company continued to advertise "Barking Dog: The Friendly Cigarette." The new cigarette was, "Good and mild. . . . blended to the modern taste . . . a richer, smoother, more pleasing smoke. Try Barking Dog Cigarettes for a few days and learn the difference between smoking from habit and smoking from choice!"

The official position of the American Medical Association was that Dr. Barber's statement was "utterly without any scientific basis and foolish."[2] But was it?

221

"Don't take off your shoes," shouted "Doc" Rucker in his medicine show in Herrin, Illinois, to a member of his audience who complained of pain from foot corns. "This cures right through the leather." He applied a copious flow of a liniment made of gasoline, camphor gum, and sassafras. The "doc" guaranteed that the liniment would cure anything from corns to fallen arches. "Don't you feel the relief?" he cried. "Of course you do, if you'll tell the truth." The gasoline, soaking through the leather, provided a temporary coolness to the aching corn. "Sure I do," called out the afflicted sufferer. "There you are," shouted "Doc" in triumph as his assistants hustled through the crowd selling the liniment at fifty cents a bottle.[3]

Medical Quackery or Alternative Medicine

Because electricity in the 1920s was widely viewed as an open door to a new utopia, many gadgets, some with distinct medical benefits, but others of dubious merit, were widely available. It was difficult for the medical consumer to know which was which. Medical charlatans had a field day in marketing their wares. In many drugstores in 1927 one could buy metal plates, one of copper, the other of iron, so that the "electricity" of the body was grounded. When the plates were placed in shoe heels, rheumatism disappeared. One could likewise buy an electric belt for the purpose of relieving rheumatism, backache, kidney, liver, and bladder trouble. A pharmacist might dispense an Addison galvanic electric belt for $2.50 each which he bought for $1 a dozen or an Owens electric belt to "cure stomach trouble" while the Sanden belt would cure anything at all. Dr. Morris Fishbein, editor of the *Journal of the American Medical Association* deplored the "magic collars, electric belts, and mysterious cure-alls" that were touted by quacks who grew rich by preying on the all-too-human desire to be quickly and painlessly cured.

By 1927, however, medical quackery was on the wane. The Food and Drug Administration, established in 1906, was gaining in its attempt to curb the more egregious examples of medical charlatans. But as one device was forced off the market by the FDA, another was offered as a permanent and painless cure-all. "Bravado, selflaudation, a ready wit and a double tongue, shrewdness, a knowledge of the foibles of men, a blunted conscience and an ignorance of the very things in which they claimed competence always have characterized the quack."[4] Quackery, in the form of medical vaudeville shows and other gimmicks, were still widely practiced as unscrupulous practitioners saw continuing opportunities to get rich. Opportunities abounded to provide medicine and mechanical devices of questionable value to the growing demands of the gullible "new" woman and the "new" man to look virile, slim, vibrant, and energetic. "There seems indeed," lamented Dr. Morris Fishbein in 1927, "a veritable craze for reduction which has passed the bounds of normality and driven women and young girls to a type of self-mutilation impossible to explain on any other basis than the faddism of the mob."[5] The fashion of the day was such that women were expected to be flat-chested as well as pencil-thin. Unlike the days of the Gibson girl, the stereotype of the flapper let loose a flood of advertising hawking the slimming benefits of a host of questionable medications.

The most notorious of these products was Marmola promoted by Edward Hayes. The product was made up of dried thyroid glands of various animals in an attempt to hasten the body's metabolism and so lead to weight reduction. The nostrum really worked and initially had been based upon considerable research. However, as early as 1907, the side-effects of the thyroid medication were such as to make reputable doctors shun this medication altogether. Not so the hucksters of quack medicine.

Instead, they continued to make the most outlandish claims for Marmola and similar weight reducing medicine. The caption underneath the picture of a heavy, huge-breasted woman read, "Take off the fat where it shows." If one used Marmola regularly ladies might indulge in a "lifelong loaf," drink liquor "not illiberally," abandon "table restraint." "Beneath your fat a graceful figure dwells," insisted an ad for Marmola which would bring that figure out. [6]

Despite modifications of the formula, the fraud division of the post office insisted that the boasts of Marmola were inaccurate at best and deceptive at their worst. It called upon Hayes to demonstrate why a fraud order should not be issued against the Marmola Company. Early in 1927, Hayes signed an affidavit that he had absolutely abandoned his business and would not again resume it at any time in the future.

The I-On-A-Co, or Wilshire ring, was described as a "simple and effective method of using magnetism for the cure of human ailments." It was advertised as "a new pathway to the cure of disease" that did not require dieting, opiates, pills, powders, purgatives, or exercise. All the patient needed to do was place the electronic harness over her shoulders, sit back, read a newspaper, light a cigarette, and the magnetic force permeating the body would begin an effective cure within fifteen minutes. The Better Business Bureau estimated that the medical gimmick cost about $5.75 to manufacture but sold for $58.50 for cash or could be bought in easy payments for $65.00.

While one satisfied customer declared he would not part with his I-ON-A-CO for $10,000, the American Medical Association denounced the therapeutic value of the device. It was, the AMA said, about as useful as "the left hind foot of a rabbit caught in a churchyard in the dark of the moon." The Rockefeller Institute for Medical Research deplored the fraudulent use of its name in endorsement of the product. The institute declared that it had nothing to do with the belt and no connection with its inventor.[7] And writing in the distinguished health journal *Hygeia* in February 1927, Dr. Arthur J. Cramp, a dedicated foe of medical quackery, denounced the way in which even intelligent people were duped into using it. By 1927, the combined attacks of the Better Business Bureau and the American Medical Association began to have an impact. Dissatisfied users increased in numbers, radio and newspaper advertising declined rapidly, the I-ON-A-CO offices were closing, and on September 7, 1927, Gaylord Wilshire died, and with him died the infamous Wilshire Ring.[8]

But were these nostrums medical quackery or the 1927 version of alternative or even holistic medicine? In fairness, it should be said that what medical charlatans sought to profit from for the most part did little good but also did little harm. Then as today, the chief danger was not so much the adverse effects of the medical gimmicks being huckstered but the belief in a cure they provided. While waiting for a medical miracle to cure them simply, painlessly, and quickly of their ailments, the sick and the ailing postponed seeking help from legitimate medical practitioners.

The Health of Americans

Writing in the *New Republic*, Stuart Chase, author and social critic, observed:

Here is Richard, a practical man, living in the United States of America as the Year of Our Lord 1927 begins. . . . [Yet], his body does not make sense. He is too fat, too short winded, his blood pressure is too high. His sexual life is out of rhythm. . . . He combines artificial abstinence with an occasional debilitating orgy. His vision is poor, his skin is pasty, his arteries are hardening before their time. He negatives the good effects of his golf with too many highballs and cigars. He negatives the spacious leisure of his home and his office, with a nervous pressure which hounds him as remorselessly as does his shadow. He changes from subway local to express to save two minutes which he does not need; he seriously damages his efficiency by trying to answer the telephone and dictate a careful memorandum simultaneously; and if no elevator goes by him, he is out of sorts for the balance of the day. His diet is, hygienically speaking, absurd. In short, a pretty unpractical body.[9]

Yet by 1927, substantial progress had been made in medicine as well as considerable improvement in the health of Americans.

In his annual report, the Surgeon General of the United States declared that "The health of the people of the United States was generally good for the fiscal year ending July 11, 1927." Medical progress was made in the treatment of rickets, pernicious anemia, goiter, and erysipelas, a painful inflammation of the skin. Good progress was made in the immunization of children against diphtheria. By 1930 diphtheria had almost disappeared. According to the Metropolitan Life Insurance Company, "beyond question the greatest single public health fact in 1927 was the large reduction of mortality from tuberculosis to a new minimum for all time." The company also noted an "unprecedently low mortality from pneumonia."[10] The decline in tuberculosis was attributed in part to the country-wide campaign of the National Tuberculosis Association, which made use of billboard advertising, motion pictures, radio, lectures and printed matter to encourage early diagnosis and prompt treatment. There was likewise some decline in venereal disease. Life expectancy in the United States in 1927 was 58 years, with a goal articulated by the American Public Health Association to extend it by twenty years. It is worth noting that this goal has been achieved.

However, in 1927, more smallpox was reported in the United States than in any country except India. Diphtheria and scarlet fever were both slightly more prevalent than in previous years. Little noteworthy progress was made in controlling heart disease, cancer, or blindness.

But "if a barber-surgeon of medieval times had gone into a deep sleep, such as that experienced by Rip van Winkle, and had awakened in the year 1927 within a modern hospital or clinic, he might have been at least mildly surprised. For in the highly organized institution of the present time is found a spectacular example of changes brought about by the scientific renaissance."[11] There were more practicing physicians in the United States in 1927 than ever before. In 1927, there were 149,500 physicians and in that year 4,045 new physicians graduated from medical school. The number of general practitioners continued to shrink as an increasingly large number of physicians chose to specialize.

Yet, in 1927, there was serious concern with the adequacy of medical education, the costs of medicine, the shortages of nurses and equipment, and the foot-dragging by physicians in the area of preventive medicine and treating contagious diseases. At a meeting of the American Hospital Association, Professor J. A. Myers of Preventive Medicine and Public Health of the University of Minnesota, deplored the harsh and seeming indifferent treatment to which tuberculosis patients were often subject. In words that are reminiscent of treatment of AIDS patients during the early years of the epidemic, Professor Myers cited the case of a young farmer who was sent by his physician to the local hospital to determine why his lungs had hemorrhaged. When the diagnosis of tuberculosis was reached, "The hospital immediately demanded his removal from its walls and did little less than throw him into the streets. . . . When I saw the man a few months later he had passed through a period without care after his dismissal from the hospital, which was completely disastrous. When he was admitted to another general hospital . . . his chances of recovery were gone. . . . More humane treatment on the part of the first general hospital might have saved his life."[12]

There was growing interest in the new discipline of psychiatry. A highlight of the year in this field was the joint meetings between members of the American Psychiatric Association and religious leaders to ascertain whether or not a common ground might be found.

The role of sterilization as a means of improving the human race was given a boost in 1927 when Associate Justice Oliver Wendell Holmes Jr., son of a physician, upheld a 1924 sterilization law in the state of Virginia. In a nearly unanimous opinion Justice Holmes spoke for the court when he upheld, in Buck v. Bell, the right of the state of Virginia to eugenically sterilize mental defectives. The case involved a twenty-one-year-old inmate of the Virginia State Colony for the Feeble Minded. The woman was both the mother of a "feeble-minded" child and the daughter of one. "Three generations of imbeciles," said Justice Holmes, "is quite enough." The judge went on to say that the rights of the patient must be carefully considered in every procedural way. The justice, as well as his seven other colleagues, were convinced that in this case the state of Virginia had carefully considered the patient's rights. Since sterilization involves only minimum surgery and does not diminish sexual pleasure, Holmes felt that preventing mental defectives to have children was a sacrifice upon which the nation was justified in insisting. "It would be strange," wrote Holmes, "if [the nation] could not call upon those who already sap the strength of the state for these lesser sacrifices . . . in order to prevent our being swamped with incompetence."

Americans at School

If universal literacy was the goal of American education, then by 1927 the United States had almost achieved it, at least among whites. For the 28 million American children, the one-room, little red school house was, by 1927, almost a thing of the past as 37,000 of such schools vanished between 1918 and 1926. The average number of days in the school session was approximately 160 while the average daily attendance was about 136. "Secondary and higher education were offered to almost as many students in the United States as in all the world. . . ."[13]

Secondary education was rapidly becoming the rule rather than the exception. According to George S. Counts, 1927 "stands in the center of one of the great revolutionary epochs in the history of the secondary school."[14] The junior high school, essentially a downward extension of the secondary school, was already in full swing. Its intent was to establish an environment which focused on the needs of the early adolescent and which encouraged them to go on to high school. The junior college, representing an upward extension of the high school, was a parallel movement intending in part to encourage further attendance at institutions of higher education. By 1927, 153 junior colleges existed in thirty-one states.

The nation was spending about $3 billion a year for education and public school property was valued at $5 billion. But was this enough? Do dollars alone measure the value Americans placed on education? The qualitative state of the buildings children attended left much to be desired and the salaries their teachers earned were shameful.

In the largest cities, elementary school teachers averaged $2,000 a year; high school teachers, $2,500. Teachers in rural areas often earned but $700 to $800 a year. Little wonder, then, that often the ill-prepared were attracted to teaching. In some rural areas, elementary school teachers lacked even a high school education. "In hardly any city was a grade-school teacher's pay equal to the minimum standard of living as proclaimed by trade unions and social reformers."[15] With wages similar to those paid longshoremen, it is not surprising that men (upon whom the bulk of the burden to support a family fell) left elementary school teaching in large numbers, thus making elementary education largely female in character. Only administrative positions were still held by men. Teachers were expected to set examples of the highest moral character as determined by the mostly Protestant, white, male board members. Women teachers led a very circumscribed life. They could not bob their hair, go out on dates, wear short skirts, or become engaged to be married. In smaller communities spinsters were the mainstay of the teaching staff. Although teachers were rebelling, in some communities a curfew for teachers was still in effect. North Salem, New York, for example, had a ten o'clock curfew for public school teachers. But the teachers made their hostility known by flouting the curfew and spending the evening at the movies, where they had gone to see "Beau Geste." Charles Keeler, a member of the North Salem Board of Education, insisted that his community had no curfew. Instead, it asked teachers to agree to be in bed by ten o'clock three nights a week. Mr. Keeler explained his views: "We may be old-fashioned, but we think teaching is like any other business. When a girl enters it we believe that her mind and energies should be on her school first and on movies and dancing second. At least three nights a week."[16]

Here is how Robert and Helen Lynd described life in and out of school in their classic study of Muncie, Indiana, during the mid-1920s.

The school, like the factory, is a thoroughly regimented world. Immovable seats in orderly rows fix the sphere of activity of each child. For all, from the timid six-year-old entering for the first time to the most assured high school senior, the general routine is just the same. Bells divide the day into periods. . . . As they grow older, the taboo upon physical activity becomes stricter, until by the third or fourth year practically all movement is forbidden except the marching from one set of seats to another between periods, a brief interval of prescribed exercise, and periods of manual training or home economics once or twice a week. . . . For nearly an hour the teacher asks questions and pupils answer, then a bell rings. On the instant books bang, powder and mirrors come out, there is a buzz of talk and laughter as all the urgent business of living resumes momentarily for the children, notes and 'dates' are exchanged, five minutes pass, another bell, gradually sliding into seats, a final giggle, the last vanity case snapped shut . . . another class is begun.[17]

The Lynds point out that the apple of the educational system of Muncie is the vocational education program, designed to prepare students for the world of work, and the basketball games, designed to entertain the community. Teachers were expected to teach loyalty to the country, often as interpreted by conservative extremists. Thus it was not surprising that in a Middletown questionnaire students asserted that "the white race is the best on earth," that "the United States is unquestionably the best country on earth," and that every good citizen should act according to the statement "My Country right or wrong!" Conformity was behind the steering wheel and on the gas pedal and drove the school systems of the nation.

In 1927, Abraham Flexner delivered a lecture at Harvard University entitled: "Do Americans Really Value Education?" His response has a familiar ring. Americans, he said, value education but not scholarship. We value, he said, spreading educational opportunities and giving young men and women a chance to develop intellectually. But what this means in practice is not "that we value education, but that as a people we value the prolongation of youth. . . . Abundance of opportunities to go to school and college can therefore be in part interpreted as meaning that we value comradeship, fun, sport, in a word—happiness, at an easy unproductive non-energized level. . . ." The scholar in other countries such as Scotland, Scandinavia, France, and Germany, Flexner continued, "is surrounded by something faintly resembling 'the divinity that doth hedge a king. . . .'" Not so, he concluded, in the United States.[18]

While Europe was remembering the one hundredth anniversary of the death of the great Swiss pedagogue and philosopher Johann Pestalozzi (1746–1827), American pedagogues were scarcely aware of his influence.[19] Yet, an American philosopher who was well-versed in Pestalozzi would have, for good or ill, a lasting impact on America's schools.

John Dewey and American Education

In 1927, the Executive Committee of the Progressive Education Association invited the philosopher John Dewey (1859-1952) to become its honorary president. "More than any other person," declared the letter of invitation, "you represent the philosophical ideals for which our Association stands."[20] Dewey occupied the office until he died in 1952. His name is intimately associated with progressive education, an approach to teaching which by 1927 was already under fire. Although progressive education lost its sense of direction early on, it left a permanent mark on American schools in terms of what is taught, how it is taught, who shall be taught, and who shall teach.

In 1859, the year John Dewey was born in Vermont, Horace Mann, the foremost American leader in education, died. Dewey would extend the work of Horace Mann and reinterpret what universal education meant for a new era. And in the same year, Charles Darwin published *The Origin of Species*, a work that signaled the triumph of science and scientific modes of thought. Dewey would adapt scientific concepts to education.

In 1879, Dewey received his B.A. from the University of Vermont. He obtained a doctorate in philosophy from the Johns Hopkins University and between 1894 to 1904 served as Chairman of the Department of Philosophy, Psychology, and Pedagogy at the University of Chicago. It was from this professional springboard that he became a national, even an international leader in education.

By 1927, he had written his great work, *Democracy and Education* (1916) and with his eldest daughter, Evelyn, *Schools of Tomorrow*. In 1927 he wrote on general philosophical issues of his day in *The Public and Its Problems*. Because Dewey's turgid writing style was "damnable; you might say God-damnable," as William James declared, most of his critics and most of his supporters did not read the exhaustive literature he left behind. His ideas were often misinterpreted and the practices he preached were even more often inexpertly applied by teachers and administrators, but his influence cannot be undervalued. While the professional organizations established to promote and interpret his ideas have vanished, many of his techniques to dispel the schools' conformity remain in place to this day.

In 1927, Dewey visited the Soviet Union to inspect first-hand the influence of education on making social changes. Writing in the *New Republic*, Dewey expressed satisfaction with how his theories of education were put into practice in Russian schools. "The Russian educational situation is enough to convert one to the idea that only in a society based on the cooperative principle can the ideals of educational reformers be adequately carried out."[21] Yet, Dewey's bedazzlement with the Soviet Union was short-lived. In 1931, the Central Committee of the Communist Party adopted a resolution declaring its opposition to progressive education. Dewey's reputation in the Soviet Union was further eroded when he was chairman of the Commission on Inquiry into the Charges Made Against Leon Trotsky in the Moscow Trials during 1937–1938. By declaring Trotsky not guilty, Dewey came under bitter attack as an imperialist warmonger and a tool of Wall Street.[22]

"Dewey believed that democracy would be achieved only as schooling was popularized in character as well as in clientele. . . in the reform of education he saw the first and foremost work of an 'intentionally progressive' society."[23] According to Lawrence Cremin, former president of Teachers College, progressivism in education meant:

1. Broadening the program and function of the school to include direct concern for health, vocation, and the quality of family and community life.

2. Applying in the classroom the pedagogical principles derived from new scientific research in psychology and the social sciences.

3. Tailoring instruction more and more to the different kinds and classes of children brought within the purview of the school.[24]

Among those who were being increasingly brought into the school system were African American children. To the extent to which they were left out, or were forced to drop out, they were being failed by the nation's schools.

Educating African American Children

In October 1927, 1,400 boys and girls in the high school of Gary, Indiana, went on strike protesting the presence of twenty-four black children in their classes. "This handful of Negro children," explained the *Chicago Tribune*, "was assigned to the Emerson High School because of the great distances they would otherwise have to travel each day in going to and from school."[25] The newspaper went on to compare the attitude of the students of Emerson High with the caste system in India, in which "Untouchables" were excluded from social intercourse with the rest of the community. The proportion of African American to white children, one to fifty, was something the Emerson students viewed with horror. In a stormy special session of the Gary City Council, the new students were assigned to Schloebel High School until a separate high school could be built. Black Alderman A. B. Whitlock complained about the council's action. "You are setting an awful example by yielding to these striking students. My people are taxpayers and have a right to as good an education as any one."[26]

In the 1927 case of Gong Lum v. Rice, the awful example of the Gary City Council was reinforced by the United States Supreme Court, which sustained the separate but equal doctrine established by the 1896 case of Plessy v. Ferguson. Martha Lum, a Chinese resident of Mississippi, objected to a school board order requiring her to attend a school maintained for African Americans. Since there was no separate school for Chinese children, she held that her child was entitled to attend school with whites. The Supreme Court held that for purposes of education, all those who were not white were, therefore, "colored" and could be assigned to a segregated school. The Supreme Court could have reversed Plessy v. Ferguson if it chose. But the Supreme Court did not choose to weigh the rightness of previous decisions. The shortsightedness of the Supreme Court led to the continuation of separate school systems all over the South and in parts of the North. "For all practical purposes the separate but equal concept had achieved *de facto* constitutionality in the field of public education as a minimum constitutional requirement."[27]

"After a half century of Negro public schools in the South," lamented W. E. B. Du Bois, "there are states where the expenditures for Negro schools are less than a fifth of those for whites and yet the white schools are not good."[28] In the South the disparities in expenditure between white and black education were marked. The average expenditure per educable white child in the "Upper South" was $25.80 while for the educable black child the expenditure was $11.31. In the "Lower South" the contrast was even greater. Here but $5.60 was spent on the educable Negro child while $30.82 was spent on the educable white child.

Even in the North, to which blacks were migrating in ever larger numbers, their children were confined mainly to segregated schools. And, in these schools, black attendance was far more sporadic than that of whites. The average number of days attended by black children was but 115.4 while that of whites was 138. Few were the resources available to assist African Americans academically and weak was the will to do so. Concluded E. George Payne, who made a study of black education in the North, "Equal educational opportunity is not present. . . ."[29]

Higher Education

By 1927, about one-eighth of Americans between eighteen and twenty-one were attending one of 975 institutions of higher education. The lavishly endowed elite institutions remained selective, even discriminatory in their admissions but the state colleges and universities took in many students seeking higher education closer to home and at lower cost.

The great public institutions were gathering momentum and some of them outstripped the elite private colleges and universities in enrollment and physical facilities. The Morrill Act of 1862 established agricultural and land grant universities: by 1927, one writer could insist that because of these publicly supported institutions, geologists, chemists, physicists, and engineers were "creating wealth through the discovery and organization of the forces of nature."[30] Despite these achievements, higher education came in for its share of criticism.

While Arthur J. Klein of the United States Bureau of Education could write in 1927, "under present conditions the costs are not a decisive factor in determining whether students shall or shall not attend college," parents were not so sure.[31] In an article entitled "The Revolt of a Middle Aged Father," I. M. Rubinow questioned the value and the costs of a college education for his daughter in terms that sound familiar in our own day. On his visits to his daughter's college he was at first favorably impressed with the alluring old buildings, the loud talking, singing and "innocent spooning" of the happy boys and girls at this co-educational institution. Then it struck him that the scene was more like a summer camp, with children enjoying a vacation rather than adults pursuing an education much less a vocation. Was this worth the astronomical sum of $1,500 a year? And, as he needed to pay for the college education of three children, was it worth the sacrifices he must make to spend the $18,000 on their education? This devoted father lamented, "Into this went almost all the savings of a lifetime, and most of the income during their college years. I do not run a car. . . . We have sacrificed many opportunities for vacation and travel; opportunities for saving for our old age which is not so very far off. . . . Was it necessary? Was it wise? Was it fair to us? And was it worthwhile for them?" Rubinow concluded: "A further increase of the college population from 600,000 to a round million, to three or five million full-time students, might spell economic catastrophe."[32] Despite Rubinow's misgivings, pressure mounted from women, blacks, and immigrants for colleges to open their doors and to provide an equal opportunity for a higher education.

If parents were grumbling about the high cost of higher education, college professors were complaining about low salaries. A study of the salaries of college and university professors concluded that "as a rule, the salaries of these university professors did not pay their living expenses," and that most professors required supplementary income to live modestly.[33] To supplement their income, some teachers became taxi drivers and, as the *New York Times* noted, they did a fine job doing so.[34] Teachers might serve from twelve to twenty-five years and be close to fifty years of age before they may be sure of getting $3,000 to $4,000 annually.[35]

Women and Higher Education: "Do You Teach 'em Dancing?"

That women had achieved equal opportunity for secondary education was evidenced by the statistical data of the United States Bureau of Education. *Bulletin 39* of the year 1927 reported that in 1925–1926 there were 1,971,083 girl and 1,786,383 boy students. But this data was somewhat misleading. Girls were encouraged to take courses leading to entry level vocations (clerk, typist, secretary) while boys more often found the college-bound curriculum more readily open to them.

Co-educational colleges were becoming increasingly popular even while remaining controversial. Commented one observer of a co-educational class taught by Bernard De Voto: "Good Lord! I was expecting a college, not a sample room. That front row! It looked like a hosiery window at a spring opening or the finale of a *Varieties* first act. What do you teach em, dancing?" But De Voto's defense of co-education was condescending. He argued that for men, colleges and universities remained little more than feeding schools for those about to enter law and medicine. A liberal education, he concluded, was just right for young women who had no such aspirations! "The women," he declared, "see no need to prepare themselves for law or dentistry. . . . They have time for wisdom— and knowledge—and truth and beauty—and cultural development and individuality. That is why they are so significant for the future if society has any use for liberal education and expects the colleges to have anything to do with it."[36] De Voto concluded his comments by asserting that if America's college were to preserve all that was lovely and admirable in their past, it would be "the coeds, those irresponsible and over-dressed young nitwits, who will save it unassisted."[37]

In higher education, while the number of women attending public and private colleges and universities was growing rapidly, many of the older established universities made the admission of women especially difficult. The result was that women's colleges grew greatly in both numbers and prestige. While many of the public colleges of the southern states gradually opened their enrollments to women, the rate at which they did so was by no means uniform. Thus, the University of Virginia, for example, continued to deny admission of women except under some important restrictions and then only as candidates for vocational degrees.

An important study by Byrd Kennon in 1927 for the American Association of University Women found that college women were effectively squaring marriage and careers. They were not making a statement about women's prerogatives, but sought to use the education and training they had acquired to improve the living standards of their families. Many worked with their husbands, some in occupations that did not require fixed hours or leaving the home, but whatever accommodation they made, they appeared to be doing so successfully.

Should undergraduate education for women include study that would help them become better wives and mothers? The controversy was never fully resolved, but women's colleges did add courses on nutrition, family life, and mental hygiene. But if domestically relevant courses were but of marginal interest to college-going women, the campus was not yet ready for "women's studies." This was a development that would have to wait for more than fifty years.

African Americans and Higher Education: "Too Much Kissing in the Dark"

On October 8, 1927, students at Hampton Institute in Virginia gathered for the traditional Saturday evening movie. When they learned that the lights were to be left on at the rear of the auditorium because there was "too much kissing over there in the dark," they expressed their disapproval by shouting "lights out" and scraping their feet. This seemingly minor incident launched a protest that shook the very foundations of Hampton Institute and African American higher education in America. The protest may also be viewed as an example of widespread anxiety on the campuses of other historically black institutions, as these institutions gradually became aware of a changing social climate they did not understand and were in a dilemma about how to react appropriately. In general, white administrators of black colleges sought to hide in the secure, if shameful, embrace of Jim Crow whose rules they at least understood, while students exuberantly heralded and pressed for social and educational changes their administrators and faculty were reluctant to encourage or even recognize.

By 1927, there were 13,580 students enrolled in seventy-nine black colleges. This number marked a six-fold increase over the number enrolled a decade earlier. In *The New Negro on Campus: Black College Rebellions of the 1920s*, Raymond Wolters traces with flair and scholarship the issues that were involved in the student protests at Fisk, the leading liberal arts college for African Americans; Howard, the only black multiversity; Tuskegee and Hampton, the nation's most prominent industrial institutes; Florida A & M and Lincoln (Mo.), which were state supported land-grant colleges; Wilberforce, which was managed by an

African-American church; and Lincoln (Penn.), which was controlled by a white church board. Throughout the twentieth century leaders in the movement for civil rights were products of these institutions: W. E. B. DuBois (Fisk), Martin Luther King Jr. (Morehouse), and U.S. Supreme Court Justice Thurgood Marshall (Lincoln, Penn.) This section of this chapter relies heavily on Wolter's distinguished study.

The issues in the student protests of the 1920s had to do with campus governance, curriculum, and the parietal rules under which African American students were expected to live. But the black student protest movement was part of a larger controversy which had been going on since the Civil War over the kind of education, if any, that ought to be made available to the recently enslaved men and women. Are African Americans and the nation best served by providing blacks only a vocational education designed both to help them perform the menial tasks which they were likely to be called upon to do and to accept cheerfully a lower place in white America? Or, should a more traditional education in the classics be made available to them so as to enable some to rise in society as high as their talents can take them while developing a cohort of African American leadership? The followers of Booker T. Washington favored the former course while those of W. E. B. Du Bois agitated for the latter.

The Washington position, though favored in the South and by Northern conservatives, was fatally flawed in that the dividing line between an industrial and a classical education could not always be so sharply delineated. In the very attempt to provide even vocational training for Negroes, a cadre of leaders in the form of teachers and administrators had to be developed and this required a background in the academic disciplines. Neither teachers, administrators, nor the successful graduates of their programs could be expected to accept the status quo indefinitely. The very rapid increase in black enrollment in black colleges testified to the need for black leadership.

As DuBois saw it, black colleges were to train their students for leadership positions in the white as well as the black community. The colleges were, moreover, to be a source of black identity and a means of building black self-esteem. Raymond Wolters writes, "DuBois was a fastidious black Brahmin—a connoisseur of the best of Western culture, a devoted chronicler of African contributions to civilization, and also an exhorter urging Negro Americans to make their own special gift to the world. . . . Negroes should be both black and American."[38] DuBois became the philosopher and sometimes the strategist of the African American student protest movement of the 1920s.

Hampton Institute had been founded in 1868 by the American Missionary Association. James Edgar Gregg, the white principal of Hampton Institute, who had been appointed in 1918, could boast that his institution, with an endowment of $8,500,000, was the richest among black schools and seventeenth among the 176 American colleges with endowments of more than a million dollars. But this financial success had been achieved at high cost. Wealthy donors eagerly supported the "Hampton Idea," according to which African American students could be inculcated with high moral values while being trained for subordinate positions in American society. Blacks were to acquiesce in Jim Crow laws, and the school's rules and regulations which conformed to those laws.

At Hampton, the color line was drawn with segregated dining rooms and guest houses. Hampton Institute's principal inaugurated a system of interracial etiquette that was "so intricate and baffling that it took more time and energy . . . than to teach carpentry and farming."[39] Student life was ordered in such a way that young blacks would willingly, even eagerly, accept a lower place in the American social order. Thus according to an administrative order:

> Students must be in bed when the lights are out, no talking or whispering is allowed. . . . Every student is expected to bathe at least twice a week. . . . No student is allowed north of the line passing through the center of the Principal's house except when on school business. . . . Students are forbidden to use tobacco or intoxicating liquors in any form. . . . Rowing, sailing and bicycle riding on Sundays, except on school duty or by special permission is forbidden.[40]

Students lived by the bell which told them when to get up, go to classes, meals, work, and sleep. All students were required to attend daily chapel services, and janitors and matrons were authorized to inspect students' rooms at any hour of the day or night. Outside observers such at Paul Hanus of Harvard, who was asked to do a study of the institution, were shocked by the rigidity they found on the campus. In this way, the institute's administration sought "above all to make the right kind of men and women."[41] But in making its students the "right kind" of men and women, was a classical or vocational program to be adopted? Campus traditions encouraged the latter. A changing America required the former. But could Hampton Institute change? Would its administration have the vision to do so? Would its alumni and donors allow it to do so? The administration, as it turned out, lacked the vision; alumni and donors preferred the status quo, and so change was in the hands of the students. Reluctantly they took up the challenge and success was unevenly achieved.

Under Gregg's leadership, Hampton Institute was changing despite itself while hiding those changes from itself. While it retained the name "Institute" and insisted that it had no intention of abandoning the Hampton Idea, it was doing so nevertheless. When in 1927 Hampton was accredited as a college by Virginia's Department of Education, Gregg insisted that Hampton Institute was not a liberal arts college and had no intention of becoming one.[42] But Hampton was becoming a kind of Potemkin Village. While the facade seemed to reassure donors, Southerners, conservative Northerners that the Hampton Idea was still alive and well, there was enough classical education available to placate those who urged a curriculum as found in the best white institutions of higher education. Thus, the student protest movement of 1927 came about not because the administration of Hampton sought to inhibit kissing in the movies, but because they saw in a duplicitous administration barriers to the higher aspirations of black students.

When on Sunday, October 9, 1927, Hampton students followed up on their Saturday night protest by refusing to sing the traditional plantation songs, Gregg became furious, especially in view of the fact that two potential donors had been invited to the entertainment. On October 10, Gregg suspended classes and held separate meetings for male and female students. The scolding students received did not help matters, and a Student Protest Committee made up of twenty-one young men was organized.

On Tuesday, October 11, students boycotted classes and insisted that Gregg discuss their grievances with the Student Protest Committee. Gregg said that he would not meet with the committee unless the students returned to classes and called off the strike. This the students agreed to do, and drew up "the Petition of Hampton Students," seeking a less regimented social life on campus and more academic rigor. While Gregg agreed to discuss matters, he warned that he could not negotiate unless the students understood that some of them would have to be punished for the strike. This the students would not accept. The protest had been orderly, no property of Hampton Institute had been destroyed and so they could not accept punishment for what they believed to be a legitimate and orderly approach to Hampton's problems. On Friday, the students resumed their strike and Gregg announced a lockout of students when he declared "Hampton Institute is closed until further notice and that students are expected to leave the campus promptly."

Gregg cranked up his community relations and before long he won the general support of alumni, newspaper editors, and even parents of students. Yet, despite a generally favorable climate of opinion in support of Hampton Institute's administration, there were many who acknowledged that the "New Negro" could not be dealt with as one would customarily do years ago. The *Washington Tribune* noted that "The student of today is not like the rough fellow from the pine woods of fifty years ago. . . ."[43]

With public support leaning in favor of Gregg and students locked out, the protest collapsed and Hampton Institute was reopened on October 25, 1927. Gregg suspended some sixty-nine students and hundreds of others were placed on probation, notwithstanding the fact that he was punishing the most able students on the campus. Although the school was open and the protest movement officially over, the climate on campus remained contentious. Unrest on the campus remained high, and a student beat up a white teacher. During the course of the student protest, Gregg had not consulted with his faculty, but when the institute reopened he made it clear that he expected his teachers to remain loyal to the institution and not to the students. Faculty resignations grew, campus problems mounted, and "by the spring of 1929 Hampton was on the verge of anarchy and Gregg submitted his resignation.[44]

Gregg was replaced by George P. Phenix, another white administrator. Unlike Gregg, however, he welcomed the transition of Hampton from a vocational institution to a traditional college. But the issue of whether an institution for black students should be headed by a white and staffed by a mostly white faculty went unresolved for twenty years.

At Hampton Institute and at other black schools, students gave notice that the nineteenth century educational goals of Booker T. Washington were inadequate for the twentieth century. Yet if one applies the rule of unintended consequences, the outcome of even the narrowly focused educational goals of conservative blacks and whites could not contain the inalienable rights of a now-free people. The queen's observation in *Through the Looking Glass* that "it takes all the running you can do to stay in the same place" aptly applies to educational developments in 1927. The year was marked by interminable debate on the aims, costs and techniques of teaching and administering the public schools. In professional and popular literature the low level of pupil achievement, the inadequate preparation of teachers, the inefficiency of school organization, and the mounting costs of education were widely commented upon in terms that echo criticisms of education in our own day. For example, Henry Holmes found that public dissatisfaction with public education might be traced to "confusion as to purposes . . . [and] the lack of a coherent system of schools. . . ."[45] He continued, "Our schools form a maze, a labyrinth, with any number of entry points and exits. . . . It is a sprawling, spineless confusion of educational 'opportunities.' "[46]

The author went on to urge the greater use of scores on aptitude tests as administered by the College Board as a means of improving college standards and making sure that high schools, too, raise their academic sights. Pedagogy also came under considerable criticism as a subject not worthy of study and much less one worthy of the description "science." In fact, according to many critics, the schools of 1927 were not as good as they once were but as Will Rogers put it, "they never were."

[1]*New York Times,* September 24, 1927.

[2]*New York Times,* September 25, 1927.

[3]W. A. S. Douglas, "Pitch Doctors," *American Mercury* 10 (February 1927): 224–225.

[4]Arthur William Meyer, "The Vogue of Quackery," *Medical Journal and Record* 125 (1927): 736.

[5]Morris Fishbein, *The New Medical Follies* (New York, Boni and Liveright, 1927), p. 91.

[6]See James Harvey Young, *The Medical Messiahs: A Social History of Health Quackery in Twentieth-Century America* (Princeton, N.J.: Princeton University Press, 1967), pp. 123–129.

[7]*New York Times,* June 24, 1927.

[8]See Stewart H. Holbrook, *The Golden Age of Quackery* (New York: The Macmillan Company, 1959), pp. 135–145.

[9]Stuart Chase, "The Practical Man and His World," *New Republic* 49 (January 5, 1927): 184.

[10]William F. Ogburn, ed., "Public Health and Medicine," in *Recent Social Trends in the U.S. Since the War and Particularly in 1927* (Chicago: University of Chicago Press, 1929), p. 115.

[11]Harry H. Moore, *American Medicine and the People's Health* (New York: D. Appleton and Company, 1927), p. 33.

[12]Quoted in T. Swann Harding, *Fads, Frauds and Physicians* (New York: The Dial Press, 1930), pp. 292–293.

[13]Preston William Slosson, "The Great Crusade and After," in Dixon Ryan Fox and Arthur M. Schlesinger, ed., *A History of American Life* (New York: The Macmillan Company, 1930), p. 321.

[14]George S. Counts, "Education," in William F. Ogburn, ed., *Recent Social Changes in the United States Since the War Particularly in 1927* (Chicago: University of Chicago Press, 1929), p. 192.

[15]Slosson, "The Great Crusade and After," p. 322.

[16]*New York Times,* September 21, 1927.

[17]Robert S. Lynd and Helen Merrell Lynd, *Middletown: A Study in American Culture* (New York: Harcourt, Brace and Company, 1929), in Marvin Lazerson, ed., *American Education in the Twentieth Century: A Documentary History* (New York: Teachers College Press, 1987), pp. 87–93.

240 GERALD LEINWAND

[18] Abraham Flexner, *Do Americans Really Value Education?* (Cambridge: Harvard University Press, 1927), pp. 7-20.

[19] T. N. Gillespie, "Masters of Pedagogy," *American Mercury* 11 (May 1927): 1–12.

[20] Quoted in Lawrence A. Cremin, *The Transformation of the School: Progressivism in American Education, 1876–1957* (New York: Vintage Books, 1961), p. 249.

[21] John Dewey, "New Schools for a New Era," *New Republic LVII* (December 12, 1928): 91.

[22] William W. Brickman, "John Dewey's Life, Work, and Educational Influence," in *John Dewey and Evelyn Dewey, Schools of Tomorrow* (New York: E. P. Dutton and Company, Inc.), p. xiii.

[23] Lawrence Cremin, *The Transformation of the School*, p. 126.

[24] Ibid., pp. viii-ix.

[25] Quoted in "The Gary School Strike," *Literary Digest* 25 (October 22, 1927).

[26] Quoted in ibid.

[27] Albert P. Blaustein and Clarence Clyde Ferguson Jr., *Desegregation and the Law: The Meaning and Effect of the School Segregation Cases* (New Brunswick: Rutgers University Press, 1957), pp. 102–103.

[28] W. E. B. Du Bois, "Race Relations in the United States," *Annals of the American Academy of Political and Social Science* 140 (November 1928): 8.

[29] E. George Payne, "Negroes in the Public Elementary Schools of the North," *Annals of the American Academy of Political and Social Science* 140 (November 1928): 233.

[30] J. C. Schmidtmann, "State Universities Add Billions to Nation's Wealth," *Current History* 26 (May 1927): 204.

[31] A. J. Klein, "Higher Education," *Bureau of Education Bulletin*, No. 34, p. 10.

[32] I. M. Rubinow, "The Revolt of a Middle Aged Father," *Atlantic Monthly* 139 (May 1927): 593–604.

[33] Jessica B. Peixotto, *Getting and Spending at the Professional Standard of Living: A Study of the Costs of Living An Academic Life* (New York: The Macmillan Company, 1927), p. 252.

[34] *New York Times*, September 23, 1927.

[35] Peixotto, *Getting and Spending at the Professional Standard of Living*, p. 261.

[36] Bernard De Voto, "The Co-ed: The Hope of Liberal Education. With Some Reflections Upon Her Male Classmates," *Harper's Monthly Magazine*, pp. 452–459.

[37] Ibid., p. 459.

[38] Raymond Wolters, *The New Negro on Campus: Black College Rebellions of the 1920s* (Princeton, N.J.: Princeton University Press, 1975), p. 24.

[39] Quoted in ibid., p. 231.

[40] Quoted in ibid., p. 235.

[41] Quoted in ibid.

[42] Ibid., p. 236.

[43] Quoted in ibid., p. 265.

[44] Ibid., p. 272.

[45] Henry W. Holmes, "Chaos or Cosmos in American Education," *Atlantic Monthly* 140 (October 1927): 403.

[46] Ibid., p. 404.

10
That's Entertainment

October 10, 1927

Earl Carroll, the flamboyant New York City theatrical producer, having been con-
victed of perjury and having served four months of his sentence of a year and a day in
a Federal penitentiary in Atlanta, Georgia, was paroled at 6:25 P.M. Despite his
denials to the grand jury, Joyce Hawley, a chorus girl, had bathed naked
in a bath tub of champagne at a Washington's Birthday celebration held at Carroll's
theater.

According to eyewitnesses, two jazz bands furnished the music. Long tables were set
with food and drink and three tubs containing liquid juices occupied prominent places
on the stage. Three men served drinks to the guests while one man served food. At 4:30
A.M. a huge cake was cut. Carroll then announced that he had a great surprise for his
five hundred guests and ordered everybody to the orchestra seats.

A bathtub set on a wheeled platform was rolled on to the stage from the wings. Two
men poured wine into the tub, the naked chorus girl stepped in, and the men crowded
around to drink from the tub. After twenty minutes, the tub with the girl in it was
wheeled off the stage. The party continued until 6:00 A.M.

The impresario was accused of violating both the prohibition law and the law
against immoral exhibitions. Joyce Hawley, through her attorney, held that Earl Car-
roll had promised to pay her $1,000 for the bathtub act and to give her a part in one of
his productions. She alleged that after promising these things Carroll gave her twenty
dollars and advised her to "take a drink and forget it."

✺

There was a drizzle in New York on May 19. Lindbergh had all but decided
to wait for better weather before making his historic attempt to cross the Atlantic
alone. But by early evening, he received a call from the New York Weather

Charles Lindbergh.
Courtesy New York
University.

Bureau indicating that for the next few days, at least, no storms were anticipated over the North Atlantic. Before dawn Lindbergh made final preparations for his flight. Assured in his methodical way that wind, weather, power, load, were all as he had planned, he advanced the throttle and the plane clumsily raced down the muddy runway. With twenty feet to spare, *The Spirit of St. Louis* lifted off, barely clearing the telephone lines at the end of the airport. He flew hour after hour into the dark. Cotton wool in his ears eased the pain on his eardrums made by a noisy motor. His greatest problem was fighting sleep. "Sleep is winning," he wrote in his book *The Spirit of St. Louis.*

But sleep did not conquer. As daylight came up, he could make out the Irish coast, then the English Channel, Cherbourg, France, and, on May 21, 1927, with no map of the airport, using only a flashlight to illuminate his instrument panel, and with absolutely no experience in landing a plane at night, Lindbergh astounded the world with his safe landing in Paris, thereby launching the heroic Lindbergh of myth and legend.

The American ambassador in Paris, Myron T. Herrick, cabled Lindbergh's mother: "Warmest congratulations. Your incomparable son honored me by becoming my guest. He is in fine condition and sleeping sweetly under Uncle Sam's roof."[1] A few days later he struck just the right note when he said at a reception for the young hero: "Lindbergh brought you the spirit of America in a manner which it could never have been brought in a diplomatic sack."[2]

The Lone Eagle: The Hero as Entertainer

Six men had died in an attempt to win the $25,000 prize money put up by Raymond Orteig, a Frenchman living in America, in the name of Franco-American friendship. The Orteig prize not only encouraged well-known pilots to compete but served to ignite widespread interest in air travel. By 1927, there was enough enthusiasm for aviation that it only required a spark to move the center of interest from the barnstorming tricks of daredevil pilots, of which Lindbergh was one, and the delivery of mail by air which Lindbergh likewise did, to regular air travel by ordinary people.

The prize did not require that the flight be solo, but because it was, because the flight was undertaken by this tall, skinny, Midwestern youth with a boyish grin who, upon landing, urged that "somebody call mother"—the man and the event touched the heroic nerve-endings of America. Radio, telephone, cable, and talking motion pictures, all the new communications technologies of the day made the most of it. Charles Augustus Lindbergh became the first superstar of the media.[3]

So great was Lindbergh's exposure to the media that the glare of publicity tended to trivialize an otherwise genuine act of courage, daring, and technical brilliance. In the end, Lindbergh became a source of entertainment as the media destroyed the man and the triumph.

Lindbergh was not the first to cross the Atlantic Ocean. In May 1919 the first crossing was made by a United States Navy NC-4 seaplane. The pilot, Lieutenant-Commander Read, left Rockaway, New York, on May 8. Stops were made at Newfoundland, the Azores, and plane and pilot arrived in Lisbon on May 27. A month later (June 14–15) John Alcock, a Canadian, and A.W. Brown, an American, flew non-stop from Newfoundland to Ireland in 15 hours and 57 minutes. And on July 6, 1919, the R-34, a British dirigible, successfully completed the first lighter-than-air non-stop crossing of the Atlantic from England to New York City.

In mid-April of 1927, Commander Richard Byrd in the tri-motor *America* took off from Roosevelt Field on Long Island for Paris only to crash. Byrd survived with but a broken wrist. Two weeks later, another tri-motor flown by two of the Navy's outstanding pilots took off from Langley Field, Virginia, for Paris. The plane, with four tons of fuel, rose seventy feet into the air and crashed, killing both pilots. Two French pilots, Charles Nungesser and François Coli, took off from Paris for New York only to disappear somewhere at sea.

Based on the experiences of these pilots, Lindbergh believed that a light plane, not a heavy one, operated by a single pilot, not a crew, fueled with just enough gas to make the trip, would succeed where the others failed. When Lindbergh arrived in New York his tiny plane, *The Spirit of St. Louis,* was a refreshing alternative to the highly charged commercialism which seemed to dominate the efforts of his rivals. That Lindbergh flew alone added to the glamour of the event. As a result, crowds instantly followed wherever he went. Journalists would not let him get the rest he needed before his historic journey. Lindbergh was already tired when he took off.

Lindbergh (1902–1974) was a strange hero to America of the 1920s. This son of Swedish parents, who came from the rural Midwest, who neither drank, swore, nor smoked, "did much to reassure the 1920s that youth was not going to the dogs."[4] He seemed to embody the old truths—the lone adventurer who was self-reliant, who could make do or do without, who could master machines without being mastered by them, a boyish, self-confident, self-effacing youth, who was decent and respectable and who stood for God, mother, and country. This young man seemed to be a welcome alternative to the flapper, the dandy, the fop, the bootlegger. He comforted America by suggesting that the Charleston, bootleg whiskey, and hare-brained stunts were not the only values America held.

As Lindbergh soloed across the Atlantic, even Will Rogers, America's outstanding humorist, became serious. "No attempt at jokes today. . . . A . . . slim, tall, bashful, smiling American boy is somewhere over the middle of the Atlantic Ocean, where no human being has ever ventured before. He is being prayed for to every kind of Supreme Being that had a following. If he is lost it will be the most regretted loss we ever had."[6]

In the *New York World* the otherwise cynical Heywood Broun wrote about the Lindbergh flight and the world's reception of it: "I think it was a triumph over fear which moved us to celebration. . . . Nature can't bully us indefinitely with wind and wave and perils of vast oceans. One of our boys has put the angry sea in its place. The big pond, hey? Why, after this it is a puddle and we may step across as neatly as Elizabeth upon the cloak of Walter Raleigh."[7]

In religious services throughout the land prayers of thanksgiving were offered for Lindbergh's safe landing and moral lessons for America were drawn. Dr. Raymond L. Forman, of St. Paul's Methodist Episcopal Church declared, "While others were wrangling, a young boy slipped quietly away and beat them to the goal." The Reverend Dr. Selden Delany, of the Episcopal Church of St. Mary the Virgin, said, "It has been a striking thing that while everyone else 'jockeyed' for money and for publicity and waited for the weather this young man simply flew. . . . While others are paralyzed by doubt and fear the mystic makes the adventure . . . into the unknown, trusting to God." Dean Howard Chandler Robbins, of the Cathedral of St. John the Divine, asserted that no greater deed of personal prowess and adventure appeared on the pages of man's conquest of nature than this lonely, epic flight. "The heroic adventure of the Christian life," he insisted, "depended upon self-discipline such as that which Lindbergh exhibited but which seemed to be absent from the hedonist expressions of a seemingly undisciplined America."[8] Thus the legend and the Lindbergh mystique.

After celebrations and honors abroad, Lindbergh and *The Spirit of St. Louis* returned aboard the cruiser Memphis. As the vessel steamed up the Potomac, a band played martial airs and Lindbergh received a twenty-one-gun salute, an honor ordinarily reserved for heads of state. He was received by President Calvin Coolidge in a festive ceremony in which he was awarded the Distinguished Flying Cross from the president's hands. His welcome in New York was greater than the welcome given to soldiers returning from the Great War. The crowds were greater, the adulation unreserved, the radio and newspaper coverage ever more thorough. Receptions and awards followed one another in quick succession. At the Hotel Commodore, New York City gave him a dinner which was probably the largest ever given an individual in modern history. Thirty-seven hundred guests feasted on six thousand pounds of chicken, two thousand heads of lettuce, one hundred twenty-five gallons of peas, and eight hundred quarts of ice cream.[9] Charles Evans Hughes, the former secretary of state and soon to be chief justice of the United States Supreme Court, had this to say: "We measure heroes as we do ships, by their displacement. Colonel (a position to which he had been immediately promoted) Lindbergh has displaced everything. . . . He has displaced everything that is petty, that is sordid that is vulgar. . . . We are all better men and women because of this exhibition in this flight of our young friend. Our boys and girls have before them a stirring, inspiring vision of real manhood. What a wonderful thing it is to live in a time when science and character join hands to lift up humanity with a vision of its own dignity!"[10]

Lindbergh received offers to endorse products, to star in the emerging movies, and enter business partnerships. For the most part he refused those offers in a laudable attempt not to commercialize on his success. He did allow his name to be used to encourage air travel and his book *We* produced substantial advances and royalties. With the booming stock market and the scandals of the Harding administration as a backdrop, Lindbergh's integrity and genuine achievement seemed to stand out all the more.

Lindbergh's was a period variously described as the "Roaring Twenties," the "Jazz Age," the "Age of Ballyhoo." New journalistic techniques demonstrated the power of the media to rivet popular attention "on one intrinsically trivial person or episode after another—a golfer, a tennis player, a prize fighter, a movie star, a sordid murder, an old man's lewd adventures with a young mistress, to the virtual exclusion of events and trends out of which a tragic destiny for the whole of the Western world is being inexorably shaped."[11] Such an environment was made to order for an accidental hero.

Newspapers and radio gave attention to every detail of the famous flight across the Atlantic. The *New York Times* devoted all of its first five pages to Lindbergh and his achievements. In breathless prose, the *New York Times* reported the well-publicized take off of the solo flight of the "Lone Eagle" across the Atlantic to LeBourget airport in Paris. "A sluggish gray monoplane lurched its way down Roosevelt Field yesterday morning, slowly gathering momentum. Inside sat a tall youngster eyes glued to an instrument board or darting ahead for swift glances at the runway. . . . Death lay a few seconds ahead of him if his skill failed or his courage faltered."

When he landed safely in Paris, the *New York Times* exulted, "Lindbergh Does It! To Paris in 33 1/2 hours." In an editorial the staid newspaper lost its cool altogether: "What is the greatest story of all time? Adam eating the apple? The landing of the Ark on Arat? The discovery of Moses in the bulrushes? . . . But Lindbergh's flight, the suspense of it, the daring of it, the triumph and the glory of it . . . these are the stuff that makes immortal news."

And the ballyhoo continued. "He has exalted the race of men!" shouted the *Baltimore Sun* when Lindbergh landed at LeBourget. "He has performed the greatest feat of a solitary man in the records of the human race!" declared the *New York Evening World.* Lindbergh had taken his place "among the great pioneers of history," was the opinion of the *Ohio State Journal.* The *New York Times* devoted fifteen pages of copy and photographs to the landing. The *New York American* devoted ten pages, the *Herald Tribune,* nine pages, the *World* weighed in with eight pages. As for the tabloids, the *Daily Mirror* gave twenty-three pages of story and pictures while the *Daily News* provided readers with sixteen pages. "During the first four days of the Lindbergh story about 250,000 more stories were published about him than about any other single event in the history of American journalism, and it has been estimated that in that period the newspapers devoted to him something like 30,000 columns and approximately 36 million words, or enough to fill almost one hundred books the size of Theodore Dreiser's *An American Tragedy*."[12]

Newspapers as Entertainment

In 1927, the English poet William Butler Yeats wrote to a friend, "I am still of the opinion that only two topics can be of least interest to a serious and studious mind—sex and the dead." Sex and death surely fascinated Americans during the 1920s and the mass media were not squeamish about giving their readers and listeners a great deal of both.

On January 12, 1928, the *Daily News*, a tabloid newspaper founded in New York City in 1922, published a photo showing Ruth Snyder hooded and strapped in the electric chair. To get the first and only photo of an electrocution the *Daily News* smuggled an out-of-town photographer past prison officers and into the death chamber at Sing Sing. Tom Howard had strapped a small camera on his ankle and at the fatal moment he reached into his pocket and pressed the cable release. Howard had time for only one exposure and that was all he needed.[13] He had photographed the first woman to die in an electric chair.

Sensationalism such as this led Herbert Asbury to describe 1927 as "The Year of the Big Shriek." He continued, "Not since the close of World War has there been a year which produced such an amazing crop of news as 1927, scarcely had one stupendous occurrence been embalmed in journalistic traditions as the great story of the age than another appeared to take its place, and forced frenzied editors and reporters to new heights of hysteria and hyperbole, while above the din of competition rose the mellow baying of the publicity hound and the raucous bleat of the politician as he knelt before the glory of the front pages and welcomed the heroes returning from the scenes of their exploits."[14]

"If Americans were not having fun in 1927 it was hardly the fault of the nation's press."[15] When, in 1927, President Calvin Coolidge announced that he did not choose to run in 1928, he made headlines that were unusual for a president who prided himself on his silence and who insisted that reporters never quote him directly. Although his meaning seemed clear enough to the average American reader, his announcement was interpreted as being ambiguous and there followed a spate of commentary in an attempt to ascertain what he really meant.

But with a man in the White House who loathed publicity, or at least seemed to (see pp. 16–17), the newspapers of the day freely drew on the exploits of private individuals such as stunt pilots, flag-pole sitters, marathon dance participants, goldfish swallowers, film stars, sports figures, and captains of crime. In the 1920s, the spotlight shifted from public men such as presidents to another kind of hero, a celebrity from the world of sports, entertainment, even crime.

1927 started with the tail end of the salacious story of Daddy Browning, the real estate tycoon and his thirteen-year-old child bride Frances Heenan, "Peaches." The marital difficulties were vividly portrayed with smirk and smear as the attempt to inform was suffocated with the desire to titillate and sell papers. William Randolph Hearst's the *New York Daily Mirror* led the way with the entire front page given over to five inch streamers: "Peaches' Shame!" "Oh!-Oh!-Oh! Daddy Browning." The *Graphic* tried to do even better, or worse. The tabloid serialized Peaches' "private diary," and the caption under a picture of Daddy and Peaches playing in bed was: "Woof! Woof! Don't be a Goof!"

As the Peaches/Daddy Browning case became less and less newsworthy, the newspapers made the most of what they had in the bloody murder by Ruth Snyder and her corset-salesman lover, Judd Gray (see pp. 131–132). The accused were not members of high society but ordinary, unglamorous people who were inept in committing the crime. But the newspapers tried to make the most of what for a time they labeled, "the dumbbell murders."

On the opening day of the trial, fifteen Western Union operators transmitted 62,711 words to the press rooms of the *Daily News* and *Mirror*. On May 6, 1927, there was no other story in the first fourteen pages of the *Daily News*. Newsprint was backed up by a host of photographs in keeping with the traditions of the tabloids.[16] On May 9, 1927, the jury found Ruth Snyder and Judd Gray guilty of first degree murder and were later sentenced to death in the electric chair.

From a journalistic viewpoint, perhaps the most interesting and significant phenomenon of the trial was the amazing concentration of celebrities, so-called experts, and commentators drawn in to comment, analyze, and interpret the human emotions and the motivation of this ordinary couple who committed so heinous a crime. The prominent historian/philosopher Will Durant, impresario David Belasco, the Reverend John Roach Stratton, W. E. Woodword, the historian and biographer of George Washington, were all made offers they couldn't refuse and added their illustrious voices to an interpretation of this sordid event.

By 1927 there were nearly 2,200 daily newspapers with a combined circulation of nearly 40 million, or about one newspaper for every two literate persons over the age of ten. And competition among them for circulation and advertising was keen. Sensational newspaper stories were important circulation builders and even the most stolid of newspapers did their best to trumpet the news as best they could. In 1927, Silas Bent, a journalist of the day, wrote *Ballyhoo,* a book in which he criticized the techniques newspapers used to exaggerate the import of the news they were peddling.[17] Bent was particularly critical of the boastfulness of the newspapers.

An example of how newspapers ballyhooed the news was their reportage in 1927 of an alleged wave of youthful suicides. When two students, sons of prominent families, killed themselves, the newspapers began writing about "waves" or "epidemics" of youthful suicides. This, despite evidence from a statistician for a life insurance company which showed that the percentage of suicides among youths under twenty years had been falling for a period of sixteen years. But newspapers tended to ignore this critical statistic as they brought in experts who attempted to "explain" the suicide phenomenon. When a thirteen-year-old school boy hanged himself at the height of suicide ballyhoo, a physician who investigated the case drew the conclusion that the "boy had succumbed to newspaper suggestion; and a part of the press was so callous as to headline the tragedy as 'imitative' suicide."[18] Likewise, newspapers reported a crime "wave" when in fact crime declined during the 1920s.

To attract readers, sports news became ever more important. By 1927 relatively conservative newspapers such as the *New York Times* and the *Herald-Tribune* were devoting twenty-five or more columns a day to sports. A report in 1928 to the American Society of Newspaper Editors concluded that the sports sections of the newspaper had become "the most important classification of news."

And ballyhoo followed in the sports pages as much or more than it did in the news sections of the paper. Dempsey, the *World* exulted, was "a sort of legend . . . a superhuman colossus of brawn." The *New York Times* asserted that Babe Ruth of the New York Yankees, "wears the laurel amid the deafening plaudits of the American nation."

In 1928, Ben Hecht and James MacArthur wrote a Broadway hit, "The Front Page." The drama established the image of the indifferent, hard-drinking, hard-driving, newspaper man who connived in every way to "get the story" but was indifferent about the story he wrote. The chaos of the newsroom, the clatter of the typewriters, the incessant ringing of the telephone, the shouted orders of city-editors, their salty language and cigar or cigarette smoke, all were glamorized as the world of journalism. J. L. Morrill, of the staff of the School of Journalism of Ohio State University, described what went on in the newspaper room as follows:

Turn to the press—its steaming sheets survey,
Big with wonders of each passing day;
Births, deaths and weddings, forgeries, fires and wrecks,
Harangues and hailstones, brawls and broken necks. . . .
Lively or sad, life's meanest, mightiest things,
The fate of fighting cocks or fighting kings.[19]

But it was not in the full-sized newspapers that the gamey world of gossip-as-news reached its crescendo but in the world of tabloid journalism—which, in 1927, was at its zenith.

Tabloid Journalism

By 1927, leadership in journalism was coming from the tabloids. From New York City, the *New York Daily News* and its mirror image, Hearst's *New York Mirror,* and Bernarr McFadden's scandal sheet the *Graphic,* the tabloid newspaper spread from one community to another throughout America. So ubiquitous had tabloids become that one editorial called tabloids the "black plague" of American journalism.[20] In addition to a smaller format of four to five columns, making it more conducive to reading in crowded places such as on public transportation, the essence of tabloid news involved making the ordinary appear extraordinary, and hyping the extraordinary into sensationalism.

Thus, the Peaches Browning affair, the Hall-Mills Murder, the Snyder-Gray murders were made to order for tabloid newspapers. Stories such as these gave them the opportunity to do what they did best, namely, to cover an event by providing harrowing details of sordid murders, assorted burglaries, arson, rapes, sexual misconduct, and varied highjinks. Full of pictures, many composite in nature so as to distort while titillating, the great emphasis in the tabloids was on scantily clad women in lingerie, bathing suits, or short skirts barely covering seductively crossed legs. Tabloids paid for tips on stories they felt would have wide readership. At the *Daily News,* every caller got fifty cents irrespective of the fact that some of the callers were reporting stale information. Many tipsters received $2 to $5. "By 1927 the *Daily News* was dishing out $1,000 a week to callers."[21]

Among the headlines one could find in the 1927 *Daily News* were the following:

SNYDER POISON PLOT (March 25)
FORD MURDER PLOT (March 31)
SHAKES OFF WIFE'S GRIP LEAPS 5 STORIES (August 26)
SLAIN, BEHEADED, LEFT NUDE, IN WOODS (August 27)

DROWN BOY FOR $140,000 (September 1)
"HEART BROKEN" MOVIE EXTRA SUES THAW (December 13)
TELL OF KRESGE LOVE NEST (December 17)

Using headlines such as these, with lurid pictures to match, the tabloid newspaper prospered mightily. By 1927, after but six and a half years of publication,
the 1,082,976 daily circulation of New York's *Daily News* was the largest ever
achieved by a daily in the United States. Initially, the traditional newspapers
sought to welcome the tabloids as worthy competitors. They could do so because
the readership of such papers as the *New York Times,* the *World,* or *Herald Tribune*
was unaffected. The steady diet of the lurid and the smutty, appealed to those
who never read newspapers before—laborers, shop-girls, stenographers, house-
wives, and often school children. In 1927, the New York bureau chief of United
Press declared, "It hardly matters what the newspapermen think of the tabloids.
The people are showing what they think by the way they buy them."[22] As one
writer put it, tabloids won readers by appealing to "large numbers of adult
infants."[23] Nevertheless, tabloids influenced not only the kind of coverage the
more staid and traditional newspapers would give to news but changed the very
meaning of what constituted news in the first place.

Before long, however, the more traditional newspapers realized that they
would have to change with the times and change not only their conception of
what constituted news but how to report it. Thus, the *New York Times* "devoted
to the Hall-Mills trial more space than it had ever given to any other story in its
history. . . . In wordage the *Times* outstripped the three tabloids combined."[24]
And so on April 3, 1927, the *New York Times* could report that its circulation
reached the highest figure in its history. With smug satisfaction the *Times* editorial declared:

> The demonstration is complete that a large public desires a newspaper that
> preserves its sanity in the midst of clamor, that seeks and prints news which
> counts from all parts of the world, and that does not insult the intelligence
> of its readers by assuming that they cannot read or understand anything not
> in big type or in a picture, and that their daily desire is not to be amused or
> scandalized rather than informed.[25]

To stimulate circulation, tabloids resorted to every kind of contest imaginable.
With beauty contests making up their stock in trade, there were tongue teasers,
tongue twisters, crossword puzzles, pasting together parts of presidents or of film
stars, prettiest legs, most popular barber, scantiest bathing suit. The *New York*

Daily News started a lottery contest with a prize of $1,000 which the *Daily Mirror* matched and increased. The lottery reached a peak of $20,000 until the government put an end to the lottery. The *Daily News* paid $1.00 to $5.00 to readers who sent in jingles, limericks, bright sayings, embarrassing moments, malapropisms. As many as 20,000 readers a day responded to the contests. The *News* honored a city policeman and fireman for heroism each month. Each citation carried an honorarium of between $100 to $250. Its readers were invited to vote for their favorite movie stars. In 1927, the Movie King was John Gilbert with 12,715 votes, while the Movie Queen was Vilma Blanky with 10,000 votes.[26]

"Don't tell my mother I'm working on the *Graphic*. She thinks I'm a piano player in a whorehouse," was a popular sentiment among journalists. Launched in 1924 by Bernarr Macfadden, the hugely successful magazine publisher of *True Stories* and similar confessional journals, the *Graphic* was often referred to in the trade as the "porno-Graphic" and the New York Public Library refused to give it rack space in the newspaper room. Macfadden thought he would use the profits from his publishing empire to promote his ideas of physical culture, health, fitness and alternative approaches to medicine.[27] The *Graphic* became the most lurid of the New York tabloids and outdid other tabloids in its emphasis on sex, mayhem and murder. Under the guise of promoting bodily health, fitness, athletic ability, physical stamina, and vigor, the *Graphic* was quick to show bulging muscles in women as in men. Its main endeavor was to identify the perfect man and woman and "pair them in the interests of eugenics under the benevolent auspices of the paper."[28]

Despite its unsavory reputation, the *Graphic* launched the careers of many celebrity journalists. It was at the *Graphic* that Walter Winchell honed his peeping-tom technique of journalism. In a column called "Your Broadway and Mine," he wrote about new mistresses, "secret" rendezvous, lavish weddings, spectacular funerals, society events, and general gossip of popular sports and entertainment personalities. It is estimated that one-third of the *Graphic*'s readers bought the paper to read Winchell's column. Because his readership grew, he seemed worth the $300 a week he was paid. Although he was often inaccurate, and was not above tailoring the facts to make a better story, he was forgiven by a devoted readership. Among the features of his column, the best known was forthcoming "blessed events" of famous people. In 1927, one such column announced that his wife June Winchell had given birth to a baby girl, Walda.

Sometimes his columns were almost incomprehensible to all but the most loyal of readers. Thus, he wrote in a *Graphic* column:

Nursed the sheets till late, being weary from a strenuous tear the night before, having hoofed at a White Light Place with Bobbie Folsom and other charming wretches. So to breakfast with Lovely Kent, who is as sweet as her Christian monicker . . . Up betimes and broke fast with a baby doll from 'Artists and Models'. . . In the rain to keep a rendezvous with Mary Thomas, who coryphees for a living. . . .[29]

Yet, when writing in 1927 for the more literary journal *Bookman* here's how he described "The Real Broadway":

(Broadway) is a sublimated Coney Island or county fair or street carnival, with its mummer-plays and catch-penny devices, its cacophony and gaudy lights, its peep-shows and wax figure museums, its skating rinks, hooch dances, freaks and fol-de-rol all brought to a degree of refinement and dignity and yet still, in essence, only the merry-go-round with the steam calliope on which the adult infant spends his nickels away from his schoolbooks and other serious activities of life.

As a standard of moral comparison it is at once an enticement and a hell, a Circe's cavern of lascivious and soul-destroying delights, an unholy place where producers are the seducers of women, where stars without talent are made meretriciously overnight, where pure girls succumb to rich admirers for diamond brooches, furs, imported automobiles, apartments and other luxuries—a Babylon, a Sodom and Gomorrah all within the confines of a garish district extending from just below Forty-second Street to Columbus Circle at Fifty-ninth. . . .[30]

When Winchell left the *Graphic*, his column was taken over by Louis Sobol. When Sobol left he was followed by Ed Sullivan who later became the popular TV personality of the "Ed Sullivan Show" which in turn was the making of many entertainers who were given a chance to show off their talents before huge audiences.

Although tabloids came under considerable criticism they defended themselves vigorously. They pointed out that they appealed to those who would not otherwise read a newspaper. Moreover, they declared that the "yellow journalism" of which they were accused used techniques not developed by them but primarily from the tactics of William Randolph Hearst, whose newspapers sensationalized the Spanish-American War. Defenders of tabloids held that they simply appealed to basic human emotions. Thus, W. D. Walker, who worked in the publicity department of one of New York's large department stores, declared: "These people (ninety-five percent of the population) are intensely human. . . . They tread the daily grind in the home, the office, the workshop; but they are potential adventurers. . . . And the tabloids dish up to them, every day, food which keeps alive an unexpressed part of their nature, makes them feel they belong in the human chorus, though not in the spotlight."[31] And Professor Robert A. Millikan, in a lecture at Yale, held: "The beauty of women, the strength of men, the flavor of strawberries, the aroma of flowers, the love of friends, courtship, marriage and divorce, the race track, the wrestling match and the boxing bout, all of these played almost exactly the same role in the lives of the people of Rome as they play in the lives of the people of New Haven or New York. And it is around these things too that about ninety percent of the interests of the average man revolve."[32] And the defenders of the tabloids held that they catered to these long neglected interests of the majority of Americans.

In the 1927 conference of the Newspaper Institute, A. H. Holcombe, managing editor of the *New York Herald Tribune,* voiced a concern shared by many in the newspaper business, namely, that the search for sensationalism had gone well beyond the limits of good taste and that in the absence of self-imposed censorship government censorship would be invoked. "The law prohibits the sale of rotten eggs," Holcombe declared, "not the sale of rotten news."

The Tower of Babel

Before the newspaper extras hit the streets, urban America knew of Lindbergh's successful non-stop flight across the Atlantic from New York to Paris in *The Spirit of St. Louis.* While they later read the details avidly in their newspapers, they first heard the essential facts about the flight over radio. When he decorated Colonel Charles Lindbergh with the Distinguished Flying Cross, President Calvin Coolidge spoke over a national hook-up of fifty stations to an audience estimated at thirty million.[33] Through radio, the voice of Calvin Coolidge was heard by more people than that of any previous president (see pp. 22–23). His unseen audience was equal to the entire population of the United States in 1865.

What newspaper publishers should or could do about the advent of radio was puzzling to many of them. In a decade when fads such as flagpole sitting, mahjong playing, marathon dancing, and gold fish swallowing were popular, was radio likewise merely a novelty? If so, it could be ignored, as the public would soon tire of it. But was radio a competitor? If it was, then the wise thing to do was to throw obstacles in the way of its development. Was radio an important medium of communication? If so, newspapers had better get on board and buy radio stations and otherwise print schedules of radio programs in their newspapers.

H. G. Wells, the British novelist, futurist, and jack of all (mostly wrong) predictions, was wrong about radio. In an article for the *New York Times Magazine* on April 3, 1927, Wells predicted the "speedy decline" of radio. "Broadcasting," he wrote, "is an inferior substitute for better systems of transmitting news and evoking sound. . . . I am afraid that the future of broadcasting . . . is a very trivial future indeed."[34] Lee Deforest (1873–1961), frequently called the "father of radio" and "pioneer of television," along with other giants of the early days of radio, launched a counter-attack. "No, H. G., radio is here to stay. . . . It will become a more and more indispensable part of our daily and nightly home life. For radio has worked and is now working too profound a change in our national culture, our musical tastes, ever to be cast aside."[35] By 1927, it was evident that radio was an important medium for entertainment, news, information, and offered opportunities for making money by selling air time for advertising. Clearly radio could not be ignored.

Whether it was called "wireless," "wireless telephone," "wireless musicbox," or "radio telephone," in the 1920s America was in love with radio. What went out over the air had something to please everyone: music, news, drama, opera, soap opera, play-by-play descriptions of football or baseball games, or blow-by-blow descriptions of boxing matches. Around the radio the family gathered to be informed, amused, entertained, and sold the latest fad or fantasy of American industry. Radio united the nation in a common, if not always elevated culture. The airwaves partially eliminated the economic divide between urban and rural America and gave both greater opportunity to share in the nation's prosperity.

All America, for example, shared those daily hilarious fifteen minutes when Freeman Gosden and Charles Correll, both white, created their sympathetic black characters, first as "Sam 'n' Henry" and later, in 1928, as "Amos 'n' Andy." On any Monday through Saturday night, a phenomenal sixty percent of all Americans could be found in front of their radio listening for fifteen minutes at 7:00 P.M. to the antics of "Sam 'n' Henry." On a wintry Tuesday evening in Chicago, January 12, 1926, thousands of families of the American Midwest heard Sam declare, as the pair made their way to Chicago from Mobile, Alabama, "I hope dey got faster mules dan dis up in Chicago." "Thus Sam 'n' Henry focused right away on the most dramatic development in Afro-American life between the two World Wars: the Great Migration of Southern blacks to large cities, largely in the North."[36]

The racist implications of two whites playing black roles in which the latter were held up to ridicule for their naiveté, simplicity, and the difficulties of their adjustment to city life, remained for a another generation to contemplate.

Indeed, some African Americans objected, sometimes strenuously, about how they were made fun of, but in the America of the 1920s whites and blacks shared a common joke in the series. Whites recognized in "Sam 'n' Henry" problems that they, as immigrants from abroad or migrants from rural areas, shared as they adjusted to urban life. Blacks, by laughing through their tears, sought to take the hurt out of their perilous existence in the ghettoes of urban America.

In 1927, there were 732 broadcasting stations in the United States. Fewer than a hundred of these were affiliated with a network. The average radio set was in operation for two hours and twenty-five minutes each day. Most people tuned between 8:00 P.M. and 10:00 P.M. Battery-operated radio sets were important in rural America in 1927, but in urban areas, radios operating on regular house current were growing in number. While Zenith promoted radios for operating on house current, Philco began manufacturing radios for cars.

The total number of radio stations grew until they reached a peak in 1927. Initially, many radio stations were owned by churches and educational institutions. However, when the potential for making money through advertising was genuinely grasped, radio entrepreneurs rapidly entered the field of radio. By 1927, David Sarnoff had already established the National Broadcasting System and in that year the fledgling Columbia Broadcasting System was launched with twenty-six-year-old William Paley at the helm. But radio in America was chaotic. Partly as a result of that chaos, purchases of sets and parts declined in 1927, as the following figures illustrate:

1925	$430,000,000
1926	506,000,000
1927	425,600,000
1928	650,550,000

It was not until the Federal Radio Commission was established in 1927 that some order was brought out of the radio industry and radio sales continued their climb.

On February 23, 1927, the Federal Radio Act, after a substantial legislative battle in the Sixty-ninth Congress, was signed by Coolidge. The adopted legislation created a Federal Radio Commission, described as a "traffic cop" of the air. The commission it established was a many-faceted compromise between industry and government in which the radio entrepreneurs lobbied against federal regulation altogether. It was a compromise between those who sought to give regulatory powers to the Secretary of Commerce, Herbert Hoover, and those who insisted upon a separate commission so as not to depose too much authority with the commerce secretary. The legislation was also an attempt to appease populist sentiment, which feared monopoly control of radio by such emerging networks as NBC and later CBS.

In the debate over the need for regulating the airwaves it is interesting to note that the Secretary of Commerce, ordinarily thought of as an unreconstructed philosopher of the free market in industry, sought substantial regulation of emerging radio. As early as 1922, in his opening address to the first National Radio Conference Hoover declared: "It is inconceivable that we should allow so great a possibility for service, for news, for entertainment, for education and for vital commercial purposes to be drowned in advertising chatter, or for commercial purposes that can be quite well served by other means of communication."[37] In the five years after that speech Hoover remained a consistent and strong advocate of broadcast regulation. For his efforts in bringing order to the broadcasting industry, Hoover has sometimes been described as the father of the broadcasting industry.

While still nominally lodged in the Commerce Department, the Federal Radio Commission that was established had far less power than Hoover wished. The commission's primary responsibility was to supervise only the "technical" aspects of radio broadcasting. This included the issuance of licenses, the classification of stations, allocation of wavelengths, specifications on power and hours of operation and the prevention of interference. The act lacked any regulatory standards for the commission to follow except the vague mission to regulate broadcast radio for the "public interest, convenience, and necessity." Moreover, the commission had to justify its existence and its authority had to be renewed annually by Congress.

When the NBC and CBS networks began full broadcasting in 1927, it was still unclear whether radio in America would be sponsored by commercial advertising or rely on government subsidies. Those who opposed the commercialization of radio believed that if left to advertisers, radio would debase its main mission of informing, enlightening, and uplifting Americans. Educational programming, they feared, would be lost in the welter of claims and counterclaims as dulcet-voiced announcers urged listeners to buy this, invest in that, and do so now.

These fears were not without merit. In 1927, the first false radio advertising case came before the Federal Trade Commission. The case involved the alleged false advertising of The Omaha Tanning Company and its president, W. C. (Harness Bill) Kalash. The FTC asserted that the claim by "Harness Bill" that its saddle gear were made by hand and sold directly to the consumer, avoiding the costs of middlemen, was false. In his radio talk, "Harness Bill" insisted:

Now folks I want you to understand that I am positively not selling you harness made from anyone else's leather, but I am only offering you harness which is made in my own tannery from leathers which I have tanned myself and have watched the process of the tanning every step of the way from the green hide to the finished leather here in my own tannery.

The statement, the Federal Trade Commision determined, was false and misleading.[38]

Despite very real potential for abuse, advertising made radio accessible without cost to the masses of Americans and the programs they sponsored reflected American interests and tastes. Advertising made possible an expansion of a range of offerings and encouraged the networks to expand and improve their facilities. Because radio advertisers were forced to find common ground among all listeners, more than print or film, politics or laws, radio united the nation.

"You Ain't Heard Nothing Yet!": America Goes to the Movies

If the movies were "the opiate of the people" then the theaters in which they were shown were the "people's palaces." The glitzy $12 million Roxy which opened in New York City in 1927 made the others fade in comparison. Six thousand two hundred people could sit in its auditorium, with room for an additional 2,000 in the lobbies. On its stage several hundred performers could display their talents. There were dressing rooms for two or three hundred entertainers, three organs, and an orchestra pit that could hold a hundred musicians. The Roxy incorporated a fully-equipped hospital and ushers carried first aid kits should the need arise. "The Cathederal of the Motion Picture," as it came to be called, opened on March 11, with *The Love of Sunja* with Gloria Swanson. Nor did the financials of the Roxy disappoint. Its gross business in one week in its first year was $135,000.

The Golden Years of Hollywood began in 1927. In that year, there were 743 new movies playing in 21,660 theaters, with an average weekly attendance of some 57 million. But by 1927, admissions appeared to be falling off. With an average admission ticket costing about 60 cents, the cost of attending a movie for a family of four was somewhat out of reach for many Americans. Rather than spend money on going to the movies, why not make do with an evening's entertainment provided free on radio? Hollywood moguls cast about for new ways of making the movies more exciting for more people. They found just what they were looking for in "the talkies."

Warner Brothers—Harry, Jack, Sam, and Albert—was the smallest, most poorly financed movie studio in Hollywood. As box office receipts fell, the brothers knew they would have to take greater risks than larger studios if they were to increase their box-office revenue. Thus, when the owners of Vitaphone patents came around to see them, the Warner brothers were interested. Vitaphone demonstrated its wares in New York City with a program of musical short subjects from renowned musical celebrities such as Mischa Elman and Giovanni Martinelli, plus a silent film, *Don Juan* with John Barrymore. Because the music came from behind the screen rather than from live musicians sitting in front of the screen as in the case of silent films, the Warner brothers thought that a film's musical accompaniment enhanced the quality of the movie. At the same time, they might be able to sell Vitaphone as a way of providing "canned" music in lieu of the more expensive live musicians. Because the audience liked the music they heard, the Warner brothers were encouraged to risk everything on a full length sound film.

Because their capital was so limited, they implored Al Jolson to accept stock in their company in lieu of salary for a movie that came to be called *The Jazz Singer*. Jolson refused and insisted upon a $75,000 fee, thereby making the mistake of a lifetime. *The Jazz Singer* has to do with a young New Yorker, Jakie Rabinowitz (Al Jolson), a cantor's son, who prefers the stage to the pulpit. He leaves home and returns as Jack Robin, a successful singer in musical reviews but a failure in his father's eyes. Because of his father's terminal illness, Jack must choose between singing the Kol Nidre chant performed before the Day of Atonement, the holiest holiday of the Jewish calendar, or appear on Broadway. He chose Broadway.

As a film, the movie was mediocre. Most of it remained silent, but Al Jolson did put over three songs and a bit of dialogue. Once it was released in October 6, 1927, the audience was ecstatic. When Al Jolson ad-libbed: "Wait a minute, wait minute. You ain't heard nothing yet!" the audience went wild. Al Jolson spoke fewer than 350 words, but a revolution in the movies had begun. But had it?[39]

The production chief at MGM, Irving Thalberg, didn't think so. "Novelty is always welcome," he declared, "but talking pictures are just a fad."[40] One studio producer scoffed at the "talkies." "I don't think," he said, "that there will ever be the much dreamed-of talking picture on a large scale. To have conversation would strain the eyesight and the sense of hearing at once, taking away the restfulness one gets from viewing pictures alone." Another film tycoon predicted the end of the "talkies" "because sound will keep fans awake—they come in to relax and, maybe, catch a nap!"[41] Even Harry Warner was not entirely convinced.

"Who the hell wants to hear actors talk?" he wondered. But desperation forced him to join with his brothers and take the gamble.

Sam Warner died the day before *The Jazz Singer* opened and he never knew that the gamble paid off. Within a year, Warner Brothers became a major studio and a force to be reckoned with in the motion picture industry. "By the spring of 1927, the movement of the public toward talkies was unmistakable; by the autumn of 1927 it was a stampede."[42] Warner Brothers leaped to the front rank of the film industry. From one theater in 1927, they gained control of over seven hundred three years later. The assets of Warner Brothers rose from $5 million in 1927 to $160 million in 1929; their net profit for 1929 was $17 million, a record high for the industry, and nearly 900 percent greater than the previous year.[43]

When movie fans entered their favorite movie "palace" they suspended reality for a time and saw projected on the silver screen what they would like to be—a handsome lover, a financial baron, a flirtatious woman, a brilliant scientist, a quick-on-the-draw cowboy, a nimble prize-fighter, a zealous cop, or even a notorious crook. Under the sway of movies were traditional values suspended or even upended? Because the barons of the movie industry discovered early on that sex and violence sold, how much of each could be used to titillate an audience?

During the 1920s, the motion picture industry was rocked by sex scandals, sensational divorces, and accusations that sex was for sale in exchange for roles in movies. Because of concern that the movie producers might corrupt America with the power of their films, religious groups and self-appointed moral vigilantes were pressing for government censorship of films. The Reverend William Sheafe Chase, for example, in a text entitled *Catechism on Motion Pictures in Inter-State Commerce . . .*, asked rhetorically, "Shall no effective control be exercised over these Jews to prevent their showing such pictures as will bring them the greatest financial returns, irrespective of the moral injury they inflict upon the public?"[44]

In 1915, in Mutual Film Corporation v. Industrial Commission of Ohio, the Supreme Court ruled that making movies was a business as any other business, and so movie producers were subject to prior censorship and could not claim the protection under the First Amendment to the United States Constitution which guarantees freedom of expression. Moreover, by 1927 the threat of government regulation loomed over the movie industry. There were those in Congress who felt that recent consolidations in the movie industry had been in violation of the anti-trust laws and they threatened government investigation. What the movie industry wanted was a means of regulating and censoring itself while keeping government imposed controls at bay. Faced with pressure to offer more uplifting fare, the newly created Motion Picture Producers and Distributors of America (MPPDA) in 1922 turned to William Harrison Hays, President Warren G. Harding's postmaster general, to direct their organization.

In Will Hays, the man and the mission were well suited to each other. Hays was a non-smoker, a teetotaler, an elder of the Presbyterian Church, and a staunch opponent of pornography in the mails. In short, he was a man in whom middle America could have confidence. Hired at $100,000 a year, this popular, glib, and well-connected politician became the czar of the movie industry. The Hays Office, as it nearly universally came to be called, dominated the film industry of America for a generation.

Between 1922 and 1927, Hays fought a war on two fronts. He sought to make friends with the forces urging movie censorship by offering them ample opportunity to voice their objections, and he encouraged movie producers and directors to make compromises where they could. But Hays' early efforts to clean up the film industry met with resistance from the members of the very association that had hired him in the first instance. By 1927, because proliferating censorship boards were adding to the costs of making movies with their demands for cuts, directors and producers were convinced "clean movies" were unprofitable and unpopular. In April 1927, Universal president Carl Laemmle expressed concern that movie producers would lose money because of "namby-pamby" movies. "Invariably they (the movies) are too damned clean."[45] For his movie *White Shadows in the South Seas*, Hunt Stromberg wanted "lots of tits."[46]

When film writer Ben Hecht came to Hollywood to write film scripts in 1927, he was advised by his colleague Herman Mankiewicz, "In a movie . . . the hero, as well as the heroine, has to be a virgin. The villain can lay anybody he wants, have as much fun as he wants, cheating and stealing, getting rich and whipping the servants. But you have to shoot him in the end." Ben Hecht would take few chances; he wrote films mostly about villains.[47]

After a series of false starts, the Hays Office developed a statement of movie "Don'ts" and "Be Carefuls." While God was satisfied with ten commandments, the list of "Don'ts" included eleven items which could not be shown on the screen. These included profanity, licentiousness or suggestive nudity, illegal drug traffic, and inference of sexual perversion, white slavery, miscegenation, sex hygiene and venereal diseases, childbirth, children's sex organs, ridicule of the clergy, and willful offense to any nation, race, or creed. The list of "Be Carefuls" included twenty-five subjects about which movie producers were to exercise special care. Producers were to be careful about the use of the flag, international relations, arson, firearms, theft, robbery, brutality, murder techniques, methods of

smuggling, hangings or electrocutions, sympathy with criminals, sedition, cruelty
to children or animals, the sale of women, rape or attempted rape, first-night
scenes, man and woman in bed together, deliberate seduction of girls, institution
of marriage, surgical operations, the use of drugs, and excessive kissing. The codification of "Don'ts" and "Be Carefuls" was unanimously adopted by MPPDA in
October 1927 "to the end that vulgarity and suggestiveness may be eliminated
and that good taste may be emphasized."[48] Thus, in the motion picture industry
a creative tension continued to exist between fans who expressed their preferences as they paid their money, what movie makers wished to explore as a commercial and artistic effort, and what moral exemplars believed needed to be
curbed.

On January 11, 1927, thirty-six people gathered in the Ambassador Hotel in
Los Angeles with a view toward establishing an organization to speak on such
issues as the role of the emerging sound films, demands for censorship of movies
by religious and community improvement groups, threats by government to sue
the industry for alleged violation of anti-trust laws, and most importantly, to
respond to the demands of employees in the movie industry to join unions. The
movie producers were determined to keep Hollywood an open shop. In the latter effort they failed. By May of 1927, the founders of the Academy of Motion
Picture Arts and Sciences developed a constitution and set of by-laws and
selected their first officers. A charter was granted to the academy by California
and the board of directors chose Douglas Fairbanks as its first president.

To curtail costs and to respond to falling revenues, the studios attempted to
impose a ten percent salary cut on all talent. In light of the uproar that followed
and threatened strikes, the studios withdrew the proposed cut and sought other
ways to economize. Ten years later, the academy withdrew from all labor-management matters. But its role in bestowing "Awards of Merit" so as to "encourage
the improvement and advancement of the arts and sciences" of motion pictures
stimulated worldwide interest.

The first "Oscars" were awarded in 1927. The Academy Awards, covering
films opening in Los Angeles between August 1, 1927, and July 31, 1928, went
to *Wings*, a picture based on World War I, to Emil Jannings and Janet Gaynor
for best actor and actress, and to Frank Borzage as best director. The awards were
not announced until February 18, 1929, and were not presented until May 16 of
that year. The awards of that year paid tribute to the passing of the silent film
while recognizing in *The Jazz Singer* that revolutionary development in movies
had taken place. The first awards were presented by Douglas Fairbanks and
William C. de Mille, the elder brother of Cecil B. In a ceremony that lasted four

minutes and twenty-two seconds, the awards were scarcely noted by the media.

By 1927, at least forty percent of Hollywood's films were sold overseas. To the chagrin of other countries, films made in America had enormous appeal. Some nations tried to impose a quota on American-made films or, as in the case of England, to require that exhibitors show a fixed percentage of films labeled "Made in England." "But no foreign film company could hope to equal the technical perfection, and cash resources, of Hollywood."[49]

The distinguished character actor, Lionel Barrymore, expressed the view that the motion picture was "not a medium for serious reflection and never will be."[50] Serious reflection, in his view, was reserved for the theater.

Broadway in Lights and Shadows

In 1927, $10 million worth of electric and billboard ads flashed their messages upon the throngs of the ever-popular Times Square, Broadway and Forty-Second Street in New York City. From a "magic lantern" on top of the Capitol Theater at Fifty-first Street and Broadway, letters 150 feet high could be read up to two miles away.[51] But as *Variety* described it, beneath those lights, "Every gimmick imaginable goes on . . . from fake auction rooms to shell games; speakeasies operating openly; creepers and badger workers with improved methods; undercover rendezvous of intermediate sex luring Freudian students and everything else the former vice belts ever had. . . . Hubert's freak show on 42d Street. . . . The Garment Exchange with its models. . . . Street fakers offering their wares and watching for cops . . . handbook men, three-card monte boys, touts, tipsters and steerers for speaks. . . ."[52] To Cardinal Spellman, New York was the city of sin. "And Broadway," he said, "was not for your daughter."[53] But Broadway's footlights continued to attract the talented, the ambitious, the mischievous, and those who sought vicarious thrills.

With 270 recently opened plays, 1927 was "Broadway's biggest theater year ever." Nightclub hostess Texas Guinan's *Padlocks of 1927* was a garish, raucous offering, while *Good News* evoked memories of collegiate days. George M. Cohan's *The Merry Malones* was still going strong. When the *Ziegfeld Follies of 1927* opened on August 16, it featured for the first time a single star, Eddie Cantor (in blackface), and most of the songs were by only one composer, Irving Berlin. Mounted for the then-staggering sum of $289,000, it featured, among other things, a live ostrich that carried Claire Luce across a jungle-like set alive with cobras, tigers, and flamingos. In 1927, the hardy perennial *Abie's Irish Rose*, a play which popularized America as a melting pot of immigrants, was still on Broadway and still filling the house. The play opened in 1922 and ran for five years, five months, and 2,327 performances.

When *Showboat* opened in 1927, it was a different kind of musical. It dealt
with serious subjects, in serious ways. As the curtain rose, a formidable looking
group of black men sang:

> Niggers all work on de Mississippi,
> Niggers all work while de white folks play,
> Loadin' up boats wid de bales of cotton,
> Gittin' no rest till de Judgment Day.

Based on a novel by Edna Ferber, the musical traced the lives of three generations of a show business family and in the process dealt with such issues as race
relations, family strife, alcoholism, and miscegenation. When the curtain fell for
the first time no one applauded; no one knew what to do or say; everyone left
silently. The next day's reviews pronounced the show the greatest musical of all
time.[54] Ferber had been reluctant to have her story made into a Broadway musical which would feature fifty scantily clad show girls dancing on the deck of
"Cotton Blossom," the showboat of her story. But when she heard the music, she
wrote in her memoirs. "The music mounted, mounted, and I give you my word
my hair stood on end, the tears came to my eyes. I breathed like a heroine in a
melodrama. That was music that would outlast Jerome Kern's day and mine."[55]

The Pulitzer Prize in theater for 1927 went to Paul Green's play *In Abraham's
Bosom*, a story about race relations in rural North Carolina between 1885 and
1890. At that time, the Jim Crow laws held sway and the rigid separation of the
races was deeply entrenched. In the *Herald Tribune*, theater critic George Gold-
smith wrote that while the play was charged with "primitive emotion," it was also
"preachy, repetitious and faulty in construction." Perry Hammond, also writing for
the *Herald Tribune*, observed, "It is a sad play, so well written and so well acted
that even the near-Southerners who applaud 'Dixie' the loudest may be urged to
tears." Hammond wrote, however, that the play may be "a little tiresome to the
average playgoer." Even the Pulitzer Prize Award Committee noted that the
award was made not because the play was faultless, but because it "came up out of
the soil of the South, and with a passionate sincerity tried to say something important about the Negro problem, and because it seemed to us that the prize, if given
to Green, might be of great encouragement to regional American drama. . . . ."[56]

Titillating plays remained an important aspect of the theatrical scene of 1927.
The sex symbol of the year was Mae West, who offered *Sex*, a play she had written for Broadway. Bob Sisk, writing for Variety, wrote: "Never had disgrace fallen
so heavily on the 63d Street Theater as it did Monday night, when a nasty red-
light district show . . . opened. . . . Many people walked out before its first act was

over. . . . The second act saw many withdrawals, and the third act played to lots of empty seats. . . . [It] is a show so vile and strongly resembling the dramatic garbage of the year." The play was raided and Mae West was sentenced to ten days in the workhouse.[57]

In 1927, Billy Minsky's burlesque show *Irish Justice*, having provoked the "decent" people of New York, was raided for showing hard bodies and bare breasts. The show was performed in court before Magistrate Simpson so that he could judge the extent of its indecency. "One lame-brained show girl lifted her skirt, waved a neat limb at Magistrate Simpson, and simpered, 'How about meeting me at 7:30, Judgie?'"[58]

During 1927, consolidation among competing burlesque shows eliminated jealousy between rival shows and burlesque made a commitment to offer its audience "low gags and long legs." As a result, *Variety* reported that "the girls on the runway are grinding more vigorously."[59] Where police could be bought, burlesque went the limit with the "shake," "cooch," "shimmy" and striptease which prompted *Variety* to comment in 1928 that burlesque "is the most disgusting stage show ever presented."[60]

Police raids of "blue" plays scared those best able to pay for relatively expensive theater tickets, thus often forcing the actors to take a pay cut or to close down altogether. Reformers in New York clamored for a bill that would shut down for one year theaters that showed salacious plays. Governor Al Smith refused to sign such a bill. A "Committee of Nine" consisting of actors, managers, and authors, was established to act as a board of self-censorship but within a few months it disappeared.

Popular Music: "Let's Blow!"

When the novelist F. Scott Fitzgerald called the decade of the '20s the "Jazz Age" he meant the lifestyle, the mindset, the often delicious nonsense, serious rebellion, and protest against convention, which the often improvised music clearly reflected. Because its origins lacked respectability, because jazz mirrored the riproaring values of the twenties, it was initially by no means universally welcome. As reported in the *New York Times:* "The Salvation Army of Cincinnati obtained a temporary injunction today to prevent the erection of a moving picture theater adjoining Catherine Booth Home for Girls, on the ground that the music emanating from the theater would implant 'jazz emotions' in the babies born at the home."[61]

Throughout the twenties, newspapers reflected consistent concern about the negative influence of jazz upon Americans, especially young Americans. Just as in the 1990s the public and the press viewed with alarm the seeming encouragement rap lyrics gave youths to rebel, so too jazz was widely condemned for corrupting America's youth. To many, the music appeared to be not merely a musical craze, but a challenge to conventional morality, parental authority, and community values. Because jazz spoke for women's liberation, "flaming youth," sensuality, urban life, modernity, scientific and social experimentation, it was suspect in rural and traditional America even as they listened and were moved. Middletown could not escape the values of Broadway and Tin Pan Alley, whose publishing houses churned out music to which the populace could listen, sing, and dance as they heard beloved melodies played over and over again on the radio, phonograph, at the movies, or on the stage.

Here's how one newspaperman described Memphis's Beale Street, the home of the blues and the forerunner of jazz. It was, he said, "a street of business and love and murder and theft—an aisle where . . . merchants and pawnbrokers, country Negroes from plantations, Creole prostitutes and painted fag men, sleepy gamblers and slick young chauffeurs, crooks and bootleggers and dope peddlers and rich property owners and powdered women . . . and labor agents and blind musicians and confidence men and hardworking Negroes from sawmills and cotton warehouses and factories and stores meet and stand on corners and slip upstairs to gambling joints and rooming hotels and barber shops and bawdy houses."[62]

When the United States Navy closed down Storeyville, the infamous red light district of New Orleans, black musicians joined the migration northward to Kansas City, Chicago, and New York. If the 1927 slums of Memphis and New Orleans had any redeeming qualities, it was for the distinctively American music whose roots may be found in the talent of African American musicians of those cities. Jazz differs from other music in that it is sometimes improvised and, therefore, indefinable. It can assume such musical forms as ragtime, blues, work songs, African American spirituals, and brass band music.[63]

Jazz was perfectly suited to the illicit surroundings of roadhouse, speakeasies, private saloons, cabarets, where many Americans, high brow and low-, sought escape from the limitations on behavior imposed by Prohibition. In this environment, jazz became all the more suspect and all the more attractive at the same time. Jazz could go to one's head, touch one's soul, move one's feet, sway one's body, provide a touch of naughtiness, and allow Americans to blow off steam—like the liquor that was legally unobtainable. Jazz "loosened libidos and corsets and there seemed to be no end to the variety of dances that the flapper could do. From the intimate waltz to the sultry black bottom, the Charleston, and the shimmy, to the endless series of animal dances, experimentation was the order of the day." The underlying tempo of jazz is one "that makes shoulders twitch, that bedevils hips, that provokes wiggles and twists on the dance floor, and causes blue noses to cry out that jazz is a great immoral influence."[65] Because the origins of jazz were in the slums, because there was music to match every mood, jazz served to hide the grim reality that the "Roaring Twenties" did not roar for all Americans.

"A goodly part . . . of what we know as jazz is Jewish. Without Irving Berlin, Jerome Kern and George Gershwin (jazz) would be sadly lacking in light and shade."[66] To Brooklyn-born George Gershwin (1898–1937), jazz was a respectable music form which reflected, he said,

> the soul of the American people. . . . It is jazz developed out of ragtime, jazz that is the plantation song improved and transformed into finer, bigger harmonies. . . . it is a combination that includes the wail, the whine, the exultant note of the old 'mammy' songs of the South. It is black and white. It is all colors and all souls unified in the great melting pot of the world. . . . I do not know what the next decade will disclose in music. No composer knows. But to be true music it must repeat the thoughts and aspirations of the people and the time. . . . I am sure of but one thing: that the essence of future music will hold enough of the melody and harmony of today to reveal its origin. It will be sure to have a tincture of the derided yesterday, which has been accepted today and which perhaps tomorrow will be exalted—jazz.[67]

The jazz king of 1927 was Louis "Satchmo" Armstrong. With his Hot Five group of musicians (banjo, piano, clarinet, trombone) the Satchmo clowned around and made money with his hits of that year, "Muskrat Ramble" and "Heebie Jeebies." Louis Armstrong's remark to white trumpeter Jack Teagarden: "You an ofay, I'm a spade. Let's blow" may be apocryphal. But nevertheless, it suggests that to musicians, music's the thing, not race.[68] Fats Waller, the three-hundred pound Harlem-born pianist, "was the personification of the hedonism of the times. . . . He loved luxury and his capacity for pleasure was even larger than his size suggested."[69] In 1927, he wrote *Keep Shufflin'*, his first Broadway show, but *Hot Chocolates* (1928) was one of his biggest stage successes.

On December 4, 1927, Washington, D.C.-born Edward Kennedy "Duke" Ellington (1899–1974) began his reign at the Cotton Club. Located at 644 Lenox Avenue in New York's Harlem, the Cotton Club's all-black reviews were as glamorous and as lavish as anything on Broadway. The opening almost didn't take place. The Ellington band had a signed contract to appear in Philadelphia, but the well-connected mobsters who owned the Cotton Club knew what to do. They sent a well-built emissary with bulging pockets to the theater owner in Philadelphia

Duke Ellington. Courtesy the Schomburg Collection, New York Public Library.

"requesting" him to tear up the contract. "Be big or you'll be dead." Ellington opened in the Cotton Club right on schedule and played to its usual audience of gangsters, white and African American celebrities.[70] His performances added to the lore and lustre of the city and gave Gotham much of its irreverent character.

That the entertainment industry of the 1920s was marred by its intimate relationship with mobsters became evident in the vicious attack in November 1927 on popular cabaret singer Joe E. Lewis. The reasons for the attack were never made clear, but may have resulted from rivalry between competing cafe owners. Lewis was assaulted in his room at Chicago's Commonwealth Hotel by several men who slashed him so mercilessly that *Variety* reported in a headline, "Joe Lewis Survives Cutting/Minus Voice, Arm and Mind." "The deepest gash" the story continued, "was in his throat; another deprived him of his right arm and hand, while the most serious is the skull fracture. With Lewis's life now seemingly saved, the doctors are concentrating on saving his voice. . . ."[71] Lewis did survive, but he could no longer sing. He became a popular comic instead. The assailants were never apprehended.

But the more controversy jazz engendered, the more it appeared to grow. In 1927, the F. W. Woolworth five- and ten-cent stores challenged Tin Pan Alley when Woolworth began to sell ten cent disks with a hit song on one side and a non-copyrighted, and thus royalty-free, song on the other. In that year, the biggest hit on records was Gene Austin's "My Blue Heaven." It remained a best seller until it was superseded by Bing Crosby's recording of "White Christmas." *Variety* worried about the graft that was being paid by music publishers to singers, band leaders, masters of ceremonies, and to any who would push their songs and propel them into popularity.

Of all the big bands of the 20s, none rivaled that of Paul Whiteman (1890–1967). Whiteman, one of the band leaders who gave jazz its most exquisite expression, expounded, "What is jazz? Is it art, a disease, a manner, or a dance? Has it any musical value? After twelve years of jazz I don't know. . . . In this country especially, the rhythm of machine, the over-rapid expansion of a great country endowed with tremendous natural energies and wealth have brought about a pace and scale of living unparalleled in history. Is it any wonder that the popular music of this land should reflect these modes of living?"[72]

Between 1920 and 1934, Whiteman had thirty-two number one records, far more than any other band. Between 1925 and 1927, some 500,000 Americans listened to Paul Whiteman's orchestra play 400 jazz programs.[73] Among the recordings of 1927 that were voted into the Hall of Fame by the membership of the National Academy of Recording Arts and Science was George Gershwin's "Rhapsody in Blue."

Whiteman included in his band some of the best jazz players and singers of the period. Among the great band leaders who had their learning experiences with Whiteman were Jimmy and Tommy Dorsey. In 1927, crooner Bing Crosby joined the Whiteman band and became a hit on his own a few years later. But the singing sensation of the 1920s was Rudy Vallee.

After graduating from Yale in 1927, Rudy Vallee became the heartthrob of the Jazz Age. With a cheery "Heigh-ho Everybody" he led his Connecticut Yankees for a record-breaking ten years on radio. Among the super-stars who got their start with Rudy Vallee were George Burns, Gracie Allen, Edgar Bergen, and Charlie McCarthy, and Alice Faye. Ruth Etting, Helen Morgan, and Libby Holman, competing for best-selling female artist of 1927, made the torch song famous. The torch song was a kind of paradox in an age of flappers, in that the singers' lyrics pined for an unrequited love and implied slavish submission to the men who spurned them.

In 1927, the Metropolitan Opera House in New York presented *The King's Henchmen* to appreciative audiences. With a libretto written by Edna St. Vincent Millay, the opera drew on an old Saxon legend of chivalric ideals. The opera company took thirty-seven curtain calls on opening night. But it was another sort of "opera," which made a tremendous impact in years to come, that first debuted in 1927.

By 1927, station WSM in Nashville had been successfully producing a radio show called "Barn Dance" for two years. It was presided over by George Dewey Hay, sometimes known as "the solemn old judge," who allegedly referred to his program as the "Grand Ole Opry" because it followed an opera broadcast. On December 10, 1927, the name stuck and has been used ever since. It became the oldest continuous show in the history of radio. Initially seeking an audience in the rural south with hillbilly music, the Grand Ole Opry began to draw on religion and country music and to expand its audience far above the Mason-Dixon line.

A Golden Year in Sports

The 1920s was a golden age for sport in America. In journalist Grantland Rice, sports heroes found a wordsmith who could capture "their color and their crowd appeal, their vivid splash against the skyline, their remembered deeds. . . . Ruth, Dempsey, Bobby Jones, Man o' War, Hitchcock. . . . They had that indefinable quality that comes from championship ability plus the love and admiration of the masses on the personal side, which sport has never approached since—and probably never will again in the life span of this generation."[74] In a year of ballyhoo, Rice reported the triumphs of sports heroes and endowed them with virtues that made them worthy idols among the fans.

"In 1927 the sports world wore seven-league boots," wrote Grantland Rice; here's why.

• Baseball's biggest salary ever, $210,000 for three years' worth of work for the New York Yankees, went to Babe Ruth. "He is now the largest-salaried swatter that ever swung a bat."[75]

• At Wimbledon, Helen Wills triumphed in tennis.

• Johnny Weissmuller remained America's leading amateur swimmer.

• Although the Davis Cup was lost to France in 1927, "Big" Bill Tilden remained America number one tennis player. (During the many years during which Tilden was America's tennis hero sports writers rarely commented upon his homosexuality.)

• World War I flying ace Captain Eddie Rickenbacker bought the Indianapolis Motor Speedway and in 1927, George Souders, driving a Duesenberg, won the Indy 500 with an average speed of 97.545 miles per hour.

• The Harlem Globetrotters were organized by Abe Sapperstein. "On a crisp January day in 1927," wrote Wendell Smith, sports editor for the *Pittsburgh*

Courier, an important black newspaper, "[Sapperstein] . . . took five players, a ramshackle flivver . . . and a tattered road map and started one of the most amazing careers of sports the world over." Although the first journey out of Chicago was but forty-eight miles to Hinckley, Illinois, the travels of this team took it to the far corners of the earth. As the team's first manager and coach, Sapperstein outfitted the Globetrotters with red, white and blue striped uniforms made in his father's tailor shop. In that first winter of 1927, the team played before spectators who minimally understood the game. They won 101 of 117 games.

Walker "Toots" Wright, Byron "Fats" Long, Willis "Kid" Oliver, Andy Washington, and Al "Runt" Pullins developed a unique basketball style designed to win and to entertain. Spectators roared in amusement when players spun the ball on their fingers, bounced the basketball off their heads into the basket, or dribbled the ball between their legs. Despite these tactics, it was not until almost a decade later that the Globetrotters were taken seriously as a competitive and formidable basketball team.

• When in 1927 Gertrude Ederle met President Coolidge he said, "I am amazed that a girl of your small stature could swim the English Channel." As the first woman to swim the English Channel (1926) she smashed the existing men's records.

• In a water carnival sponsored by chewing gum magnate William Wrigley Jr., ninety-six swimmers, one man and one woman swimming nude, dived into the cold waters off Catalina Island to attempt to swim the 22 miles to the California mainland. Norman Ross of Chicago was the only one to complete the ordeal and to claim the $25,000 prize.

• Bobby Jones, a student at Emory Law School, defended his title in the British open by playing at the historic St. Andrews course in Scotland. More than 20,000 spectators walked the links with the 25-year-old when he won. The Scots were impressed with his level of play and did not hesitate to call him "the greatest golfer in the world." After Jones won the U.S. Amateur championship in 1927 for his fourth major title in two years, Grantland Rice wrote for the *New York Herald-Tribune*, "Bobby Jones . . . proved beyond all question that he is the greatest golfer that ever lived . . . in the span of time that dates back 500 years there has been only one Jones."[76] More than two billion dollars was invested in golf in the the United States alone. Three thousand professional instructors and over a hundred thousand workers were employed to maintain the courses.

• At Meadow Brook, Long Island, polo became a popular spectator sport and an American polo team led by Tommy Hitchcock defeated the English team to retain the International Cup for the United States.

• Collegiate, not professional, football dominated the year with 200,000 young collegians participating. Early in the 1920s, the center of college football shifted from the Ivy League schools of the Northeast to the universities of the mid- and far west. "Red" Grange, of the University of Illinois, dubbed the "Galloping Ghost" by Rice, remained the most popular player, but by 1927 he was playing professional football.

But the football hero of the year was not a player, but a coach—Knute Rockne of Notre Dame. In 1927, his Notre Dame team, spurred on by legendary inspirational locker-room talks, won seven games, tied one and lost one. His record to 1927 was sixty-four games won, six lost, and two tied. The roster of the teams he fielded and inspired reflected America as a nation of immigrants and was in marked contrast with the WASP players of the Ivy League.

Collegiate football in 1927 was, indeed, big time. So much so, that in those days as today, professors resented the pressure to allow academically marginal students to play. They deplored the vast sums invested in football and the fig leaf of amateurism that barely covered the near-professional reality of the way the game was viewed on many college campuses. Heywood Broun wrote in 1928 that college football should become frankly professional, a resolution to the problems that haunt institutions of higher education to this day as they continue to reconcile academic and football excellence.

• Boxer Jack Dempsey, according to Grantland Rice, with "steel fists and an iron jaw, was a killer in the ring. Outside he was gentle, courteous, patient, considerate." In 1926, Dempsey, the "Mannassa Mauler," lost by a decision in a ten-round bout with Gene Tunney, who became the new heavyweight champion of the world. Tex Rickard, boxing's impresario, promoted a return match between the two formidable boxers. On September 22, 1927, the Dempsey-Tunney "fight of the century" took place at Soldier Field in Chicago before a record crowd. To the Dempsey-Tunney rematch wealthy spectators came by plane and less well-to-do Americans came by special trains. The Twentieth Century Limited, the luxury train from Grand Central Station in New York to Chicago, stretched three times its normal length. At the 71st Armory at Park Avenue and Thirty-fourth Street in New York, two fighters reenacted the fight as Graham Mac-Namee called it on radio. Some fans were seated so far from the ring they could scarcely see the boxers. More favored fans including Charlie Chaplin, Douglas Fairbanks, Harold Lloyd, John Barrymore, Al Jolson, Florenz Ziegfeld, David Belasco, financier Bernard Baruch, steel magnate Charles M. Schwab, and retail mogul Julius Rosenwald were among those who could see boxing history being made.

Approximately fifty million intense fans heard Graham McNamee describe the infamous seventh round on radio:

> Dempsey drives a hard left under the heart. Jack pounded the back of Tunney's head with four rights. Gene put a terrific right-hardest blow of the fight-Gene beginning to wake up—like a couple of wild animals—Gene's body red-hits Dempsey a terrific right to the body—Jack is groggy—Jack leads hard left—Tunney seems almost wobbling—they have been giving Dempsey smelling salts in his corner—Some of the blows that Dempsey hits make this ring tremble—Tunney is down—down from a barrage—they are counting—six, seven, eight—.[77]

By Illinois boxing rules, Dempsey should have retired at once to a neutral corner. But by instinct, he hovered over his downed rival. Referee Dave Barry paused while he rushed Dempsey to a neutral corner, thus delaying the start of the count. The two extra seconds gave Tunney a chance to regain consciousness and eight seconds in which to rest. At the count of nine, Tunney rose to his feet. In the remaining three rounds, Tunney out-boxed a frustrated and angry Dempsey, and retained the world's boxing championship.

But as the headlines in the *New York Times* implied, controversy stalked the 1927 encounter:

GENE TUNNEY KEEPS TITLE BY DECISION AFTER TEN ROUNDS DEMPSEY INSISTS FOE WAS OUT IN THE 7TH AND WILL APPEAL.

The judgment of boxing lore remains inconclusive.

The Battle of the Century became legend not only because of its controversial conclusion but because it represented spectator sport at its most spectacular. 104,943 boxing fans paid a staggering $2,658,000 to see the second Dempsey-Tunney fight. Gene Tunney's purse for defeating Jack Dempsey was an equally astonishing $990,445, or $8.87 million in 1996 dollars. Jack Dempsey garnered $884,500 and retired from the ring.

*The mightiest of all Yankee teams had a crack pitching staff, a formidable "Murderers Row" of batters: Ruth, Lou Gehrig, Bob Meusel, Tony Lazzeri, and in Ruth, Meusel, and Earle Combs, a "perfect" outfield. In October, with 110 games won and 44 lost, the Yankees were nineteen games ahead of the second place A's, and in the World Series the Yankees trampled the Pirates in four straight games. On July 4, 1927, at Philadelphia, the turnstiles clicked 72,641 times for the Yankees-Athletics double-header. The twenty-two games played between these two teams alone attracted more than a half million paid admissions.

The 1926 Yankees. Reproduced from the collections of the Library of Congress.

In a year that worshipped athletic "greats," thirty-two-year-old Babe Ruth was a sports icon to Americans. On September 30, 1927, Babe Herman Ruth hit homer number sixty off southpaw Tom Zachary of Washington in a game at "The House that Ruth Built," the Yankee Stadium. It was Ruth's last time at bat, the score was 2-2 with one Yankee on base. The first pitched ball was a called strike, the second was high, a ball. The "Bambino" connected with a home run on the third pitch.

Babe Ruth found a worthy competitor in Lou Gehrig. Where Ruth was brash and often vulgar, Gehrig was a college-educated gentleman but with the same determination to win in a game he loved. In 1927, Gehrig hit forty-seven home runs.

If the Dempsey-Tunney re-match was the most spectacular sporting event of 1927, it was by no means the only one that attracted fans to the grandstands as sports became big business. "Babe Ruth played in ball parks before more than 30,000 spectators where attendance before had dropped below 1,000. Jack Dempsey fought before more than $10,000,000 worth of customers in what otherwise would have been a rather drab time for the ring."[78]

Upwards of 100,000 fans viewed the Notre Dame-Southern California battle in Chicago, and the total number of spectators for the entire football season, from September to Thanksgiving, was 30 million who paid $50 million in gate receipts. Attendance figures such as these appeared to justify the building of new college stadiums for as many as 80,000 spectators at one time. Higher admissions fees meant that the monies handled by college athletic directors were significantly greater than in 1926.

Horse racing, with a new single-day attendance record of 48,000, was at its most popular. Polo, more popular as a spectator sport in 1927 than today, golf, tennis, rowing, hockey, and virtually every sport on the calendar reflected startling increases in spectator attendance.

In reflecting on play in America, Stuart Chase estimated that Americans in 1927 spent approximately $21 million for all forms of diversions including driving for pleasure, listening to the radio, boating, hiking, hunting, and fishing. "Not far from one quarter of the national income of America is expended for play and recreation, broadly interpreted."[79] While the figure is a rough estimate only, it demonstrates that play became an important part in American life and that Americans were prepared to spend their affluence in having a good time. The prosperity of the 1920s, the increase in leisure time made possible by technological improvements, and fewer work hours gave Americans more leisure. Freed from Puritanical restrictions that equated play with sin, Americans came to recognize and to luxuriate in the utility of play.

※

[1]Kenneth S. Davis, *The Hero: Charles A. Lindbergh and the American Dream* (Garden City, New York: Doubleday and Company, Inc., 1959), p. 212.
[2]Ibid., p. 207.
[3]A. Scott Berg, *Lindbergh* (New York: G. P. Putnam's Sons, 1998), p. 6.
[4]Dixon Wecter, *The Hero In America: A Chronicle of Hero-Worship* (New York: Scribner's, 1941), p. 28.
[5]Geoffrey Perrett, *America in the Twenties: A History* (New York: Simon and Schuster, Inc., 1982), p. 283.
[6]Quoted in Berg, *Lindbergh*, p. 121.
[7]Quoted in *Literary Digest* 93 (June 4, 1927): 6.
[8]Davis, *The Hero*, p. 213.
[9]Berg, *Lindbergh*, p. 159.
[10]Davis, p. 233.
[11]Ibid., p. 120.
[12]Herbert Asbury, "The Year of the Big Shriek," in *Mirrors of the Year 1927-1928* (New York: Frederick Stokes and Company, 1928), p. 204.
[13]John D. Stevens, *Sensationalism and the New York Press* (New York: Columbia University Press, 1991), p. 126.
[14]Asbury, "The Year of the Big Shriek," p. 191.

[15]Robert A. Rutland, *The Newsmongers: Journalism in the Life of the Nation 1690–1972* (New York: The Dial Press, 1973), p. 319.

[16]Stevens, *Sensationalism and the New York Press,* pp. 152-153.

[17]Silas Bent, *Ballyhoo: The Voice of the Press* (New York: Boni and Liveright, 1927).

[18]Ibid., p. 31.

[19]J.L. Morrill. "What Goes on in the Newspaper Office." *Some Phases of Journalism.* Columbus, The Ohio State University, 1927, p. 37.

[20]"Tabloid Poison," *Saturday Review of Literature* 3 (February 19, 1927).

[21]Stevens, p. 123.

[22]Quoted in Stevens, p. 128.

[23]Oliver H.P. Garrett, "The Gods Confused," *American Mercury* 12 (November, 1927): 327.

[24]Ibid., p. 331.

[25]Ibid., p. 332.

[26]*New York Daily News,* April 8, 1927.

[27]Quoted in Robert Ernst, *Weakness is a Crime: The Life of Bernarr Macfadden* (Syracuse: Syracuse University Press, 1991), p. 89.

[28]Aben Kandel, "A Tabloid a Day," *Forum* 77 (March 1927): 383.

[29]Quoted in Bob Thomas, *Winchell* (Garden City, New York: Doubleday and Company, Inc., 1971), p. 43.

[30]Quoted in ibid., p. 37.

[31]Quoted in Martin Weyrauch, "The Why of the Tabloids," *Forum* 77 (April, 1927): 496.

[32]Ibid.

[33]*New York Times,* September 4, 1927.

[34]H. G. Wells, "Mr. Wells Bombards the Broadcaster," *New York Times Magazine* (April 3, 1927): 3 and 10.

[35]"Radio Men Counter-Attack H. G. Wells's Bombardment," *New York Times,* May 8, 1927, p. 16.

[36]Melvin Patrick Ely, *The Adventures of Amos 'n' Andy: A Social History of an American Phenomenon* (New York: The Free Press, 1991), p. 2.

[37]Quoted in Daniel E. Garvey, "Secretary Hoover and the Quest for Broadcast Regulation," *Journalism History* 3:3 (Autumn 1976): 67.

[38]"First False Radio Advertising Case," *Editor and Publisher* (August 13, 1927): 4.

[39]Al Jolson frequently performed in blackface. He did so when he sang in *The Jazz Singer,* and as a consequence today is often seen as racist. But, "Al Jolson opted for blackface to enhance the theatrical qualities of his performance, not to degrade blacks." Ted Gioia, "A Megastar Long Burned Under a Load of Blackface," the *New York Times,* October 22, 2000, p. 34.

[40]Peter Hay, *Movie Anecdotes* (New York: Oxford University Press, 1990), p. 3.

[41]Quoted in Abel Green and Joe Laurie, Jr., *Show Biz from Vaude to Video* (New York: Henry Holt and Company, 1951), p. 265.

[42]Benjamin B. Hampton, *A History of the Movies* (New York: Covici-Friede Publishers, 1931), p. 383.

[43]Robert Sklar, *Movie Mad America: A Cultural History of the American Movie* (New York: Vintage Books, 1994), p. 152.

[44]Ben Yagoda, "Hollywood Cleans Up Its Act," *American Heritage* 31 (1980): 15.

[45]Quoted in ibid.

[46]Leonard J. Leff and Jerold L. Simmons, *The Dame in the Kimono: Hollywood, Censorship and the Production Code from the 1920s to the 1960s* (New York: Grove Weidenfeld, 1995), p. 6.

[47]Barry Norman, *Talking Pictures* (New York: Hodder and Stoughton, 1987), p. 79.

[48]Quoted in Robert H. Stanley, *The Celluloid Empire: A History of the American Movie Industry* (New York: Hastings House, 1978), p. 185.

[49]Green and Laurie Jr., *Show Biz from Vaude to Video*, p. 253.

[50]Lionel Barrymore, "Will the Movies Ever be Different?" *Ladies Home Journal* (May 1927): 14.

[51]*New York Times*, November 8, 1927.

[52]Green and Laurie Jr., pp. 326-327.

[53]Ibid.

[54]Ibid.

[55]Quoted in Chuck Mancuso, *Popular Music and the Underground: Foundations of Jazz, Blues, Country, and Rock, 1900-1950* (Dubuque, Iowa: Kendall/Hunt Publishing Company, 1996), p. 48.

[56]John L. Toohey, *The Pulitzer Prize Plays* (New York: The Citadel Press, 1967), pp. 58-59.

[57]Green and Laurie Jr., pp. 288–289.

[58]Green and Laurie Jr., p. 305.

[59]Ibid.

[60]Green and Laurie Jr., p. 306.

[61]Quoted in Kathy J. Ogren, *The Jazz Revolution: Twenties America and the Meaning of Jazz* (New York: Oxford University Press, 1989), p. 3.

[62]Quoted in Thomas Childers, "Memphis," *American Heritage* (October 1998): 104.

[63]Russell Nye, *The Unembarrassed Muse: The Popular Arts in America* (New York: Dial, 1970), p. 332.

[64]Mancuso, *Popular Music and the Underground*, p. 49.

[65]Paul Whiteman, "In Defense of Jazz," *New York Times*, March 13, 1927.

[66]Isaac Goldberg, "Aaron Copland and His Jazz," *American Mercury* 12 (September 1927): 63.

[67]George Gershwin, "Jazz is the Voice of the American Soul," *Theatre Magazine* (March 1927). In Gregory R. Suriano, ed., *Gershwin in his Time: A Biographical Scrapbook 1919–1937* (New York: Gramercy Books, 1998), pp. 47-49.

[68]Richard M. Sudhalter, "A Racial Divide that Needn't Be," *New York Times*, January 3, 1999.

[69]Carl H. Giles, *1927: The Pictorial Story of a Wonderful Year* (New Rochelle, N.Y.: Arlington House, 1971), p. 117.

[70]Marshall W. Stearns, *The Story of Jazz* (New York: Oxford University Press, 1958), p. 183.

[71]Quoted in Arnold Shaw, *The Jazz Age: Popular Music in the 1920s* (New York: Oxford University Press, 1987), pp. 198-199.

[72]Paul Whiteman, "In Defense of Jazz," *New York Times*, March 13, 1927.

[73]Gilbert Seldes, "What Happened to Jazz," *Saturday Evening Post* (January 22, 1927): 25.

[74]Grantland Rice, "The Golden Panorama," in Allison Danzig and Peter Brandwein, ed., *Sport's Golden Age: A Close-up of the Fabulous Twenties* (Freeport, New York: Books for Libraries Press), p. 7.

[75]"Babe Ruth's $210,000 for Three Years of Swat," *Literary Digest* 92 (March 19, 1927): 67.

[76]Mark Inabinett, *Grantland Rice and His Heroes: The Sportswriter as Mythmaker in the 1920s* (Knoxville: The University of Tennessee Press, 1994), p. 54.

[77]Quoted in Allen Churchill, *The Year the World Went Mad* (New York: Thomas Crowell, Inc. 1990), p. 263.

[78]Rice, "The Golden Panorama," p. 2.

[79]Stuart Chase, "Play," in Charles A. Beard, ed., *Whither Mankind: A Panorama of Modern Civilization* (New York: Longmans Green, 1928), p. 338.

11

WRITERS AND READERS

November 5, 1927:

William Hale "Big Bill" Thompson, mayor of Chicago, had his eye on the White House. He thought he saw a lack of patriotic resolve in Chicago's libraries and schools, an issue which he could use to further his presidential aspirations. In pursuit of this goal, Mayor Thompson called upon the trustees of the Chicago Public Library to resign and to pressure William McAndrew, the reform-minded superintendent of Chicago schools, to do likewise.

The mayor's concern was that library books on American history were "tainted" with a pro-British slant and that American heroes like George Washington were described as rebels and as traitors and not treated with the veneration they deserved. In Mayor Thompson's view, it was the responsibility of the Chicago libraries to promote "Americanism" and this, he said, they were not doing. At one point he even threatened to burn the pro-British volumes on the shores of Lake Michigan.

To Mayor Thompson, William McAndrew was "that stool pigeon of the King of England" and a "bunk-shooting educator."[1] Among the mayor's criticisms was that the textbooks in use in Chicago schools were teaching "the false and insidious doctrines of alienism."

Thompson had been elected to his first term in 1915 and then again in 1919. He was defeated in 1923 by reform-minded William E. Dever but he was reelected in 1927. Because the thrice re-elected mayor seemed to personify Carl Sandburg's "Chicago: City of the Big Shoulders," because Mayor Thompson was the "Barnum" of politicians, what took place in Chicago elicited national interest and what he said attracted national attention.[2] Although his was a divisive voice, his words resonated well in some quarters of 1920s America. "My election," he pledged, "means that Chicago will be an example of patriotic devotion to American ideals—not a pest-hole of anti-Americanism. My election, thank God, means that our boys will not be cannon fodder for European battlefields. We will send these lackeys back to England where they can sing "'God Save the King.'"[3]

In her book *Paris France* (1940) Gertrude Stein declares, "After all everybody, that is, everybody who writes is interested in living inside themselves in order to tell what is inside themselves. That is why writers have to have two countries, the one where they belong and the one in which they live really. The second one is romantic, it is separate from themselves, it is not real but it is really there."[4] For most of the expatriates the second country was France and the second city Paris, where Americans found the creative climate to develop their literary or artistic bent. The Fifth and Sixth Arrondissements on the Left Bank of the Seine were more exciting than Greenwich Village, New York. Where the Boulevard Montparnasse crosses the Boulevard Raspail, students and artists from the Sorbonne and the Beaux Arts mingled with aspiring American writers and artists to form the core of Bohemian life in Paris.

In his memoirs, Matthew Josephson describes his second trip to Paris to do the research for his biography of Emile Zola. He notes, "The American invasion was seemingly at its flood tide when we arrived in Paris again in the spring of 1927; our ship alone had brought 531 American tourists in cabin class."[5] The United States Chamber of Commerce estimated that there were 15,000 Americans living in Paris in 1927. But this was probably an underestimate. How does one count the uncountable? That is, those who hang-out, who have no visible means of support, who hold no steady job, the unpublished writer, the artist who has not had a show, the musician who has not yet had his or her music performed in public, or the actor whose talent has yet to be recognized? The Paris police estimated that there were probably 35,000 Americans living in Paris. But were they really expatriates?

The Expatriates

"I feel more American than I have ever felt before," wrote Louis Bromfield in 1927 from the vantage point of living in what he called a "sick and weary" European continent. "Having known America intimately for the greater part of my life, I am familiar with the spectacle from the inside, and now I am seeing it from the outside, which is more illuminating than one might suppose. . . I have discovered things I could never have noticed in the midst of an Iowa cornfield or in the soda-fountain-bound crowds of Fifth Avenue and Forty-second Street." However, he concluded, "there isn't any such thing as an American Expatriate."

The American, he writes, is instead more like the ancient Roman. He is everywhere, flinging his money about, and he feels the power of an immense and wealthy nation. American money, Bromfield reported with pride, was saving Versailles and the Grand Trianon from ruin and repairing roofs and restoring walls of half the national monuments of France. Like the Roman citizen, the American, he wrote, was respected everywhere, even if it was only the respect that comes from wealth and power. Where once daughters of wealthy Americans went to Europe in search of marriageable men with titles of nobility, the American woman of his day, better dressed than the best Parisienne, was sought after by impoverished noblemen now in search of her wealth.

Those to whom the term "expatriate" has been applied included the newcomer Ernest Hemingway, the cartoonist James Thurber, that eccentric literary couple Zelda and Scott Fitzgerald, and the novelists Edna Ferber and William Faulkner. Those writers, and other Americans who lived in Paris in 1927, made frequent trips back to the United States. They loved Paris and what it had to offer but they had no desire to become French. When their child was about due, the Hemingways returned to America so that it would have American, not, French citizenship. The Americans living in Paris were not cut off from home. They spoke "American" with one another and had easy access to English language newspapers. "There were certain quarters of Paris that summer where one heard nothing but English spoken with an American accent."[6] If an expatriate is one who lives in permanent exile from his or her native land, then the term is not an accurate description for American writers who lived in Paris in 1927.

Publications as diverse as the *Brooklyn Daily Eagle, Vogue,* the *Saturday Evening Post,* and *Vanity Fair* had editorial offices in Paris. The most important literary review in Paris was *Transition,* the first number of which appeared in April 1927. "With its 150 pages of small type it appeared almost encyclopedic and gave representation to every tendency in the literary spectrum of modern Europe, America and the antipodes." James Joyce, Franz Kafka, and William Faulkner were among those who appeared in its pages. *Transition* achieved a circulation of four thousand and gave the doyenne of American expatriates, Gertrude Stein, ample representation. In the late spring of 1927, Nathalie Clifford Barney, an heiress from Cincinnati and an old Parisian resident who belonged to the preceding generation of American expatriates, gave a great tea party in honor of Gertrude Stein. In Miss Barney's resplendent mansion, located in the rue Jacob in the old St. Germain quarter, Ford Madox Ford read "Homage to Gertrude Stein" to some two hundred guests. Because so many of the guests were Americans, the few French writers among them bid a hasty retreat.[7]

Many Americans in 1927 were, however, critical of American writers who lived abroad. How could one write a novel about America while sipping coffee in a Parisian bistro or in a Roman street cafe? But, Bromfield reminded his readers, the young novelist without a ready audience must find a place he could afford to live. In 1927, that place was often in Europe.

For the wastrel, the opportunist, the eccentric, the hanger-on, for the talented but as-yet-unrecognized struggling artist and writer, the American dollar in France went a long way. While Paris in 1927 was not so cheap as Rome or Berlin, with 25.545 francs to the dollar, American expatriates could live comfortably if not elegantly in small, inexpensive hotels near the Boulevards Saint Michel and Saint Germain. A hotel room might cost as little as a dollar a day. For the equivalent of fifty cents one could buy a decent dinner including an acceptable *vin ordinaire*. In cafés such as the Café du Dome, Le Select, and La Rotonde, "wannabe" writers and artists could gather and linger and drink without the restraints imposed in America by prohibition.

The Writers

In a letter he wrote to Charles Green Shaw, who was doing a book on leading personalities of the 1920s, H. L. Mencken wrote, "I hope to write at least one good book before I die. Those that I have done are all transient and trivial. . . ."[8] But the "bad boy of Baltimore," as he was called, was being too modest. In an age when many worried that writers like factory workers were churning out standardized products, Mencken spiced the decade with his iconoclasm. He had little faith in democracy and unrelentingly scorned the "homo boobiens" of middle America. Yet his rejection of democracy may have been more apparent than real. He had enough faith in Americans so that he, along with them, ridiculed Puritanical inhibitions, opposed censorship, and championed individual rights. He opposed the Ku Klux Klan, prohibition, book burning, and postal regulations that prohibited the flow of reading materials considered salacious.

In 1927 he wrote: "I am completely devoid of religious feeling. All religions seem ridiculous to me, and in bad taste . . . I do not believe in the immortality of the soul, nor in the soul. . . ."[9] He thumbed his nose at fundamentalism and believed Christianity to be a mob religion. To show his disdain for religion he sometimes stole Gideon Bibles from hotel rooms and sent them to friends inscribed "With regards from the author." He ridiculed women's rights declaring, "Women can make men perfectly happy, but they seldom know how to do it. . . . Women are also the cause of the worst kind of unhappiness."[10] "I have little belief in human progress. The human race is incurably idiotic. It will never be happy. . . . I believe the United States will blow up within a century. Being an American seems amusing to [me], but not exhilarating."[11] He attracted young readers to his *American Mercury* because they agreed with him and older readers because he exasperated them. Little wonder, then, that Sinclair Lewis dedicated *Elmer Gantry*, a scathing satire of religious fundamentalism, to H. L. Mencken.

Elmer Gantry was one of a series of books by Lewis in which he satirized many aspects of conventional American life. In *Main Street* (1920), Lewis scorned the small town that centered on such self-satisfied, conventional fraternal organizations as Kiwanis and Rotarians. He worried about the unimaginative outlook of the men and women of Gopher Prairie, the fictional site of Lewis's *Main Street*, of the apparent reluctance of small town America to come to grips with modernism and pluralism. In *Babbitt* (1922), he satirized American business, and in *Arrowsmith* (1925), he scorned the medical profession, whose fee for service mentality gave second place to medical research while distributing medical services unevenly among Americans. For *Arrowsmith*, Lewis was awarded the Pulitzer Prize. But the forty-year-old writer cavalierly turned it down, thereby stimulating ever more controversy while enhancing his image as a breaker of idols and, not least, assuring his place among publishers as a controversial and marketable writer.

"If He is a Fundamentalist God, Let Him strike me dead within ten minutes," declared Sinclair Lewis as he ridiculed Christian Fundamentalism in his 1927 speech to the Linwood Boulevard Christian Church in Kansas City. Inasmuch as his challenge to God was uttered shortly before the appearance of *Elmer Gantry* (1927), he attracted even more than the usual thunder and lightning, this time from evangelists and fundamentalists and the faithful to whom they preached. In *Elmer Gantry*, he satirized the growing commercialism and dubious morality of a host of Christian preachers. While it is not clear at whom especially he aimed his satire, he may have had in his sights the swashbuckling evangelist Aimee Semple McPherson of Los Angeles (see pp. 199–205). But there were some who thought that in creating *Elmer Gantry*, Sinclair Lewis went too far. William Lyons Phelps believed that "Elmer Gantry is not a representative clergyman, he is not even human."[12]

Despite the criticism, *Elmer Gantry* struck a responsive note among the book-buying public. With an initial printing of 100,000 copies and sales of over 200,000 in the first ten weeks, *Elmer Gantry* became the number one best seller in 1927 and Sinclair Lewis the year's most popular American novelist. *Elmer Gantry* was the unanimous choice of the Book-of-the-Month Club, which had been formed the year before. The judges felt that the book was not so well written as Lewis's *Babbitt* but, wrote one of the members of the selection committee, "Many will be shocked by it, but everyone will wish to read it."[13]

The Bridge of San Luis Rey by the thirty-year-old dramatist Thornton Wilder was among the best novels of the year and remains a literary classic. The bridge in Wilder's story, built by Incas in the seventeenth century, was "the finest bridge in all Peru. . . ." It had been woven with loving care by skillful fingers, "a mere ladder of slats that swung over the gorge. . . ." But on July 20, 1714, the bridge collapsed and five travelers were thrown into the ravine below. Brother Juniper, a Franciscan monk with a mission to convert the Incas to Christianity, witnessed the horror. As Wilder's story unfolds, the author traces the lives of the five who were killed. By the story's end, Brother Juniper is convinced that death was the best possible outcome for the victims in view of the circumstances they faced.

Wilder looked to another time and place for the setting of his story. Yet his story had wide appeal because he dealt with the continuing search for spiritual meaning. Was it God's plan that those five perish or did they die by accident? In 1927, Americans were grappling with the seeming erosion of traditional values, the pluralism brought about by immigrants, the growing migration of rural whites and Southern blacks to the cities of North and South. Americans were not yet entirely comfortable with the new machinery readily available to them; radio, automobiles, and the labor-saving household appliances electricity wrought. Were men and women meant to fly? Was the backseat of an automobile a suitable place for the young to make love? If not married, should the young be making love? Should women be working outside the home? Need religious America be at war with scientific America? Was rural America dying and was urban life better? What entertainment was suitable for the airwaves and for the movies? Was drinking alcoholic beverages altogether wicked?

Hemingway's *Men Without Women* is a book of short stories in which the author shows that without the softening influence of women men are likely to be more violent in their behavior. "The Undefeated" is the story of an aging bull fighter who is looking for just one more opportunity to step into the arena. He is reluctantly given the opportunity to do so and in the encounter, vividly described by Hemingway, although he is gored, he continues to fight until he kills the bull. Perhaps the best story is "Killers," in which two gunmen come to a small restaurant frequented by a Swede, Ole Anderson, whom they are determined to kill. Ole is warned by a boy that the killers are in town, but Ole makes no move to leave his spartan room.

William Faulkner, John Steinbeck, Ezra Pound, and Edwin Arlington Robinson, were among the young writers who were not yet well known in 1927. The veteran writer Booth Tarkington wrote *The Plutocrat* in 1927, which some consider his best book. Edgar Rice Burroughs, who conceived his *Tarzan* books in 1913, continued to write and sell them in 1927. Burroughs, writing in Chicago, far from the African jungles, wrote of a white boy who was brought up by apes. The stories were popular throughout the twenties and the books were eventually translated into fifty-six languages.

Crime novels were extraordinarily popular in 1927 perhaps because of the growing awareness of lawbreaking as Americans sought to thwart the inhibiting influences of prohibition. Of the crime novels, the best were those of S. S. van Dine. His *The Canary Murder Case* of 1927 sold well and *The Greene Murder Case* by the same author made the best-seller list of 1928. S. S. van Dine advanced the mystery story by introducing elements of psychology and psychiatry which were still essentially new developments. In van Dine's view, every murder had not only the fingerprint of the murderer, but bore his or her psychological imprint as well. Thus, if the behavior of a suspect could be verified and interpreted one was nearer to the solution of the crime. In *The Canary Murder Case*, for example, a game of poker is arranged with the thought that the way one behaves in playing poker is similar to the way one behaves in planning murder. Through the poker game Vance discovers the killer.

In non-fiction it is not surprising that Charles A. Lindbergh's account of his flight, *We*, made the best-seller list of 1927. But it may be more of a surprise that so much serious non-fiction sold so well. Will Durant's *The Story of Philosophy*, published by Simon and Schuster was the number one non-fiction best seller in 1927. The author proposed to "study not merely philosophies, but philosophers; we shall spend our time with the saints and the martyrs of thought, letting their radiant spirit play about us until perhaps we too, in some measure take part in what Leonardo called 'the noblest pleasure, the joy of understanding.'"[14] In eleven succinct chapters *The Story of Philosophy* introduces its readers to the giants of philosophy. While the Book of the Month Club did not make *The Story of Philosophy* a "book-of-the-month," it did recommend the book to its members. "It is good reading for the least philosophical of nations."[15]

In 1927, Oswald Spengler published his pessimistic *The Decline of the West* which foresaw the end of Western civilization. Vernon Parrington published *Main Currents of American Thought* which, in three volumes, probed the work of American poets, historians, novelists, orators and pamphleteers. Charles A. and Mary R. Beard published their popular history of the United States, *The Rise of American Civilization*. It influenced what students and scholars of American history read, thought, and argued about for two generations. The journalist Mark Sullivan wrote the second volume of his *History of Our Times*, a popular treatment of American society. André Siegfried, a French critic of America, made a number of important observations of conflicts in American culture in

1927. His book, which loosely translates as *America Comes of Age*, is especially concerned with conflicting racial problems in America.

Biography was especially popular for American readers in 1927. Carl Sandburg's life of Lincoln, *The Prairie Years*, was described by one writer as "a masterpiece." André Maurois, the French novelist and biographer, wrote a life of the British prime minister, *Disraeli*, and Philip Guedalla wrote one of the British prime minister, *Palmerston*. Emile Ludwig's biography *Napoleon* was described as the most interesting of a number of biographies written by the author. But by current standards, it is far from a satisfactory treatment of its subject.

Women Writers

Mark Twain insisted that Helen Keller along with Napoleon were the two most interesting characters of the 19th century. Helen Keller, blind and deaf from a childhood illness, was tutored by Anne Sullivan and the two of them were well known to Americans through numerous lectures and vaudeville acts. Helen Keller published *My Religion* in 1927.

Among the best sellers of the year was *Lost Ecstasy*, by fifty-one-year-old Mary Roberts Rinehart, better known as a prolific writer of popular mystery. *Lost Ecstasy* is a more general novel of a loving relationship between a cowboy and a lady. Using a fountain pen rather than a typewriter, Rinehart wrote sixty novels, many of which are still readily available today. Among her readers and admirers was secretary of commerce and later President Herbert Hoover.

Willa Cather became well known for her *Death Comes for the Archbishop*. It is the story of two missionary priests who seek to convert the Indians in "territories yet unknown and unnamed" in New Mexico and Colorado. The plot of the story is secondary to the character descriptions of the missionaries, the Indians, the Mexicans, the clash of religious beliefs, and the pageantry of the Spanish Catholic heritage. Edna Ferber wrote *Showboat*, which shortly thereafter became an operetta on Broadway (see p. 264). Among the poets, Edna St. Vincent Millay wrote *The King's Henchman* which was made into an opera and Sara Teasdale wrote a slender volume of meditations, *Dark of the Moon*.

Edith Wharton, already popular for her novels *Ethan Frome* (1911) and *The Age of Innocence* (1920), wrote *Twilight Sleep*, a popular satire of New York's fashionable society, which made the list of best sellers for 1927. Yet, Wharton complained that "the great American novel" was reflecting an American era that had passed rather than one that was emerging. In 1927 she wrote: "America's sedentary days are long since past. The whole world has become a vast escalator, and Ford motors and Gillette razors have bound together the uttermost parts of the earth. The universal infiltration of our American plumbing, dentistry and vocabulary has reduced the world to a playing field for our people. . . . We have . . . internationalized the earth, to the deep detriment of our picturesqueness." Yet, she went on to note, publishers of 1927 were asking for manuscripts which represented life in America as if we were still "tethered to the village pump." Great American novels, she insisted, should instead reflect "the intense social acquisitiveness and insatiable appetite for new facts and new sights."[16]

Dorothy Parker and the Algonquin Round Table

Her *New York Times* obituary described Dorothy Parker (1893–1967) as a "literary wit," and "sardonic humorist." She, like Mencken, challenged the conventional wisdom of her day. As a writer of advertising copy for *Vogue* she honed a spare writing style; as in, "Brevity is the soul of lingerie." With rapier-like wit she reached for the jugular and found it. When a pompous young man declared, "I cannot suffer fools gladly." Her instant repartee was, "That's funny. Your mother could." When looking for a writing assignment she wrote, "Salary is no object; I want only enough to keep body and soul apart." Pressed by the *New Yorker* for overdue book reviews she replied, "I am too fuckin' busy and vice versa."

In December 1926, Horace Liveright published *Enough Rope*, a book of Dorothy Parker's mostly light and sparkling poetry which eventually went through an unprecedented eleven printings. Of her book of verse, the *New York Times* had this to say: "Miss Parker's is not society verse . . . it is flapper verse. And as such it is wholesome, engaging, uncorseted and not devoid of grace."

In October 1927, she began writing book reviews for the *New Yorker*. Identifying herself as "Constant Reader" she wrote influential weekly book reviews through May 1928, and occasionally until 1933. Through her stinging columns she enhanced the reputation of some authors while destroying that of most others. Dorothy Parker admitted that it was easier to criticize those you hate than to praise those you love. Of one novel she wrote, "This is not a novel to be tossed aside lightly. It should be thrown with great force."

If 1927 was the height of the flapper era, then Dorothy Parker was its essence. She regretted that she could not claim to be a native New Yorker because at the time of her birth the family was at its vacation home in West End, New Jersey. Her father was J. Henry Rothschild, a prosperous clothing manufacturer, and her mother was the former Eliza Marston, of Scottish descent. She recalled that she was "a plain and disagreeable child with stringy hair and a yen to write poetry." Her marriage to Edwin Pond Parker was a turbulent one, and the couple divorced in 1928. She was married and divorced again, drank too much, had numerous devastating love affairs which resulted in two abortions. She made several attempts at suicide. She was arrested and fined $5 for "sauntering" in a demonstration at the Massachusetts State House against the electrocution of Sacco and Vanzetti. She was a little woman possessed of a dollish face and basset hound eyes. As the writer Alexander Woolcott put it, she was a blend of "Little Nell and Lady Macbeth."[17] In 1967, Dorothy Parker died alone in her suite at the Volney Hotel in New York City, with only Troy, her poodle, at her side.

Parker was a founding member of the Algonquin Round table, an informal gathering of literary wits who met at the Algonquin Hotel to drink, dine and insult each other. The Round Table took shape in June 1919 and included such literary notables as Alexander Woolcott, Harold Ross, who became founding editor of the *New Yorker*, the columnist Heywood Broun, the journalist/historian Margaret Leech, Robert Benchley, Robert Sherman, and Frank Adams, who wrote the then-popular column "The Conning Tower." The novelist Edna Ferber was a participant, as was Edna St. Vincent Millay, the Canadian-born humorist Stephen Leacock, and Damon Runyon, the quintessential newspaper reporter. While the participants around the table varied daily, they formed a literary network which could get jobs, produce plays, launch magazines, and publish fiction, non-fiction, and poetry. They all took great pleasure in skewering one another and others with literary pretensions with one-liners, using scathing wit that bordered on insult.

The Round Table participants ladled up a witches' brew of ideas, some of which would eventually find expression in the syndicated columns they wrote, the magazines they edited, the plays and books they wrote and criticized. While most were not originally from Manhattan, they viewed themselves and were so regarded by others as savvy, debonair, urbane, ultra-modern urbanites who pried New York, and perhaps most of America, from its conventional moorings. By 1927, the Algonquin Round Table began to break up. But the influence of its participants on the lively arts lingered on well beyond the decade of the twenties. Margaret Case Harriman, the daughter of the owner of the Algonquin Hotel, observed: "Nothing like the Round Table—for color, interest, and lasting influence—had ever been seen before; and nothing like it has been known since."[18]

H. L. Mencken and the Harlem Renaissance

In a portrait of her friend Alexander Woollcott, the literary critic and radio host, Dorothy Parker wrote in *Vanity Fair* in 1934, "Then he came to New York ... Didn't we all?"[19] In the aftermath of World War I, among those who came to New York were Southern blacks who began to shed their rural lifestyle. From the farm they moved first to Southern cities and then to Chicago, Cleveland, and Detroit.

But New York's Harlem was the mecca that beckoned. In 1890, one in seventy people in Manhattan was black; by 1930, it was one in nine. In other cities, black enclaves were carved out of white neighborhoods and white resentment mounted. Between 1916 and 1930, New York was one of the few large cities that did not experience violence between the races. In his 1927 book, *The Decline of the West*, Oswald Spengler identified New York as a world city and only such a city could absorb the great African American migration that came to it.

Jimmy Walker, the suave mayor of New York City in 1927, reflected "the New York style incarnate."[20] Debonair, pleasure-loving, flamboyant, and fashionable, "His Honor" spent as much time in nightclubs, with someone else picking up the check, and on vacations, paid for by others, as he did behind his desk at City Hall. Criticized for his high salary, he quipped, "Think of what it would cost if I worked full time."[21] But New Yorkers didn't care.

New Yorkers loved him because he loved them, all of them, and they knew it. African Americans in New York's Harlem knew it. He removed restrictions on hiring African American doctors at Harlem Hospital and otherwise showed himself to be racially and ethnically sensitive. And it was none too soon, because in the decade of the '20s New York became the culture capital of the world and Harlem became the Harlem we know today. Black Manhattan, as the African American writer James Weldon Johnson described Harlem, became home to talented blacks who contributed to what the *Herald Tribune* called the Negro Renaissance.

In 1927, while waiting to go to work, a black youth loitered in a bank lobby in Memphis. Perfunctorily, he picked up a newspaper, and as he glanced through it, he suddenly fixed his attention upon a very strange article. Here in front of his bewildered eyes was a vicious verbal attack on a man who was not black, and yet the vehemence of the language was of the kind that was usually reserved for blacks. Why did the South hate this man so much, the youth wondered. His curiosity piqued, he borrowed a library card from a white co-worker and forged a note. "Will you please let this nigger boy," read the astonished librarian in charge, "have some books by H. L. Mencken." Why would any Southerner want a book by H. L. Mencken, much less a "nigger?" Reluctantly, she gave Richard Wright the books he sought.[22]

Little wonder that to the white South Mencken was its nemesis. In an article entitled, "The Sahara of the Bozart," Mencken described the American South as a intellectual wasteland as barren as the Sahara. The South he said, in 1917 "is almost as sterile artistically, intellectually, culturally as the Sahara Desert."[23] It is a "gargan-tuan paradise of the fourth-rate. There is not a single picture gallery worth going into, or a single orchestra capable of playing the nine symphonies of Beethoven, or a single opera-house, or a single theater devoted to decent plays, or a single public monument worth looking at, or a single workshop devoted to making of beautiful things . . . you will not find a single Southern prose writer who can actually write . . . when it comes to critics, musical composers, painters, sculptors, architects and the like, you will have to give it up, for there is not even a bad one between the Potomac mudflats and the Gulf. Nor a historian. Nor a philosopher. Nor a theologian, Nor a scientist. In all these fields the South is an awe-inspiring blank. . . ."[24]

Ten years later, in the *American Mercury* for October 1927, H. L. Mencken acidly announced that America had entered the "Coon Age" in recognition that during the decade of the 1920s "the Negroization of American culture became something like a recognized phenomenon."[25] While unselfconsciously using the term "darkey," "blackamoor," "coon," Mencken asserted that so much of what passed for American music and dance, cooking and language, the cabaret and the church, had its origins in black influences. He believed that African Americans were in a better position than whites to describe the realities of their life, to reveal the truth about the harshness of their conditions, and the tensions such conditions created for raising families, going to school, getting and keeping jobs, realizing ambitions, releasing creativity, and achieving recognition.

It is difficult to understand in our time that Mencken should also be considered a friend by many African Americans. Perhaps he was acceptable because he was critical of the South as well, and if he criticized African Americans, as he often did, they listened. "He was their cup of tea precisely because he was a bitter brew." He was tough-minded, unsentimental, honest, and in him blacks found a man who told them, "with zest and humor that these attitudes were necessary for the writing of great literature."[26]

Among the early major white publishers to publish the works of African American writers were Horace Liveright who in 1922 published Jean Toomer's *Cane*, an examination of the lives of blacks in America. Albert and Charles Boni published Alain Locke's *The New Negro*, an anthology of essays on Negro life in 1925, and upon Mencken's urging, Alfred A. Knopf in 1927, reissued James Weldon Johnson's 1912 *Autobiography of an Ex-Colored Man*. Mencken was among the first to open the pages of his *American Mercury* magazine to black writers, and to recognize and welcome the literary contributions of African Americans to the cultural mosaic of America. Between 1924 and 1933, Mencken published fifty-four articles by and about blacks in his *American Mercury*.

George Schuyler became the most published author, black or white, in the *American Mercury*. Between 1927 and 1934, nine of Schuyler's essays appeared in that popular monthly. He complained that African Americans were becoming less black as they took medication to lighten their color and used hair ointments to straighten their hair. "As a group we have year by year been getting lighter and lighter, both as to complexion, morals and brains."[27] He was the most acid-tongued critic of black life—not only in the *Mercury* but in other publications as well.

"Nineteen twenty-seven seems to have been the year for satire," and the *American Mercury* was the perfect vehicle for satirical pieces. [28] In "Our White Folks," published in the *American Mercury*, George Schuyler viewed the white not as a monster, but as one who is lazy, hypocritical, and often stupid. The Southerner's knowledge of blacks was mostly superficial while blacks' knowledge of whites was detailed and intimate.[29] In an article "Blessed are the Sons of Ham," published in the *Nation*, Schuyler wrote how he relished the discomfort of waiters who lied to him by saying all tables were occupied in a dining room, or of ticket sellers who said the show is a sell-out when he tried to buy a theater ticket.[30] (see also pp. 154–156). In "Our Greatest Gift to America," published in *Ebony and Topaz*, he wrote that the black presence flatters the white into believing that he is better than the black "buffoons" he sees in minstrel shows.[31]

Writing in *Forum* in 1927, the black sociologist E. Franklin Frazier wrote a satire, "The Pathology of Race Prejudice." Frazier finds that the pathologies associated with insanity are similar to those associated with race prejudice. Southerners construct a theory to prove "that white blood is responsible for character and genius in mixed Negroes"; then they find an equal and opposite theory that "white blood" harms blacks. Like the insane who do not give up their fixed beliefs no matter what the evidence, so too the racists do not surrender their views that white blood is superior to African American blood, or that the African American is a ravisher of women. Frazier ended his essay with a quotation from Nietzsche, "Insanity in individuals is something rare—but in groups, parties, nations, and epochs, it is the rule."[32] Such is the case, he concluded, in the American South.

In 1922, with Mencken's encouragement, Walter White wrote *The Fire in the Flint*. For two years it remained unpublished until Mencken intervened on White's behalf and prevailed upon Knopf to release it. By 1926, some reviewers were describing White's novel as "the greatest novel yet written by an American Negro."[33] But not Mencken. "He had gotten it (the novel) published and then he saw it praised beyond its meager merits."[34] Even as he opened the pages of the

American Mercury to African American writers, by 1927 he began to feel that the promise of the Harlem Renaissance would fall short.

On the one hand, Mencken felt that the Negro Renaissance had failed to produce that great American novel written by an African American, and on the other, it had failed to develop a black audience for black writers. "By 1927, many felt that the Harlem Renaissance had simply come and gone, without much happening in between."[35] It was Mencken's view that the inability of the African American to write such a novel was a litmus test of the artistic capacity of the black race and it had failed the test.

In a July 17, 1927, article that he wrote for the *New York World*, Mencken quickly comes to the point: "So far, it seems to me, his accomplishments have been very modest. . . . He [the Negro] has done little of solid value. . . . The best jazz and ragtime are being created by George Gershwin and Paul Whiteman. . . . As to poetry, with the exception of James Weldon Johnson, they have done very little." As for novels, "No Negro has ever written a novel even remotely comparable to such things as *Babbitt* or *Jurgen*. No Negro writing short stories rises above the level of white hacks." Then in an about face, Mencken abandoned the wait-and-see attitude which marked his views earlier in the decade and asserted, "I am not altogether sure that his prospects in the fine arts are as good as the more optimistic partisans seem to think."[36] Two months later in another piece for the *New York World* he continued his criticism.

While some African Americans viewed Mencken's comments as a stab in the back, others accepted them because Mencken, being Mencken, was simply telling the truth in his own pugnacious style. George Schuyler in a piece for the *Pittsburgh Courier* declared, "Indeed, I have said much the same thing myself." But Schuyler did not let Mencken off so easily. "On the other hand, it seems to me that Br'er Mencken's attitude is a little pontifical." American writers, Schuyler insisted, had not for the most part, achieved the levels of great European writers, nor did composers achieve the level of Beethoven, Wagner, or Liszt. "The fact is that this is a young country just emerging from the pioneering stage." And so, it was not surprising that white America's literary output had been mediocre.

Other blacks were not so kind to Mencken. The black press accused him of slander, others of sophistry, of being a source of evil, an infidel, of being mesmerized by the "tar-baby" image of the American black. W. E. B. DuBois was more restrained, but he did say that Mencken "did not understand where the shoe pinches." Du Bois noted that the African American artist was expected to write about "fools, clowns, prostitutes," and that subtle discrimination remained against him by the leading publishing houses. DuBois asserted that Mencken unfairly overlooked Toomer, Dunbar, McKay, and Hughes, and concluded, "despite a stimulating critic's opinion, we Negroes are quite well satisfied with our Renaissance. And we have not yet finished."[37]

What H. L. Mencken forgot or chose to overlook was that the Harlem Renaissance was a protest movement as much as it was a literary and artistic movement. Driven from the ballot box by poll taxes and other restrictions, blacks of the 1920s lacked political clout. With discrimination in the workplace denying them economic power as well, the artists of the Harlem Renaissance sought to prove that their talents were as good as those of whites and that in this arena they could fare competitively on their own merits and in strict conformity with the best literary talent. The Harlem Renaissance was a movement toward self-discovery as blacks sought to adapt to both urban environment and modernity. In a sense, the writers who did achieve recognition as part of the renaissance were American expatriates who found in Harlem and even in Paris an environment which could hone their emerging talents. Writing in 1927, African American sociologist E. Franklin Frazier noted that blacks, as other minorities, at first attempted to lose themselves in the majority, sometimes even at the expense of giving up unique characteristics. When this fails, as it always does, "a new valuation is placed upon these very characteristics, and they are glorified in the eyes of the group."[38] Thus, the Harlem Renaissance initiated a wave of black nationalism which expressed itself in the Marcus Garvey movement which urged a return to Africa and the black power movement of our own time.

Emanuel Haldeman-Julius and the Little Blue Books

In 1926 the Book-of-the-Month Club was born and was followed in 1927 with the establishment of the Literary Guild. Both sought to take advantage of a growing readership among the American people. By making explicit recommendations of books by a panel of literary critics, and by promoting them heavily in bookstores and through direct mail, the book clubs contributed to the growth of a book-buying public. By offering free memberships in the clubs, discounts on popular books, premiums and special offerings for members who purchased a stipulated number of books annually, the book clubs helped substantially to create a mass market for books. Once a cottage industry, book publishing leaped into the commercial mainstream and developed sophisticated techniques in book production, distribution and promotion. A maverick publisher, E. Haldeman-Julius drew on these techniques to make his "little blue books" among the most widely read during the 1920s.

Emanuel Julius was born in 1889 in Philadelphia to immigrants who had come to America from Odessa, Russia, ten years earlier. Although his parents were Jewish, Emanuel remained an atheist throughout his life. His father had been a binder of fine books and had bound a set of books for Theodore Roosevelt. Emanuel had a helter-skelter kind of schooling, but with a father in the bookbinding business, books were available to him and he read very widely. In his late teens he joined a branch of the Socialist Party in Philadelphia and before he was twenty he had met some of the giants in the socialist movement in America. He moved to New York City where he earned a meager living as a reporter for the progressive newspaper the *Call*. He pursued several jobs as a reporter on socialist newspapers in Chicago and Los Angeles but eventually moved to Girard, Kansas, to try to salvage the journal *Appeal to Reason* whose chief editorial writer was the noted Eugene Debs.

In 1915, while working on *Appeal to Reason*, he met Marcet Haldeman, the daughter of an affluent banker in Girard, Kansas. The niece of Jane Addams, founder of Hull House, a pioneering settlement house in Chicago, Marcet Haldeman was a no-nonsense, rather hard-nosed social worker who was trying to write while addressing the needs of the poor. In 1916, Marcet and Emanuel were married and a year later, as the circulation of the *Appeal to Reason* continued to dwindle, they bought the paper. Marcet supplied the money and Emanuel the managerial and editorial skills. The hyphenated name, Haldeman-Julius reflected their marital and business partnership.

The new publishing venture, *People's Pocket Series*, printed good literature in paperbound editions which sold for twenty-five cents. The idea was modeled after a German publisher, Universal Bibliothek, which successfully published a list of seven thousand inexpensive small books in red paper covers. Initial success was modest because production costs were high. It was not until after 1924 when Haldeman-Julius could invest in new printing and binding equipment, that his publishing effort, renamed the Little Blue Books, seemed assured. While he was initially guided by intuition, Haldeman-Julius eventually relied heavily on analysis of sales data, responses to advertising, and questionnaires designed to elicit the literary tastes of the mass of Americans.

The Little Blue Book idea drew on both socialism and capitalism. The socialist part was based on the then-novel idea that the proletariat would read good books if manufactured cheaply enough and if they could be carried in their work clothes for reading during a rest from the assembly line or on a lunch break. The capitalist part was that Haldeman-Julius was determined to make the venture a profitable one by controlling costs, advertising heavily and using modern marketing and management skills. He sharpened his manufacturing techniques so that his Little Blue Books could be manufactured for a penny a book and sold for a nickel.

By 1927, he had sold a hundred million Little Blue Books and his printing plant in Girard, Kansas, became the largest mail-order book publishing company in the world. When asked whether he considered himself a philanthropist or a capitalist he declared forthrightly, "I invested my capital in the Little Blue Book idea because I thought it was a sound business venture. . . . I was as interested in making a profit as Henry Ford."[39]

The journalist Louis Adamic described the Little Blue Books in the journal *Outlook and Independent* as "a weathercock which shows which way the breezes of public taste were blowing." And an article in the *New Republic* declared that the Little Blue Books were "a barometer of plebeian taste."[40] In his 1928 book *The First Hundred Million*, Haldeman-Julius asserted that the most interesting part of the story he was about to tell was not how he manufactured and marketed the Little Blue Books but what they told about "what America wants to read."[41] The Little Blue Books, he insists "represent a democracy of literature" [42] An overview of the titles and sales of Little Blue Books in 1927 offers a good perspective both on what he published and, more importantly, on the nature of American popular literary tastes in that year.

On January 1, 1928, there were 1,260 titles in the Little Blue Books of length varying from 32 to 128 pages, with most having 64 pages. In the nine years of the existence of the Little Blue Books as many as 2,000 titles were published, some of which were dropped because of lack of sales, cost considerations, or marketing research that suggested a particular title was not popular. In 1927, 20.7 million Little Blue Books were sold for a nickel, with customers ordering from magazine and newspaper advertising a dollar's worth of books, that is twenty books, at a time. While the titles in the Little Blue Book list are infinitely varied, most might be classified under sex, self-improvement, religion, and classical literature.

Haldeman-Julius discovered that "Americans were not afraid of sex," and that they would buy books which improved their sexual techniques, relieved sexual anxieties, or overcame sexual dysfunctions. Since his books were sold exclusively through the mail, he had to be careful that what he published could legally be sent through the post office. He was concerned that censorship was inconsistently applied and he could not always be certain that what he wanted to publish and mail would not run afoul of the law. Among sex related books the following were sold:

Prostitution in the Modern World	129,500
What Married Women Should Know	112,000
What Married Men Should Know	97,500
What Every Young Man Should Know	95,000
What Every Young Woman Should Know	90,000
Woman's Sexual Life	97,000
Man's Sexual Life	78,500
The Art of Kissing	60,500

"Sales figures," declared E. Haldeman-Julius, "demonstrate that the desire for self-improvement on the part of American readers is not an idle dream."[43] Included in this category were books offering instruction in a foreign language, and others on history, anatomy, astronomy, physics, botany, art, music, and sculpture. There were books on grammar, quotations, and various kinds of dictionaries. And for the farmer there were books on fertilizers, husbandry, or poultry, among others. Among the best selling self-improvement titles in this category were the following:

How to Improve Your Conversation	77,000
How to Improve Your Vocabulary	76,000
How to Write Letters	53,500
Care of Skin and Hair	52,000
Hints on Public Speaking	46,500
How to Psycho-Analyze Yourself	43,000

Judging from sales of books on religion, E. Haldeman-Julius concluded that religious fundamentalism was waning in 1927. He pointed not only to the sales reception given Sinclair Lewis's *Elmer Gantry*, but also to his own sales.

Haldeman-Julius was most proud of the classics he published as Little Blue Books. The works of Friedrich Nietzsche and Plato were among his best-selling philosophers. His books included American and English poets, the works of Shakespeare as well as *The Rubaiyat of Omar Kahyyam* translated by Edward Fitzgerald, which was the oldest among the series. Haldeman-Julius also claimed credit for introducing the public to such contemporary authors as Will Durant, Theodore Dreiser, Ben Hecht, Fannie Hurst, Sherwood Anderson, and Clarence Darrow, to mention a few.

Haldeman-Julius observed that by 1927, Americans were more willing to read heretical books "now that the shadow of the rack has faded into nothing." But, he conceded, "The passion for burning 'dangerous' books still survives even if this is the twentieth century."[44] Indeed, in America in 1927 some books were still forbidden.

Forbidden Books

During the 1920s, the Carnegie Foundation shifted its attention away from building libraries for the public toward a greater concern with the role of libraries in public life and the nature of the materials a library should acquire and make available to readers. Librarianship adopted the trappings of a profession as the Carnegie Corporation funded a library research program at the University of Chicago which led to a doctoral degree. But if librarians were becoming more "professional" would they be in a better position to acquire books that would reflect the clash of the new modernity with the old morality? What books should be available for the flapper and the new man? How best should works of the writers of the Harlem Renaissance be incorporated into a library's collection and should such books be available to all? Should patrons expect to find on the shelves of public libraries information on birth control? On sexuality? On socialism? On communism?

In 1927 censorship in libraries was in the saddle and caution the watchword. "Every public library in the United States places restrictions on the use of fiction."[45] Fiction was widely regarded as "trivial" reading and so was not to be encouraged. Emily Post's book on etiquette was "serious" reading while Sinclair Lewis's *Babbitt* was not. The Buffalo library had only one book of fiction and it could be drawn by one reader at a time. In New Jersey, Newark's libraries would buy no fiction for its main library while New York removed chairs from the room devoted to fiction so that readers could "Grab it and get out of here!"[46]

It was easier for librarians to say "No" to books deemed controversial than to be courageous and acquire books which a host of community groups might oppose. In an article entitled, "Three New England Libraries" in the *American Mercury*, the libraries were roundly criticized for failing to include in their collections works by Theodore Dreiser, Carl Sandburg, or Rachel Lindsay. Nor could one find works by Flaubert, d'Annunzio, Lawrence, Joyce, or Huxley.[47] In 1927, the exasperated editor of *Library Journal* deplored the growing "craze for suppressing books on evolution and the trend of certain classes of citizens against this or that class of books. . . . Free libraries should be free in a double sense, and in this sense free libraries like a free press are essential to our continuing progress as a free people."[48]

In Chicago, in 1927, Mayor Thompson, who made Chicago a safe haven for the likes of Al Capone (see pp. 132–140), fanned anti-British sentiment with the view of purging from school and public libraries those accounts that appeared to show a pro-British bias or a lack of patriotic fervor. In 1927, he charged the American Library Association and the Chicago Public Library with spreading pro-British propaganda. When the ALA listed in a document called "Reading with a Purpose" the books of such scholars as David Saville Muzzey, and Arthur M. Schlesinger, he vowed to remove and burn any number of similar books from the school and public libraries. The mayor was particularly incensed that the libraries were urging upon readers the writings of Edward Bok, who advocated United States membership in the World Court and Andrew Carnegie of the Carnegie Foundation, who was urging a union of English-speaking people. "Your whole 'reading with a purpose' course should be severely scrutinized and considerable portions at least, should be eliminated."[49]

When "Big Bill" Thompson found himself faced with a lawsuit when he threatened to burn the pro-British volumes he found objectionable, he relented. But if he could not burn the books he would remove them from the shelves of the Chicago Public Library. He sent one of his hacks to the Chicago Public Library to remove *The American Nation* by Alfred Bushnell Hart, originally published in 1907, Willis M. West's *The Story of American Democracy*, and two books by Claude H. Van Tyne, who interpreted the American Revolution as a civil war between competing factions.

It is to the credit of the trustees of the Chicago Public Library that they rebuked the mayor and defended the ALA. "This exchange of freedom of thought we consider the primary function of a library and in keeping with the American ideal of a free press. Any other course would lead to an arbitrary censorship as detrimental to American political liberty as to academic thought."[50] In later accounts Carl Rodent, the Chicago librarian, chose to see his role in heroic proportions, asserting that he "strode into the room" where the mayor's acolyte was preparing the books for removal, he "ordered the man out of the library, never to return; he never did."[51] Actually, in the spirit of the time, Rodent's position was more conciliatory. Instead of ordering the mayor's representative out of the library he urged that the books be withdrawn from circulation and not be burned, but indicated he would essentially do as he was told. "Rodent, who would be ALA president in 1928, was offering the classic compromise, discretionary circulation, when this was the norm for large libraries and their definition of freedom."[52]

On May 1, 1927, librarians, including those of Boston, protested when censors tried to delete such classics as *The Scarlet Letter*, *Adam Bede*, and *Tess of the d'Ubervilles*. An editorial in *Library Journal* deplored the fact that Dreiser's *American*

Tragedy continued to be excluded. Librarians, the editorial declared, had a "responsibility of the shelves" especially when it came to literary classics which they could not be compelled to remove.[53]

Nor was censorship confined to public libraries alone. Boston's Watch and Ward Society and the police aggressively suppressed books being sold by booksellers as well as those selected by libraries. The Boston police suppressed Percy Marks's *The Plastic Age* and nine new novels. In April of 1927, they banned Sinclair Lewis's *Elmer Gantry,* Theodore Dreiser's *An American Tragedy,* and Warwick Deeping's *Doomsday.* When publisher Horace Liveright sued to protect *An American Tragedy* in the courts he lost his case.

In October 1927, the distinguished attorney Morris L. Ernst sought in vain to defend a novel of high school and college life by John Hermann entitled, *What Happens.* The verdict upheld the Government's action in seizing three hundred copies of the book which had been published in English in Dijon, France, and shipped to this country. Ernst's argument was that "what is obscene today is not what the customs and the laws of the '90s define it." The presiding judge in the U.S. District Court refused Ernst's request to read passages from Shakespeare. "You are here," said the judge, "to show that this book is not obscene, not that Shakespeare is." The judge congratulated the jury for finding the Hermann book obscene and seemingly concurred with the view of Assistant United States Attorney John Ryan: "I have heard," the prosecutor said, "of the freedom of the age, but don't you want to protect the morals of the young? The hearth, the family are what we are saving in seizing this book."[54]

As 1927 waned, librarians and booksellers refused to grovel before the censors. In *New York Libraries,* a quarterly journal distributed among the libraries of New York State and made widely available farther afield, a distinguished librarian sought to explain what freedom meant in public libraries. It meant first, "Freedom to use the library without paying money each time we use it. . . . Freedom means also the right to use the library in any way one likes. . . . Freedom means to read with a purpose. . . . Freedom means to read without a purpose, freedom to read for joy, freedom to linger at will with the ones you like best among the great company of the wise, the brave, the heroic, the tender and true, who can make for us a new heaven and a new earth."[55]

But American readers in 1927 were finding a way out of library censorship. For two or three cents a day they could borrow whatever they wanted to read from the growing number of private lending libraries. These were not so fastidious as to the fare they offered their general readers. According to *Publishers Weekly,* sixty-seven new rental libraries were established in 1927. They outnumbered the new bookstores by five to three and the free libraries by seven to one.[56] The rental libraries more readily catered to the needs of new readers, including shop girls, clerks, and stenographers. These readers wanted entertainment, adventure, and perhaps some love and sex in the materials they read.

Librarians were aware that their clientele was slipping away to rental libraries and for this they blamed the increase in the number of volumes offered by publishers and the failure of their budgets to keep up with the books available. Librarians demonstrated that in 1914 in libraries of large cities expenditures were twenty-two cents per capita and in 1926 expenditures were forty-six cents per capita. This increase, however, while double that of 1914, was not enough to keep pace with library needs and fell woefully behind expenditures for public schools which increased four-fold over the same period. Librarians also pointed out that the one dollar book of previous years had become the three dollar book of 1927 and the seventy-five cents book had become two dollars. These increased costs, they insisted, rather than censorship, explained why librarians had to be selective in what they purchased, what they made available, and what they protected from excessive use.

In 1927, perhaps concerned that censorship in libraries, bookstores, and newsstands had become a growing problem, the journalist Heywood Broun and the historian Margaret Leech collaborated on a biography: *Anthony Comstock: Roundman of the Lord.*

Heywood Broun warned his readers about the problems of censorship. After noting H. L. Mencken's concern that "moral endeavor has become a recognized profession in this country," Broun observed that, while Comstock "reduced the quantity of erotic literature, his campaign of suppression did much to increase eagerness and curiosity about forbidden books." Broun concluded, "Nobody but fools and censors believe so devoutly in the power of pornography. . . . It is pretty safe to assume that any given censor is a fool."[57]

⚜

[1] *New York Times*, November 5, 1927.
[2] Ibid.
[3] Ibid.
[4] Quoted in Frederick J. Hoffman, *The Twenties: American Writing in the Postwar Decade* (New York: The Viking Press, 1955), p. 25.
[5] Matthew Josephson, *Life Among the Surrealists: A Memoir* (New York: Holt, Rinehart and Winston, 1962), p. 314.
[6] Ibid.

[7]Ibid., p. 324.

[8]Guy J. Forgue, ed., *Letters of H. L. Mencken* (Boston: Northeastern University Press, 1981), p. 307.

[9]Ibid., p. 306.

[10]Ibid., p. 307.

[11]Ibid.

[12]William Lyon Phelps, "Some Books of 1927," in *Mirrors of the Year 1927* (New York: Frederick Stokes Company, 1928), p. 256.

[13]Al Silverman, ed., *The Book of the Month: Sixty Years of Books in American Life* (Boston: Little, Brown and Company, 1986), p. 17.

[14]Will Durant, *The Story of Philosophy* (New York: Simon and Schuster, 1926), p. 4.

[15]Silverman, *The Book of the Month*, p. 14.

[16]Edith Wharton, "The Great American Novel," in *Mirrors of the Year 1927–1928* (New York: Frederick Stokes and Company, 1928), pp. 167–168.

[17]*New York Times*, June 8, 1967.

[18]Margaret Case Harriman, *The Vicious Circle: The Story of the Algonquin Round Table* (New York: Rinehart and Company, Inc., 1951), p. 79.

[19]Ann Douglas, *Terrible Honesty: Mongrel Manhattan in the 1920s* (New York: Farrar Straus and Giroux, 1995), p. 17.

[20]Ibid., p. 12.

[21]Quoted in ibid.

[22]Richard Wright, *Black Boy: A Record of Childhood and Youth* (New York: Harper & Row, 1937), pp. 267-270.

[23]H. L. Mencken, "The Saharha of the Bozart," *New York Evening Mail* (November 13, 1917). In Huntington Cairns, ed., *The American Scene: H.L. Mencken, A Reader* (New York: Alfred A. Knopf, 1965), pp. 157–168.

[24]Ibid., p. 159.

[25]Douglas, *Terrible Honesty*, p. 77.

[26]On Mencken and African Americans during the 1920s the author is indebted to Charles Scruggs, *The Sage in Harlem: H. L. Mencken and the Black Writers of the 1920s* (Baltimore: The Johns Hopkins University Press, 1984), p. 22.

[27]George Schuyler, "Shafts and Darts," *Messenger* 9 (November 1927), p. 230.

[28]Scruggs, *The Sage of Harlem*, p. 72.

[29]George Schuyler, "Our White Folks," *American Mercury* 12 (December 12, 1927), p. 387.

[30]George Schuyler, "Blessed Are the Sons of Ham," *Nation* 124 (March 23, 1927): 313–314.

[31]George Schuyler, "Our Greatest Gift to America," in Michael W. Peplow and Arthur P. Davis, ed., *The New Negro Renaissance: An Anthology* (New York: Holt, Rinehart and Winston, 1975), p. 67.

[32]E. Franklin Frazier, "The Pathology of Race Prejudice," *Forum* 77 (June 1927): 856-862.

[33]Scruggs, p. 121.

[34]Ibid., p. 122.

[35]Ibid., p. 139.

[36]Quoted in ibid., pp. 123-124.

[37]Quoted in ibid., p. 129.

[38]E. Franklin Frazier, "Racial Self-Expression," in Charles S. Johnson, ed., *Ebony and Topaz: A Collectanea* (New York: Opportunity: Nation Urban League, 1927), pp. 119-121.
[39]Quoted in Dale M. Herder, "Little Blue Books as Popular Culture: E. Haldeman-Julius' Methodology," in Russell B. Nye, ed., *New Dimensions in Popular Culture* (Bowling Green, Ohio: Bowling Green University Popular Press, 1972), p. 32.
[40]Quoted in ibid., pp. 33-34.
[41]E. Haldeman-Julius, *The First Hundred Million* (New York: Simon and Schuster, 1928), p. 1.
[42]Ibid., p. 2.
[43]Ibid., p. 37.
[44]Ibid., pp. 86-88.
[45]Fletcher Pratt, "A Glance at the Public Libraries," *American Mercury* 14 (June 1928): 133.
[46]Ibid.
[47]Evelyn Geller, *Forbidden Books in American Public Libraries, 1876–1939* (Westport, Conn.: Greenwood Press, 1984), pp. 131-132.
[48]*Library Journal* 52 (February 15, 1927): p. 200.
[49]*New York Times*, November 5, 1927.
[50]Quoted in Geller, *Forbidden Books in American Public Libraries*, 134.
[51]Ibid.
[52]Ibid., pp. 134-135.
[53]*Library Journal* 52 (May 1, 1927): 478-479.
[54]*New York Times*, October 5, 1927.
[55]Paul M. Paine, "The Library Must Be Free," *New York Libraries* 11 (February 1928), pp. 42–44.
[56]Pratt, "A Glance at the Public Libraries," p. 133.
[57]"Broun on Censorship," in Heywood Broun and Margaret Leech, *Anthony Comstock: Roundsman of the Lord* (New York: Albert and Charles Boni, 1927), pp. 265-275.

12
YESTERDAY'S TOMORROWS

December 17, 1927

The forty-man crew of the United States submarine S-4 died when the ship attempted to surface about a mile outside the harbor of Provincetown, Massachusetts. In the attempt to rise from the ocean depths, the S-4 collided with the Coast Guard destroyer Paulding and sank. For three days, members of the ill-fated submarine tapped on the interior hull of the ship and pleaded for food and water. But stormy seas and gale force winds prevented divers, who heard these cries of despair, from reaching the crew in time. The last definite message from the S-4 was a series of three taps from Lieutenant Graham Newell Fitch, the officer in charge of the torpedo room where the last six survivors were entombed, to his wife and mother.

Even as President and Mrs. Calvin Coolidge extended their good wishes for the Christmas season to the nation, Secretary of the Navy Wilbur made a Christmas Eve visit to the site of the disaster. It was not until January 4, 1928, that the first of the bodies of the submarine crew were removed.

Mrs. M. T. Stevens, mother of one of the victims, assailed the navy and sharply criticized the nation's rescue attempts. The Secretary of the Navy, however, insisted that everything that could be done had been done to try to rescue the crew.

❧

A child born on New Year's Day 1846, when James K. Polk, a slave owner, was the eleventh president of the United States, would be eighty-two years old in 1927. One would think that there would be few surprises left given the historic, scientific, and technological developments through which he or she had lived during those years. If America of 1927 was almost unrecognizable to our eighty year old, how did he or she view the future?

Tomorrow in Fiction and Fact

If yesterday is history, tomorrow is a *tabula rasa,* a blank slate, upon which fact and fiction vie for minds of men and women. Because the dividing line between what science and technology may produce and what the brain of humankind can imagine is often murky, what writers wrote and what Americans read may give us some insight into what our predecessors imagined the future might be like.

Amazing Stories, first published in April 1926, hit its stride in 1927. The magazine, devoted to "scientifiction," as its owner and editor Hugo Gernsback called it, was a pioneering effort in the field of science fiction. In its pages could be found a brew of stories with elements of fiction, prophecy, science, in various proportions. In its editorials Gernsback expressed his belief that his magazine was providing instruction while identifying future avenues of further scientific research. As the motto on the cover boldly asserted: "Extravagant Fiction Today—Cold Fact Tomorrow."

In 1927, Gernsback published the first *Amazing Stories Annual, The Yearbook of Scientifiction.* The stories were not so much an expression of what Americans actually expected to happen, but they did exemplify the prevailing philosophy: if we could imagine it we could do it and, moreover, ought to.

The worldwide depression which began in 1929 hit Gernsback and other journals especially hard. His limited advertising revenue dried up and his would-be readers found other ways to spend what discretionary money they still had. Barely three years after its founding, *Amazing Stories* was forced into bankruptcy and by 1933 it was forced from the field altogether. "But his impact on the field was profound."[1] During the 1930s some of his readers formed fan clubs. The Hugo Awards—SF achievement awards comparable to the Oscar or Emmy— first given in Philadelphia in 1953, are named for him.

Yet, because the level of science his magazines projected was too low and the fiction often banal, Gernsback as a progenitor of the field has all but been forgotten. As science fiction as a literary genre rose, Gernsback's reputation fell. Gernsback is often scorned because he could see no farther than the literary "ghetto" of pulp magazines as vehicles for his "scientification." But, it was from the covers of Gernsback's magazines that artist Frank R. Paul designed his imaginative spaceships, which became the most widely identified symbol of the field of science fiction. Moreover, Gernsback served as a transitional figure from the early comic series of *Buck Rogers in the 25th Century* and *Flash Gordon* to *Star Trek* and *Star Wars.* Little wonder that those who remember still hail him as "The Father of Modern Science Fiction."[2]

In these and other tales of science fiction may be found recurring pessimistic and optimistic themes in which some deplore the arrival of the machine age and some welcome it. There are fears for the methods of emerging warfare including the use of air power, poison gas, enhanced explosives. Will planets, like nations, make war upon one another? But how much of science fiction was based on sheer imagination and how much on hard-headed science? Some writers during these formative years for science fiction tried to remain faithful to realistic possibilities of science and technology some let fantasy and romance dominate their interpretation. But, as we shall see, fact is often stranger than fiction.

Televox, Algernon, and Mrs. Twitchel

When her partner kicks her under the table for making a stupid bid, Mrs. Twitchel's mind returns to her bridge game. She had been unable to concentrate. Had she turned off her oven? Was her home warm enough so that the pipes do not freeze and burst? To alleviate her concerns she calls home and leaves orders for precisely what she wants done. Here is how the science writer Waldemar Kaempffert described how she might proceed:

Mrs. Twitchel excuses herself for a few moments and uses the Televox at her bridge club. She lifts the telephone and calls home in the ordinary way. "Give me Main 2350," she tells the operator. When the bell in Mrs. Twitchel's home rings, a sound sensitive relay lifts the receiver-hook and starts up the station signal-buzzer that sets up the whole apparatus for action. When she hears the now familiar combination of buzzes which signals her that indeed the connection has been made to her own home, "she is ready to talk electrical Esperanto. . ." that is, a language system developed by R. J. Wensley based on three notes which are sounded by electrically generated tuning forks.

"Tweet," sings one of Mrs. Twitchel's pitch pipes. Which means, "I'm ready, what do you want?"

"Tweet, tweet, tweet," say Mrs. Twitchel's pitch pipes, which this time means, "Connect me with the electrical stove."

"Buzz, buzz, buzz," the Televox replies, which means "You are connected. It might interest you to know that the switch is open and there is no heat."

Mrs. Twitchel pushes another button. "Br-rung," which means "close the switch and start the oven."

"Tweet, tweet, tweet," hums Mrs. Twitchel which commands, "Connect me with the furnace down in the cellar. . . ."

Mrs. Twitchel commands the furnace with a series of tweets, buzzes, and bells and, when she blows her third pitch-pipe she says, in effect, "Thanks. Goodbye." She returns to her bridge game and, presumably, with a clear mind, she will make no more mistakes.

This technique, the inventor believed, could work across the country, across the ocean, and across town to offer remote control of assembly lines and power plants.[3]

Algernon, the robot, however, had reason to be jealous. From at least medieval times, inventors have sought to make a mechanical person that can write a name, play a tune, serve a cup of tea. Even the most ingenious inventor could not contrive a robot with a brain. But a mechanical device could be created with arms and legs (wheels) and could move stiffly about in response to programmed commands. It could be run by a small dynamo or battery mounted on its back while photo-electric cells would serve for eyes, and telephone receivers for ears. A thermostat would enable it to feel heat and its multiple "arms" with "fingers" could be made sensitive enough to feel the difference between say a sheet of paper and a block of wood. Algernon, a huge electro-mechanical doll, could probably be programmed to lift weights, vacuum a rug over a specified area, turn the gas on and off in the kitchen, open and close windows, or start and stop a motor. But, would you trust Algernon to lift the baby from the crib and bring it to the living room?[4]

While today's computers have unceremoniously pushed aside the technology of Televox and Algernon, reading about them helped Americans imagine the shape of things to come.

The Shape of Things to Come

Because a comet became visible in the northern hemisphere in December 1927 when Christians were honoring the Christ child and all Americans were preparing for a more secular celebration of the new year, some sought to read in the appearance of the comet portents of what the future might hold. As comets go, the ninth comet of the year was not a particularly spectacular one. But for thousands of years, comets have been regarded as divine messengers or as omens for good or evil. And so if there were in 1927 no magi to herald the event, there was no shortage of soothsayers who sought to take a squint at what might lie ahead for America.

Nearly all projections of the future are bound to be wrong. Seers get it wrong because they project current trends into the distant future. Thus, if a population is growing they assume it will always grow and therefore, perhaps, create a population problem. If cities are growing, some futurists make the assumption that they will continue to grow and that green space will altogether disappear. "Nearly everyone who writes about the future assumes that the most marked tendencies of our own time will go on asserting themselves without ever being checked by opposing tendencies."[5]

Futurists with a utopian perspective also get it wrong because likely as not they tend to describe an emerging world with values and practices of which they approve. Some project a worldview in which religion is absent; others one in which religion is central. Some offer a vision of a world in which marriage is sacred; others in which it is an encumbrance. Some utopians urge a world in which children are cared for in the bosom of the family; others, in which children are cared for in some central institution. Some project a world from which work or pain are forever banished, while others see a future of continued toil, drudgery, and anguish.

Although it is not surprising that most of the prognosticators got it wrong, a review of some of the insights of those who had the temerity to venture a leap into the distance may offer some idea of the hopes and fears of 1927 mortals. What men and women hope for tomorrow, or fear for tomorrow, more than what they can realistically expect of tomorrow, often determines how they live today.

Herbert George (H. G.) Wells (1866-1946), the British writer and scientist, got it wrong. In an essay for the *New York Times Magazine,* he anticipated that as medical advances lengthened the span of life, sex would become less important as men and women would then be free to engage in more mature pursuits. Since the death rate for prehistoric men and women was so high, he reasoned, and the human life span so short, our distant ancestors he insisted, needed to be "almost as sexual as a cat" simply to maintain the race and the family. Medicine, he predicted, would restore adult vigor, prolong human life, reduce infant and child mortality—and so the early human preoccupation with sex would likewise diminish. "The average man and woman," H. G. Wells declared, "will be of riper years, far maturer in outlook, and far less deeply immersed in sexual and family affairs."[6] How little Wells appeared to realize that the 1927 flapper and "new man," with more sophisticated knowledge of birth control available to them, with Margaret Sanger to encourage them, and new sex manuals to instruct them, would make recreational sex the modern norm.

Count Hermann Keyserling got it wrong. Despite rising standards of living and labor saving machinery, Keyserling anticipated a new "dark age" for humankind. On the eve of his visit to America, this founder of the Darmstadt (Germany) School of Wisdom asserted, "Cultural traditions, however beautiful they may be, no longer carry their old convictions, be they religious, social, political, or artistic. What I have called the chauffeur type . . . is everywhere becoming the model and the ideal. " The "chauffeur," he insisted, was his symbol of what humankind had become—not cultural, but primitive, violent, and while full of vitality also arrogant. "America," he said, as the paradigm of the chauffeur type, "represents today an island sundered from the rest of the world. . . ."[7]

In a follow-up essay he asserted that America's history up to 1927 was nothing more than an extension of European colonial roots and that a real American type was just emerging. A new "American race" was developing and a unique American history was beginning. Because in the United States and in South America there was an admixture of blood from many groups, the American soul is "out of harmony with itself," and so Americans were a restless people. The revolt of modern youth in America says Keyserling "bears a clear resemblance to the spirit of the Russian Revolution than to that of traditional America."[8] While conceding that America was becoming the envy of the world, in a contradictory way he nevertheless believed "the Americanization of the world is an increasingly remote possibility."[9]

Clearly Keyserling was wrong. But more disturbing was his emphasis on blood, race, and "pure stock" to describe some of the original settlers in the New World. What he failed to see was that in its pluralism may be found America's future strength, not its weakness. Aldous Huxley (1894-1963), had a clearer vision. 'The future of America," he wrote, "is the future of the world. . . . For good or evil, it seems that the world must be Americanized."[10]

But, in other respects, Aldous Huxley likewise got it wrong. Because of the complexity he saw in the emerging machine age, he proposed a society in which human beings were divided into different psychological types and educated and governed accordingly. In his 1927 essay, Huxley anticipated a theme that he would develop in *Brave New World* (1932). In this volume he portrays a civilization of the twenty-fifth century chilling in concept, nightmarish in its control of the destinies of children, women, and men, and pessimistic in its expectations for the intelligence of human beings. Here too, may be found a linkage with George Orwell's 1949 prophetic and equally pessimistic vision of humankind, *1984*. According to Orwell, machines could raise living standards and all people could, therefore, become equally educated. But, were this to happen, the hierarchical nature of societies would be threatened and so war, as a chronic state of affairs, becomes highly desirable as it sucks up the excess capacity machines make possible. Therefore, "War is Peace," "Freedom is Slavery," and "Ignorance is Strength."

Even H. L. Mencken got it wrong, at least thus far. "I believe," he wrote in 1927, "that the United States will blow up within a century. "I have little belief in human progress," Mencken observed. "The human race is incurably idiotic. It will never be happy."[11] As usual Mencken was spitting against the prevailing winds in America. Most Americans of that year were more optimistic, were avidly pursuing happiness, and many even thought they had found it in the material prosperity of the times.

In 1927, the economist Rexford Tugwell (later one of the theorists of Franklin Roosevelt's "New Deal") wrote *Industry's Coming of Age* in which he acknowledged the maturing of American industry and its enormous productive capacity. We twist our hopes out of shape. We long for a past presumably simple, a past that never was, or we anticipate a future utopia which we cannot mold. The paradox of 1927, as Tugwell saw it, was that while the bitterness of technological alienation may be expressed in literature, escape from bitterness would be found in the productivity American technology made possible.

America's concern with the future was based on a mixture of hope, fear, and faith. The hope was that cherished lifestyles, traditional moral virtues, habits of right thinking of an imagined, idyllic, past, would sustain America despite a flood of technological change. The fear was that an America with too many people would exhaust its natural resources, that its food supply would be inadequate to sustain its people. Yet, in 1927 hope overcame fear as Americans looked to the future with faith that all technological advance was progress and tomorrow would always be better. If fundamentalism in religion could offer visions of a spiritual utopia in a city of God then a secular utopia based on technology would make a city of man likewise a reality.

Metropolis

As interpreted by the director Fritz Lang in his film *Metropolis*, moviegoers of 1927 could see a mechanized and frightening concept of city living in the not-too-distant future. Lang's $2 million silent film, a German import, the costliest and most ambitious picture ever screened in Europe, is the grim story of what the future may hold for urban life. It is one in which the machine lives and ant-like masses are subject to its whims. While the rich live high above the noise and soot and smells of the machinery and the transportation network that make the city work, the joyless urbanites are chewed up by the grinding gears that makes all else possible.

A caricature of Henry Ford appears to preside over "Metropolis" with Maria, a female robot, obeying the industrial despot's every command. Although Maria eventually attempts to relieve the urban slaves of their brutish toil, the revolt is unsuccessful: she cannot break the chains that bind them to machines. Disaster follows and the "proles" are worse off than before. Machines, like the monster of

Frankenstein, control humankind. As the final caption in the black and white film warns: "There can be no understanding between the hands and the brain unless the heart acts as mediator."

If the fantasy of film offered escape from reality, the reality of the Holland Tunnel offered hope that urban America could be made to work. Named in memory of Clifford M. Holland, the young engineering genius who designed it but did not live to see it completed, the tunnel was opened for motorists on November 13, 1927, at 12:01 A.M. It was an example of how the hand, the brain and the heart came together to build "A Modern Marvel"[12] During the first twenty-four hours 25,747 vehicles had gone through from Jersey City, New Jersey, and 25,538 vehicles had passed through from New York City. Built in eight years at a cost of $48.4 million, the world's longest twin tube tunnel burrows its way under the Hudson River from Canal Street in Manhattan to 12th Street in Jersey City, connecting Manhattan with the rest of America. For the pleasure of taking the tunnel instead of waiting for a ferry, motorcycles, cars, passenger buses, and trucks paid tolls ranging from 25 cents to $1.25, depending upon the size of the vehicle. The expectation was that as soon as the tunnel's capital expenditure and interest are paid off, it will be open to the public free of charge.[13] Still waiting.

"When Thomas Edison speaks, everybody listens." In the March issue of *Popular Science Monthly*, Thomas Edison inveighed against the continued building of skyscrapers in the city and the resulting dangers of overcrowding. Although he warned that "disaster must overtake us" unless there was a halt to the building of ever taller buildings," there were few who listened. Plans continued to be made for ever taller buildings.[14]

One such was the proposed Larkin Tower of 110 stories, another was the proposed eighty-story Book Tower in Detroit, Michigan, and the Union Terminal Tower in Cleveland, Ohio. At the 1927 International Art Center in New York, some of the world's most prominent architects displayed models and plans for other skyscraper towers in other sections of the country. Edison's reservations notwithstanding, the building of ever higher buildings appeared to be the wave of the future.[15]

Indeed, the skyscraper was widely viewed as an instrument of urban renewal. In some visions of an urban future, an occupant need not come down again, once ensconced in an office. Thus, John K. Hencken, a New York engineer, proposed a sixteen-mile elevated speedway, a highway in the sky, as a means of alleviating New York's traffic problem. A number of city planners believed that from an engineering perspective it was altogether possible to build a boulevard through the heart of the city. Speedy moving platforms, elevated playgrounds for children, underground railways service for cargo would all be part of a livable urban environment.[16]

"Think of future cities, or groups of skyscrapers," declared Harvey Wiley Corbett of New York City one of the greatest architects of 1927, "as you think of coral islands or trees with human beings playing merely the part of coral insects . . . Compare the New York skyline to a coral reef or a bunch of skyscrapers to a grove of trees, and you can get an idea of how much a city like New York will grow and change in another three quarters of a century." He visualized sidewalk bridges hundreds of feet above the streets by the year 2000. "From the fortieth story, or perhaps the eightieth, men of 2000 A.D. will walk straight to the corresponding floor of the building across the way. . . . The end of skyscrapers is not yet anywhere near in sight." [17]

Despite his inventiveness and his imagination, Thomas Alva Edison did not get the city of the future quite right. He correctly visualized a future city of enormous size and identified the automobile as the chief obstacle to making living in the city less cramped. He identified the need for synchronized traffic lights and he proposed to solve the problem of corner intersections by elevated crossings. He visualized the helicopter as a means by which the traffic problems of a city might be alleviated.

At the fiftieth anniversary of the Engineers Club of Philadelphia, Samuel Rae, the retired president of the Pennsylvania Railroad envisaged a sunny, smokeless city, with double and perhaps triple-decked streets heated and cooled with centralized fuel and power plants. Mr. Rae anticipated that in fifty years, in 1977, small and inefficient power plants would be closed and heat and power will be obtained from central plants. Heating of individual homes, he predicted, would be a thing of the past. A central unit could distribute energy more efficiently, inexpensively, and more cleanly than could the individual systems for heating and cooking. "We may realize a smokeless city, and added sunlight will greatly improve the health of urban dwellers."[18]

To the Moon

In its first issue of 1927, an article in *Popular Science Monthly* reported that "Man's fascinating dream of reaching the moon is progressing from a Jules Verne fancy to a cold problem of mathematical and engineering calculations." The author continued, "What would it be like to travel through space in a ship (rocket) of this kind? In the first place, once the regions beyond gravity had been gained, the passengers would float like spirits in mid-air- a detail the moon voyagers have provided for by supplying straps with which the passengers will be fastened to the walls. Since no liquids would flow, the passengers would be forced to suck their drinks through bottles through rubber nipples. . . . How the return voyage would be accomplished are problems apparently unsolved."[19]

On May 8, 1927, the *New York Times* reported that Ivan Fedorof, a Russian mechanic from Kiel and a member of the "All-Inventors Vegetarian Club of Interplanetary Cosmopolitans," will fly to the moon in September in a "rocket" half airplane half giant projectile. He will be accompanied by Max Valier, the German moon fan and the three who prove most fit of the seventy-five Moscow volunteers. A future line of airbuses is likewise contemplated. However, while Fedorof insisted that his "moon machine" is already half built, he has only a wooden model to show visitors.[20]

If a journey to the moon held little practical interest then perhaps "New York to Paris in an hour and a half," would tickle the popular imagination. This was the vision of Max Valier, a German aviator and astronomer, who believed such travel in a rocket would be feasible before long. According to the inventor, a passenger would, "climb into the cigar-shaped central cabin . . . the pilot jerks a lever. With a tremendous roar the rocket airplane races up an almost vertical runway, flings itself free, and heads straight into the upper air. At an altitude of fifty miles the pilot flattens his course; now he can put on full speed without any danger of burning up the craft like a meteor. Hardly more than an hour after leaving New York you are over Paris; the craft slows, and descends, and auxiliary rocket motors bring it gently to earth."[21]

If these visions of moon flight seem absurd, fantastic, or pre-mature, it is important to note that parallel with these flamboyant projections more serious work was going on in the theoretic underpinnings of rocket science. In 1927 much of this work was undertaken by The Society for Space Travel which was founded in that year. Among its early members, and clearly an emerging leader in rocketry, was Wernher von Braun who later developed the first rockets to travel in space. After first contributing to Hitler's rocket program, he was later brought to the United States where he continued to make important contributions to America's own efforts to reach the moon.

In 1927, the airplane was still fighting to secure its place as the foremost means of global rapid transportation. If travel by rocket was still a fanciful dream, travel by zeppelin was viewed by many as having the more promising future. Dr. Hugo Eckener, head of the great zeppelin works in Friedrichshafen, Germany, and pilot of the airship ZR-3 which flew to America in 1924, was one who was sure that the future lay with lighter than air transportation. Eckener was convinced that a zeppelin could be developed relatively quickly to circumnavigate the globe non-stop, something the airplane could not yet do. The future this zealot visualized was one in which zeppelins would sail over continents, oceans, and cities, bringing them closer than could be achieved by railways or steamships."[22]

New methods of transportation continued to stir the imaginations of Americans in 1927. Glenn Hammond Curtis envisioned "a personal airplane so individual so compact and so flexible so that it will compare with airplanes as the motorcycle does with automobiles."[23] Transportation of this nature would, he believed, contribute to the development of suburbs and so relieve crowding in central cities. While the "flying motorcycle," with a range of about fifty miles might be suitable for individual transportation needs, for commuting distances of several hundred miles, Curtis anticipated the "flying bus." The flying bus, moreover, would have the capability of hovering over one spot, that is to stand still in the air so to board and unload passengers. He thought that the hovering bus more practical than either the dirigible or the helicopter, both projects in experimental stages at that time. Curtis anticipated the development also of the "flying boat," appropriate transportation for crossing large lakes, wide bays and gulfs. The transatlantic airliner, however, Curtiss believed to be in the more distant future since it would be too difficult to provide for the safety and comfort of many passengers during a flight of some eighteen hours.

While Lindbergh crossed the Atlantic alone and made it safely to Paris, Clarence Chamberlain, flying in the Bellanca monoplane Columbia, accompanied by Charles Levine, his financial backer, flew the 4,100 miles to Germany just two weeks later without mishap. Levine thus became the first transatlantic air passenger and thereby raised the possibilities of regular transatlantic crossings by air. Some predictions for large-scale transatlantic air transportation were clearly more optimistic than the state of the art warranted. Major General Mason M. Patrick, chief of the U.S. Army Air Corps, declared, "Ocean airlines will be organized and ten years will make commercial air traffic over our oceans the rule rather than the exception."[24] Some had visions of mid-ocean fueling stations and landing strips, while other anticipated the need for more accurate weather forecasting. Others recognized that before travel across oceans could be made widely available, multi-motored aircraft would be needed. Eddie V. Rickenbacker, America's flying hero, was overly optimistic about the short-term possibilities of travel over the ocean. Within five years, he predicted, "Americans will have available a regular oceanic service, of forty hours, with greater safety and comfort than that available today on our finest ocean liners."[25] Commander Richard E. Byrd, however, was less optimistic. After paying tribute to the courage and skill of

Lindbergh and Chamberlain, Byrd, the first to fly over the North Pole, cautioned, "It will be some twenty years," Byrd insisted, "before regular commercial trans-Atlantic air service is established."[26] Admiral Byrd recognized the need for better weather information and multi-engine planes. However, he also believed that ocean landing strips would be needed where planes could refuel and where passengers could rest, eat, and sleep.

In 1927, it still took five days to cross the continent by rail. William P. Mac-Cracken Jr., assistant secretary for aeronautics in the department of commerce and the recipient of the first airplane pilot's license issued by that department, anticipated that a combination of air and rail travel could bring a traveler from New York to San Francisco in a little over two days. Such a coast to coast trip would be something like this:

> Leaving New York at 2:45 P.M., Eastern Time, on Sunday . . . a traveler will arrive in Chicago at 9:45 Central Time, Monday morning after bath, shave and breakfast on his all-Pullman train. He will be whisked to Chicago's new lakefront municipal flying field and take off for Cheyenne, Wyo., at 10:30 o'clock. His plane will land him in Cheyenne at 6:50, Mountain time, that evening, slightly more than thirty hours from the Atlantic sea board. An all-rail trip, by existing schedules, would have consumed fifty-two hours of travel. A traveler will leave Cheyenne by rail at 7:40 P.M. reaching Ogden, Utah at 9:20 A.M. Mountain time, next morning. A swift flight from Ogden, starting at 9:20 A.M. Pacific time, Tuesday, will place him in San Francisco at 4:30 P.M. in time for dinner—a little more than two full days after his departure from Manhattan Island. No strain of the imagination is required to picture this journey as one of the everyday prospects of the early future.[27]

The Next War

"One more war in the West, and the civilization of the ages will fall with as great a shock as that of Rome," declared Stanley Baldwin, Great Britain's prime minister.[28] While he could not know of the resiliency of Western civilization, he could visualize monster bombers, anti-aircraft batteries, machine guns spraying bullets farther than those used in World War I. Charging tanks, incendiary shells, deadly gases, bacterial attacks, were to be the weapons of the next war. A German general predicted that the next war would be one in which the enemy will be "the entire civil population rather than a combat of armed men."[29] Many American army officers agreed with this judgment. David Sarnoff, vice president of the Radio Corporation of America, predicted the development of pilotless planes and unmanned ships capable of delivering a fearsome load of bombs and shells. Yet, in 1927, America was by no means in the forefront in the development of what was then called "scientific warfare." In his farewell address, General Pershing insisted that "armies must still fight our battles and to win, must overcome the opposing force. Since the beginning of history man has overestimated his newest accomplishments. This has been particularly true of the means of making war." And, Major General Charles P. Summerall, chief of staff of the Army, declared, "In the final analysis war is the problem of a soldier with a bayoneted rifle . . . in his hands, going somewhere to take a piece of land held by another soldier with a bayoneted rifle . . . in his hands."[30]

Just as we worry today about the possibility of an attack by an intercontinental ballistic missile, so Americans in 1927 expressed some concern that ocean-spanning planes could attack America. In mid-1925, President Coolidge's aircraft board was asked whether the United States was in danger of being attacked from the air by "any potential enemy of menacing strength." The short answer was a reassuring "No." But obviously, the answer had to be qualified with the statement that it was "based on the facts as they now are." "No airplane capable of making a transoceanic flight to our country with a useful military load, and returning to safety, is now in existence."[31] Yet air travel was developing so fast that there remained plenty to worry about. In a frightening scenario, one writer conceived the possibility of an air attack by an armada of four thousand planes— seaplanes, mono-motored planes, and multi-motored bombers "battleships of the air." Such an armada, the writer estimated, could drop two thousand tons of high explosives, and perhaps large quantities of poison gas as well, enough to paralyze the heart of the nation. In such an attack New York would be the focus of intensive destruction, Chicago's railroad network would be ruined, and the Gary steelworks wrecked, as would be the water supplies of great cities. The author went on to detail a "possible" but by no means "probable" outcome.[32]

Unlimited Resources

In a year in which Werner Heisenberg arrived at his uncertainty principle— which holds it is impossible to measure both the position and momentum of a particle at the same time, that the very act of measurement disturbs a particle's values—there were plenty of confident seers.

"Some day, perhaps a hundred years from now, perhaps sooner—our children's children will read of the doings of the year 1927, and will wonder at the wastefulness of those quaint people of the olden days who shoveled lumps of coal into

316   GERALD LEINWAND

WE ARE NOW FULL BROTHERS TO THE GOLDFISH
—Ireland in the Columbus *Dispatch*.

furnaces to get heat and power, and who depended on wells dug into the ground
to supply oil and gasoline for their motors."[33] The sun, winds, and waves would
provide unlimited sources of energy, one Hyatt E. Gibbon, writing in *Popular Science
Monthly*, predicted.

He pointed, for example, to a demonstration before the French Academy of
Sciences that not only the ocean waves, but the temperatures of sea water held
out possibilities of limitless power sources. He quoted Marconi, the inventor of
the wireless, who predicted that cities could be illuminated without wires and
that electric power carried from waterfalls to towns and factories without the
need of cables.

At an International Conference on Bituminous Coal held at the Carnegie
Institute of Technology at Pittsburgh, Pennsylvania, experts discussed ways to

produce efficient quantities of synthetic gasoline and oil, and new ways of distributing and utilizing coal. "They pictured the engines of industry and transportation eventually propelled by cheap synthetic oil, and cities free from coal smoke."[34]

"Tomorrow," wrote Alden P. Armagnac in *Popular Science Monthly*, "radio beams of power may light and heat your home . . . [and may] drive airplanes, automobiles and trains." The author reached this conclusion after a demonstration by an engineer of Westinghouse Electric and Manufacturing Company before members of the New York Electrical Society. The transmission of power without wires was viewed as a real possibility for the near future by both Guglielmo Marconi and Dr. Charles Steinmetz. The former was quoted as saying, "The transmission of power without wires is not a theory or a mere possibility. It is a fact which I myself have demonstrated in numerous practical experiments, conducted on a large scale. . . ."[35]

The British scientist Archibald Montgomery Low took perhaps the greatest leap of faith. In his book *The Future*, he asserted "Certainly the present is only the very beginning of an age of discovery."[36] As summarized by Robert E. Martin, Professor Low predicted a fantastic future "more fantastic than anything most of us could imagine."

The typical man of the future . . . will be called by a radio alarm clock in the morning to take a few moments' radio light treatment or massage. Then he will jump into his synthetic felt one-piece suit. He will wear his hat almost continuously because everyone will be bald. He will have to watch out lest he put on his wife's clothing by mistake, for men and women will dress almost alike.

During breakfast a loudspeaker will tell him of news events, and he will watch some of them as they occur on television. By altering the wave length, he can hear the kind of news he wishes. His breakfast may come from the communal kitchen by tubes. Telephone messages that were automatically recorded while he slept will then be read, and so too will the news received on his radio tape machine.

The business man of the future, traveling to his office in his car, will get in touch with it on the way by radio and dictate to a pocket dictaphone. An elevator will carry the car to his floor. All office buildings will have moving stairways, the streets moving sidewalks, and the stores moving floors. Most of his travel will be by air. . . .[37]

A. M. Low further anticipated that the world would be quieter, radios carried in the pocket, the automobile streamlined, possessed of a flexible body enclosed in flexible glass and air-cushioned. Some day too, the automobile would be able to fly. But Professor Low was aware that "the advance of science must be accompanied by an equivalent progress of moral and ethical ideas."[38] He was also sensitive to the changing role of women "who are adapting themselves successfully to all masculine pursuits. It is only natural to expect that they will play an equally important part in future warfare, sharing all the dangers on complete equality with their men folk until the sexes are indistinguishable."[39]

The Drift of Civilization?

In 1928, Joseph Pulitzer's *St. Louis Post-Dispatch* marked its fiftieth birthday by attempting at least a partial answer to that question. The newspaper commissioned a series on the theme "The Drift of Civilization." In the first essay, the Russian writer and philosopher Maxim Gorky observed that 1927 marked the two hundredth anniversary of the death of Isaac Newton, one of the world's great geniuses. Newton's tomb in Westminster Abbey bears the following inscription: "Let all mortals rejoice that so great an adornment of the human race ever existed."

Gorky went on to note that man, likewise, is an adornment of the world, and that while he has every reason to be amazed at his accomplishments, he no longer wonders about them. "Man's riddance of amazement at the invention of his reason at the creation of his hands," Gorky observed, "I consider to be a fact of immense importance and I imagine that the man of the twentieth century begins to think in this way:

"I can fly in the air, swim under water, move upon the earth with a speed that seemed incredible before, I have discovered radium, the mysterious, and found the way to use it—I can speak with any spot on my planet by means of the wireless—it seems that I will soon find out the secret of life eternal. What is there else that is concealed from me?"[40] What else indeed?

⚶

[1]Thomas D. Clareson, *Understanding Contemporary American Science Fiction: The Formative Period, 1926-1927*, (Columbia, S.C.: University of South Carolina Press, 1990), p. 16.
[2]Ibid., p. 17.
[3]Waldemar Kaempffert, "Science Produces the Electric Robot," *New York Times*, October 23, 1927.
[4]Ibid.
[5]J. B. Priestly, "A Mistake About the Future," *Harper's* 155 (June, 1927): 114.
[6]H. G. Wells, "The Way the World is Going," *New York Times Magazine* (January 9, 1927).

[7]Count Hermann Keyserling, "A New Dark Age Foretold for Man," *New York Times Magazine* (November 27, 1927): 3.

[8]Ibid.

[9]Ibid., p. 18.

[10]Aldous Huxley, "The Outlook for American Culture," *Harpers* 155 (August 1927): 265.

[11]"Letter to Charles Green Shaw, December 2, 1927," in Guy J. Forgue, *Letters of H. L. Mencken*, p. 307.

[12]*New York Times*, October 9, 1927.

[13]"Motoring Under the Hudson River," *Literary Digest* 95 (December 10, 1927): 13.

[14]Robert E. Martin, "Forty Thousand People Within Four Walls!" *Popular Science Monthly* (March, 1927), p. 18.

[15]Ibid.

[16]"A Highway on the Roof Tops," *Popular Science Monthly* (July 1927).

[17]Myron M. Stearns, "Babies Born Today May," *Popular Science Monthly* (October 1927): 21.

[18]"Smokeless Cities Predicted by Rae," *New York Times*, December 18, 1927.

[19]H. C. Davis, "To the Moon at 7 Miles a Second," *Popular Science Monthly* (January, 1927): 29.

[20]*New York Times*, May 8, 1927.

[21]"To Europe by Rocket," *Popular Science Monthly* (September 1927): 41.

[22]T. R. Ybarra, "The Zepplin's Builder Forecasts Its Future," *New York Times*, July 31, 1927, p. 2.

[23]Frank Parker Stockbridge, "Glenn Curtiss Sees a Vision of Aviation's future," *Popular Science Monthly* (July 1927): 32.

[24]George Lee Dowd, Jr., "The First Plane to Germany," *Popular Science Monthly* (August 1927): 14.

[25]Ibid., p. 15.

[26]Richard E. Byrd, "Why We May Wait 20 Years for Ocean Air Lines," *Popular Science Monthly* 3 (August 1927): 9.

[27]William P. MacCracken Jr., "Air-Rail Lines May Span U.S.," *Popular Science Monthly* (December 1927): 12-15.

[28]Quoted in George Lee Dowd, Jr., "Getting Ready for the Next War," *Popular Science Monthly* (December 1927): 26.

[29]Ibid.

[30]Quoted in ibid., p. 17.

[31]Quoted in Caleb Johnson, "Could Air Invaders Destroy Us?" *Popular Science Monthly* (September 1927), p. 18.

[32]Ibid., p. 19.

[33]Hyatt E. Gibbon, "Vast Stores of Future Power," *Popular Science Monthly* (February 1927): 24.

[34]Ibid.

[35]Alden P. Armagnac, "Wireless Power—the Next Great Invention." *Popular Science Monthly* (July 1927): 9-10.

[36]A.M. Low, *The Future* (New York: International Publishers, Inc., 1925), p. 5.

[37]Robert E. Martin, "An Amazing Vision of the Future," *Popular Science Monthly* (June 1927): 29.
[38]Low, *The Future*, p. 6.
[39]Ibid., p. 132.
[40]Maxim Gorky, "Man," in *The Drift of Civilization* (New York: Simon and Schuster, 1929), p. 3.

SUGGESTIONS FOR FURTHER READING

Ables, Jules. *In the Time of Silent Cal.* New York: G.P. Putnam's Sons, 1969.

Allen, Frederick Lewis. *Only Yesterday.* 1931, reprinted New York: Bantam Books, 1959.

Asbury, Herbert. *The Great Illusion: An Informal History of Prohibition.* Garden City, New York: Doubleday and Company, Inc., 1950.

Baldwin, Neil. *Edison: Inventing the Century.* New York: Hyperion, 1995.

Barry, John M. *Rising Tide: The Great Mississippi Flood of 1927 and How it Changed America.* New York: Simon and Schuster, 1997.

Berg, A. Scott. *Lindbergh.* New York: G. P. Putnam's Sons, 1998.

Bergreen, Laurence. *Capone: The Man and the Era.* New York: Simon and Schuster, 1994.

Chesler, Ellen. *Woman of Valor: Margaret Sanger and the Birth Control Movement in America.* New York: Simon and Schuster, 1992.

Clareson, Thomas D. *Understanding Contemporary Science Fiction: The Formative Period (1926–1927).* Columbia, S.C.: University of South Carolina Press, 1990.

Dinnerstein, Leonard. *Antisemitism in America.* New York: Oxford University Press, 1994.

Douglas, Ann. *Terrible Honesty: Mongrel Manhattan in the 1920s.* New York: Farrar, Straus and Giroux, 1995.

Epstein, Daniel Mark. *Sister Aimee: The Life of Aimee Semple McPherson.* New York: Harcourt, Brace, Jovanovich, 1993.

Ernest, Robert. *Weakness is a Crime: The Life of Bernar Macfadden.* Syracuse, N.Y.: Syracuse University Press, 1991.

Ferrell, Robert H. *The Presidency of Calvin Coolidge.* Lawrence, Kansas: University Press of Kansas, 1998.

Galbraith, John Kenneth. *The Great Crash.* Boston: Houghton, Mifflin Company, 1961.

Giles, Carl H. *1927: The Picture History of a Wonderful Year.* New Rochelle, N.Y.: Arlington House, 1971.

322 GERALD LEINWAND

Green, Abel and Joe Laurie Jr. *Show Biz from Vaude to Video.* New York: Henry Holt and Company, 1951.

Handlin, Oscar. *Al Smith and His America.* Boston: Little, Brown and Company, 1958.

Haynes, John Earl. *Calvin Coolidge and the Coolidge Era: Essays on the History of the 1920s.* Washington, D.C.: Library of Congress, 1998.

Hoffman, Frederick. *The Twenties: American Writing in the Post-War Decade.* New York: The Viking Press, 1950.

Johnson, Paul. *Modern Times: The World from the Twenties to the Eighties.* New York: Harper and Row, 1983.

Josephson, Matthew. *Life Among the Surrealists: A Memoir.* New York: Holt, Rinehart, and Winston, 1962.

Kennedy, David M. *Birth Control in America: The Career of Margaret Sanger.* New Haven: Yale University Press, 1970.

Lacy, Robert. *Ford: The Men and the Machine.* Boston: Little, Brown and Company, 1986.

Larson, Edward. *Summer for the Gods: The Scopes Trial and America's Continuing Debate over Science and Religion.* New York: Basic Books, 1997.

Levy, Daniel S. *Two-Gun Cohen: A Biography.* New York: St. Martin's Press, 1997.

Lynd, Robert and Helen. *Middletown: A Study in American Culture.* New York: Harcourt, Brace and World, 1956.

Macaulay, Neill. *The Sandino Affair.* Durham, N.C.: Duke University Press, 1985.

Sklar, Robert. *Movie Mad America: A Cultural History of the American Movie.* New York: Vintage Books, 1994.

Slosson, Preston William. *The Great Crusade and After: 1914–1928.* In Dixon Ryan Fox and Arthur M. Schlesinger. *A History of American Life,* New York: The Macmillan Company, 1930.

Sobel, Robert. *Herbert Hoover and the Onset of the Great Depression. 1929–1930.* Philadelphia: J. B. Lippincott Company, 1975.

Sobel, Robert. *Coolidge: An American Enigma.* Washington, D.C: Regnery Publishing, Inc. 1998.

Soule, George. *Prosperity Decade: From War to Depression (1917–1929).* New York: Harper and Row, 1968.

Wecter, Dixon. *The Hero in America: A Chronicle of Hero Worship.* New York: Scribners, 1941.

White, William Allen. *Calvin Coolidge: The Man Who is President.* New York: The Macmillan Company, 1925.